They Called Him

Second Edition, revised and enlarged

They Called Him

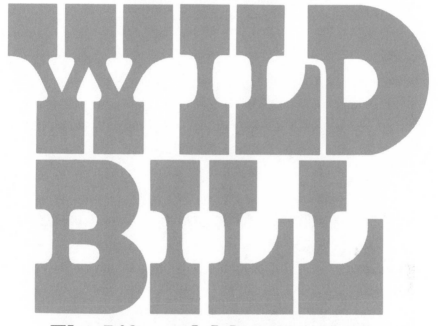

WILD BILL

The Life and Adventures of JAMES BUTLER HICKOK

by Joseph G. Rosa

UNIVERSITY OF OKLAHOMA PRESS : NORMAN

By Joseph G. Rosa

They Called Him Wild Bill: The Life and Adventures of James Butler Hickok (Norman, 1964; second edition, 1974)
Alias Jack McCall (Kansas City, 1967)
The Gunfighter: Man or Myth? (Norman, 1969)
The West of Wild Bill Hickok (Norman, 1982)
Rowdy Joe Lowe: Gambler with a Gun (with Waldo E. Koop) (Norman, 1989)
Wild Bill Hickok, Gunfighter (College Station 2001; paperback edition, Norman, 2003)

Library of Congress Cataloging-in-Publication Data
Rosa, Joseph G.
   They called him Wild Bill.
   Bibliography: p. 354.
   1. Hickok, James Butler, 1837–1876. I. Title.
F594.H627   1974   917.8'03'20924 [B]   74-5958
ISBN: 0-8061-1538-6

8   9   10   11   12   13   14   15   16   17   18   19   20   21   22

To the late GARY COOPER (1901–61),
Whose portrayal of Wild Bill Hickok in *The Plainsman*
Inspired the research that led to this book.

Preface

AT THE CONCLUSION of the Introduction to the first edition of this book, I wrote: "As more and more documents become available, perhaps my book will have to be replaced in its turn." At that time I did not think that I would be the one to do it, but such has been the accumulation of new material since its publication that my publishers have kindly agreed to revise it, and this present volume is the result.

Much of the material for the original edition was obtained by mail. It was donated by many unselfish persons or institutions who believed that such a project, from such a distance, deserved all the help it could get. I realized just how true this was when, in 1965, I first crossed the Atlantic and saw for myself the vastness of the United States in relation to the ground I had covered by mail.

Since then I have spent a great deal of time personally checking newspapers, court records, and other material on file at state historical societies and archives. And I have made visits to places such as Rock Creek, Topeka, Abilene, Hays, Deadwood, and other towns or locations that knew Wild Bill. From many of these places I have gathered the material used in this book.

During 1965 I made one special visit that was perhaps the most important of all: I went to Troy Grove in Illinois and met members of the Hickok family. There I found Wild Bill's nephew Horace and his wife Louise (now both deceased), who showed me great courtesy. Through Horace I was introduced to his sister Ethel. In the past nine years I have returned six times to see her and discuss at length the exploits of her uncle James, with the result that she allowed me access to letters and materials which had never been made public. So far as I know, I am the first person, outside the family, to be privileged to see them.

Among the numerous letters received by the family over the years is the following historic communication from J. W. Buel, requesting information for his book:

Sт. Louis, March 9th, 1881

Horace D. Hickok
or Lorenzo B. Hickok

DEAR SIR. I am now engaged writing a new and more complete life of your lamented brother James, under the title of "Heroes of the Plains," which I hope to have issued some time in May. The book will also contain a sketch of Buffalo Bill; will comprise between 400 and 500 pages and about 100 illustrations. I was actuated to this work by two causes: first, I met James' widow in September last and have since visited her at her home in Cincinnati; she has given me so much assistance by lending me her scrap book full of "Wild Bill's" adventures, besides telling me so much that is [illegible] wholly new that I have the subject matter for an exceedingly interesting book; secondly, my interest in the pamphlet I wrote entitled Marvellous Adventures of Wild Bill, was obtained by a Chicago firm under fraud, and is bringing them a veritable harvest. My new book, "Heroes of the Plains," will be issued in elegant style, with 12 or 16 beautiful lithographed engravings printed in five colors.

My principal object in writing you now is to obtain a rough drawing of the house in which James was born, as I wish to make an engraving from it. Either of you can make a representation of the house that will give my artist sufficient idea to perfect it. In addition to this please tell me the exact location of the house; whether in the woods, or prairie, and in what township it stands, or if not standing now tell me when it was torn down.

In looking over the memoranda you sent me one year ago I find that you omit giving any account of James between the time he was constable of Monticello township, Johnson County, Kansas, and 1860 when he vanquished the McCandlass gang at Rock Creek.

This book will be of great value to you because it preserves this history of so near a relative, who was unquestionably one of the greatest characters this country ever produce[d]. Its value to the people generally is attested by the very great sale my pamphlet life of him attained.

Will you have the kindness to write me at your very earliest convenience, and give a brief mention of some of the adventures of your brother, which have escaped my notice in the pamphlet, also tell me, of course, how he spent his youth, where he attended school; any anecdotes of his early life or afterwards, etc. In short, any incident you can call to mind, for in this book it is needful that no interesting fact should be omitted.

By replying to these questions you will very greatly oblige me and the result will prove honorable to you. I was thinking of visiting your home but the distance is great and my time just now is very precious, besides my second thought tells me that you can readily supply the information which I feel assured you will not neglect doing. Please write me as soon as possible, as I am even this day badly in need of the facts I ask for.

viii

I am with much regard and thanks for past favors, Yours truly,

J. W. BUEL

address me at No. 2643 Park Avenue. See card I enclose. I will, of course, send you each a book as soon as it appears.

J. W. B.

So far as I can gather, no copies of *Heroes of the Plains* ever reached Troy Grove, or if they did no one today knows what happened to them. Neither is it known how much information the family may or may not have given to Buel, for no acknowledgment was given them. However, this correspondence does suggest that Buel was not the villain some writers make out. Admittedly his book contains a great deal of fiction, but no more than was common at the time: remember, he was writing for an audience that wanted blood and thunder rather than factual history or biography. Nevertheless, there is factual material to be found in his book if one is prepared to sift through the obvious changes of names, dates, and places made to suit his narrative. I believe that if Buel's original notes, correspondence, and other material were to be found, perhaps a great deal more would be known of Hickok's actual exploits than has yet been published.

Buel stated: "I was fortunate in securing Wild Bill's diary from his widow, Mrs. Agnes Lake Hickok, of Cincinnati, from which I have drawn my facts concerning him, that there might be no mistakes or omissions in recounting the marvelous exploits of his life in this publication."[1] But this statement has been disputed by Horace Hickok, who told me that neither his father nor his uncle Lorenzo believed their brother kept a diary. However, belief in such a document or journal does have some contemporary backing. In 1876 it was claimed that:

Bill was always a very difficult fellow; hundreds have offered him large sums for a record of his adventures, but he always replied to such applicants that he kept a diary of every act of his life, and when he died the public should have the whole thing in full, but not till then.[2]

Assuming that the above was the document which Buel claimed to have had in his possession in 1881, where is it today, or was Wild Bill indulging in his well-known habit of legpulling? There seems little doubt that Buel did know Hickok. In the late 1860's and early 1870's Buel was a newspaperman in Kansas and Missouri. In 1872 he took over as city editor of the Fort Scott *Monitor*, following a

---

[1] *Heroes of the Plains* (Author's Preface), 10.
[2] Jefferson City (Missouri), *People's Tribune*, Aug. 23, 1876.

period with the Spring Hill *Enterprise*,[3] and during his sojourn with the *Monitor* he would have had ample opportunity to have familiarized himself with reports published in that paper and the *Democrat* about Wild Bill in the 1850's. By 1876, Buel was city editor of the St. Louis *Evening Dispatch*. He wrote several other books and traveled extensively, eventually settling in Philadelphia, where he died in 1920.

In the 1920's another "biographer" of Wild Bill came upon the scene. Frank J. Wilstach, a former independent theatrical manager in New York, became general press representative for Sam H. Harris, a prominent Broadway manager, in 1924. In his correspondence with William E. Connelley, which covered several years, Wilstach stated that he had seen Hickok on stage with Cody, which could have been true. As late as September 14, 1925, Wilstach wrote to Connelley saying that Walter Noble Burns had advised him that Connelley was to do a book on Hickok, and "that same idea has been in my noodle for a long time. If I could get hold of certain material, I might make a start at it." His problem was verifying the origin of the family and establishing other facts.

Wilstach's book was published in 1926 and went into three or four editions, but Wilstach intimated that he did not take it seriously, referring to it at one point as "absurd," which may have been a facetious comment. Nevertheless, his major contribution was the discovery of Sarah Shull, the girl involved in the Rock Creek fight, and the unearthing of Hickok's last two letters to his wife, at that time in the possession of Wild Bill's son-in-law Gil Robinson.

But it was to William E. Connelley, for sixteen years secretary of the Kansas State Historical Society, that historians looked for the definitive book about Wild Bill. Nationwide press publicity brought letters from scores of old-timers, and Connelley himself dispatched hundreds of letters to likely contributors. By 1928 the book was completed, but on July 14, 1930, Connelley died without seeing it in print.

Following his death, his daughter Edith visited his rooms at the Society and removed a mass of material which she claimed as his "private" property. Today much of this material is scattered. In 1933 his book was published as *Wild Bill and His Era*, edited by his daughter. So much has been cut (and badly) that the result was a disaster.

In the belief that Connelley's material would provide answers to

[3] Topeka *Daily Commonwealth*, Apr. 26, 1872.

innumerable questions, I joined the search for it that has lasted almost forty-two years, and learned recently that some of it had been purchased by the Western History Department of the Denver Public Library. The collection is contained in five boxes—the first devoted to material on Quantrill, and the remainder to Hickok. Three of these latter boxes are filled with large envelopes containing letters, clippings, and rough drafts of the chapters of the book. But in one box are to be found completed copies of the manuscript, typed copies of letters received, complete with an index, and typed copies of books and magazines, all prepared for Connelley by a typist on the staff of the Kansas State Historical Society.

In October, 1972, I went to Denver to examine this collection in the hope that some of the material would aid my present revision, and found that in establishing where Connelley got his material, the collection is a gold mine, for it contains masses of information that clarifies his thinking and motivations. But after two days of intensive reading and sifting of the evidence, it became obvious that Connelley was as much to blame for the disaster that befell his book as was his daughter.

His claim that he began collecting material on Wild Bill in 1884 when he lived in Springfield, Missouri, and interviewed old-timers who were there when Hickok shot Dave Tutt may be true, but none of these comments were written down, or if so they have disappeared. An examination of his correspondence and material does not inspire confidence. He did not seriously contemplate a book until very late. In a letter to Walter Noble Burns dated January 5, 1923, he wrote: "I have all the information necessary to write a complete account of the life of Wild Bill. It would take me thirty days to write the book, but I am pretty much pressed for time and the cost of publishing is so great that I have not been able to see any money in it." It was 1928 before the manuscript was complete, and he admitted that his daughter wrote five chapters of the book because he was too busy to do it himself.

In his original foreword dated January 7, 1928, he stated: "The most brilliant chapters of this book were written by her—The Man as He Was—Cowboys and Trails and Cowboy Life—Wild Bill's Show Life—Calamity Jane—Wild Bill's Death—and Conviction and Execution of Jack McCall. These sparkling chapters are unapproachable by any writer within my knowledge."

I searched through a copy of his original book and his material in the hope of establishing the truth about some of the Civil War adventures, but I soon realized that what was not taken from Buel's highly colored account was based upon old-timers' recollections and not upon official records. Connelley did not have access to the material available today; otherwise, I am sure some of his absurd statements and conclusions would have been discarded.

All through his voluminous correspondence Connelley exhibited an arrogance that today would not be tolerated. His dealings with various publishers (in particular Yale University Press, with whom he had a contract to publish the book, but which was later canceled) and his tactless demands for material and assistance have to be read at length to be appreciated. Even the Hickok family did not escape from his unceasing demands, but only one member, Howard L. Hickok, was prepared to assist him. It was Howard who furnished him with copies of Wild Bill's letters written from Kansas in the 1850's (some of which I have reproduced in the text from copies made available by Ethel Hickok), thereby convincing Connelley that there was no marriage between Hickok and Mary Owen.

On January 25, 1928, in thanking Howard for the copies of the letters, Connelley made further demands for material which the other members of the family did not wish to disclose, adding: "Please tell your folks that they will be ashamed of themselves one of these days for their attitude." Understandably, when Connelley wrote on July 15, 1929, requesting "the gun carried by your uncle and copies of all papers and letters that he wrote," the Hickoks were not impressed. However, he did have the good sense to admit on January 20, 1930, that the relatives had been imposed upon so often that they could hardly be blamed for thinking some people were anxious to exploit them.

Connelley, while producing good material, aroused bitter feelings in other areas, too. His disclosure that David C. McCanles had disappeared from Watauga County, North Carolina, with state funds and in the company of Sarah Shull caused an uproar amongst the McCanles family and faction. And allegations that George W. Hansen had been hired by certain "millionaires" to discredit Hickok brought a spirited denial from Hansen. Even J. B. Edwards of Abilene, who had known Hickok, questioned Hansen's motives and hinted at what such detrimental digging would cost and who was paying the bill. Prior to dispatching his letter, Edwards allowed Connelley to read it, and it was promptly copied and returned for dispatch. In the letter Edwards, while condemning Hickok's morals (as he did those of most of the men of the border), pointed out that Wild Bill was a man of his time and indicated that he had no personal reason to debunk Hickok. But the Connelley-Hansen feud continued until Connelley's death, neither side being prepared to give an inch.

Connelley's motives and conclusions about Hickok deserve a study that is beyond the scope of this book, but at least I hope that the foregoing will explain something of the problems encountered by historians anxious to establish the origin of his material and statements. In my own study of this material I have been able to solve a few of the mysteries, and these are incorporated in my text.

Readers of the first edition of this book will note a number of changes in the text but not in the format. The original introduction has been revised and stories of doubtful validity have been replaced by more reliable information.

Among the major discoveries, apart from the inclusion of material made available by the Hickok family, is the true identity of Captain Honesty of *Harper's* fame, McCall's Pardon File, and additional proof that Wild Bill did serve as a deputy United States marshal.

Criticisms of the first edition of this work were few and were confined to two basic points: that I relied too much on newspapers of the day, and that instead of discussing the "psychological implications of the callousness, cruelty and selfishness that crop out repeatedly in the man's [Hickok's] career,"[4] I preferred to publish flattering descriptions of him from contemporary admirers. I make no apology for continuing to include such reports because disregarding the flattery of some and the inaccuracies of others, the fact remains that they are contemporary opinions and not modern conclusions. Also, they frequently provide clues that lead a diligent researcher to better things.

As for "psychological implications," such a suggestion is dangerous. It is impossible to psychoanalyze a dead person; if Wild Bill is to be judged at all, it must be by the standards of his own time and not by so-called twentieth-century behavior patterns.

There are still many gaps in Wild Bill's life, and these are not helped by the great number of other "Wild Bills" who were known to be around at the same time. In his extensive research into the origin of various nicknames, Waldo E. Koop has found thirty-two men called "Wild Bill," none of whom had anything to do with Hickok, the earliest one being a "youth captured in the woods in 1809 near Pinckneyville, Mississippi . . . born about 1800, [and]

4 The New York *Times* (book review), May 31, 1964.

xiii

died in 1818 . . . [known also] as the 'Mississippi Orson.' " Mr. Koop logically concludes that those who appeared in the 1860's and later were so-called because "Hickok may have popularized the title to such an extent [that] some persons who affected the long-haired style may have been nicknamed Wild Bill as a matter of course."[5]

How James Butler Hickok became "Wild Bill" is still subject to speculation. Family recollections tend to agree with the accepted version that the name was acquired following an attempted lynching in Missouri. But in 1877, United States Attorney William Pound suggested that the title was fastened upon him by the guerrillas of Arkansas and Missouri during the Civil War, out of respect for his "fearless and efficient service as a Union Scout," and that he "had no reason, during his life to be ashamed of it."[6]

With time, more of the gaps may be filled, but it is my hope that this volume will prove to be the most comprehensive to date.

JOSEPH G. ROSA

Ruislip, Middlesex, England
January 23, 1974

[5] Waldo E. Koop to the author, Nov. 30, 1971.

[6] William Pound to the Hon. Alphonso Taft, attorney general, Feb. 7, 1877 (Records of the Office of the Pardon Attorney, No. F–307, Records Group No. 24, National Archives, Washington, D.C.).

Acknowledgments

Revised Edition

MY DECISION to revise this book was influenced largely by the reaction toward the first edition by the Hickok family. They believed that the publication of some of the material in their collection would refute some of the tall stories and set the record straight. Therefore, I wish to thank three members of the family who went to great lengths to aid me in my research: Ethel Hickok, to whom I owe a great deal for graciously agreeing to the publication of extracts from letters written by her uncle James in the 1850's, and letters from his wife to his mother and sister dated 1876—together with other material she has placed at my disposal, she has also agreed to the publication of two rare family portraits of Wild Bill as a young man; her niece, Edith Harmon, whose unique research into the family's history has unearthed information hitherto unknown or ignored; and Major James Butler Hickok, United States Marine Corps, for permission to quote from his father Howard L. Hickok's unpublished manuscript.

In particular I should like to thank Joseph W. Snell, assistant archivist of Kansas, who kindly read this manuscript and besides offering helpful suggestions has, over the years, been a tower of strength on this and other projects; Nyle H. Miller, secretary, and the staff of the Kansas State Historical Society who, each time I have visited the Society's building, have gone to great lengths to see that I received every assistance possible.

Others to whom I owe a tremendous debt are Clifford and Doris Leonard; C. Leland Sonnichsen; Jessica Nashold; William B. Secrest; Don Russell; Ramon F. Adams; Waldo E. Koop; William Peacock, Jr.; Lucile Stevens; Paul D. Riley; David Dary; Mrs. Ellen Anderson Mitchell (daughter of "White-Eye Jack"); the late Earle R. Forrest; R. Larry Wilson; Frank Aydelotte; Joseph Balmer; Haldeen Braddy; Oliver Knight; Tim Bannon; the late Mary E. Everhard; the late Sir William Charles Crocker; Leland D. Case;

the late J. Leonard Jennewein; Claude D. Coe; Mrs. Mary Coe; Arthur Carmody; Paul and Penny Dalton; Mrs. Betty Plummer; Richard Dillon; Frank Forster; Leo Oliva; Charles Parsons; Stanley J. Smith; Karl F. Stephens, M.D.; Agnes Wright Spring; William B. Shillingberg; Gary L. Roberts; Stewart P. Verckler; Clifford P. Westermeier; Robert R. Dykstra.

And to the following people and organizations: John Mullane, Cincinnati Public Library; Mrs. Katherine Halverson, Wyoming State Archives; Pat Wagner, Western Publications; Mrs. Alys Freeze and James Davis, Western History Department, Denver Public Library; G. M. O. Briegal, Royal Courts of Justice, London; C. W. Ringrose, librarian to the Honorable Society of Lincoln's Inn; Elmer O. Parker, Old Military Records Branch, National Archives, Washington, D.C.; Roy P. Basler, Manuscripts Division, Library of Congress; John E. Wickman, director, The Dwight D. Eisenhower Library, Abilene, Kansas; Mildred M. Roblee and Steva Carter, The Springfield Public Library; Mark G. Eckhoff, director, Legislative Judicial and Diplomatic Records Division, National Archives; W. Neil Franklin, chief of the Diplomatic, Legal, and Fiscal Branch, National Archives; R. Reed Whitaker, chief, Archives Branch, and Delbert A. Bishop, director, Federal Records Centers at Kansas City and Denver, respectively; Frederick R. Goff, chief, Rare Book Division, Library of Congress; Robert W. Hill, keeper of manuscripts, The New York Public Library; Major General James A. Weir, M.C., Commanding, Fitzsimmons General Hospital, Department of the Army, Denver, Colorado; Mrs. Arline G. Maver, retired curator, Connecticut State Library; The Dickinson County, Kansas, Historical Society; Marjorie Kinney, Missouri Valley Room, Kansas City Public Library; Carol M. Dean, reference librarian, Troy (New York) Public Library; Keith D. Jones; Anthony Garnett; and the late Vincent Mercaldo.

To all these people and institutions (many of whom received acknowledgment in the first edition) and to those people whom I may have inadvertently neglected to mention, my grateful thanks.

First Edition

No work of this nature could possibly be undertaken as an independent venture. Only with the assistance of great numbers of helpful and generous people have I been able to assemble the material needed for this book. Perhaps two hundred persons have contributed in some way toward its completion, and though I could not hope to acknowledge their help here (although some are credited in the text), I made a point of acknowledging their assistance personally or by letter, and they will, I know, find some satisfaction in seeing their efforts put to good use.

In particular I should like to thank the following, to whom I owe so much for encouragement, for advice and guidance in selecting material, and for their unselfish efforts to see that I got all available assistance: C. L. Sonnichsen, who kindly read the manuscript and suggested several constructional and editorial alterations; Nyle Miller, secretary, Mrs. Lela Barnes, treasurer, and the staff of the Kansas State Historical Society; Joseph Balmer, Earle R. Forrest, Don Russell, Raymond W. Thorp, William B. Edwards, E. B. Mann, Howard L. Hickok, Horace A. Hickok, L. G. "Pat" Flannery, Russell Thorp, Herschel C. Logan, George Jelinek, Robert Dykstra, Mr. and Mrs. William L. McPherrin, Cliff and Doris Leonard, Joe Koller, Mrs. Zoe A. Tilghman, Mrs. Jessica Nashold, F. Maurice Speed, Henry Newcombe, Colin W. Rickards, Bryan W. Haven, Clarence S. Paine, and Hamilton B. Mizer.

I am grateful to the following persons and organizations, for supplying information which would otherwise have been unobtainable: Professors S. J. Sackett and Paul K. Friesner, the Kansas State College at Fort Hays; Mrs. Agnes Wright Spring, Colorado State Historical Society; Harry Svanda and Miss Lyn Bessmer, the Federal Records Center, Kansas City, Missouri; Miss Ruth Cibulka, the Chicago Historical Society; Mrs. Alys Freeze, the Denver Public Library; Miss Nell Perrigou, the Deadwood Chamber of Commerce; Mrs. Lola M. Homsher, the Wyoming State Archives and History Department; Donald F. Danker, the Nebraska State Historical Society; the Illinois State Historical Society; the South Dakota State Historical Society; the New York Historical Society; The New York Public Library; Miss Emma Swift, the Rochester, New York, Public Library; The Westerners of Chicago, Kansas City, and England; Colt's Patent Fire Arms Manufacturing Company; the National Archives and the Library of Congress, Washington, D.C.; the Greater Niagara Falls Chamber of Commerce; and Lloyd's Register, London and New York. I received much help from the chiefs of police of Yankton, South Dakota; Abilene, Kansas; Sydney, Nebraska; and Evanston, Wyoming.

And last, but by no means least, I am indebted to Miss Hilda Phillips, who assisted in the typing of the manuscript, to Joan Whitford, who kindly read the proofs; and to the vital link in the chain of communication, the United States postmasters, who are always more than willing to assist—in particular, the postmasters of Utica, New York; Ulysses and Hickok, Kansas; New York City; Springfield, Missouri; Chicago, Illinois; Troy Grove, Illinois; and Rochester, New York.

My thanks to them all.

J. G. R.

Contents

Illustrations

They Called Him

WILD
BILL

Under the sod in the land of gold
　　We have laid the fearless Bill;
We called him Wild, yet a little child
　　Could bend his iron will.
With generous heart he freely gave
　　To the poorly clad, unshod—
Think of it, pards—of his noble traits—
　　While you cover him with the sod.

　　—From *The Burial of Wild Bill* by
　　Jack Crawford, "The Poet Scout."

Introduction

In 1929 the state of Illinois raised the sum of $10,000 and erected a permanent memorial to Wild Bill Hickok. The bronze tablet, fixed to a rugged and unhewn mass of granite, was dedicated in the New State Park at Troy Grove on August 29, 1930. It reads as follows:

JAMES BUTLER "WILD BILL" HICKOK,
PIONEER OF THE GREAT PLAINS, BORN HERE MAY 27, 1837, ASSASSINATED AT DEADWOOD AUGUST 2, 1876. SERVED HIS COUNTRY AS A SCOUT AND SPY IN THE WESTERN STATES TO PRESERVE THE UNION IN THE CIVIL WAR. EQUALLY GREAT WERE HIS SERVICES ON THE FRONTIER AS EXPRESS MESSENGER AND UPHOLDER OF LAW AND ORDER. HE CONTRIBUTED LARGELY IN MAKING THE WEST A SAFE PLACE FOR WOMEN AND CHILDREN. HIS STERLING COURAGE WAS ALWAYS AT THE SERVICE OF RIGHT AND JUSTICE. TO PERPETUATE HIS MEMORY THIS MONUMENT IS ERECTED BY THE STATE OF ILLINOIS.
A.D. 1929.[1]

Wild Bill did not, and does not, need such a memorial. He long ago became immortalized in American folklore, and his exploits have been fictionalized to such an extent that the facts are hard to establish. Yet the real Hickok, the man of action, cool, reserved, ruthless, and at times unscrupulous, was every bit as deserving of a reputation as the figure of legend.

Here was a man whose friendship was sought by many and prized by few; a man who inspired loyalty and freely gave it; a man whose friends admired him with an affection that bordered upon adulation. There were also those among his contemporaries who branded him a bully, a braggart, a cheat, and a rogue; some, who grew up after his death, called him a coward. But no man of his time ever called him that to his face, for he was perfectly able to take care of himself on the wild frontier of the American West

1 The Connelley Collection in the Denver Public Library contains correspondence between Connelley and Dr. Otto Schmidt and H. H. Cleaveland, director of the Department of Public Work and Buildings of Illinois, which led to the inscription on the monument.

in the 1860's and 1870's. Challenged by all manner of glory hunters, he was always armed and practical; he never bluffed or took unnecessary risks, sure in the knowledge that an unguarded moment could be his last.

Like all truly dangerous men, Wild Bill Hickok was quiet, soft-spoken, and let actions speak louder than words. Catlike in movement, he was gifted with a coolness and presence of mind that enabled him to co-ordinate his phenomenal reflexes in the split second allowed for decision in a gunfight. When Hickok was forced into pulling a gun on another man, he had already anticipated the outcome: he not only shot to kill, he also fought to stay alive.

Here was a man who was proud, egotistical, and yet not a braggart, but always conscious of his effect upon others; a man who recognized his own faults and vices, but had enough strength of character to laugh at himself and what his legend had made him— for he became a legend in his own lifetime. The real James Butler Hickok was that kind of a man. And most of his detractors did not start their character assassination until he was safely underground.

This man and the manner of his life has long been the subject of bitter dispute. His reputation as a man-killer has been grossly magnified; he was quoted (or misquoted), in 1867, as having counted "considerably over a hundred" white men. Naturally, his detractors were quick to ridicule this figure. Perhaps they were right, although four years of hiding, fighting, and killing in the forests and mountains of Missouri and Arkansas during the Civil War might have produced at least half this total. But when he died his alleged personal claim was only thirty-six.

At this date the record shows seven known victims and several probables. To reach anything like the total of thirty-six would mean the inclusion of a number of legendary killings which, without names, dates, and other facts, cannot be considered. One significant fact does emerge when the circumstances behind each of those killings (with one exception) are examined: Wild Bill was provoked. Contemporary references to the man and his character indicate that Hickok was a mild-mannered, courteous, and peaceful individual when left alone. His quiet, self-assured, and almost ministerial appearance misled many into the belief that perhaps, after all, he was only a legend. All too often they learned to their cost that he was indeed "a bad man to fool with." Some even compared him with a stalking tiger, for when he was aroused, "he was as ferocious and pitiless as one."[2]

Here was a man who courted women with dash and charm, and

4

they quickly warmed to him. Children, too, were attracted to this man who, despite his reputation for violence, was surprisingly gentle with those from whom he knew he had nothing to fear. He consorted with prostitutes, whom he rarely trusted; gambled incessantly; and consumed whisky in large quantities but never got drunk. Yet generals and great ladies were proud to know him.

Of his love life it was once said: "He was . . . without morals to speak of,"[3] and another wrote: "Hickok's morals were much the same as those of Achilles, King David, Lancelot and Chevalier Bayard, though his amours were hardly as frequent as David's or as inexcusable as Lancelot's."[4] Of his character one declared that he was "generous to a fault, swore like a trooper at certain stages . . . [and] was the only frontiersman who would take his pistols off and fight a square fight with any one who wanted to settle a dispute in that way."[5] Others, too, noticed this tendency to use his fists instead of his pistols on occasion; he had been known to "beat up a Mule Skinner in a fist fight."[6]

We have said that he gambled, but there was a wide divergence of opinion on his pasteboard capabilities. To some his reputation as a gambler was good, but to others it was bad. "He would rather indulge in poker than eat," said John Malone, and "on one occasion . . . played in his last earthly possession[,] a black and tan terrier."[7] Charles Gross, his friend in Abilene, noted that "he would gamble the shirt off his back,"[8] and others, too, suggested that gambling was a passion rather than a profession.

Wild Bill attracted attention wherever he went. He stood six feet or over, and was broad-shouldered, tapering to a lithe, narrow waist and loins, and wore his hair, parted in the middle, shoulder length in the manner of the plainsmen and Indian scouts of his day, openly defying the red men to take it. The color of his hair has led to some dispute. George Ward Nichols wrote of his "fine dark hair," and Custer recalled that his "hair and complexion were those

[2] Frank A. Root and William Elsey Connelley, *The Overland Stage to California*, 146, citing an unnamed writer in the St. Louis *Republic*.

[3] Charles F. Gross to J. B. Edwards, Apr. 26, 1922, Manuscripts Division, Kansas State Historical Society.

[4] E. C. Little, "A Son of the Border," Topeka *Mail and Breeze*, Sept. 13, 1901, reprinted from *Everybody's Magazine*.

[5] John Malone, quoted in the North Topeka *Times*, Aug. 31, 1876.

[6] Luther North, *Man of the Plains*, 310.

[7] Malone, *loc. cit.* Reference to Hickok's terrier touches upon a trait that was common among frontiersmen—a liking for animals, especially dogs. As early as 1856, Wild Bill's most prized possession (apart from his gun and a fiddle) was his dog.

[8] *Loc. cit.*

5

of the perfect blond." But a Kansas editor who noted his "fine auburn hair," and a writer in the St. Louis *Republic* who wrote that "his hair was auburn in hue, of the tint brightened but not reddened by the sunlight,"[9] were closest to the color the family remembers. As if to support this conclusion, his eyebrows and mustache were also of a lightish color and rarely show up in photographs without retouching. There also exists a lock of his hair, taken from him after death, and now preserved in New York, which is "judged to be auburn."[10]

Notwithstanding his enormous stature, his hands and feet were small, the former bony and supple with long tapering fingers. When he walked his tread was firm, controlled, and deliberate, and his movements graceful.

Wild Bill had clean, clear-cut, and strong features, with high cheekbones and a thin nose slightly ridged at the top, curving down to a flattened tip with flared nostrils, giving him a somewhat predatory look. In expression his face seemed almost benign, although the slightly cynical mouth, surmounted by a straw-colored mustache that curled wickedly around it (occasionally complemented by a goatee) and eyes that stared one right in the face without wavering, denoted a firm and deliberate manner that suggested a great strength of character. But it was his eyes that commanded most attention. They were a translucent blue-gray in color, surprisingly gentle in normal conversation, but when he was aroused, they became coldly implacable.

A pioneer Western photographer, who also studied phrenology, made a particular note of Hickok's features: "Temperamentally," he wrote, "the motive of bone and muscular system predominates, as indicated by the oblong square-shape of the face. The remarkable thing about this face, however, is the absence of curved lines. It is made up of straight lines and sharp angles. . . . The whole face shows resolution, courage and determination, in a marked degree. The expression of the face is one of sadness and kindness."[11]

In dress as in manner Wild Bill attracted attention. He favored Prince Albert frock coats, and "salt-and-pepper" trousers which he sometimes wore pulled down over his boot tops, or tucked in so that the half-moon or spiral designs he occasionally effected were

[9] Manhattan (Kan.) *Independent* (Oct. 26, 1867). Root and Connelley, *Overland Stage*, 146.

[10] Robert W. Hill, Keeper of Manuscripts, The New York Public Library, to the author, Jan. 6, 1966.

[11] DeLester Sackett, cited in The Westerners' *Brand Book* (Chicago), Vol. III, No. 4 (June, 1946), 24.

shown to advantage. These boots were made of the finest calfskin and fitted with two-inch heels and were alleged to have been custom-made for him in Leavenworth. Covering the boiled white shirt front was a fancy brocaded vest, often worn with the top button undone, not through carelessness, but to allow easy access to the two .41-caliber Williamson derringers in concealed pockets inside. Around his waist he sometimes sported a scarlet embroidered silk sash which supported a pair of engraved ivory-handled .36-caliber Colt 1851 Navy revolvers, weapons that were almost as well known as Hickok himself. He was rarely without them, and he wore them butts-forward for the "Cavalry" or old-time plainsman's "Twist" draw. Early in his career he had worn holsters, but later he preferred to use just a belt, a sash, or his waistband.

Wild Bill was as fastidious about cleanliness as he was about dress. He was known to be fond of baths; he liked to wear clean clothes; and one man recalled meeting Wild Bill when he had something in his eye: "Bub, come here and take this handkerchief and get the gnat out of my eye," Hickok ordered. "Hold on! your hands are not clean, go in and wash them." I did so and then removed the gnat, and he gave me a 'shin plaster' quarter. I have his picture which he also gave me."[12]

Wild Bill's personal opinion of his awesome reputation received little publicity. In 1873 he wrote: "I have never insulted man or woman in my life but if you knew what a wholesome regard I have for damn liars and rascals they would be liable to keep out of my way." Later, when confronted by his reputation as a man-killer, he replied: "I suppose I am called a red-handed murderer, which I deny. That I have killed men I admit, but never unless in absolute self-defense, or in the performance of an official duty. I never, in all my life, took any mean advantage of an enemy."[13]

Despite his reputation as a man-killer or "bad man," Wild Bill had a great sense of humor—this is evident in his letters home—and his brothers claim that in later years "James" loved practical jokes and legpulling. That he must have been good at it is evidenced by the fun he had with various journalists—assuming that everything they published came from him and not from others.

It was the gentlemen of the press who, while eulogizing or de-

[12] Louis Charles Laurent, "Reminiscences by the Son of a French Pioneer," Kansas State Historical Society (hereinafter cited as KSHS) Collections, Vol. XIII (1913–14), 369.
[13] Mendota (Ill.) Bulletin, Apr. 11, 1873; Annie D. Tallent, The Black Hills; Or the Last Hunting Ground of the Dakotahs, 100.

flating the Hickok legend, also contributed greatly to it. They coined several titles for him, including "The Prince of Pistoleers," "Beau Brummell of the Frontier," "Gunmaster of the Border," or "Gentleman Jim." But these are all of more recent origin. The old-time editors were more facetious, and vied with each other to invent something new. As a result "Wild Bill" became "Gentle William," "Tempestuous William," "William Severe," and other humorous variations. Yet for all this Hickok was unknown to the multitudes east of the Mississippi until the middle 1860's.

In 1865, Colonel George Ward Nichols[14] met him in Springfield, Missouri, and decided that he was good "copy." Their interview was published in the February, 1867, issue of *Harper's New Monthly Magazine*, and the Colonel immortalized Wild Bill and his battles. Although time and patient research have proved most of the story to be grossly inaccurate, it did serve to launch "Wild Bill" on the road to fame.

In the melodramatic and highly colored style of the day, Nichols described his parting with Wild Bill:

"If you have no objection I will write out for publication an account of a few of your adventures."

"Certainly you may," he replied. "I'm sort of public property. But, Kernel," he continued, leaning upon my saddle-bow, while there was a tremulous softness in his voice and a strange moisture in his averted eyes, "I have a mother back there in Illinois who is old and feeble. I haven't seen her this many a year, and haven't been a good son to her, yet I love her better than any thing in this life. It don't matter much what they say about me here. But I'm not a cut-throat and vagabond, and I'd like the old woman to know what'll make her proud. I'd like her to hear that her runaway boy has fought through the war for the Union like a true man."

[William Hitchcock—called *Wild Bill, the Scout of the Plains*—shall have his wish. I have told his story precisely as it was told to me, confirmed in all important points by many witnesses; and I have no doubt of the truth.—G. W. N.]

In spite of such comforting assurance, the Colonel made statements that annoyed Hickok and upset his family back home in Troy Grove, for Nichols magnified his prowess as a scout, spy, and fighting man. The article was widely read, creating much interest in

---

[14] See note 24, Chapter Four. This appears to be the Colonel's only venture into Western literature. The remainder of his life was devoted to music; when he died in 1885, he was president of the Cincinnati College of Music (Cincinnati *Times-Star*, Sept. 15, 1885; Cincinnati *Commercial Gazette*, Sept. 16, 1885; Cincinnati *Daily Enquirer*, Sept. 16, 1885).

the East and even in England where *Harper's* had a limited circulation. As a result it became, in fact, Hickok's death warrant. Until his death nine years later, he was besieged by journalists and others; though eager for more details, few of them were interested in the truth. Hickok became a target for all manner of comment or abuse, and was constantly obliged to prove himself the equal of all comers. Small wonder that the man who lived with and tried to play down the legend grew embittered by the cruelties of fate, and was far removed from the carefree, devil-may-care boy of the Kansas border wars, or the scout of the early 1860's. This man's legend, promoted by Nichols, has down the years snowballed into monumental size.

The proportion of truth in even the verifiable stories is hard to determine. Wild Bill himself seems to have been guilty of purposely enlarging upon his adventures, doubtless never dreaming that much of what he said would be faithfully reported as truth. Many of the scriveners went away convinced that Wild Bill Hickok was a superman. Only a few were skeptical. And so the legend grew. Friends and enemies contributed to it, passing on stories of doubtful validity, exaggerating the list of killings, asserting and denying his prowess as a pistoleer, plainsman, and persuader of women.

Almost a century has passed since James Butler Hickok died, yet his name[15] still lives as one of the greatest in American folklore. But long, long ago the real man was overshadowed by Wild Bill Hickok, his legend.

[15] During World War II there was launched at the Permanente Metals Corporation Shipyard No. 2 at Richmond, California, on February 26, 1943, a ship named the *James B. Hickok*. After a distinguished war service she was sold into civilian ownership and underwent several changes of name: *James B. Hickok* (1943–48), *President Pretorius* (1948–52), *Centurion* (1952–54), and *Prodromos* (1954–58). While on passage from Montreal to Helsinki, she collided with the *King Minos* in the English Channel on December 3, 1958, in dense fog. The stern section was cut off and sunk off Dungeness, and the fore section was beached off Rye and later refloated and towed to Boulogne and broken up (I am indebted to Lloyd's Shipping Editors' Department, who searched their Casualty Reports to provide some of this information).

-⋅◦◦{ **1** }◦◦⋅-

The Boy and the Man

HE WAS BORN IN HOMER,[1] La Salle County, Illinois, on May 27, 1837,[2] and baptized James Butler Hickok after his mother's father. His first home was a small frame house in a remote frontier village, but for all this he came from sterling stock. It was believed originally that his ancestors came from Ireland, but probably they were descended from the Hiccox family of Stratford-upon-Avon, Warwickshire, England. The family name of Hiccox, Hiccocks, Hitchcock, and other variant spellings was common in the Stratford area during the sixteenth and seventeenth centuries. Some members of the Hiccox family were tenants of William Shakespeare, for it is recorded that Thomas and Lewis Hiccox farmed on 107 acres of land in Old Stratford bought by William Shakespeare from a John Combe in 1602.[3]

An illustration of a coat of arms in the possession of the Hickok family which bears the name Hiccox has been traced to an "Edward Hiccox, Esq.," of Stratford, but research at the College of Arms in London has revealed that the arms were never officially registered. However, on November 30, 1707, arms were granted to John Hiccocks, Esq., of Lincoln's Inn, County of Middlesex, one of the masters of the High Court of Chancery. The son of William Hiccocks of South Lambeth, Surrey, John Hiccocks was admitted to the Middle Temple in 1683, was admitted to the Bar in 1690, and

[1] By the early 1860's, Homer was known as Troy Grove. The change came about because it was realized that there was another and larger Homer in the same state.

[2] Kent Ladd Steckmesser, in *The Western Hero in History and Legend*, 105, claims that the page from the Hickok family Bible recording James's birth is missing, but he does not indicate where the Bible is located. The family records in Troy Grove show the date as May 27, 1837. Another Bible, in the possession of the descendants of Lydia Hickok Barnes (and said to be the one owned by William and Polly Hickok), shows the date as 1838. However, this and other entries in the volume have been amended by an unknown hand to conform with the accepted versions. One conclusion is that the original entries were made from memory some years later, necessitating correction (Laurence W. Lindberg to the author, Mar. 23, 1972).

[3] H. S. A. Smith, M.A., borough librarian, Stratford-upon-Avon, to the author, Jan. 10, 1959; The Shakespeare Birthplace Trust to the author, Jan. 22, 1971.

was called to Bench in 1709. He served as master of the High Court of Chancery from 1703 to 1723. He died on April 5, 1726, and was buried in the Temple graveyard.[4] The design of both arms bear certain similarities which suggests that there was a family link.

No connection has yet been established between the Stratford branch of the family and that in London, yet some members of the Stratford family may have moved to London about 1567.[5]

A branch of the family is believed to have taken root in America when William Hitchcock[6] embarked on the *Plaine Joan* which sailed from London for the northern continent on May 15, 1635. When he settled down, he chose Farmington, Connecticut. After a hard life as a farmer he died about 1645, leaving a widow Elizabeth and two sons Samuel and Joseph, both born in Farmington. Elizabeth later remarried to a William Adams in 1648. Joseph died at Woodbury, Connecticut, in 1687, and Samuel died about 1694. Many of their descendants remained in Connecticut, but they were prolific and lusty, and soon spread all over New England.[7]

Perhaps the most interesting of all the early members of the family was Aaron Hickok, great-grandfather of Wild Bill. He was born at Woodbury, Connecticut, in 1742. When he was eighteen years of age the family moved to Lanesborough, Massachusetts, and then to Pittsfield, Massachusetts, where he made his home during the Revolutionary War. During the uneasy period which led up to the Declaration of Independence, Aaron fell afoul of a local Tory landowner who wanted his property, and by devious means obtained it. Although the injured party, Aaron was found in the wrong "and his body taken to the Gaol House!"[8]

Aaron was a colorful character and from his physical description his great-grandson must have borne some resemblance in looks as well as in characteristics: five feet eleven inches in height, of light complexion and sandy hair. When the Revolutionary War started, Aaron and his brother Ichabod enlisted and thereby started a tra-

[4] *Burke's General Armory*; W. J. G. Verco, C.V.O., Chester herald of arms, College of Arms, London, to the author, Nov. 5, 1970; Records of the Middle Temple Library, London.

[5] Charles Nelson Hickok, *The Hickok Genealogy, Descendants of William Hickocks of Farmington, Connecticut*, Foreword; Richard Savage (ed.) *Stratford-upon-Avon Parish Registers* (1558–1812).

[6] This spelling is used in the New England Register, Vol. II, 212 (Boston, Mass., n.d.). Other variants suggest that it was William Hickocks (Edith Harmon to the author, Dec. 16, 1970).

[7] "The Hickok Family," unpublished genealogical record compiled by Edith Harmon (hereinafter cited as Harmon, "The Hickok Family," *loc. cit.*).

[8] Edith Harmon to the author, July 16, 1971.

dition: there has been a Hickok present in each of America's wars, from those patriotic minutemen of 1775 even to those engaged in the Vietnam conflict of the present generation. Aaron served as a private in Captain Asa Barn's company of Colonel Patterson's Regiment of minutemen, which marched on April 22, 1775, in response to the Lexington Alarm when Paul Revere made his famous ride. Aaron is believed to have been present at Bunker Hill but may not have engaged in the actual fighting. Ichabod joined the cause a little later as a member of the contingent from Pittsfield which joined the Continental Army in 1777.[9]

Aaron Hickok married twice and had nineteen children. He was a farmer, and also owned and operated a sawmill and an iron forge. His third son of the first marriage, Oliver, was born about 1774, and he married sometime before 1801, but the record of the marriage has not yet been found. When America went to war with Great Britain in 1812, Oliver answered the call to arms. Oliver, only thirty-eight years of age, died at Sackett's Harbor, New York, on October 3, 1813, from wounds received in battle. His father Aaron died the following year.[10]

Oliver Hickok's son William Alonzo was born on December 5, 1801, at North Hero, Grand Isle County, Lake Champlain, Vermont. In his youth William was inclined toward the church, and his parents worked as hard as they could to get him the necessary education. He studied for the Presbyterian ministry at Middlebury College, Middlebury, Vermont. Following his father's death, his mother remarried, to a man named Oliver Gibbs. When school terms were over, William would return home and spend his vacations busying himself around the property. His grandson wrote:

He was tall, well over six feet in height, had a fine physique, had dark hair, high cheek bones and a roman nose; a distinguished looking man ably suited to his chosen calling. He had worked in the forests and on the farm during his vacations, could split a chalkline with a handaxe and had considerable experience in the rough carpentry of the time. The seminary that grandfather attended was in New York state, and it was there he met pretty Polly Butler, she was an aunt of Gen. Ben Butler of Civil War fame. Polly was born in Bennington, Vt. Her father was one of the Green Mountain Boys with Ethan Allen. Her brother Lorenzo had moved to New York and it was while on a visit with Lorenzo that she met grandfather and soon after [on June 23, 1829] married him. He took her with him to North Hero. . . .

9 Harmon, "The Hickok Family," *loc. cit.*
10 *Ibid.*

North Hero had a typhoid fever epidemic and grandfather contracted the disease, was severely ill, and also contracted brain fever. After a lengthy convalesence he partially recovered. He had a complete amnesia and very poor health. All hopes for the ministry were lost . . . the young couple turned to his mother for help and advice. She furnished [them with] enough money to start a small store in Bro[o]me County, New York.[11]

William actually took his bride to Cornwall, Vermont, before moving to Maine, Broome County, New York, where on May 1, 1830, Oliver was born. A child born on October 9, 1831, and named Lorenzo Butler, died shortly afterwards, and when another son was born on November 23, 1832, he was also given the name Lorenzo Butler. One year later the family moved to Illinois, settling at Union Grove, or Union Center, Putnam County, but soon moved to Bailey Point, now Tonica. Horace was born on October 5, 1834, and in 1836 the family moved to Homer, Illinois, and settled down.

The scene of several Indian skirmishes during the Black Hawk War, the area had not been considered safe for some time after the treaty, but by the time William and his family arrived settlers were once more moving into the area.

Homer was laid out by members of the Wixon family. Close by was the little Vermilion River and plenty of timber. Between 1834 and 1837 there was a steady demand for town lots and farm land. William built a home and opened the first store. His friends from college days, Nahum Gould and William Dewey, organized the local church, but as time went on, William grew away from what he soon realized were fanatical beliefs and became more and more liberal in his religious thinking. Gould taught his children his religious doctrines, but William encouraged them to think for themselves and form their own conclusions.[12]

Close by the Hickok store a man named Levi Brown built a tavern which served as a stage stop. This was the Green Mountain Inn (or House). William's aspirations to succeed in his new venture were doomed to failure, for the 1837 financial panic ruined him. He lost his store and his home just after the fourth boy, James, was born. He was left with no alternative but to go to farming, and moved to a little place north of Homer. Two more children were

[11] Howard L. Hickok, "The Hickok Legend," an unpublished manuscript in the possession of his son, Major James Butler Hickok, U.S.M.C., 2 (hereinafter cited as Hickok, "The Hickok Legend," *loc. cit.*).
[12] Harmon, "The Hickok Family," *loc. cit.*; Hickok, "The Hickok Legend," *loc. cit.*, 3.

13

born, both girls—Celinda on September 3, 1839, and Lydia on October 29, 1842.[13]

Hard years were to come, but the young Hickok children were able to receive some education along with helping out on the farm. William's health and memory were much improved and he was able to encourage his children in their many pursuits. By 1844, William had moved to a new place at the head of the grove where the timber was much heavier, but as time went on his health again began to fail. His sons assumed control of the farm, and built themselves a small cabin on the Abner Westgate farm, but made regular trips home. This was some four miles from Homer. By the late 1840's the youngsters were very independent, and with money he had earned on the surrounding farms James purchased a firearm.

Even as a small boy James was to show that trait which was to mark him for the rest of his life—an inborn fondness for handguns. Whether his first weapon was a single-shot pistol, musket, or shotgun is not known, but at every opportunity he would disappear into the woods to try it out. This desire for loneliness, this feeling of confidence in himself, and belief in walking on his own were to stay with him for the rest of his life.

Talk of the abolition of slavery, and the cruelties and injustices that went with it, made a deep impression on William Hickok. The latter part of his life was spent in fighting for their freedom. His friend Gould was a rabid Abolitionist, but William was generally sympathetic with any oppressed people. Nevertheless, he joined Gould and his Quaker friends who were engaged in the dangerous business of assisting escaped slaves.

Some of the slaves were brought to Homer from Lowell by crossing the river at Utica or La Salle, but most of them were helped by the Lowell Quaker settlement and went through Ottawa. One of the female slaves named Hannah stayed with the Hickok family for many years, and the family still owns a tintype of her.[14] She later moved to Malden, Illinois, where she married.

The Hickok home in Homer was equipped with a hidden cellar which was used as a hiding place for the slaves. Howard Hickok first heard of it in 1906:

Grandfather built two cellars in his new home, one a false hidden cellar which was lined with hay. This was used as a station of the Underground. I lived in this house . . . and was not aware of this hidden cellar. It was brought to my attention by my father, who had me remove some

[13] Harmon, "The Hickok Family," *loc. cit.*
[14] The tintype is now owned by Ethel Hickok.

boards in the living room floor and under this floor was a dry earthern room, probably six foot square, and it was still lined with stems and traces of prairie hay.

Running the Underground was a serious and dangerous undertaking; besides the Provost Marshals, who were legally bound to reclaim the slaves, there were several men in the neighborhood who made the undertaking more difficult and dangerous. These were the kidnappers and bounty hunters. The kidnappers recaptured the slaves and resold them. The bounty hunters returned the slaves to their former owners for the bounty paid by them. . . . Gould was lame and grandfather was ill but both gave freely of their time and effort to help hundreds of slaves to their northern goal. Frequently they were fired upon by the bounty hunters. Dad told me that while riding one dark night they were fired at by a group of men, in an attempt to stop them.

Grandfather pushed dad and uncle Jim from the wagon seat into the bed of the wagon with the negroes. The speed of the team and grandfather's knowledge of the country, enabled him to turn into a side road and return home while the disgruntled hunters went on toward Wedron.[15]

With the death of William Hickok on May 5, 1852, the running of the farm was left in the hands of James and his brothers Horace and Lorenzo. Oliver had left home in 1851 and gone to California in the wake of the gold rush. He became a teamster on the rough trails around Placerville and Folson. Following a fall from a wagon he lost an arm, but was still able to handle horses.[16] Horace and Lorenzo took over the mundane chores. Providing the food supply fell to James, and he spent the greater part of his time out in the woods and fields shooting squirrels, rabbits, deer, and prairie chickens, which must have been welcome additions to a hard diet.

When Oliver left for California, James took his place working on the farm of a neighbor named Carr. It was there that he first showed the mettle and spirit that was to mark him for life. Howard describes it:

He and his brothers had spent many hours swimming in the little river near their home [the cabin on the Westgate farm]. He was a fine swimmer. Few were the days in summer that did not find him in the water. The following was told to me by James Wylie in 1897. Another small stream, the Tomahawk creek ran through the Carr property. One day after a hard rain Jim and the boys of the neighborhood were swimming in the then swollen stream. One of the young men from the party was from Peru, Ilinois. He was a good swimmer, and amused himself by bullying the younger boys, and ducking them under the water. Wylie,

15 "The Hickok Legend," *loc. cit.*, 4–5, 7–8.
16 *Ibid.*, 9.

the son of a Scotch [sic] immigrant, could not swim, but amused himself by wading and splashing in the shallower puddles. The Peru joker shoved him into deeper water, and Wylie promptly went under. The bully frightened, left the water, and started dressing. Uncle Jim jumped in and rescued Wylie, brought him safely to shore, and then walked over to Mr. Bully picked him up clothes and all and threw him into the stream.[17]

When William Hickok died, the family moved back to Homer. Lorenzo and Horace pooled their resources and bought a home in the village (it is not certain if this was the one where James had been born or if the re-purchase of that came later). For James, life in the village was dull. His avid interest in all sorts of adventure (as a boy he had read stories about Daniel Boone and Kit Carson) had left him with a yearning to follow Oliver's move and head west. But his other brothers persuaded him to wait a year or so until they had provided for their mother and sisters. James agreed and meantime sought employment away from home. In 1854 he went to Utica, Illinois, where he spent some time as a driver on the Illinois and Michigan Canal. The job came to an end when he threw his employer into the canal for mistreating his team.[18] This incident later gave rise to the legend that Hickok fought a man named Charles Hudson on the canal bank and ended by almost drowning the man. It is alleged that James ran away from home in a panic, but it is now believed that this story was a Buel invention.

By 1855, James's dreams and ambitions were centered upon the new Kansas Territory. With the opening of Kansas Territory in 1854, the question of slavery was uppermost in the minds of the people who planned to settle there, for they would have to decide whether Kansas would be a free or a slave state. Missourians who supported slavery crossed the border by the hundreds to claim land, believing that if Kansas became a free state the slaveowners in Western Missouri would lose many slaves, who would then flee to Kansas. So began the struggle between the Kansas "Free Staters" and the Missouri "Border Ruffians."

The new land appealed to the Hickoks because of its farming potential, and from an examination of family documents it is evident that this was the reason James and Lorenzo left for Kansas. Family recollections gave the year as 1855 and the 1859 territorial census states that James had been in the state since 1855, but on September 28, 1856, James wrote to his mother and stated that he had

17 "The Hickok Legend," loc. cit., 10.
18 Ibid., 11.

been away from home a little over three months. Therefore, it is probable that James and Lorenzo left home in June, 1856.

News of the departure of the Hickok brothers was a blow to their many friends in the neighborhood. The McLaughlin family who lived near by had two daughters, Sarah and Josephine. Although it was Sarah who was to receive mention in James's letters home, it was Josephine who, as a very old lady, claimed to be his childhood sweetheart and constant companion.[19]

The brothers set off on foot, journeying to St. Louis, Missouri, following the Illinois River for some distance and then going across country to the city. They found the town a busy place, overflowing with hunters, trappers, and all manner of people. Wrote Howard:

The boys were amazed and bewildered. At the post office they found letters from home and the news that their mother was ailing. Lorenzo did not take kindly to the crowds and the bustle of the busy town. He worried about his mother and finally decided to return home. He was a quiet orderly man, dignified, much like his father. He was more of a realist than uncle Jim. So the brothers parted. Lorenzo went back to Homer after giving uncle Jim money enough to prove up on the homestead he was to take for the family. Uncle Jim had a faculty for making friends and keeping them; and he was a popular member of any crowd he met.

He engaged passage on the first [available] steamboat bound up the Missouri river. Among the adventurous spirits on the boat were men that had heard him call Lorenzo by the nickname of Bill [family tradition states that Lorenzo, for some indeterminate reason, became known as "Billy Barnes" during his teens] and from that time on he himself became Bill Hickok, or Shanghai Bill on account of his slim and supple form. He was much over six feet in height, strong and self confident, still attuned to a code of quiet gentle speech and manner: trained to a skill seldom attained in the use of firearms: skilled in woodcraft: taught to champion the weak, but encouraged never to let himself be "put upon." He was taught to believe in the freedom and equality of men.[20]

Arriving at Leavenworth, James found that the boat was besieged by a hostile crowd of proslavery men who refused to allow passengers off but did let the freight come ashore. Having little baggage, James slipped into a line of stevedores and came quietly ashore and disappeared into the crowd. Work was hard to find, and he was determined not to spend the little money Lorenzo had given him toward their homestead. But it would not be easy. Armed

[19] Edith Harmon to the author, Sept. 9, 1970.
[20] "The Hickok Legend," *loc. cit.*, 12.

bands of proslavery men were making life difficult for would-be settlers, and in retaliation they themselves formed militant groups.

For a time James worked for various persons; a man named Williams employed him as a plowman, and it is claimed that he also worked for a man named Richard Budd, who lived west of Leavenworth.[21] Howard claims, as did others, that James joined General James Lane's Free State Army, winning his place by beating others at marksmanship for prizes. James won first prize, having paid thirty dollars to compete. He was allowed to join and had three dollars of his own money left, but still had not touched the money Lorenzo had given him.[22]

While it is evident that James was actively engaged in the Free State movement, his letters home do not suggest that he was so employed until later in the year. In a combined letter to his mother and his sister Lydia, he hints at the hazards of Kansas. To his mother he wrote, on September 28, 1856:

You say write us often[,] how can I when it has been more than three months since I left home and only received to letters from home . . . the excitement is purty much over. I have seen since I have been here sites that would make the wickedest hearts sick[,] believe me mother[,] for what I say is true[.] I can't come home til fall[,] it would not look well.

To his sister he wrote:

You requested me to write to you. I returned to the border yesterday, and went right strate to the post office expecting to get several letters from Illinois but I was disappointed only getting one where I expected several[,] but I was glad to get one from you and mother[.] I have wrote letters to George[e] Mc[Laughlin] Hi Higgins, Daniel Carr[,] liberty Mc[Laughlin] from all those I have not received an answer[.] George Mc I can excuse[,] he has the care of a family to attend to which engages the most of his time and mind I suppose. he agreed to write to me often if I would write to him[.] Tell him[,] Lydia[,] that he need not look for letters from me till he answers letters[s] I have wrote[.] [portion missing from the original] . . . In your next leave out Riling Carr and so forth.

> Your brother
> J. B. Hickok[23]

---

21 William Elsey Connelley, *Wild Bill and His Era*, 14–15.

22 Hickok, "The Hickok Legend," *loc. cit.*, 13–14.

23 The original letters are owned by Ethel Hickok. In this letter, as in other originals reprinted here, the spellings have not been altered, with the exception of occasional obscure misspellings, which I have corrected in brackets. I have also added punctuation in brackets, where it seemed necessary for clarity.—J. G. R.

The next letter is dated November 24, 1856, and is addressed to his brother Horace. In this letter James was irritated, yet also showed something of his sense of humor, together with a rare insight into his personal philosophy:

I received your letter, dated 7th, and was glad to hear from you and always will be glad to get letters from home. But when you get ready to wright to me again, please leave it off another week and maybe you can think of noncence enough to fill a letter without writing capital letters. You mentioned . . . Marry Ann Masterman married Mr. Hunt[.] I was sorry [to] hear it though I was glad to hear that you had a chance to enjoy a few lesure moments at an evening party and am very much obliged to you for dancing with Sarah Mc[Laughlin] for me and I hope that you will continue to do your duty for I concider it is your duty to dance with the girls for me while I am absent from home. You never mention how George Mc and his wife get along. . . . there is a damn niger sitting ahere before me and I can't think of anything to wright. she is a free colored lady[.] You said something about that damd old shot gun of mine I left the locks out at Bill Whiley's to be sent to old [illegible][.] I do not know whether or not they were ever sent or not and if you want to get it there is a card on the gun with my name on it. I opened your letter when I was coming home this evening to see who it was from and the first thing I read you wanted to no what was going on in Cansas[.] I looked ahead of me to where the roads crossed and saw about 500 soldiers agoing on and I looked down the river and saw some nice steamers and they wear [were] all agoing onn and that is the way with all the people in Cansas[,] they are all a going on[.] I guess they are going to hell so you see I have told you what is going on in Cansas. If I had none [known] as mutch one month ago as I do now I would have had a deed to 160 achres of land now but never mind there is more land to be sold in Cansas yet[.] there is the finest country in Cansas I ever saw[,] nice roling priry[,] nice timber on the cricks[.] you mentioned something about my being in governor protection but I aint nor have not been[,] but iff uncle Sams troops had been at hickery point [Hickory Point] 15 minutes sooner than they were I might have had the honor of riding with uncle Sams troops but captain harvey [James A. Harvey] had given orders that scouts should be sent towards Leavenworth city to see where abouts the companys of captain dun [Dunn?] and miles [Miles or Mills?] Company were camping[,] for you must no that they were camping all the while only when provisions got scarce they could not help marching[,] and that is the way with all the pro slavery companys[.] thare is 29 of our company in custody at Lacompton [Lecompton] yet[.] I have been out to see them once[.] I had as good a horse and as good a gun as thare was in our company[.] thare was a man living on Crooked Crick who furnished me with a horse and rifle and revolver and what I have told you is true. I have rode night after night without getting out of my saddle. There is no roads[,] no cricks[,] no trails[,] no groves[,] no crossings[,] no springs[,] no partys of any kind between Leavenworth and Lorance [Lawrence] or Lacompt [Lecompton]. . . . the land sales commenced this first of November[,] there is more speculators than you can have any idea of[.] these men don't trouble the squatters at all but take every foot of vacant land ruff or smooth[.] our troubles are at an end[,] things are very peacable now governor gary [John W. Geary] told Judge Lacompt [Samuel D. Lecompte] that he had no further use for him nor marshall donalson [Israel B. Donaldson][.] that caused . . . [some] excitement . . . [amongst] the proslavery party but they know better than to make much fuss about it[.] you talk as if you thought if you were here that I would hunt with you[.] I have something else to do[,] I can kill the game we want before sunrise and by moonlight so what would be the use for me to hunt animore[,] and that you could not do for you don't get up early enough[,] and you never scouted any[,] so you could not hunt well at night[.] I must quit for tonight again for that dammed niger has got here before me again (25th) the 26[th.] I have been in masuria [Missouri?] every day for a month and stopping in Kansas every night[.] I am a pilgrim and a stranger and I am a going to wonder [wander] til I am twentyone and then I will tarry a little while. . . . 27th of 1856

Now my dear brothers I want you to excuse these few lines I have written to you and also those bad mistakes and bad spelling for I have written them by candelight. . . . I have got a bad cold otherwise I am well weighing 180 pounds[.] now I will tell you a few lyes[.] I have quit swearing now[,] though take care though Bill [William Simpson][.] I have quit drinking but tut bill I have quit dancing etc[,] I have quit chewing tobacco and dont touch any lager beer and I dont speak to the girls at all[.] I am getting to be a perfect hermit[,] my fiddle[,] my dog[,] and my gun I almost worship. I hold no intercourse with the world around[,] everything looks dark about me and a round but there is a bright spark ahead[,] and it I see[,] it I persue til my fiddle strings brake and my dog dyes and my gun bursts that is so. I want Lydia and Celinda both to wright to me every week without fail[.] . . . I wish this sheet of paper were a little larger for I would like to wright a little more and shure will have to quit and only these few lines[.] I am sorry but can't help it.

From your brother James to H. D. Hickok

HICKOK[24]

A number of interesting facts emerge from this letter. James was something of a musician. His nephew Howard stated: "Uncle Jim loved music. He used to whistle and sing 'Buffalo Gal,' 'Oh! Susan-

[24] *Ibid.* "Captain dun" was probably H. C. Dunn, who was promoted to Captain, "Union Guards," Fourth Regiment, Northern Division, Kansas Militia, on September 1, 1856.

nah.' One letter I had [from someone not identified] told of his love for dancing . . . of seeing him in a square dance, swinging the girls around, a pair of guns at his belt, his frock coat swirling out like a lady's skirt."[25]

Of more importance is James's reference to Hickory Point. The remark "thare is 29 of our company in custody at Lacompton" refers to the aftermath of the Pottawatomie Massacre. Following an attack on Lawrence on May 21, 1856, John Brown in company with three of his sons and three other men set off to Pottawatomie Creek on May 23, and on May 24 brutally murdered and mutilated five proslavery men. This act resulted in a border war.

Attempts to capture John Brown failed and a succession of battles took place. Federal troops were brought in and found themselves engaged with both Free Staters and proslavery militants. By August the situation was desperate and the recently appointed governor of Kansas, Wilson Shannon, resigned on August 21, completely shaken by the state of affairs in the territory. Proslavery Daniel Woodson, territorial secretary, assumed the office of acting governor until the election of a new governor, and promptly proclaimed the territory in open rebellion. David R. Atchison, a proslavery extremist, marched into Kansas with a "Grand Army" of Missourians, and some of his men fought John Brown, while James Lane led a Free State Army toward Lecompton. A pitched battle was prevented by the arrival of Colonel Philip St. George Cooke with troops from Fort Leavenworth.

On September 11, John W. Geary, the new governor, arrived at Lecompton. He disbanded the militia organized by Woodson and went with Cooke to intercept Atchison and others, dissuading them from again entering Kansas. At this time other federal troops captured some Free Staters commanded by Colonel James A. Harvey, who had fought a minor engagement with proslavery men at Hickory Point. These men were probably those mentioned by James Hickok.[26] It is quite probable that he was employed as a scout by Harvey's command.

During the summer of 1856 or 1857, James made the acquaintance of John M. Owen. Born in Tennessee in 1813, Owen emigrated to Missouri in 1833, but three years later moved to what became Kansas. For a time he was employed by the American Fur Company near Silver Lake, and then moved on to what is now known as Monticello, Johnson County. Later he was adopted into

25 "The Hickok Legend," *loc. cit.*, 29.
26 William Frank Zornow, *Kansas: A History of the Jayhawk State*, 68–75.

the Shawnee tribe and in 1840 married Patinuxa, a Shawnee woman, a descendant from a family named Logan. They had one child, Mary Jane. Owen's marriage and purchase of land from an Indian named Toley were probably responsible for his adoption into the tribe. When he actively supported the Free State cause, the tribe disowned him and he lost his rights. In 1856 he settled on a small tract of land on Mill Creek, where he and James Hickok first met.[27]

Old-timers noted that during the period while he was with Owen, Hickok seemed to be without any particular occupation, never had any money, "and spent his time principally in having a good time with the boys, and astonishing them with his dexterity in hitting a target with a pistol. It was a common feat with him to take a stand at a distance of a hundred yards from an oyster can, and with a heavy dragoon revolver send every bullet through it with unerring precision. He had not then commenced his practice upon human beings."[28]

But James soon had an opportunity to use his pistol on other targets. Joining with John Owen, he made his way to join James H. Lane's Free State Army. Prior to his arrival in Kansas, where he became the leader of the Free State cause during the territorial period, and one of the first two United States senators, Lane had won renown in the war with Mexico (1846–48) and later achieved considerable notoriety in the Civil War. Lane was not the organizer of the famous "Red Leg" band of guerrillas—a misconception shared by many, including the Hickok family.

For over a year Hickok and Owen followed Lane, and legend says that they became his bodyguard. It is claimed that they were with Lane at Highland, Kansas, in 1857, when the general made a Free State speech there in the fall. Bayless S. Campbell stated that he saw two men dismount from their horses and lie down on the grass near some stone-masons who were building the foundation of a hotel. "These two men were General Lane's bodyguard, and one of them was Hickok."[29]

Buffalo Bill Cody also claimed to have seen Hickok in 1857. According to Cody, Hickok was a member of the ill-fated Lew Simpson wagon train, which was attacked by Mormons on October 5 and reduced to cinders. Later Cody recalled that this was the first time he had met the future Wild Bill, claiming that as an eleven-year-old boy he had been saved by Wild Bill from a beating at the

[27] E. F. Heisler and D. M. Smith, *Atlas Map of Johnson County Kansas*, 44.
[28] *Ibid.*
[29] Connelley, *Wild Bill and His Era*, 17–18.

hands of camp bullies. From then until Hickok's death they were friends.

In any event, by the end of 1857, Hickok was back in Monticello, and early in the new year the local township elections took place. No doubt Hickok had made some name for himself as a supporter of Lane, or perhaps he was simply known and respected in the little community. In the election of March 22, 1858, the following township officers were elected: R. Williams, chairman of the Board of Supervisors; W. Mason, supervisor; John Owen, supervisor; and J. B. Hickok, constable. These commissions were issued by the Acting Territorial Governor, James W. Denver, effective April 21, 1858.[30]

During this period James interspersed his duties as a constable with farming, and also filed a claim on some land which he worked during his spare time. That he was a keen farmer is proved by his letters home—letters which describe fully his daily tasks and hopes for the future. Sadly, few of those letters now survive, but those that do, provide an interesting insight into his many activities. He had now been joined by his cousin Guy Butler, who spent most of his time at Lawrence during the border wars.[31]

Writing from Monticello on August 14, 1858, probably to Horace, James said:

DEAR BROTHER,
I have neglected answering your letter than I ever did a letter in my life[.] But I beg to be excused this time and I will give my excuse[.] I went to Lacomtan [Lecompton] as a witness and also on business of my own[.] I have the best lawyer engaged to tend my Claim that there is in the territory [Brumbaugh and Bolinger?—see Chapter Two,] there will be no danger but what I will get my claim some time but I will stick it out tell Bill [William Simpson] if you please that I am going to have 160 acres before [illegible—coming?] home and I think [illegible] bad luck if I dont have more[.] I have seen guy and like him first rate[.] he sings a little to much about a man by the name of brown who wore two dangling curls[.] He stayed the first time he Came to see me three or fore days[.] last Wednesday he Came to see me again and steyd [stayed] all day[.] he cant like me very well for he is always wanting to see you so much[.] you want to no whether it would be better for you to come out here in the spring or not[.] there is not mutch a doing here in the country now but I will tell you before spring when I think about it[.] second
Mother mention[ed] some thing about drinking and gambling in hur

30 KSHS *Collections*, Vol. V (1891–96), 485.
31 Howard L. Hickok to the author, Oct. 13, 1960.

letter[,] well now [illegible] I will tell you what is a fact[.] I have not drunk a pint of liquar in a year and have not played for a sent [cent] in twice that time[.] the first time I go to Lawrence I will send you my likeness and you can see whether it looks like a whisky face or not[.] I have been making hay for 4 or 5 days[.] I have got it all stacked ready for same[,] just got through [a]bout half an hour ago[.] one of my best friends lyes here sick even unto death[,] he is the man I live with [.] I think that guy will write to you, that I am mighty poor Company[.] he thinks I talk less than any man he ever see. all the time he was here I wanted to talk to him but I would get to studying sometimes two hours if he did not say anything[.] I have got an awful notion of studying lately[.] anyway I set some times two hours and think a bout one thing and a nother without speaking even when the hows [house] is full of people. . . . every time I turn over and write without moving [portion missing] tell the reason that I write so many different ways [portion missing] you that the delaware lands are Coming in to market. . . . I made you both a Clame on them lands[.] I made them last fall when every body though them lands were coming in to market[.] I live right close to these lands and when they do come in if they ever do[,] I am going to have a wipe [swipe?] at them shure[.] there is one section over that [there?] that I would like to have for us fore brothers[.] there is a bout one hundred acers of timber on the [illegible] and the great butiful priarie cant be beat in the country[.]

JAMES B HICKOK

Monday 23

Celinda says [portion missing] but a letter that she got from Ol[iver?] not got it when I got hurs[.] But I shall [missing] for it[.] if I don[']t get it you must write what news there was in it[.] I should like to know when he is coming home for if he should come home soon you could look for me shortly after[.]

Monday night 10 o[']clock

I quit writing to go a hunting[, and] I have just returned and got my supper[,] and thought I would write and tell you what luck I had[.] had one young buck [and] two turkeys which I carryed home on my back and now you may think I am tired whitch I shurly am but howsoever being herd [?] and not while setting by the fire[,] I might as well write as not[.] thare is plenty of game here more than there was on the other side of the river[;] gees[e] are plenty here in the fall[.]

JAMES

. . . MONTECELLO Tuesday 17th 1858 10 oclock

guy was here this morning a little while[,] he was on his way to the [illegible] to get some sand[.] he says gerush is married to William Simpson [Gerusha Butler, James's and Guy's cousin.] you ought to have seen him [illegible] this morning[,] for a bout half an hour he was shaved a gain[;] it make him look awfull thin[.] I tell you I did not hardly no him[.] look out that you dont all get maried[.] guy sends his respects and love to all ... a good by for this time[.]

Montecello[,] Tuesday afternoon[.] I have been of[f] on official business and now it is five oclock[.] I will write a little more. ... But I have not got my diner yet[.] guy was here ... to say he had broke a singletree and came to borrow one of[f] me[.] He says he wished Bill Simpson was here so that he could make him one[.] he sayd it would not have cost him anything[,] for it would have been all in the family. ...

Montecello Friday August 20 1858

I have been mowing or reaping hay with the machine today and break it all to pieces ... so I guess I shant have to work this afternoon[,] good luck at last[.] guy sets on the bed beside me now[,] he has been after sand again and he says if you dont write him a letter as hes lonely ... he will thrash you[.] guy dont sware any yet I believe[,] nor drink any thing but water and ale and setch other things[,] and he thinks [it] is good for his health[.] I [illegible] ears of corn last Sunday[.] my gall [Mary Owen] washed them for me and a pack of dride corn and then was hungry[.] now[,] sir[,] when you get this if you dont write me a long letter when you get this [,] [you] never will have a chance to anser another

JAMES HICKOK

MONTECELLO Friday the 20 1858

I made a mistake yesterday[,] I thought it was Friday[,] but no difference[.] guy is here again today[,] he has baught a claim in douglas county a bout 120 miles from here[.] him and a nother man together they paid $150 for it [.] thare is fore achors [four acres] of timber that will do for fire wood on it and 200 [illegible] and 400 hundred in the woods that they can have[.] he says there is a butifull spring a bout to rods from the dore [door] and a hous 14 feet square on it[.] he says he is going to fence in the whole quarter this winter[,] or the to of them is[.] I hope they may find [and] have luck on it[.] guy is at work at Manelata [?] for 18 teen dollars amount[,] driving a bull team with Sandys[.] [That is] a gentleman ox team [if] there are any [ladies] that reads this that they can read the middle line if they are bashfull[.] I must go to puttin up hay....

JAMES HICKOK[32]

In another letter headed "Montecello Monday 16th [August] 1858" (evidently James wrote when he found time, and probably was careless of his dating), he wrote:

I will Write a few minutes While diner is cooking. I have been and served three summonses this morning. There has been 25 horses stolen here Within the last ten days by to men by the name of Scroggins and Black Bob[.] They have narry one been taken yet[,] but I think they

---

[32] In the possession of Ethel Hickok.

will ketch it soon. if they are caught About here they Will be run upawfull soon to the top of Some hill[,] I guess[,] where they wont steel Any more horses[.] I am going out to see guy next Sunday . . . he is turning out an awfull mustache and goatee but I think my mustache and goatee lays over hisen Considerable[,] the fact of it is hisen ain't no Whare[.] I went to see my gall yesterday[,] and eat 25 ears of Corn to fill up with. You ought to be here and eat some of hur buiskits[.] she is the only one that I ever Saw that could beat mother making buiskits and you no I aught to no for I can eat A few you no. I have got to go this afternoon and suppeany a dozen witnesses[,] so I will quit[,] eat my diner and go[.]

JAMES BUTLER HICKOK[33]

On an undated sheet James expressed his opinion of the situation that then existed in Kansas. While getting some water he saw a fight break out, which he carefully avoided. The incident does indicate that he had a strong sense of justice and a belief in law and order:

. . . it was the first time in my life that I ever saw a fight and did not go to see it out[,] and I am glad of it now[.] you dont no what a Country this is for drinking and fighting[.] but I hope it will be different some time and I no in reason that will when the Law is put in force[.] there is no Common Law here now hardly at all[.] a man Can do what he pleases without fear of the Law or any thing els[.] thare has been two awful fights in town this week[,] you dont no anything about sutch fighting at home as I speak of[,] this is no place for women and children yet[,] all though they all say it is so quiet here[.] . . . if a man fites in kansas and gets whiped he never says anything more A bout it[,] if he does he will get whipt for his trouble.

On August 23, James again referred to his girl friend, Mary Owen:

I would have finished this Letter yesterday But was not at home[.] I was over at John Owen[.] I go thare when I git hungry[.] Jest the Same as I youst to Come home to mothers to git some thing good to eat[.] mary Cut off a Lock of my hare yesterday and Sayed for me to Send it to my mother or Sisters[.] if she had not thought a good deal of you all She would not have Cut it off for She thinks a grate deal of it[.] At least she is always Coming and Curling it[—] that is when I am Hare.

JAMES B. HICKOK[34]

The relationship between James Hickok and Mary Owen has led to the false assumption that they married. William E. Connelley

[33] Ibid.
[34] Ibid.

believed this until Howard L. Hickok provided him with copies of James's letters which proved otherwise. "Subsequently," wrote Howard, "Connelley did change his mind and wrote me that he believed that I and my father and uncle were right, and also stated that of the many western characters of his time, James Butler Hickok was almost the only one without Indian progeny."[35]

Toward the end of 1858, Hickok left Monticello, and until now the reason has remained obscure. But the answer lay in his letters. When they reached the family in Illinois great concern was felt over his obvious infatuation for Mary Owen and the fact that he no longer seemed decisive about his future plans. The family discussed it and decided to take action:

> Lorenzo, wise enough to read between the lines, immediately decided to go to Kansas and try to break the infatuation. He visited Jim just after a raid had been made, and Jim's cabin burned by Pro-slavery men. . . . the advent of Lorenzo changed Jim's mind and pride of family, and pride of race advocated by Lorenzo, eventually overcame the budding romance. They gave up the idea of farming at this time and both went to Leavenworth.[36]

James's own feelings have never been known, but Howard had some thoughts on the matter:

> . . . wonder if this interference by the older brother was not a serious mistake. Owens was a prominent citizen his daughter an intelligent and beautiful girl. Had Jim remained on the farm, and married he might have been a prominent civic minded member of the community as have many men that married women of Indian extraction. Under ordinary circumstances one might think that a quiet life on the farm, would have saved him from the adventures and exciting tenure of life. . . . it was inevitable that he was destined for the short period of service alloted him in this vale of tears.[37]

While Lorenzo secured employment as a civilian teamster, which occupation he continued during the Civil War, at one point working for General Frémont, James got a job with Russell, Majors, and Waddell, and for nearly two years he drove their stagecoaches and wagons.

Driving in those days was not just a matter of driving: it was a fight for survival. There was always the danger of meeting road agents, but other perils beset the driver. The roads themselves were

---

[35] Howard L. Hickok to the author, Oct. 13, 1960.
[36] Hickok, "The Hickok Legend," *loc. cit.*, 14–15.
[37] *Ibid.*, 15.

a menace. Most of them were little better than rough tracks, but despite deep ruts, rocks, and hidden stumps, they were passable, and once clear of passes, narrow defiles, and rocky tracks, passage across prairie and mesa country was much easier.

At its best, however, stage travel was an ordeal. During the summer, with the sun at its peak, dust was a ceaseless irritant. Great clouds of it would billow around the coach, almost smothering the driver, guard (sometimes called "messenger" or "conductor"), and passengers. These early coaches had no glass windows—only leather curtains which could be rolled down over the openings. The coach was suspended on heavy leather thorough braces slung under the body and attached to spring-steel brackets at either end of the chassis. These absorbed some of the shock, but the stage traveler had indeed to be hardy.

It is believed that during 1859 and 1860, Hickok drove both freight wagons and coaches. It was on a trip to Santa Fe (there is disagreement on what he was driving) that he may have met Christopher "Kit" Carson. Shortly before his death Hickok is alleged to have parted with a Dragoon Colt which he said Carson had given him in 1859. According to the tale, Kit showed him some of the night life of Santa Fe and in particular warned him against fraternizing with the Mexican women. Hickok, shrewd man that he was, heeded this advice, and after a good hoisting session in the old part of the town, they parted. It is claimed that they met just once more, at Fort Lyon, Colorado, not long before the famous old plainsman and scout died on May 23, 1868.

Authentic recollections of James Butler Hickok at this time are hard to find, and although the following may have some fictional overtones, it does display certain characteristics of the man. Truman Blancett, an old-time Colorado Pioneer, wrote in 1931:

In 1860 my father, brothers and I were keeping the station at Ashpoint, Kan., between Seneca and Marysville, then the raw, western frontier. The town of Seneca was on the Nehama river, eighty miles west of Fort Leavenworth. Marysville was situated on the Big Blue river, 125 miles west of the fort.

The mail coach changed mules at our station, and was drawn by six or eight mules, depending on the load.

Mexican mules, such as were used, are not very large, oftimes running with the coach like scared rabbits. They were mean and wild critters and two Mexicans always were at the station to make the change of teams. It was figured it took one Mexican to handle one mule.

Hickok was at our station once a week for about a half hour at a time

THE BOY AND THE MAN

while mules were being changed, and we would exchange stories of our experiences during the interim, a universal custom at the time. We were both young, he being not more than 20 [sic] years old and I, 18. Both of us were trying to raise a mustache. "Wild Bill" was taciturn even at that age. He talked little of himself or about others. He was a man of action, not of words. . . .

I never saw him with his feet off the cash box which was carried under the feet of the mail coach driver. This box was of metal construction, its carrying space equal to about a bushel. The box was the particular trust of the guard and he was under orders to watch it with his life.

Hickok handled a pistol with the speed of lightning. When he wished to emphasize something he had a way of throwing his right or left hand towards you with the trigger finger pointed straight at you. His hands moved with incredible swiftness and I believe he practiced this mannerism with such purpose that it became a part of his nature, and probably resulted in making him the fastest two-gun man of his day. . . .

One day I returned to the Ashpoint station just as the coach pulled in. I was carrying a mighty good pistol, a Dragoon .45 [sic] caliber, and as I rode up to the coach I noticed Bill's eyes were directed toward my pistol.

"That's a mighty dangerous looking gun for an innocent looking man," he said, asking to examine it.

After looking it over he remarked: "It's a mighty fine gun, but I don't see any notches on the handle."

I told him I hadn't got to that yet, and he said:

"You will get to that before you cross the desert, that is if you don't get killed before you get into practice."

Anyone who wanted to make the acquaintance of Hickok would mind their own business and not get too inquisitive would find him a perfect gentleman in every way. In those days he was not known as "Wild Bill."[38]

As Blancett pointed out, Hickok was not called "Wild Bill" prior to the Civil War, but an individual of that name aroused some interest in the Kansas Press. On October 29, 1859, the following was published:

> FORT SCOTT, KANSAS TERRITORY,
> October 20, 1859.
>
> TO THE EDITOR OF THE BORDER STAR:
> I have just read the blustering cards of these northern bullies, Morrissey and Heenan, and they tickle me mightily. They are both said to be "some" in a fight and I like to feel such fellers. You are therefore authorized to say that I challenge both of these champions to single combat, until I or they are whipped, for $1,000 a side. The fight will take place at Kansas City or Leavenworth on any day the opposite party may name,

38 "The Old Frontier," Denver *Post*, Mar. 22, 1931.

giving me due notice thereof. As a guarantee of my earnestness I will deposit $500 at Northrup and Company's Banking House in Kansas City.

WILD BILL[39]

In an editorial, the paper said:

It will be seen from a communication in another column that Morrissey and Heenan are both challenged by a Western ripsnorter who has proved himself a tight customer in a bear fight. Our correspondent is a genuine character and we dare say he will make good all he has written. He is a Cheyenne chief, well known for his power and spunk. He is a white man by birth, but in early life he joined the Indians and so well was he pleased with their manners, customs, and mode of life that he became a member of the Cheyenne tribe and was finally chosen their chief. If Morrissey or Heenan desire a fight that is a fight—they will respond through the *Star* or one of the New York papers.

In September another paper had published an account of the exploits of "Wild Bill" and his ill-fated attempt at matrimony with a young lady whom he had met while she was a member of a wagon train bound for Pike's Peak. Friends persuaded her that she would be unwise to marry him, and "Wild Bill" returned in disgust to his tribe.[40]

One important fact has emerged from these newspaper stories. Reference to a bear fight and to Fort Scott suggest another classic Hickok legend. But first another episode in Hickok's life must be examined.

In his letters to J. B. Edwards of Abilene, Kansas, Charles F. Gross wrote:

. . . way back in 1859 my father was building a church at Buda, Ills & our family spent the summer there. I was sent to a farm near Tiskilwa Ills to work in the harvest field, the job being to carry water to the wheat binders[.] I was put to sleep with a young man named James B. Hickok[,] he lived near their somewhere. . . . I was [also] carrying bundles of grain into piles for me to shock, in the last work I worked with Bill who was shocking. We both talked most of the time & slept together at night[.]

[39] Westport *Border Star*; the late James Anderson of the Kansas City Westerners confirmed that the records of the bank are no longer available.

[40] Fort Scott *Democrat*, Sept. 29, 1859; John Morrissey and John Camel Heenan fought the first American heavyweight championship at Long Point, Canada, in 1858. It was a hard fight and Morrissey put Heenan down in the eleventh round. But it was Heenan who won the admiration of the crowd. Morrissey gave up fighting and eventually, in 1877, became a state senator. A disastrous love affair with and marriage to Adah Isaacs Menken, an original "Mazeppa," led to numerous defeats and an early death for Heenan in Wyoming at the age of thirty-eight (Gilbert Odd, "Adah Helped K. O. Heenan," *Fighters and Their Women*, London *Evening News*, Aug. 31, 1963).

I was than as now a very inquisitive boy, and just the age when I was much impressed by stories of any kind. Bill was a good worker, much older than I, strong & athletic[.] At noon and after work he pitched horse shoes[,] ran races[,] jumped, Wrestled and was best at the game of [the] others there.[41]

Although both Buda and Tiskilwa are very close to what is now Troy Grove, only recently has evidence been found to indicate that there is some truth in the story. Fred (Mac) Gibbs of Princeton, Illinois, stated that his father had once visited Kansas and returned with Hickok and together they went to La Salle, where they had their hair cut, were shaved, and had their pictures taken. Both then helped with the harvest. Gibbs remained in Illinois while Hickok returned west. The Gibbs family were related to the Hickoks following the marriage of Oliver Hickok's widow to Oliver Gibbs in 1814. As if to add further truth to this story, Howard Hickok described a typical harvest in Homer during the 1850's:

> Oliver and Lorenzo were tall, strong men, Dad [Horace] was shorter, but strongly built. Jim was a stripling tall and graceful. They raised wheat; when ripe it was cradled, bound into sheaves and flailed out on the granary floor. Horatio Gibbs, grandfather[']s half brother, was a powerful man, six feet three in height. Dad told me that Lorenzo was the only man in the neighborhood that could stay with Gibbs stroke for stroke, with the cradle. Dad and Fred Gibbs came behind them, and bound the sheaves.[42]

If James did come home that year, as the evidence seems to suggest, the visit has escaped all family chroniclers, but does explain another of the many gaps in his life.

Hickok was back in Kansas by the winter of 1859. Whether or not he actually met Cody on Lew Simpson's wagon train or some other place is not certain, but he was included in a list of friends invited to the Cody home known as "The Big House," which was intended for use as a hotel. His sister Julia named the guests as "James B. Hickok, Lew Simpson, John Willis and George Ross."[43]

With the coming of 1860, the future of Russell, Majors, and Waddell's empire was at stake. On April 3 they started the famous Pony Express. James Butler Hickok did not serve as a rider. He was too tall and heavy; most of the riders were under twenty-one years of

---

41 Jan. 20, 1926, Manuscripts Division, KSHS.
42 "The Hickok Legend," *loc. cit.*, 8; Edith Harmon to the author, Sept. 2, 1970. I also questioned Mr. Gibbs, but he was unable to add any more details or find the tintypes his father and Hickok had made in La Salle.
43 Don Russell, *The Lives and Legends of Buffalo Bill*, 41.

age, and the smaller and skinnier the better. His young friend Cody did ride for the Pony Express, while James continued in his capacity as stage or wagon driver.

In September, 1860, Hickok is believed to have met the terrible Joseph Alfred Slade, known as "Jack," who was employed by the stagecoach division of the company as a line superintendent. Born about 1824 in Carlyle, Illinois, Slade had served in the Fifth Illinois Volunteers in the Mexican War and had remained in the West. He was strikingly handsome and was said to have slain twenty-six men—a total which is disputed. In later years Hickok was called the "Slade of Kansas." The title annoyed him and was certainly unjustified.

Slade's looks belied his reputation. Mark Twain remarked that he was "so friendly and so gentle spoken that I warmed to him in spite of his awful history. It was hardly possible to realize that this pleasant person was the pitiless scourge of the outlaws, the rawhead-and-bloody-bones the nursing mothers of the mountains terrified their children with."[44] Twain's opinion was evidently shared by Buffalo Bill. Slade is best remembered for his feud with Jules Bene (or Reni) a French Canadian. Slade had been line superintendent of the Central Overland California and Pike's Peak Express Company for about a year when Benjamin Ficklin, the general superintendent of the company, ordered him to investigate allegations that Jules was mixed up in horse-stealing and in harboring outlaws. Slade was ambushed and shot in the back by Jules, following a dispute over who was in command. Someone shouted a warning to Slade but before he could pull his pistol, Jules shot him three times. Still on his feet, Slade was then shot twice more as Jules emptied both barrels of a shotgun into him.

Thinking that Slade was dead, Jules ordered horrified onlookers to bury him, but instead they tried to hang Jules, and were only prevented from doing so by the arrival of Ben Ficklin. Learning that Slade still lived, Ficklin gave Jules his life provided he left the country. Jules eagerly accepted and left. But later he came back and was captured by Slade, who took his revenge by tying him to a fence post and shooting him full of holes. He then cut off his ears and used one as a watch fob. The other he nailed to the post. His career with the company ended when he shot up the post canteen at Fort Halleck. On March 10, 1864, at Virginia City, Montana, Slade was hanged by the vigilantes for shooting up the town. He had been told to stop getting drunk and violent, but he had re-

[44] *Roughing It*, 75–76.

peatedly ignored the warnings. Many regretted the death of a man who, in his sober moments, was a good citizen.[45]

When Hickok met Slade, there was no friction between them. Their acquaintance began when Indians drove off the stock from Plant's Station and left some forty Pony Express riders, drivers, and stock-tenders idle. The men elected Hickok as their captain and set out after the stock. The trail led to the Powder River, on past Crazy Woman's Fort, to Clear Creek. Here the Indians reached their camp. At Hickok's suggestion the men waited until dark, then rode upon the Indian camp, shooting and shouting and causing a general stampede. They were successful in recovering all the company's stock, and about one hundred Indian ponies were counted among them. At a celebration spree at Sweetwater Bridge Station afterward, Slade made an appearance and, it is alleged, killed a stage driver after a violent quarrel. Somewhat sobered, the men broke off their fun and settled down to the business of re-establishing the stage company's service.

Among the Hickok stories there is a remarkable one which tells how he fought a bear about this time. This legend has been repeated countless times, bowdlerized, twisted, and warped, and just how much truth there is in it has always been in doubt.

This writer now believes that the bear fight probably owes its origin to J. W. Buel. The previously cited story of a Cheyenne chief called "Wild Bill" and mention of his bear encounter in the Fort Scott press is particularly significant. It is my belief that during his period as city editor of the Fort Scott *Monitor*, Buel read the stories in the files of the local press and used the incident to boost the heroics of his character.

But whatever the cause, it is evident that early in 1861, Hickok was suffering from injuries of some sort, and the company put him on light duties and sent him out along the Oregon Trail to Rock Creek Station in Nebraska Territory to complete his convalescence. So it was that James Butler Hickok came to the adventure that was to determine the course of his future life.

[45] For more details of Slade, see Joseph G. Rosa, *The Gunfighter: Man or Myth?* 22–24.

--❦ 2 ❧--

Incident at Rock Creek

ROCK CREEK is situated just six miles from Fairbury, Nebraska. It flows into the Little Blue River from the north. Today it is little more than a landmark, but in 1861 it was the scene of a quarrel which ended in tragedy—death to three men, and fame to one other. It was here that James Butler Hickok's legend really started.

No single gunfight, with the possible exception of the Earp-Clanton fight in October, 1881, in Tombstone, Arizona, has caused so much controversy as the Hickok-McCanles affair at Rock Creek on the afternoon of Friday, July 12, 1861.

Colonel George Ward Nichols wrote the first publicized account of it, in which he described how Wild Bill singlehandedly fought and defeated ten heavily armed ruffians, relating the story in Hickok's own words:

"You see this M'Kandlas was the Captain of a gang of desperadoes, horsethieves, murderers, regular cut-throats, who were the terror of everybody on the border, and who kept us in the mountains in hot water whenever they were around. I knew them all in the mountains, where they pretended to be trapping, but they were there hiding from the hangman. M'Kandlas was the biggest scoundrel and bully of them all, and was allers a-braggin' of what he could do. One day I beat him shootin at a mark, and then threw him at the back-holt. And I didn't drop him as soft as you would a baby, you may be sure. Well, he got savage mad about it, and swore he would have his revenge on me some time.

"This was just before the war broke out, and we were already takin sides in the mountains either for the South or the Union. M'Kandlas and his gang were border-ruffians in the Kansas row, and of course they went with the rebs. Bime-by he clar'd out, and I shouldn't have thought of the feller again ef he hadn't crossed my path. It 'pears he didn't forget me.

"It was in '61, when I guided a detachment of cavalry who were comin in from Camp Floyd. We had nearly reached the Kansas line, and were in South Nebraska, when one afternoon I went out of camp to go to the cabin of an old friend of mine, a Mrs. Waltman. I took only one of my revolvers with me, for although the war had broke out I didn't think it

34

necessary to carry both my pistols, and, in all or'nary scrimmages, one is better than a dozen ef you shoot straight. I saw some wild turkeys on the road as I was goin' down, and popped one of 'em over, thinking he'd be just the thing for supper.

"Well, I rode up to Mrs. Waltman's, jumped off my horse, and went into the cabin, which is like most of the cabins on the prarer, with only one room, and that had two doors, one opening in front and t'other on a yard like.

" 'How are you, Mrs. Waltman?' I said, feeling as jolly as you please.

"The minute she saw me she was turned white as a sheet and screamed: 'Is that you, Bill? Oh, God! They will kill you! Run! run! They will kill you!'

" 'Who's a-goin to kill me? said I. There's two can play at that game.'

" 'It's M'Kandlas and his gang. There's ten of them, and you've no chance. They've jes gone down the road to the corn-rack. They came up here only five minutes ago. M'Kandlas was draggin poor Parson Shipley on the ground with a lariat round his neck. The preacher was most dead with choking and the horses stamping on him. M'Kandlas knows yer bringing in that party of Yankee cavalry, and he swears he'll cut yer heart out. Run, Bill, run!—But it's too late; they're comin up the lane.'

"While she was a-talkin' I remembered that I had but one revolver, and a load gone out of that. On the table there was a horn of powder and some little bars of lead. I poured some powder into the empty chamber and rammed the lead after it by hammering the barrel on the table, and had just capped the pistol when I heard M'Kandlas shout:

" 'There's that d——d Yank Wild Bill's horse; he's here; and we'll skin him alive!'

"If I had thought of runnin before it war too late now, and the house was my best holt—sort of fortress, like. I never thought I should leave the room alive."

The scout stopped his story, rose from his seat, and strode back and forward in a state of great excitement.

"I tell you what it is Kernel," he resumed, after a while, "I don't mind a scrimmage with these fellers round here. Shoot one or two of them and the rest run away. But all of M'Kandlas's gang were reckless, blood-thirsty devils, who would fight as long as they had strength to pull a trigger. I have been in tight places, but that's one of the few times I said my prayers.

" 'Surround the house and give no quarter!' yelled M'Kandlas. When I heard that I felt as quiet and cool as if I was a-goin to church. I looked round the room and saw a Hawkins rifle hangin over the bed.

" 'Is that loaded?' said I to Mrs. Waltman.

" 'Yes,' the poor thing whispered. She was so frightened she couldn't speak out loud.

" 'Are you sure?' said I, as I jumped to the bed and caught it from its

35

hooks. Although my eye did not leave the door, yet I could see she nodded 'Yes' again. I put the revolver on the bed, and just then M'Kandlas poked his head inside the doorway, but jumped back when he saw me with the rifle in my hand.

" 'Come in here, you cowardly dog!' I shouted. 'Come in here, and fight me!'

"M'Kandlas was no coward, if he was a bully. He jumped inside the room with his gun leveled to shoot; but he was not quick enough. My rifle-ball went through his heart. He fell back outside the house, where he was found afterward holding tight to his rifle, which had fallen over his head.

"His disappearance was followed by a yell from his gang, and then there was a dead silence. I put down the rifle and took the revolver, and said to myself: 'Only six shots and nine men to kill. Save your powder, Bill, for the death-hug's a-comin!' I don't know why it was, Kernel," continued Bill, looking at me inquiringly, "but at that moment things seemed clear and sharp. I could think strong.

"There was a few seconds of that awful stillness, and then the ruffians came rushing in at both doors. How wild they looked with their red, drunken faces and inflamed eyes, shouting and cussing! But I never aimed more deliberately in my life.

"One—two—three—four; and four men fell dead.

"That didn't stop the rest. Two of them fired their birdguns at me. And then I felt a sting run all over me. The room was full of smoke. Two got in close to me, their eyes glaring out of the clouds. One I knocked down with my fist. 'You are out of the way for a while,' I thought. The second I shot dead. The other three clutched me and crowded me onto the bed. I fought hard. I broke with my hand one man's arm. He had his fingers round my throat. Before I could get to my feet I was struck across the breast with the stock of a rifle, and felt the blood rushing out of my nose and mouth. Then I got ugly, and I remember that I got hold of a knife, and then it was all cloudy like, and I was wild, and I struck savage blows, following the devils up from one side to the other of the room and into the corners, striking and slashing until I knew that every one was dead.

"All of a sudden it seemed as if my heart was on fire. I was bleeding every where. I rushed out to the well and drank from the bucket, and then tumbled down in a faint."

Breathless with the intense interest with which I had followed this strange story, all the more thrilling and weird when its hero, seeming to live over again the bloody events of that day, gave way to its terrible spirit with wild, savage gestures. I saw then—what my scrutiny of the morning had failed to discover—the tiger which lay concealed beneath that gentle exterior.

"You must have been hurt almost to death," I said.

"There were eleven buck-shot in me. I carry some of them now. I was cut in thirteen places. All of them had enough to have let the life out of a man. But that blessed old Dr. Mills pulled me safe through it, after a bed siege of many a long week."[1]

Nichols was followed by J. W. Buel and many others, but it is Nichols' story that is best remembered. What has never been satisfactorily resolved is how much Hickok actually said to Nichols and how much he got from others. Even before the *Harper's* story came out, the incident was already well known in the West. When *Harper's* appeared in Springfield, it was remarked:

We are sorry to say . . . that the graphic account of the terrible fight at Mrs. Waltman's, in which Bill killed, solitary and alone, "the guerrilla McKandlas and ten of his men"—the whole bilen of 'em—is not reliable. The fact upon which this account is *founded*, being that before the war, and while yet out in the mountains, Wild Bill did fight and kill one McKandlas and two other men, who attacked him simultaneously. These little rivulets in the monthlies, weeklies and dailies, all run into and make up the great river of *history* afterwhile; and if many of them are as salty as this one, the main stream will be very brackish at least. . . . Bill never was in the tight place narrated, and exhibited in the illustrating wood cut. . . . We must congratulate Bill on the fact that that picture and narrative was rather *not* true.[2]

Another report claimed that the Rock Creek referred to was actually a place beyond Marysville, Kansas, and that the "Mc-Kandles gang" consisted of four men, the leader and three others. In a desperate fight Hickok killed three, and the fourth ran off "and was not heard of afterward. There was no grudge existing between the McKandles gang and 'Wild Bill,' but the former had a quarrel with the Stage Company, and had come to burn the station 'Bill' was in charge of. The other men, hearing of their coming, ran off, leaving 'Bill' to defend the property alone. He did it with the greatest coolness and courage, and the Company rewarded him very handsomely for his action afterwards."[3]

Both reports seem to have been based upon more realistic information than that given Nichols. But although they reduced the number of casualties, they were still short of the facts. There was a fight at Rock Creek, and it is true that only three men died, but

[1] "Wild Bill," *Harper's New Monthly Magazine*, Vol. XXXIV, No. CCI (Feb., 1867), 282–84.
[2] Springfield *Weekly Missouri Patriot*, Jan. 31, 1867.
[3] Atchison *Daily Champion*, Feb. 5, 1867.

after sifting through the evidence, I suggest that possibly Hickok did not kill McCanles after all.

David Colbert McCanles (that is the correct spelling of the name; Nichols' version appears to be phonetic), the principal actor of this tragedy, was born on November 30, 1828, in Iredell County, North Carolina. Sometime after his birth his father James moved the family to Watauga County, also in North Carolina, and it was there that the boy grew up. His father earned a living as a fiddler, schoolteacher, and cabinetmaker. He evidently earned sufficient to give his son an elementary education and then put him in a military academy. But David's stay there was short, possibly because his inherent desire to be "top dog" proved too much for his masters. The young McCanles was gifted with great strength of body and mind. Anything he could not have for the asking, he would try to take by force. He outran, outfought, and outdanced his companions, and he had a certain feeling of superiority.

In 1849 he married Mary Green, the daughter of a neighbor, and soon the family man turned his ambitions toward politics. He got himself elected deputy sheriff of the county in 1852, but he and the County Sheriff, one Jack Horton, disliked but tolerated each other. Horton was a big man and may have resented the younger man's strength, which probably equaled his own. They agreed that Mc-Canles would not run for sheriff in any forthcoming elections, but McCanles obviously had no intention of keeping such a promise, and in 1856 announced himself as a candidate.

Horton was furious, and a heated argument ended in blows. Mc-Canles may or may not have won the fist fight, but he did win the election. Part of his job as sheriff was the collection of debts and certain taxes. It was because of some serious trouble over debts that he, his brother Leroy, and Jack Horton became involved with the law—and McCanles was forced to flee the country.

Writing an early county history, John Preston Arthur described at length the events which led up to McCanles' departure:

McCanless was a strikingly handsome man and a well-behaved, useful citizen till he became involved with a woman not his wife, after which he fell into evil courses. As Sheriff he was Tax Collector, and also had in his hands claims in favor of J. M. Weath, a Frenchman, who sold goods throughout this section in job lots. As there was no homestead then, whatever an officer could find in a defendant's possession was subject to levy and sale. January 1, 1859, came and soon afterwards came also a representative from Weath for a settlement with McCanless. On the morning of January 6th "Colb" [the name by which he was called locally] set out for Boone, accompanied by Levi L. Coffey, a near neighbor, then about twenty-seven years of age. "Colb" told Weath's man that he had made many collections for Weath, but had offsets against some of them and could settle the balance due only by an interview with Weath himself. Therefore, he would join Weath's man at Blowing Rock the following morning and go with him to Statesville. He and Jack Horton, who was on McCanless' official bond, then took a ride together, after which Horton sold his horse to one of the Hardins and McCanless immediately bought the same horse for the exact price Hardin had paid for it. During the same day McCanless conveyed certain real estate to his brother, J. Leroy McCanless. Subsequently, on the first day of March, 1859, J. L. McCanless conveyed the same land to Jack or John Horton, and on that day Jack Horton conveyed it to Smith Coffey. In a suit between Calvin J. Cowles against Coffey it was alleged, and so found by the jury, that these conveyances from D. C. to J. L. McCanless and from him to Jack Horton had been given to defraud the creditors of D. C. McCanless. . . . Horton is said also to have secured McCanless' saddle pockets with many claims in them against various people in Watauga County, these pockets having been left by McCanless in a certain store in Boone for that very purpose, thus securing Horton as far as possible from loss by reason of his liability on McCanless' official bond. McCanless also had the proceeds of a claim which as Sheriff he held against Wilson Burleson, who then lived near Bull Scrape, now Montezuma, Avery County. This money was due to J. M. Weath also, and which, for safekeeping, had been placed by McCanless with Jacob Rintels in Boone, in whose store Col. W. L. Bryan was then clerking, then known as the Jack Horton Old Store. Late that sixth of January McCanless called on Rintels for the money, with the request that as much as possible be paid in gold and silver. This was done. McCanless then started on the road to Wilkes County, where he claimed he was to pay the money over to Robert Hayes on an execution, having told Levi Coffey not to wait for him, as he was not going to return home that night. But instead of continuing on to Wilkes, McCanless went only as far as Three Forks Church, where he doubled back and went up the Jack Hodges Creek and through Hodges Gap to Shull's Mills, where he was joined by a woman. They went together to Johnson City, where their horses and saddles and bridles were sold to Joel Dyer. There they took the train for the West. After D. C. McCanless had been away several months, J. L. McCanless, his brother, followed him, but soon returned and took West with him D. C. McCanless' wife.[4]

The woman who accompanied him west was Sarah Shull, sometimes referred to as Kate Shell; she was the daughter of the mill-

[4] *History of Watauga County, North Carolina, with Sketches of Prominent Families*, cited by William Elsey Connelley in his reconstruction of the affair in his "Wild Bill—James Butler Hickok," KSHS *Collections*, Vol. XVII (1926–28), 2–3.

owner. After journeying by steamboat from St. Louis to Leavenworth, McCanles and Sarah fitted out at Leavenworth with all the equipment necessary for a plains journey.[5] Some have it that McCanles hoped to join the gold rush to Pike's Peak, but before he and Sarah had gone far they met a number of returning disillusioned gold-seekers. McCanles then concluded that he should settle somewhere, and take up ranching or farming. Passing along the Oregon Trail, he came to Rock Creek, where a man named Newton Glenn[6] had a small relay station used by the emigrants and the various freighting concerns passing over the trail. McCanles took a long look at the place and decided he liked it. Glenn was anxious to sell, and McCanles bought him out.

McCanles made great improvements in the water supply and set up a toll bridge over the creek. As traffic over the Oregon Trail at this point was heavy, his income must have been enormous—which probably accounts for the "crock of gold" he is supposed to have buried shortly before his death and which was never found. The toll was between ten and fifty cents a wagon, depending on the size of the load.

During the summer of 1859 he built a new and better ranch on the east side of the creek and dug a new well. Sarah Shull had meantime settled down comfortably at the original ranch, which became known as the "West-side ranch."[7]

The Rocky Mountain Dispatch Company used the West-side ranch until February, 1861, when they left owing McCanles money. He filed an action at Beatrice for attachment on the Dispatch Company for $318.90. The company also had four horses and two sets of harness belonging to him. Then, on April 22, 1861, McCanles sold this ranch to Wolfe and Hagenstein. They were to pay him in full one year from the date of purchase. This means that at the time of the shooting McCanles had three concerns owing him money.[8]

[5] Sarah Shull came west with six men. She and McCanles remained at Rock Creek, and the others went on to Colorado (Levi Bloyd to the author, July 27, 1958). The late Mr. Bloyd also revealed that Sarah Louisa Shull was born at Watauga River, Ashe County, North Carolina, on October 3, 1833, and was the daughter of Phillip Shull and Phoebe Wand (Fairbury, [Neb.] News, Aug. 13, 1965).

[6] Probably the William N. Glenn listed as a trader, aged twenty-two, shown in the 1860 census, "Jones Territory—36" Territory of Nebraska (microfilm copy on file, Manuscripts Division, Nebraska State Historical Society, hereinafter cited as NSHS).

[7] The census shows "Sarah Shell," aged twenty-six, "domestic." Bloyd adds the information that she kept books for McCanles (Fairbury News, loc. cit.), and he told this writer that at the time of his death McCanles owed her money.

[8] Levi Bloyd, Jefferson County History: Rock Creek Station (pages not numbered).

All through the summer McCanles continued his labors. By late July or August the new ranch was complete, and he sent word to his brother to bring his wife and family out.

On September 20, 1859, they arrived. With his brother James, his wife Mary, and the children came a cousin James Woods and an orphan boy named Billy Hughes. But soon after his arrival this poor youngster died of typhoid fever.

Once Mrs. McCanles realized that Sarah Shull was living across the creek, she was furious. Long and violent were the arguments which she and McCanles had. She accused her husband of being unfaithful—which under the circumstances was not a surprising charge—and he in turn did his best to persuade her that there was nothing between him and Sarah. Mrs. McCanles threatened to drag the woman out of the house, and it was only a halfhearted promise from McCanles not to see her again that kept her from doing so. Just how he was to avoid such meetings is not explained. Sarah, for her part, got bored on her own and told McCanles so. He had burned his bridges in Watauga County, and he now had to pacify both women.

Although McCanles never had a "gang" as Nichols portrayed it, he was something of a local bully and, according to some of the early settlers, a "noted border ruffian." His tremendous strength gave him an edge on most men, and he was something of a sadist. Naturally he was not very popular in some quarters.

On one occasion an employee named Harry Goff got drunk during working hours. McCanles had left him in charge of the station for a day, and when he returned and found him sleeping off his drunken stupor he set fire to his beard, first covering it with gunpowder. A screaming Goff was pitched into a water trough by the other men, thus saving his life. Goff threatened to shoot McCanles, who then had him tied to the back of an unbroken horse which was turned loose on the prairie. Not satisfied with this, McCanles tried to make the wretch climb a honey locust tree, the trunks of which are covered with thorns as sharp as needles and between an inch and eight inches in length. At the sight of the tree Goff collapsed and begged to be let go. Only after he had admitted that McCanles was the better man was he released.[9]

Early in the spring of 1860, when Russell, Majors, and Waddell[10]

[9] Connelley, "Wild Bill—James Butler Hickok," *loc. cit.*, 6–8.

[10] Russell, Majors, and Waddell organized on January 1, 1855. Their Central Overland California and Pike's Peak Express Company was organized in 1859 (Raymond W. and Mary Lund Settle, "Waddell and Russell: Frontier Capitalists," KSHS *Quarterly*, Vol. XXVI, No. 4 [Winter, 1960], 371, 373).

(whose Central Overland California and Pike's Peak Express Company was unofficially but generally known as the Overland Stage Company) were making plans for the Pony Express, McCanles finally completed all the additions he had been making to the East-side ranch that now housed his family. He then rented this ranch to the stage company and moved his family to yet another new ranch on the Little Blue River. It was later alleged that this move was made in preparation for his possible departure to join the South in the event of war. Here, away from the main trail, he hoped his family would be safe until his return—if he returned. McCanles, although he had rented his place as a Pony Express station, remained as superintendent until such time as the company supplied their own employees. On company instructions he built a commodious barn and a lean-to twelve feet wide on the south side, and also a bunkhouse.

It was early in March, 1861, that Jim Hickok arrived at the station. The effects of his recent battle showed in the clumsy way he walked, and his left arm was still useless. To McCanles he must have looked a sorry specimen. About the only work he could do was in the stables, so there he went. Daily he shuffled about assisting "Doc" Brink, a part-time Pony Express rider, by cleaning harness and doing small lifting jobs, keeping himself aloof from the other men who came and went. Young Jim avoided mixing perhaps because his wounds made him feel inferior. At any rate he failed to appreciate some of McCanles' humor. With the use of only one arm he could not do much when McCanles pretended to wrestle with him and threw him on the ground. It may have seemed funny to McCanles, but to Hickok it was exactly the opposite. Gradually, as Jim's wounds healed, McCanles found other outlets for his humor and left him alone.

Early in May, Horace Wellman and his common-law wife arrived at the East-side ranch. Wellman was the new superintendent for Russell, Majors, and Waddell. McCanles lingered a few days to clear up odd points and to settle arrangements for the balance of payments before he finally left.

Russell, Majors, and Waddell negotiated with McCanles in April, 1861, to buy the East Rock Creek station. They paid one-third down; the rest was to be paid in installments spread over three months.

When June came without sign of payment, McCanles rode up to the station to ask the reason of Wellman. But he had no answer because he was only a superintendent and his orders came from

Brownville. McCanles was not satisfied. He demanded that someone go and see the line superintendent and sort it out. His anger
was understandable, but his motive was not. So anxious was he to
get settled that he agreed to take supplies if there was no money.
Maybe he had heard the rumors that the company was in debt, or
maybe, as has been suggested, he wanted those supplies for his
friends who were planning to join the Confederacy. Again it was
said that he actually intended to move farther west with Sara
Shull, leaving his wife and family to fend for themselves. None of
these theories can now be proved or disproved; the fact remains
that Wellman weakened and agreed to go to Brownville. For some
reason young William Monroe, McCanles' twelve-year-old son,
went with him. Monroe recalled in later years that he "went . . .
after a load of supplies for the station and some for father. We were
gone about ten days as it was 100 miles."[11]

It is possible that Monroe went because he would be able to
recognize his father's horses and equipment then in possession of
the Rocky Mountain Dispatch Company, should they be at Beatrice
or Brownville. Monroe's story repeatedly conflicts with available
evidence.

A deciding factor in the dispute perhaps was trouble between
McCanles and a man named Holmes, the father of Mrs. Wellman.
It is alleged that Holmes stole a team and wagon and some farm
supplies or implements belonging to McCanles. Soon after Wellman left for Brownville, McCanles set off in pursuit of Holmes,
caught him about July 5, and brought him back badly beaten up—
a fact which did not escape Mrs. Wellman's attention. Although
the circumstances surrounding this incident are hazy, they do offer
a reason for Mrs. Wellman's personal dislike of McCanles.[12]

After the departure of Wellman, on July 1, Hickok became acting superintendent and moved into the station from a small dugout
which he had been occupying close by. Also in the house at this
time were Sarah Kelsey (stepdaughter of Joe Baker, a former employee of McCanles) and Sarah Shull. Both women were there to
keep Mrs. Wellman company.

Here arises a good reason for the personal bitterness between
Hickok and McCanles. While trying to pacify his wife's not un-
natural resentment against the lady at the West-side ranch, Mc-

[11] George W. Hansen, "True Story of Wild Bill–McCanles Affray," *Nebraska
History Magazine* (hereinafter cited as *NHM*), Vol. X, No. 2 (April–June, 1927),
114.
[12] Levi Bloyd, *Jefferson County History*; Connelley, "Wild Bill–James Butler
Hickok," *loc. cit.*, 7.

Canles had noticed a distinct change in Sarah. He soon learned the reason. Hickok had been making many a moonlight trip across the creek to pay court. McCanles warned him to stay away, but with his wounds now on the mend, Jim paid no attention. So when Wellman left and Hickok moved to the big house, there was trouble in the air. McCanles began making daily appearances to demand that Mrs. Wellman give up the property, but she was a hard woman. Where her husband was weak, she was strong. McCanles, she said, could go to the devil.

On the afternoon of July 11, Wellman and the boy returned. They had been to the company's office at Brownville and had been told that for the present there was nothing that could be done. The company had foundered financially, and just then William H. Russell, one of the partners, was in Washington in trouble with the government. Then there was Ben Holladay, who had loaned the company a considerable sum of money and held the first mortgage. When the company finally failed to meet its obligations, Holladay took over (in March, 1862) and officially renamed it the Overland Stage Lines.[13] All this, however, was pretty much in the balance when Wellman presented himself at Brownville. Not only could they not pay; they could not put up any supplies either. So Wellman returned empty-handed. When Monroe got home and told his father, McCanles flew into a rage.

The first person he spoke to was Sarah Shull. When Frank Wilstach found her while preparing material for his book, she was ninety-three years old.[14] What answers she did give to his questions were evasive. She claimed to have been at her own home two miles away when the shooting took place, but she was in fact at the ranch house. In all probability this means that McCanles spoke to her on the morning of the twelfth and returned again in the afternoon.

Wilstach managed to put the following questions to her:

"Was money owed by Wellman the cause of the tragedy?"
"No."
"Were you in the cabin when McCanles was shot?"
"No. I was at my home two miles away."
"In your opinion, and from what you were told at the time, did Wild Bill kill McCanles in self-defence?"
"Certainly—yes."

13 Edward Hungerford, *Wells Fargo: Advancing the American Frontier*, 85, 89.
14 Sarah returned to the Shull Mill, North Carolina, in 1897 and remained there until her death on June 1, 1932, aged ninety-eight (Fairbury [Neb.] *News*, Aug. 13, 1965).

"What makes you think this is true?"

"Because on the morning of the tragedy I heard McCanles say he was going to clean up on the people at the station."

"You say McCanles stole horses?"

"Yes, he stole horses."

"Were those horses for the use of the Confederate Cavalry?"

"Yes."[15]

Sarah Shull can hardly be blamed for denying she was in the station that day. There is no evidence to support the claim that McCanles stole horses for the Confederate cavalry. Remember, he had not openly taken sides. And there is the allegation that Sarah had some sort of monetary hold over McCanles—she may well have fobbed Wilstach off with reference to the Confederate cavalry, hoping that he would not dwell too much on her own personal relationship with Dave.

Thus it was that late on the afternoon of July 12, McCanles, his son William Monroe, James Woods, and an employee named James Gordon rode into the yard of Rock Creek Station. Across his saddle-bow McCanles carried a shotgun.[16] Dismounting near the barn, the three men spoke for several minutes; then, accompanied by his son, McCanles walked over to the house. Woods and Gordon remained, leaning on a fence rail.

The ranch house deserves description at this stage. It was a structure over thirty-six feet long east and west, and about eighteen feet wide north and south. Designed originally as a two-room dwelling, it had a partition down the middle lengthways which ended with a six-foot gap intended to serve as a door between rooms. The front door was on the south side, on the west side of the partition. At the west end were a chimney and a large fireplace. Also in the west end of the house, and north from the chimney, was another door leading into the yard. Two windows served the west room, one facing north and the other south. There were also two windows in the east room, one facing south and the other east. Dividing the east end was a calico curtain stretched across a lariat in order to shut off the view of the beds against the east wall.[17]

At the west door McCanles and his son halted. Calling for Wellman, he launched into a tirade of abuse when the man appeared. Why, he demanded, hadn't Wellman been able to get his money? Wellman was no match for the bigger man, and his explanations

[15] Frank Jenners Wilstach, *Wild Bill Hickok—The Prince of Pistoleers*, 69–70.
[16] Connelley, "Wild Bill—James Butler Hickok," *loc. cit.*, 15.
[17] *Ibid.*

were waved aside. McCanless wanted no excuses; he wanted his rights or he would take the station by force. In a panic Wellman went back inside. At this moment Mrs. Wellman came on the scene. She had not forgotten McCanles' treatment of her father, and in blunt words told him what she thought about him. More enraged than ever, McCanles told her that his business was with men and not with women. "Send Wellman out here," he demanded. Mrs. Wellman paused, and at that moment Hickok came to the step. Up to now he had remained in the background. Had he continued to do so, the next few minutes would have been very different. Instead, he took a stand. McCanles stopped talking and stared at him. The gangling youth with the pitchfork was replaced by a fellow who looked at him in defiance.

"What in hell, Hickok, have you got to do with this? My business is with Wellman, not you, and if you want to take a hand in it, come out here and we will settle it like men."

Hickok stood for a moment before speaking, then slowly replied, "Perhaps 'tis, or 'taint."

"Well, then," said McCanles, "we are friends, ain't we? I want to know. We have been, ain't we, Hickok?"

"I guess so," replied Hickok.

"Then," said McCanles, "send Wellman out here, so I can settle with him, or I will come in and drag him out."[18]

Hickok nodded, shrugged his shoulders, and went into the house. On the step McCanles paused, uncertain. This was not the kind of attitude he expected from Hickok; it was defiance, something he had not experienced before, and McCanles was worried. Telling Monroe to remain where he was, he stepped across to the south door. While talking to Hickok he had noticed Sarah Shull and Sarah Kelsey standing by the chimney which served as a kitchen. It was alleged in later years by some of the McCanles faction that McCanles had moved to avoid bringing the women into the line of fire. If this is true, then he was there armed and ready for trouble.[19]

At the south door he looked in to see Hickok arguing with Wellman. Wellman seemed a little distraught. Both stopped and looked at him. Feeling uneasy, McCanles asked for a drink of water.

[18] *Ibid.*, 16. This conversation varies only slightly from that cited by Charles Dawson in his *Pioneer Tales of the Oregon Trail*, "The Wild Bill–McCanles Tragedy," 216–17. He suggests that apart from the enmity over Sarah Shull, McCanles disliked Hickok because he believed he was a bad gambler, but this is not substantiated.

[19] Connelley, "Wild Bill–James Butler Hickok," *loc. cit.*, 17.

Hickok walked over to a pitcher and filled a tin cup and returned with it and handed it to him. Then he stepped backward toward the curtain that divided the room. McCanles turned his attention once more to Wellman, but aware of Hickok's movements, he called to him to come out and face him, and if he wanted to fight to come out and fight fair, or he would come in and drag him out. Hickok called back that he was welcome to try and drag him out, and that "there will be one less ——— when you try that."

Then McCanles made a movement of some sort. It could have been with the shotgun which it is alleged he was carrying,[20] or it may have been some other gesture, but his movement was answered with a shot from inside the house. Shot through the heart, the impact of the bullet throwing him on his back, McCanles tried to raise himself. His son ran to him but it was too late. His eyes glazed as he tried to form words; then he fell back dead.

Over at the barn Woods and Gordon heard the shot and dashed toward the house. Woods ran inside and was shot by Hickok with a Navy revolver.[21] The wound was not fatal and he staggered away to collapse in a weed patch. Mrs. Wellman suddenly rushed out of the house screaming at the top of her voice: "Kill them! Kill them all!" In her hand she clutched a grubbing hoe. And in her eyes shone the light of madness. She seemed to go completely crazy. Woods was quickly dispatched by the hoe in her hands. Then seeing the boy Monroe kneeling beside his father's body, she came at him, but he had wits enough to scramble to his feet and run, easily dodging her in the scrub. Gordon ran up in time to see Woods stagger back from Hickok's shot; then he himself was shot in the body. Running and staggering, he headed down the creek, pursued by more shots, but the brush made accurate shooting difficult.

Up from the stables came Doc Brink and George Hulbert, a stage driver. Joining Hickok and Wellman and setting loose a bloodhound, they set off down the creek after Gordon. One of them carried the shotgun which McCanles had dropped. About four hundred yards down the creek they came across Gordon trying to chase the bloodhound away.[22] One of the men with Hickok killed him

[20] Dawson, *Pioneer Tales of the Oregon Trail*, 216, seems positive that McCanles was armed with this weapon.

[21] William Monroe McCanles, "The Only Living Eye Witness," *NHM*, Vol. X, No. 2 (April–June, 1927), 47–50, alleged that Hickok used a pistol owned by the station, indicating that he had no arms of his own. It is believed that Hickok placed his weapons behind the curtain in preparation for trouble, which means that Wellman, too, had access to them.

[22] Dawson, *Pioneer Tales of the Oregon Trail*, 220, asserts that Gordon stabbed the dog and killed it.

with the shotgun. The unfortunate Gordon was later wrapped in a blanket and buried where he fell. McCanles and Woods were buried together on Soldier Hill, where they remained for over twenty years. Their remains were removed to the Fairbury Cemetery when the Burlington Railroad came along, cutting through their resting place.

William Monroe McCanles, in his version of the killing, stated emphatically that his father's party were not armed. To prove his point he said:

Woods and Gordon were not armed when they ran up to the door: if either or both of them had been armed they surely would have had their revolvers in hand, and while Jim was shooting Woods don't you think one or the other of them would have done some shooting? Do you think that if Woods had been armed he would have let Wellman knock him in the head without trying to defend himself?

Now, for more evidence that Gordon was not armed: Gordon kept a blood hound that usually followed him where he went. This dog was with him at the barn when the fracas began. After Gordon had made his getaway, being wounded, the station outfit put this dog on his trail and the dog trailed him down the creek and brought him to bay about 80 rods down the creek. When the bunch caught up, the dog was fighting Gordon, and Gordon was warding him off with a stick. Gordon was finished with a load of buck shot. Now, if Gordon had been armed don't you think he would have killed the dog?[23]

Monroe raised several important points. It is reasonable to assume that if both men were armed (writing in 1912, Charles Dawson said they were[24]) they would have defended themselves. Even supposing they were armed, the events took place too quickly. Woods was shot as he reached the door, and Gordon no doubt within moments as he ran behind him. It seems reasonable to accept the theory that Hickok took both men by surprise. Monroe, it seems, credits Horace Wellman with Woods's murder, whereas Connelley and others blame Mrs. Wellman. In his last remark, concerning the dog, Monroe merely poses the question: why should a man be attacked by his own dog? More likely he was trying to chase it off as its presence hindered his escape.

The question whether or not the McCanles party were armed can never be settled for sure. McCanles was a man of violence. He had always gone armed before this and on occasions had used his pistols. Why leave them off now? Then comes the strong point in

23 "The Only Living Eye Witness," *loc. cit.*, 15.
24 *Pioneer Tales of the Oregon Trail*, 216.

the McCanles faction's favor: why should a man expecting trouble take his small son along? Monroe himself supplied one possible reason. Charles Dawson emphasized the fact that Monroe and Wellman returned on July 11, a detail which at the time was agreed to by Monroe. But in his account written in the 1920's, which appeared in several newspapers, Monroe said that he and Wellman arrived on the afternoon of the twelfth to find his father at the Nye ranch close by.[25] Woods and Gordon were with him and all four came to the station. If this version is correct, then it makes possible a fresh interpretation of Sarah Shull's remarks to Wilstach. It means that McCanles intended to "clean up" on the station with or without supplies or money, and the fact that Monroe was there at the time could suggest a movement on McCanles' part to allay the suspicions of the people in the house. At the first sign of trouble the boy could run. Perhaps the real reason will never be known.

After the killing of Gordon, Hickok and company returned to the house, where they were met by Joe Baker. At once Hickok threatened his life, accusing him of being an ally of McCanles. Baker pleaded that he was no longer working for McCanles, and out of the house flew Sarah Kelsey to throw herself between them. "Don't kill him," she begged. Hickok let down the hammer of his pistol and smacked Baker across the head with the barrel, remarking, "Well, you've got to take that anyway." Hickok was in no mood for being charitable, and Baker's known association with McCanles embittered him toward the man; but as on many occasions during his life, he was influenced by, or because of, a woman.

The next day the McCanles family arrived to supervise the burial of the dead. Feeling ran high among partisans of both sides. Those who had hated McCanles welcomed the news of his death, but others demanded justice. Realizing the feeling in and around the district, Hickok borrowed a horse, rode to Marysville, Kansas, and asked Brumbaugh and Bolinger to defend him in the event of a trial.[26] Returning to the station, he told the others of his actions and

---

[25] Apart from the article in the *NHM*, newspapers in Kansas and Nebraska also quoted parts of his story with variations.

[26] Had Hickok been guilty of murder, he could easily have made his escape. Instead he waited and stood trial, which enhances his plea of self-defense. It is possible that Brumbaugh and Bolinger were the lawyers who helped establish his claims in the 1850's, or were recommended to him. In an effort to trace their records I enlisted the aid of Mr. William S. Eddy, an attorney at law in Marysville, Kansas. In his letter of December 4, 1956, he said: "I am afraid that there are no records that can help you in your quest. . . . Brumbaugh and John W. Bolinger were partners and their cases appear in the early day dockets in Marshall County—before Kansas attained statehood."

they waited for the law. E. B. Hendee, sheriff of Gage County, arrived on July 15 with a warrant for the arrest of Hickok, Wellman, and Brink. The warrant had been sworn out on July 13. They made the thirty-mile trip to Beatrice in a wagon, arriving that same day. The local press got wind of the affair, and it was reported:

> The following we extract from a private letter just received from a reliable and well-informed friend residing on the Big Blue:
>
> Three wagonloads of arms and ammunition passed through the neighborhood below here last week, going westward. On Friday three men were killed at Rock Creek on the Military Road about 30 or 35 miles west of this. All we know is that the difficulty originated in the distribution or division of a wagon load of stuff from the Missouri river, and it is supposed it was one of the three wagons above mentioned. During the difficulty some secessionists put a rope around a Union Man's neck, and dragged him some distance toward a tree with the avowed purpose of hanging him. He managed to escape. They then gave him notice to leave in a certain time or be hung. At the end of the time five of them went to his house to see if he had gone, when he commenced firing upon them and killed three out of the five; the other two making a hasty retreat.[27]

It is interesting to note that in this version—the first ever published—reference is made to a man's being dragged along by a lariat (as was Parson Shipley in the Nichols version). The McCanles faction state that there was no such person as Shipley, but there was a Robert Y. Shibley who lived near the place and had worked for McCanles. He died in 1923, aged over eighty and allegedly singing McCanles' praises.

Before the publication of the newspaper report, the preliminary hearing had ended. The verdict was in favor of the Hickok faction.[28]

During the hearing before T. M. Coulter, justice of the peace for Gage County,[29] it was alleged by the Hickok party that they had killed in self-defense, and that they were defending company property. Their plea was accepted. Mrs. Wellman (who was not charged with the others) was called as a witness for the territory, which move was taken by the McCanles faction as an attempt to break

27 Brownville (Neb.) *Advertiser*, July 25, 1861.
28 Dawson, *Pioneer Tales of the Oregon Trail*, 221.
29 Dawson asserts that the trial was conducted by Judge O. M. Mason, and the prosecution by David Butler, later governor of the state. No mention of Brumbaugh and Bolinger could be found in this connection, although Bolinger (then of Pawnee City) later appeared in connection with a dispute between Sheriff Hendee and Gage County over costs. From an examination of the records, it appears that Coulter acted for both parties, neither the territory nor the defendants being represented by attorneys.

down the case put up by Monroe and his uncle James (who had laid the official complaint against Hickok and his companions). For some reason Monroe was not, after all, called as a material witness for the prosecution. The trial literally collapsed, and by the time any further attempts at justice were made by the McCanles family, Hickok had left the state.

Early in the present century, when interest in the affair was once more stirred up, several attempts were made to trace the original court records. The search for these documents covered many years. They were finally unearthed by George Hansen in 1926, and formed the basis for the evidence against Hickok put up by the McCanles faction in the *Nebraska History Magazine*. While the documents in themselves are interesting, they do not throw any new light on the affair, except to indicate the names of the witnesses—George Hulbert, the stage driver, being noticeably absent. This may be because he was not associated with the affair until after Monroe ran away.

In the original warrant Hickok was referred to as "Dutch Bill," the name by which he was apparently known at Rock Creek.[30] Because of the fact that in some places the documents refer to him as "Duch Bill," it has been alleged that he was in fact known as "Duck Bill"—a name McCanles applied to him in their early encounters because of his "thin lips which protruded so noticeably,"[31] but this is hearsay and curiously only gained circulation after 1926. The name "Bill" must have been the one he used, for Hickok was elsewhere in the documents referred to as William B. Hickok—the name by which he was to be known all through the early part of the Civil War, until the more familiar "Wild Bill" tag appeared later.

The trial documents are in themselves interesting. They consist primarily of warrants, subpoenas, and accounts. Among the more important items are a complaint of murder by J. Leroy McCanles; his bond for twenty-five dollars; a warrant for the arrest of Dutch Bill, Dock, and Wellman; and various subpoenas for a number of witnesses. The following were called: Martin Ney, Jackson Ney, Joseph Baker, Mrs. Wellman, Jacob Wildeboy, Monroe McCanles, Jonah Brown, Joseph Holmes (Mrs. Wellman's father?), Ira Mott, Helen Ney, and Noah Brown. The latter was a material witness,

[30] It is noteworthy that Dawson refers to him only as "Wild Bill" in his 1912 account, indicating that no one had ever mentioned Hickok's being known as "Dutch Bill."

[31] Carl Uhlarik, "The Myth of Wild Bill Hickok," *The Prairie Schooner*, Vol. XXV, No. 2 (Summer, 1951), 131.

according to Leroy McCanles. Brown disappeared and the trial proceeded without him.[32]

Despite the evidence of the court documents, the testimony of Monroe (admittedly "recalled" fifty years later), and other evidence, the incident at Rock Creek still remains an enigma. Unless an original transcript (assuming one was made) is found, or genuine contemporary statements by the previously related witnesses turn up, it is hardly likely that the affair will ever appear in any fresh light.

Several points come to mind: McCanles was shot from inside the house—which means that Wellman and not Hickok *could* have fired the shot. The treatment of Wellman's father-in-law by McCanles might easily have sparked the fire of hatred which was still further inflamed by McCanles' bullying attitude to Wellman. Grievance over nonpayment of money owed McCanles may well have been the reason for the fight, but an even more likely cause was Sarah Shull. Here was perhaps the key to the whole affair. All through his life Hickok had fights over women, and Sarah might indeed have aroused a passionate jealousy between the two men—reason enough for bloodshed. Sarah disappeared from Rock Creek very quickly, for the day following the shooting she was put on a westbound stagecoach, and it was fifty years before her version of the incident was sought.

In later years friends of Hickok's claimed that he was greatly upset by the story of Rock Creek as publicized by Nichols.[33] But no matter how much he might deny the story, the Nichols version was firmly fixed in the public's imagination as the correct one.

It is hard to make positive judgments about the Rock Creek fight. Hickok either emerges as a hero or as the basest, most treacherous coward. No one, it seems, can put forward a clear-cut case either way. But one fact remains: from this trivial (by frontier standards) affair sprang the legend of Wild Bill Hickok, and it was to put him on the first rung of the ladder to fame.

[32] The original documents are reproduced in *NHM* (April–July, 1927), 107–12.
[33] Connelley, "Wild Bill–James Butler Hickok," *loc. cit.*, 25–26.

-⇥ 3 ⇤-

Civil War Adventures

In 1861 the trumpets of wrath blared across the nation, and America was at war. This was not the war of one nation against another, but the most bloody, cruel, and demoralizing war imaginable—civil war. Today, more than a century later, the heroes of that war are remembered with pride by their descendants. Among the Union heroes stands Wild Bill Hickok, whose heroics were of a special kind. He performed his deeds of daring under the guise of the spy, the scout, or the courier; thus his exploits are subject to legendary telling and retelling. Only brief glimpses of his services to the Union cause can be found in the official record, but the legends are still repeated and believed. Many of them are no doubt based on fact, but at this date the whole truth can never be known.

From Rock Creek, toward the end of July, Hickok left for Fort Leavenworth, where he enlisted in the Union Army as a civilian scout. In this capacity he took part in the Battle of Wilson's Creek (Missouri) on August 10, 1861. General Nathaniel Lyon, in command of 5,500 Federal troops, was beaten by the Confederate forces, and was himself killed. Hickok, together with other scouts and soldiers, made his escape as best he could. In later years his brother Horace wrote that before the battle James "was trying to locate a masked battery which opened fire the minute he discovered it. He never having been under artillery fire before said he was actually scared. The fire of that artillery brought on the battle of Wilson's Creek."[1]

Hickok next appeared as a wagon master. On October 30, 1861, he was engaged at $100 per month by N. P. Cook, quartermaster agent at Sedalia, Missouri, and later, on November 28, was transferred to Captain J. A. Swain, assistant quartermaster, Warsaw and Sedalia, Missouri. The War Department decided they were paying too much, and, on January 1, 1862, his pay was reduced to $60 per month. Hickok was transferred to Captain S. L. Brown, assistant

[1] Horace D. Hickok to the editor of the Topeka *Mail and Breeze*, Sept. 27, 1901. Nichols also notes this incident, although he spells it "Wilme" Creek.

53

quartermaster, Sedalia, Missouri, on February 10, 1862, and on March 26, was appointed chief wagon master at $100 per month. Then on June 30 he was transferred to Lieutenant S. C. Peck, acting assistant quartermaster at Rolla, Missouri. The records note that on September 20, 1862, he had been dropped, and no discharge or transfer was noted.[2]

According to one contemporary, George W. Hance, the government bought one hundred teams, six yoke of cattle to the team, from Jones and Cartwright. James Hickok was put in charge of the entire outfit and wintered the train at and near Otterville, Missouri:

Early in the spring of 1862 he partially loaded at Fort Leavenworth, Kan., and started with the outfit to Sedalia, Mo., to finish loading for Springfield, Mo., for General Curtis's army, which was then in southwest Missouri, and northwest Arkansas. When he got down into Jackson county, Missouri, the rebels captured the train. Wild Bill made his escape and went to Independence, the county seat of Jackson county at that time, and got several companions and recaptured the outfit the next morning. The train then proceeded under heavy escort to Sedalia, finished loading and went to Springfield, Mo. He then loaded for Batesville, Ark. From Batesville he went to Rolla.[3]

It is claimed that Hickok's brief sojourn in Independence waiting for assistance to recapture his train led to his gaining the name of Wild Bill. While wandering around the town, he noticed a large crowd outside a saloon and was told that there had been a brawl in the place and the bartender had supported the wrong side, wounded one of the victorious toughs, and now his friends wanted the bartender's blood. Just as the mob, full of alcoholic bravery, made its rush, Hickok drew his pistols, pushed himself to a position in front of the door, and demanded that they halt. As some moved forward he fired two shots above their heads. This time they halted, uncertain but still angry. Hickok told them to disperse or he would shoot the first man to move forward. Gradually they turned away and Hickok was able to tell the terrified bartender to come out, and after advising him about his choice of friends, went his way.

Hickok's bluff on this occasion had repercussions which he was

2 Records of the Quartermaster General, 1861–65, National Archives, Washington, D.C.

3 "The Truth About Wild Bill," Topeka (Kan.) *Mail and Breeze*, Dec. 20, 1901. What may have some bearing on this attack on Hickok's wagon train can be found in the Leavenworth *Daily Times* of November 17, 1861, which reported the arrival of a wagon master who had had fifty wagons and oxen stolen by rebels near Pleasant Hill, Missouri. All his teamsters were captured. Jennison's regiment set out from Kansas City in pursuit and recaptured the train and two others taken by the rebels.

never to forget. During a meeting that evening to form a vigilance committee, someone saw Hickok standing on the edge of the crowd. His name was taken up and amid the shouting a woman's voice was heard to say: "Good for you, Wild Bill!" The name stuck, and although this version seems to tally with that given by Hickok himself,[4] Howard L. Hickok gives another which is worthy of repetition because of its surprising twist.

According to Howard, by the early part of the war Lorenzo was actively employed as a wagon master for General Frémont. During one of his trips from Rolla to Springfield, James accompanied him, together with a man named Hayes and George Hance:

They were coming with loaded wagons from Rolla and entered a small village about supper time. They made their camp, fed their horses and started for town for their own supper. On their way to town they noticed a crowd surrounding the jail. The mob had opened the jail and taken a young man about nineteen years of age from the jailer and were preparing to hang him. The youth was charged with stealing a horse. Lorenzo did not like the looks of the crowd. They looked more like outlaws than solid citizens to him. He made inquiries; asking if the youth had been given a fair trial. The leader replied that there would be no trial and that they were going ahead with the hanging. Lorenzo stepped up to the youth, followed by Jim and the other teamsters. "You will hang him over my dead body," said Lorenzo. A woman in the crowd called out, "My God aint he wild[!]" So was the name Wild Bill Hickok coined, and from that time on there was a Wild Bill. Later developments proved Lorenzo right in stopping the hanging. The youth was found to be a Union man and his wouldbe hangmen were with the South in their sympathies. The wagon train went on to Springfield and the quiet gentle brother Lorenzo disclaimed his part in the incident. In some manner the name was given to uncle Jim in Springfield and kept by him throughout his life.[5]

George Hance, however, seems to clarify the situation concerning who actually deserved the name when he wrote: "I lived [in Rolla] where I first met Wild Bill and L. B. Hickok. In order to distinguish them they were called Wild Bill and Tame Bill and as such they were known and called by everyone from the summer of 1862 until the close of the war."[6]

The Records of the War Department have established that Hickok was officially employed as a wagon master until September,

[4] Connelley, *Wild Bill and His Era*, 46. Charles Gross to J. B. Edwards, Jan. 20, 1926, Manuscripts Division, KSHS.

[5] "The Hickok Legend," *loc. cit.*, 19–20.

[6] "The Truth About Wild Bill," *loc. cit.*

1862, but they do not indicate that he was fully employed. If his employment was intermittent, then there may be some truth in the belief that Wild Bill (as he will now be called) was present at the Battle of Pea Ridge as a scout or a courier.

In December, 1861, General John Pope had driven the Confederate General Sterling Price into Arkansas. Price was joined and reinforced by General Earl Van Dorn with two thousand men, together with about the same number of Indians under the command of Albert Pike. Also on the field staff was General Ben McCulloch. The Union forces were under the command of General Samuel R. Curtis, who commanded all the military forces in southern Missouri. On March 5, 1862, Curtis' scouts reported that the rebel army was advancing. Hickok was alleged to be one of these scouts, and for the next two days, and during the battle, he and the other scouts and couriers were dashing from camp to camp carrying dispatches and other information about the advancing enemy. During the fierce fighting on March 7, Wild Bill is said to have used up three horses and had one shot from under him.

On the morning of March 8, Curtis was gaining ground. Soon the rebels were defeated, and began a slow retreat to Pea Ridge. This was situated in Benton County, Arkansas, about fifteen miles west of Eureka Springs and three or four miles from the Missouri border. Retreating south over the Wire Road with Curtis' men in hot pursuit, Price's army made a stand at Cove Creek, south of Prairie Grove. This time the army was backed by Van Dorn's much-needed reinforcements. Not to be outflanked, Curtis deployed his troops around Cross Hollow, a narrow gorge on the Wire Road. It was from there that he finally routed the Confederates and sent detachments of his troops to take possession of various points between Fayetteville and northwest Arkansas.

About noon on the eighth, it is alleged that Hickok requested permission to station himself with a number of sharpshooters on a ridge overlooking the Confederate lines. During this sniping, a cheer went up from the men when it was noticed that a rebel officer had fallen in the trenches. There was much speculation over who it was; some even said it was Price. Who it actually was is not known, but legend has it that a shot from Wild Bill's rifle brought down General McCulloch. This was not so. The General had been killed the day before by Peter Pelican of Company B, Thirty-sixth Illinois Infantry. A newspaper reported the General's last words to be: "Oh Hell!"[7]

[7] Connelley, *Wild Bill and His Era*, 218. Leavenworth *Daily Conservative*, Mar. 26, 1862.

Curtis' losses during the battle are estimated at 1,351 men, at least half of them under the command of Colonel Eugene A. Carr, who had borne the brunt of the fight.

On the Confederate front many of the murderous Choctaw Indians commanded by Albert Pike were killed when they lingered behind the rebel retreat scalping and looting. Some said confusion in orders to retreat was to blame, but Pike always claimed that they had not retreated at all. They merely "left the enemy behind by rapid riding."

It has been claimed that Hickok was with Colonel John S. Phelps at Pea Ridge, or at least was well acquainted with him at this time.[8] Evidence of this is not conclusive, but an examination of Phelps's activities during the war indicates that this may well be true, for later in his career Hickok was to owe a great debt to him—as he was also to Phelps's regimental quartermaster, Captain Richard Bentley Owen.[9]

The scene was constantly changing during the war years. With British money and assistance the South could well have won the war, but fate favored the North. Without the assistance of Great Britain or any other European power, the Confederacy was forced to "go it alone." The industrial North, with its money, might, and man power, and most important, its machinery, had the upper hand over the slave states. But the South proved harder to conquer than the Union generals cared to admit. The only way that they could hope to defeat the South would be through decisive victories prepared by a first-class spy system. It was here that such men as Hickok played a part. After infiltrating enemy lines and gathering what information they could about troops, ammunition, and supply movements, the spies would work their way back to the Union lines and make a report. Of course, the Southern leaders had their own spies, which added greatly to the confusion.

Thus it was that Wild Bill graduated from sharpshooting to scouting and spying. Soon after the Pea Ridge battle he is alleged to have wangled himself on to Curtis' headquarters staff. Many are the glowing accounts of Wild Bill and Curtis, but documentation is lacking. Wild Bill himself, however, stated that he was at one time a member of the Eighth Missouri State Militia. This information he is alleged to have given Henry M. Stanley in 1867.[10]

Although no trace of Hickok's name has been found in the records

[8] Jay Monaghan, *Civil War on the Western Border (1854–65)*, 168.
[9] See Chapter Four.
[10] *Weekly Missouri Democrat*, Apr. 16, 1867.

of the regiment in Washington, it is probable that he was attached to the Eighth Missouri State Militia as a scout or spy. The regiment was organized in 1861 and saw active service until 1865. One of its roles was to provide scouts and spies to infiltrate Confederate-held territory. The leader of many such expeditions was Captain John R. Kelso, who by the end of the war was a Brevet Colonel. Something of a character, Kelso was described in 1883 as a desperate fighter and a desperate man:

He did a great deal of scouting service for the Federal army through-out Southern and Southwest Missouri and Northern Arkansas, and experienced numerous exciting and perilous adventures. He was fanatical in his Unionism, held all Confederates to be traitors, guilty of treason and deserving death. It is said of him that he killed many a man without cause. Stories are told of him that make him appear a Raw-Head-and-Bloody-Bones sort of fellow, fit only to be denominated a monster, and entitled only to execration. Doubtless some of these stories are exaggerations, but the fact remains that Kelso was a "bad man," and held human life in very cheap estimation. In this day Capt. Kelso would have been called a "crank." Much learning had made him mad. He was a transcendentalist and was well versed in all the dogmas of the schools of modern thought. It is said that he always carried a book of some sort in his saddle pockets, and frequently engaged in the study of mental philosophy and the subtleties of metaphysics while lying in the brush by the roadside waiting to "get the drop" on a "rebel!" He believed in diet and plenty of exercise as brain-producing elements, practiced them himself, and forced his wife and daughter to adopt the Bloomer costume.

But with all his whims and failings, Kelso had hosts of friends and admirers, especially among the soldiers.[11]

Evidently Kelso's beliefs caused his family much concern. In 1870 his fourteen-year-old son committed suicide with a pistol "because his sister had discovered that he was using tobacco, a habit which his father had forbidden him to practice, and which he had promised to abandon."[12]

This was the man who, sometime toward the end of 1862, is alleged to have led Hickok, John C. McKoan, and two of Hickok's friends, John W. Allen and "Zeke" Stone, both from the Cherokee Nation, where Allen was a squaw man, on a detail to find out the movements of the enemy in southwest Missouri and northwest Arkansas.[13]

11 *History of Greene County, Missouri*, 477.
12 *Ibid.*, 521.
13 This date has been fixed to coincide with the end of Hickok's known employment as a wagon master, following which he would be available for such activities.

Following a hazardous ride, mostly by night, via Rolla and Springfield, Missouri, then across the Wilson's Creek battlefield and through Elkhorn Tavern, the scouts headed toward Van Buren. There followed a series of adventures involving Confederates and the rescue from rebel hands of two young women, one of whom was alleged to be Susannah Moore.

Despite some intensive recent research by this writer into official records and other material, no reference to these incidents has been found. Particularly noticeable has been the lack of authentic information relative to Susannah Moore. An examination of Buel's book reveals no reference to this remarkable woman, and neither can anything be found in Eisele's contribution (his Civil War chapters are identical to Buel's). Wilstach, too, seemed to be unaware of the lady. So it is to William E. Connelley that we must look for the first generally publicized reference to her. Connelley certainly believed in her existence and based his evidence on stories he heard from old-time residents in Springfield. One of these was Mrs. Talihina Allen, widow of Wild Bill's Civil War scouting friend, who told Connelley that Susannah Moore's real name was Pruitt, but she adopted her stepfather's name of Moore.[14]

Most of the legends built around Wild Bill's exploits during the Civil War are associated with the years 1862–64, when he was in southwest Missouri. Some of these stories are beyond belief, and are probably the products of J. W. Buel's wonderful imagination. However, Buel claimed to be quoting from a journal Hickok kept all through the war. In describing how Wild Bill was captured on one occasion and sentenced to be shot, he wrote:

In a memorandum Bill made concerning this event he says: "The Rebs convicted me on mighty little evidence, and here I am now in a bad pickle; it may be that they will shoot me to-morrow, but somehow I feel that some means of escape will offer. Curtis must be very near, for he has been reported, in camp, as coming like the devil beating bark, on a straight trail for the Bluffs. Something tells me that I will get out of this, and this feeling gives me nerve. I'll keep a lookout and see what's what."

Buel was either quoting from an authentic document or demonstrating his own cleverness when he concluded: "How this entry

14 For a detailed account of the alleged trip via Rolla and on to Springfield, see Connelley, *Wild Bill and His Era*, 51–58, and the first edition of *They Called Him Wild Bill*, 38–44. The Connelley Collection at the Denver Public Library also contains a statement by William H. Gregg, a nephew of Dr. Josiah Gregg, author of *The Commerce of the Prairies*, which indicates that he is responsible for much information about Susannah Moore but adds no further verification.

was made in his journal, while he was under a close guard, is not explained, but it is probable that he wrote it after he escaped to indicate his feelings while under conviction, when the chances of escape were least favorable."[15] However, Buel seems so confused as to time and place that most of what he states is completely worthless.

Perhaps Nichols had some of the truth from Hickok during his alleged interview, or perhaps the various officers with whom he spoke gave him what they believed to be the truth; but the way the stories are set down, "in the scout's own words," they appear highly colored. Wild Bill, according to Nichols, told him many stories of his escapes and adventures behind enemy lines, of which the following is typical and the second sentence is significant:

"I hardly know where to begin. Pretty near all these stories are true. I was at it all the war. That affair of my swimming the river took place on the long scout of mine when I was with the rebels five months, when I was sent by General Curtis to Price's army. Things had come pretty close at that time, and it wasn't safe to go straight inter their lines. Every body was suspected who came from these parts. So I started off and went way up to Kansas City. I bought a horse there and struck out onto the plains, and then went down through Southern Kansas into Arkansas. I knew a rebel named Barnes, who was killed at Pea Ridge. He was from near Austin in Texas. So I called myself his brother and enlisted in a regiment of mounted rangers.[16]

"General Price was just then getting ready for a raid into Missouri. It was sometime before we got into the campaign, and it was mighty hard work for me. The men of our regiment were awful. They didn't mind killing a man no more than a hog. The officers had no command over them. They were afraid of their own men, and let them do what they liked; so they would rob and sometimes murder their own people. It was right hard for me to keep up with them, and not do as they did. I never let on that I was a good shot. I kept that back for big occasions; but ef you'd heard me swear and cuss the blue-bellies, you'd a-thought me one of the wickedest of the whole crew. So it went on until we came near Curtis's army. Bime-by they were on one side Sandy River and we were on t'other. All the time I had been getting information until I knew every regiment and its strength; how much cavalry there was and how many guns the artillery had.

"You see 'twas time for me to go, but it wasn't easy to git out, for the river was close picketed on both sides. One day when I was on picket

---

[15] Buel, *Heroes of the Plains*, 69.

[16] This seems to establish Wild Bill's use of the name Bill Barnes when it suited him, but whether the Texan was a genuine character is not known. Wild Bill may have been thinking of Lorenzo.

our men and the rebels got talking and cussin each other, as you know they used to do. After a while one of the Union men offered to exchange some coffee for tobacco. So we went out onto a little island which was neutral ground like. The minute I saw the other party, who belonged to the Missouri cavalry [Eighth Missouri State Militia?], we recognized each other. I was awful afraid they'd let on. So I blurted out:

"'Now, Yanks, let's see yer coffee—no burnt beans, mind yer—but the genuine stuff. We know the real article if we is Texans.'

"The boys kept mum, and we separated. Half an hour afterward General Curtis knew I was with the rebs. But how to git across the river was what stumped me. After that, when I was on picket, I didn't trouble myself about being shot. I used to fire at our boys, and they'd bang away at me, each of us taking good care to shoot wide. But how to git over the river was the bother. At last, after thinking a heap about it, I came to the conclusion that I always did, that the boldest plan is the best and safest.

"We had a big sargent in our company who was allus a-braggin that he could stump any man in the regiment. He swore he had killed more Yanks than any man in the army, and that he could do more daring things than any others. So one day when he was talking loud I took him up, and offered to bet horse for horse that I would ride out into the open, and nearer to the Yankees than he. He tried to back out of this, but the men raised a row, calling him a funk, and a bragger, and all that; so he had to go. Well, we mounted our horses, but before we came within shootin distance of the Union soldiers I made my horse kick and rear so that they could see who I was. Then we rode slowly to the river bank, side by side.

"There must have been ten thousand men watching us; for, besides the rebs who wouldn't have cried about it if we had both been killed, our boys saw something was up, and without being seen thousands of them came down to the river. Their pickets kept firing at the sargent; but whether or not they were afraid of putting a ball through me I don't know, but nary a shot hit him. He was a plucky feller all the same, for the bullets zitted about in every direction.

"Bime-by we got right close ter the river, when one of the Yankee soldiers yelled out, 'Bully for Wild Bill!'

"Then the sargent suspicioned me, for he turned on me and growled out, 'By God, I believe yer a Yank!' And he at onst drew his revolver; but he was too late, for the minute he drew his pistol I put a ball through him. I mightn't have killed him if he hadn't suspicioned me. I had to do it then.

"As he rolled out of the saddle I took his horse by the bit, and dashed into the water as quick as I could. The minute I shot the sargent our boys set up a tremendous shout, and opened a smashing fire on the rebs who had commenced popping at me. But I had got into deep water, and had slipped off my horse over his back, and steered him for the opposite bank by holding onto his tail with one hand, while I held the bridle rein of the sargent's horse in the other hand. It was the hottest bath I ever took. Whew! For about two minutes how the bullets zitted and skipped on the water. I thought I was hit again and again, but the reb sharpshooters were bothered by the splash we made, and in a little while our boys drove them to cover, and after some tumbling at the bank got into the brush with my two horses without a scratch.

"It is a fact," said the scout, while he caressed his long hair, "I felt sort of proud when the boys took me into camp, and General Curtis thanked me before a heap of generals.

"But I never tried that thing over again; nor I didn't go a scouting openly in Price's army after that. They all knew me too well, and you see 'twouldn't a been healthy to have been caught."[17]

The most enduring of the Hickok legends of the Civil War period is the story of Black Nell. It is said that Wild Bill became owner of the horse after killing her rider and two other rebels in a gunfight between Rolla and Springfield, Missouri, sometime during the autumn of 1863, and paying the United States government the sum of $225, a price at which she was valued as a prize of war. Having served him well for six years, she died in 1869, and was buried near Kansas City.[18]

It was Nichols who first publicized this remarkable animal in his *Harper's* article, when he gave a vivid description of Wild Bill's arrival in Springfield one afternoon. As Wild Bill galloped up the street at a swift pace he drew up opposite Nichols, swung his arm in a circular motion, and the horse immediately dropped as if hit by a cannon ball. Hickok left her there and strolled over to join Nichols and the other observers. Bets were made that she would enter a saloon and mount a billiard table, and Nichols and the other loungers immediately took Hickok up on it:

Bill whistled in a low tone. Nell instantly scrambled to her feet, walked toward him, put her nose affectionately under his arm, followed him into the room, and to my extreme wonderment climbed upon the billiard-table, to the extreme astonishment of the table no doubt, for it groaned under the weight of the four-legged animal and several of those who were simply bifurcated, and whom Nell permitted to sit upon her. When she got down from the table, which was as graceful a performance as might be expected under the circumstances, Bill sprang upon her back, dashed

[17] "Wild Bill," *loc. cit.*, 281–82.
[18] Connelley, *Wild Bill and His Era*, 70. Wilstach, *Wild Bill Hickok—The Prince of Pistoleers*, 106.

through the high wide doorway, and at a single bound cleared the flight of steps and landed in the middle of the street. The scout then dismounted, snapped his riding-whip, and the noble beast bounded off down the street, rearing and plunging to her own intense satisfaction. A kindly-disposed individual, who must have been a stranger, supposing the mare was running away, tried to catch her, when she stopped, and as if she resented his impertinence, let fly her heels at him and then quietly trotted to her stable.[19]

Wild Bill is said to have told Nichols that he owed his life time and time again to the mare, and that he had taught her many a trick. One time he had nearly been caught by a band of rebels, but the mare, true to her training, had dropped out of sight in some tall grass, and the rebels passed by.

But Nichols' story of Black Nell was refuted quickly, if somewhat humorously, by the editor of the Springfield *Patriot*, who "reviewed" the *Harper's* article for his issue of January 31, 1867:

The questrian scenes given are purely imaginary. The extraordinary black mare, Nell (which was in fact a black stallion, blind in the right eye, and a "goer,") wouldn't "fall as if struck by a cannon ball" when Hickok "slowly waved his hand over her head with a circular motion," worth a cent. And none of our citizens ever saw her (or him) "wink affirmatively" to Bill's mention of her (or his) great sagacity. Nor did she (or he) ever jump upon the billiard table of the Lyon House at "William's low whistle;" and if Bill had, (as the "Colonel" describes it on his own veracity,) mounted her in Ike Hoff's saloon and "with one bound, lit in the middle of the street," he would have got a severe fall in the doorway of the bar room, *sure*, to make no mention of clearing at "one bound" a porch twelve feet wide, and five feet high, a pavement twelve feet, and half the width of the roadway, (twenty-five feet by actual measurement) making a total of forty-nine feet, without computing any margin inside the room from which she (or he) "bounded."

Spying may have played a big part in Hickok's activities during 1863, but by 1864 his duties were more concerned with police work. In the section on "Scouts, Guides and Spies, 1861–65" in the records of the Office of the Provost Marshal General on file at the National Archives, Washington, D.C., appear the following entries:

THE UNITED STATES, TO WILLIAM HICKOK DR.
March 10, 1864 For
Services rendered as Special Police under the direction of Lt. N.H. Burns A Pro Mar Dist S.W. Mo at Springfield Mo from March 1, to

[19] "Wild Bill," *loc. cit.*, 279–80.

March 10, 1864 inclusive being 10 days at $60.00 per month

$20.00

I certify that the above account is correct and just; that the services were rendered as stated, and that they were necessary for the Public Service, as per my Report of "Persons and Articles," Abstract of Expenditures for March 1864.

N. H. BURNS
1 Lieut 1 Ark Inf. Actg. Pro. Mar.

Approved
JOHN B. SANBORN
Brig. Genl. Comd.

A similar document was made out for the period from March 11 to March 31, 1864, for which period Hickok was to be paid the sum of $40. But on the back of each document appeared the following terse sentence:

Disapproved and ordered filed by Col Sanderson, for the reason that no authority was issued by the Pro Mar Genl of Dept of the Mo, for the employment of this man.

W. K. PATRICK
July 20 '64   *Auditor*

Wild Bill is also listed as a detective employed at District Headquarters, Springfield, Missouri. S. R. Squires is shown as chief of police while Wm. Hickok, J. W. McLellan, and Herman Chapman are "police."

However, during the period that the army decided that Wild Bill should not be paid for his services as a special policeman, the records show the following:

HEAD QRS. DIST. SOUTH WEST MO.
SPRINGFIELD Mo April 3d 1864,

SPECIAL ORDERS
No. 89

. . . III. *J. B. Hickok,* will be taken up on the Rolls of Capt *Owen,* A.Q.M., as Scout, at these Head Quarters, from this date and will be furnished a horse, and equipments while on duty as Scout. His compensation will be five dollars per day.

By Order of Brigadier General Sanborn.

(Signed) N. D. CURRAN
1st Lieut & Acting Asst Adjt General.

This document establishes Hickok's association with Owen, and the relationship may well have cemented the friendship between

64

them that stood Wild Bill in good stead a year later when he stood trial following one of his most controversial gunfights.

By the late summer of 1864, the war was at its peak. In the South, General Price was massing an army estimated at ten thousand men. It was his intention to reach Fort Leavenworth, rich with medical and food supplies. When Price's army was near the Arkansas River, it got a new recruit. Wild Bill, aware of the danger he was facing, joined it near Dardanelle early in September. Price pressed on to Jefferson City, bypassing it because it was too well fortified and would have held up his advance. On September 8, General Alfred Pleasanton assumed command of the Union forces, inflicted great damage to Price's army, and pursued him. At Westport, Missouri, on October 23, 1864, with the help of Curtis, Pleasanton defeated Price. During the battle Wild Bill and a companion made their escape from the enemy ranks, pursued by a number of Confederates. It is alleged that he and his companion were betrayed by Dave Tutt, and that Hickok killed Tutt's friend as they escaped; but the evidence is not conclusive.

Apart from Wild Bill's previously related account of his swim for life across a river, there are four other stories crediting him with escapes across no man's land on horseback—all of which may be based upon one incident. Nichols gives a colorful version of such a ride (from the lips of a lieutenant of cavalry) which asserted that Hickok's companion was killed. But this incident is placed in Arkansas in 1863, when Curtis was matching himself against Kirby Smith. Further doubt of its authenticity was expressed by Wild Bill's "mate": "Tom Martin . . . swore yesterday that Nichols' pathetic description of his untimely murder in 1863, in that article, was not true."[20]

Connelley accepted the fact that such a ride took place at Prairie d'Ane in April, 1864, on the grounds that a onetime governor of Kansas, Samuel Crawford, claimed he saw it happen. The companion who was killed this time was Allen. As if to create further confusion, Connelley states that following the Westport battle Wild Bill tried the same trick, only this time Zeke Stone was killed.

A variation of the latter story was publicized in 1901 by Buffalo Bill's sister Helen. She described a meeting between her brother and Wild Bill, who was dressed as a Confederate officer ("Colonel

[20] Springfield *Weekly Missouri Patriot*, Jan. 31, 1867. Evidently Tom Martin was Thomas G. Martin, who served with Hickok under the command of Captain R. B. Owen (Records of the U.S. Army Continental Commands, 1821–1920, Department of the Missouri, District of South West Missouri, National Archives Record Group No. 393).

Hickok, to give him his real name"), during which they ate a meal and Hickok entrusted Cody with a package for General McNeil. She related that some days later, when the Confederates were advancing upon the Union lines, two horsemen were seen to dash out of the rebel lines and head for the Union forces. One saddle was emptied, but the other rider came on:

> . . . the bullets followed thick and fast. . . . As the survivor drew near, Will shouted:
> "It's Wild Bill, the Union scout."
> A cheer greeted the intrepid Colonel Hickok, and he rode into camp surrounded by a party of admirers. The information he brought proved of great value in the battle of Pilot Knob . . . which almost immediately followed.[21]

Hickok is said to have been associated with the Phelps family during the Battle of Westport, acting on the orders of Colonel John E. Phelps, son of the congressman, but this information is not documented.[22]

Hickok's actual movements after the battle are obscure. It has been claimed that he joined a band of the Red Legs and was involved in some skirmishes with them. In fact, all through the Hickok legends mention is found of this celebrated outfit, but not too much attention has been paid to their origin or activities. The Civil War inspired numerous guerrilla organizations. In the South, John Singleton Mosby's Rangers earned a reputation that made them the foremost "Grey Ghosts of the Confederacy," and up North, "Jennison's Jayhawkers" achieved considerable renown, but the most famous of the Kansas guerrilla bands were the "Red Legs" or "Red-legged scouts."

An examination of contemporary newspapers and official documents for information concerning the Red Legs reveals as much confusion at that time as exists today. John P. Duke, a cobbler in Independence in 1861, claimed that he had sent to St. Louis and got 120 sheepskins dyed red. Jennison's Jayhawkers arrived in town and helped themselves to his stock. They made themselves red leggings at his expense, or used the skins to make colorful boot toppings, hence the name "Red Legs."

But the actual origin of the organization is difficult to establish. In 1863 it was claimed that the Red Legs were organized by

---

[21] Helen Cody Wetmore, *The Last of the Great Scouts: The Life Story of Col. W. F. Cody "Buffalo Bill,"* 120–21.
[22] Monaghan, *Civil War on the Western Border*, 324–25.

Colonel William S. Oliver of the Seventh Missouri Volunteers late in 1861 or 1862 to hunt down Quantrill. Their activities grew so successful that pro-Southern Missourians, who did not wish Quantrill to be destroyed entirely, forced the authorities to arrest them, but forty days later they were released.

During 1862 the Red Legs were led by Captain Nathan L. Stout, provost marshal under Brigadier General James G. Blunt. In November of that year Stout was removed from office and his men outlawed and ordered arrested if found. But soon another leader came on the scene. This was George H. Hoyt.

Hoyt first became prominent when he gave counsel to John Brown after he was imprisoned at Harper's Ferry. Later he joined Colonel C. R. Jennison's Seventh Kansas Cavalry (often referred to as the First Kansas or "Jennison's Jayhawkers"). When a new battalion of cavalry was formed for Jennison's old regiment, Hoyt was given command, and the men were armed with Colt's revolving rifles and the new .44 1860 Army revolver. Among the volunteers were veterans who would not accept normal military discipline but would willingly serve as scouts, dispatch riders, or guides. These were the men who would carry on the tradition of the Red Legs, and soon the red leggings and boot toppings were a familiar sight. In company with men of the Sixth Kansas Cavalry, the Red Legs fiercely attacked and killed many of the Missouri bushwhackers (some of whom were led by Quantrill) on their own ground.

Guerrilla activities succeeded where military operations failed, because disciplined troops could not cope with the guerrillas' style and mode of attack, for they did not fight according to normal military tactics, "and they must be beat at their own game. Indian fighting is the only way to beat them."

By April, 1863, General Blunt became painfully aware that every thief, robber, and murderer in the territory was now adopting the red leggings, and whatever value the organization might have been to him was now lost. Again he outlawed all guerrilla bands. He took the matter further by ordering that all illegal bushwhackers or other rebel organizations out of uniform be hunted down and destroyed: "When such persons are taken prisoner—*which should, as much as possible be avoided*," they were to be tried by military commission and executed by shooting or hanging, but great discretion should be exercised to avoid executing loyal or innocent parties. General Blunt also recommended that the Red Legs should enlist in the army, and this many of them did when the Fifteenth

67

Kansas Regiment was organized in August, 1863, with Jennison in command and Hoyt as his second in command.

In place of the Red Legs, Blunt organized a company of scouts attached to the Fourteenth Kansas, and to lead them he appointed Captain William S. Tough as chief of scouts. These were the celebrated Buckskin Scouts, whose members probably included some men who had previously been Red Legs. Such was the confusion over the scouts that many historians do not realize that they were two separate organizations.

This confusion may explain why Wild Bill Hickok has been listed as a member of both the Red Legs and the Buckskin Scouts. Yet an intensive search of available records has failed to establish his membership in either group. One basis for this confusion stems from interviews given William E. Connelley by one Theodore Bartles who claimed to have led the band of Red Legs. However, little is known of Bartles, and his allegations lack foundation. In citing letters from Charles M. Chase written to and published in the *True Republican and Sentinel* at Sycamore, Illinois, in 1863, Connelley also included a list of alleged Red Legs which named Bartles and Hickok. But no mention of either was found in the original newspaper. In fact, Chase devoted most of his comments to Captain Tough, and the names on Connelley's list were all actually associated with the Buckskin Scouts rather than the Red Legs.

A careful check of Connelley's book on Quantrill reveals that between quoted portions of Chase's letter the author inserted material of his own, which at first glance appears to be part of the original. This can only be interpreted as an effort on his or Bartles' part to establish Hickok's presence in an organization that was both colorful and controversial. Later Connelley was to amend his view slightly to state that Hickok had "served with the Red Legs so frequently that he was considered a member of their organization, though he never formally belonged to it." But by that time the legend of Hickok as a Red Leg was established, as is evidenced by the accounts of Wild Bill's exploits with them, when in fact he was employed in less publicized pursuits.[23]

[23] John P. Duke, cited in the Kansas City *Journal*, June 25, 1889, and the Odessa *Democrat*, Mar. 14, 1924; Leavenworth *Daily Conservative*, Nov. 16, 23, 25, and Dec. 5, 1862, and Mar. 26, 31, Apr. 7, 9, 19, June 19, Aug. 28, 1863; Lela Barnes (ed.), "An Editor Looks at Early Day Kansas—The Letters of Charles Monroe Chase," KSHS *Quarterly*, Vol. XXVI, No. 2 (Summer, 1960), 113–51, 121n.; Lt. Col. R. H. Hunt, Fifteenth Kansas Cavalry, *General Orders No. 11*, a pamphlet published in Feb., 1908, (K369.2/M59, Pam V. KSHS); William Elsey Connelley, *Quantrill and the Border Wars*, 411–17; Connelley, *Wild Bill and His Era*, 93.

Despite a lack of documentation linking Hickok with the Red Legs, it is evident from the following newspaper report, published in 1867, that he was known to Hoyt, but probably only in his capacity as a spy:

"Wild Bill."—Since the publication of the paper in Harper's, setting forth the exploits of "Wild Bill," there has been a determined research in memory by those who participated in the closing scenes of the war in Northern Arkansas. Since the subject of the sketch in Harper has been prominently given to the country we have furbished our recollections, and the result is that we knew Bill Hitchcock in 1864 and recognize his portrait in the magazine for February. It is a fair representation for a wood cut. "Wild Bill," as he is called, rode in company with the writer, and with the Adjutant Mackle and Lt. Col. Hoyt from Newtonia, subsequent to the battle in October, to the Arkansas river, we think, but perhaps he remained at Fayetteville. . . . He came into Gen. Blunt's camp on the morning after the battle of Newtonia, having previously been with Price, and having spent several months in the camps in Arkansas, as stated in the article in question. . . . "Wild Bill" has made his mark in the war for the Union, and we accord him full credit for his risks and reward for results attained.[24]

The only definite information on Wild Bill's movements at this time is found in connection with Brigadier General John B. Sanborn, who had approved his payment for services as a special policeman. In October, 1864, Sanborn took command of the District of Southwest Missouri and fought several successful campaigns in that section, including the battle of Newtonia. During the early part of 1865, Hickok addressed the following letter to him at his headquarters in Springfield:

CASSVILLE, MO., February 10, 1865

BRIGADIER-GENERAL SANBORN:
I have been at Camp Walker and Spavinaw. There are not more than ten or twelve rebels in any squad in the southwest that I can hear of. If you want me to go to Neosho and West of there, notify me here. It was cold; I returned back.

J. B. HICKOCK

Sanborn's reply was:

HEADQUARTERS DISTRICT OF SOUTHWEST MISSOURI, SPRINGFIELD, MO., February 11, 1865.

J. B. Hickock
Cassville, Mo.:

[24] Leavenworth *Daily Conservative*, Feb. 1, 1867.

You may go to Yellville or the White River in the vicinity of Yellville and learn what Dobbin intends to do with his command now on Crowley's Ridge, and from there come to this place.

JOHN B. SANBORN
Brigadier-General, Commanding.[25]

The outcome of this correspondence is not known, but Archibald S. Dobbin was a Confederate general officer.[26]

One of Hickok's last acts of the war, according to William Darnell, was to carry the news of the surrender of Lee's armies on April 9, 1865, to himself and the other members of a wagon train approaching Fort Zarah:

When about a half a mile from the fort "Wild Bill" Hickok, on a dandy horse, came riding by on a run, shouting out as he rode by "Lee's surrendered! Lee's surrendered!" He was a striking figure as I noticed him, a large broad-brimmed hat on his head, long drooping mustache, long flowing hair that fell about his shoulders, a brace of ivory-handled revolvers strapped to his waist, and an extra pair in holsters that fitted about the horn of his saddle where he could reach them instantly. These latter were long-barreled ones, capable of carrying quite a distance. It was common talk that he had got many an enemy with them just on account of their long-rang qualities.[27]

What Hickok was doing on the plains of Kansas at this time is not explained, but he did not remain there long. By June he was back in Springfield, where the following order was issued:

HEAD QUARTERS DIST SOUTH WEST MO.
SPRINGFIELD, Mo June 9th, 1865

DIV & DEPT
HEAD QRS

June 10th 1865   SPECIAL ORDERS ⎫
                  No. 142   ⎭

1. Capt R. B. Owen A. Q. M. Dist Qr. Mr. will settle up with and drop from the roll of scouts the following named persons paying them to include this date at the rates heretofore established

J. B. Hickok
Thos. G. Martin...[28]

[25] *The War of the Rebellion: A Compilation of Official Records of the Union and Confederate Armies*, Vol. CL, Ser. 1, Vol. XLVII, Pt. 1, 810, 819. There are seven references to the name Hickock and Hickok among those who fought during the war. Correspondence with the National Archives revealed that the whereabouts of the original letter from Hickok is not known.

[26] *Ibid.*

[27] George A. Root, "Reminiscences of William Darnell," KSHS *Collections*, Vol. XVII (1926–28), 508.

Hickok, now unemployed like thousands of other veterans, had his future to think of. Springfield attracted him for a variety of reasons and he decided to remain there. In doing so, he kept a date with destiny.

[28] Records of the U.S. Army Continental Commands, 1821–1920, *loc. cit.*

⸺❦ 4 ⸺

Springfield and a Date with Destiny

SPRINGFIELD, MISSOURI, was the scene of Wild Bill's next adventure —his pistol duel with Dave Tutt on the public square on Friday, July 21, 1865.

In those days Springfield was not much of a town, even though it was the largest town in that part of the state. It was the sort of place, however, where pistol duels might have been expected to take place. George Ward Nichols noted its "strange, half-civilized people who, from all the country round, make this a place for barter and trade." They wore buckskin pants and homespun; they were dirty and lazy. Their most marked characteristic was "an indisposition to move, and their highest ambition to let their hair and beards grow. . . . The only indication of action was the inevitable revolver which every body, excepting, perhaps, the women, wore about their persons."[1]

It was in this atmosphere that Wild Bill and Dave Tutt faced each other for the last time.

Trouble between these two was no sudden outburst. All through the stories of Hickok's military service, Tutt's name crops up in one way or another. They probably first met at Yellville, Arkansas, where Dave was born. During part of 1863, Hickok stayed at the home of a Mrs. Estes, who recalled that Wild Bill was "as nice a man at her home as she ever had about her house."[2] Tutt had a sister who comes into the story two years later in Springfield. Did Wild Bill meet her while he was ornamenting Mrs. Estes' boarding-house? It could have happened. In a statement to Connelley at Topeka on January 23, 1923, J. P. (Tom) Botkin, former secretary of state, claimed that during his time as a Union Army Scout at Yellville, Hickok had had an affair with Tutt's sister. A son was born to her, and brother Dave swore revenge. Botkin later saw the girl when she was a happily married woman aged about fifty. Her husband was a physician of Marion County, and the son by Wild

---

[1] Nichols, "Wild Bill," *loc. cit.*, 274.
[2] Connelley, *Wild Bill and His Era*, 66.

Bill was then on the police force of Oklahoma City. However, no evidence has been found to verify this remarkable statement.

Actually, little is known of Dave—or Davis K. Tutt, to give him his right name—and his clan in the prewar period, although it has been established that his father took part in the Tutt-Everett feud which raged in Marion County, Arkansas, in which forty-five men are said to have died. The Tutt home was on Crooked Creek, and was known as "Tutt's Cabin." As late as 1900, Dave's mother was said to be living there.[3] By the time the Civil War ended, Dave was as desperate and as handy with a gun as most of the former scouts and guerrillas. His role in the war is confused. He was about twenty-six years of age and probably served in the Twenty-Seventh Regiment of Arkansas Infantry. There are stories that he was a Confederate spy, and that on one occasion he betrayed Wild Bill. But no evidence has so far been presented one way or the other.

It has been said that at the end of the war Dave brought his mother, sisters, and three younger brothers to Springfield, but in fact it was Lewis Tutt, his colored half-brother who was responsible. When the military fort at Yellville was abandoned, "Lewis drove his mistress to Springfield where she remained until cessation of hostilities and then returned to her old home again."[4] Evidently Dave joined them there and the family settled down. Although Springfield was not kindly disposed toward former rebels, Dave managed to avoid trouble until Wild Bill came to town.

Waiting for Hickok, some claim, was Susannah Moore. A row between them brought on a temporary parting, and it is alleged that Dave was not long in taking up where Wild Bill had left off. Hickok evened the score by taking up with one of Dave's sisters—and making a pretty favorable impression. This friendship upset Mrs. Tutt, who had little or no time for Yanks anyhow, and Dave evidently shared her feelings. He advised Wild Bill to let her alone, and they quarreled.

Trouble came to a head one night in July over a card game. The press described what happened in the "locals," and also indicated that Hickok had already established a reputation:

David Tutt, of Yellville, Ark., was shot on the public square, at 6 o'clock P.M., on Friday last, by James B. Hickok, better known in South-

---

[3] *Ibid.*, 82

[4] *Pictorial and Genealogical Record of Greene County* (photostatic copy supplied by the Public Library of Springfield and Greene County, Missouri). In 1883, Lewis had his half-brother's remains reburied in a plot he owned in the Maple Park Cemetery in Springfield.

west Missouri as "Wild Bill." The difficulty occurred from a game of cards. Hiccock is a native of Homer, Lasalle county, Ills., and is about twenty-six years of age. He has been engaged since his sixteenth year, with the exception of about two years, with Russell, Majors & Waddill in Government service, as scout, guide, or with exploring parties, and has rendered most efficient and signal service to the Union cause, as numerous acknowledgements from the different commanding officers with whom he has served will testify.[5]

The distance between the men when they opened fire is disputed. The first report of the affair established the time of the shooting but ventured no comment on the distance. Nichols gives the distance as both fifty paces and fifty yards; later writers record it as seventy-five yards. The pistols used by both Hickok and Tutt have caused some speculation. Tutt's has never been officially recorded, but Hickok's weapon has been a controversial issue in itself. Later writers have credited Wild Bill with using either a .44-caliber Colt Dragoon or a .32-caliber Smith and Wesson rim-fire No. 2 Army revolver.[6] However, Nichols stated that Wild Bill carried a pair of Colt Navy revolvers when in Springfield.

The card game took place in a room in the Old Southern Hotel or Lyon House, which stood on the east side of South Street, about a block from the public square. The only description in any detail of this game was that rendered Colonel Nichols by a gentleman calling himself "Captain Honesty"—a name which in itself casts suspicion on the man. But this worthy was accepted as a genuine character by the editor of the *Missouri Weekly Patriot* in his January 31, 1867, issue:

"Captain Honesty" (who can forget more than Nichols ever knew and scarcely miss it,) speaks very intelligible, good English. He was at least considered so capable and reliable an A. Q. M. as to be retained by the War Department for more than a year after the war had closed, and his regiment mustered out, to administer and settle the government affairs in one of the most important posts in the country.

Captain Honesty was Richard Bentley Owen, the man who had served as John S. Phelps's regimental quartermaster before being transferred to Rolla and then to Springfield. On July 20, the day before the Hickok-Tutt fight, it was announced:

[5] *Missouri Weekly Patriot,* July 27, 1865.
[6] The Smith and Wesson No. 2 Army revolver was a six-shot weapon in .32-caliber rim fire. Sometimes called the "model of 1855," it was in fact protected by Rollin White's patent of that year, but was first manufactured in June, 1861.

Lt. A. T. Baubie, Quartermaster of the 6th M. S. M., and who has been acting Post Quartermaster at this place since August last, has turned over all property in his charge to Capt. R. B. Owen.[7]

Owen was undoubtedly a personal friend of Hickok's, and it may well be that he gave information to Nichols in good faith. But it is not known whose idea it was to change his name and add a crude dialect. Perhaps, after debunking Nichols, the editor of the *Patriot* deliberately refrained from revealing "Honesty's" real name for fear of embarrassing a highly respected member of the community.

In his interview with Nichols, "Captain Honesty" claimed that "Bill had killed Dave Tutt's mate, and, atween one thing and another, there war an onusual hard feeling atwixt 'em." He further alleged that Tutt had tried to pick a row with Hickok on several occasions, and that Wild Bill finally refused to play cards with him. Tutt then gave money to every man who lost to Hickok so that he could keep playing. Wild Bill, however, won about two hundred dollars, which made Tutt mad. He reminded Hickok of a forty-dollar debt he owed him for a horse trade, which Hickok promptly paid him. Then he claimed another thirty-five dollars, a debt outstanding from a previous game.

Wild Bill disagreed with this and pointed out that it was only twenty-five dollars, at which point Tutt took Hickok's prized Waltham repeater watch from the table. Hickok stood up and faced him. Said Captain Honesty:

This made Bill shooting mad; fur, don't yer see, Colonel, it was a-doubting his honor like, so he got up and looked Dave in the eyes, and said to him: "I don't want ter make a row in this house. It's a decent house, and I don't want ter injure the keeper. You'd better put that watch back on the table."

But Dave grinned at Bill mighty ugly, and walked off with the watch, and kept it several days. All this time Dave's friends were spurring Bill on ter fight; there was no end ter the talk. They blackguarded him in an underhand sort of way, and tried ter get up a scrimmage, and then they thought they could lay him out. Yer see Bill has enemies all about. He's settled the accounts of a heap of men who lived round here. . . . But they couldn't provoke Bill inter a row, for he's afeard of hisself when he gits *awful* mad; and he allers left his shootin irons in his room when he went out. One day these cusses drew their pistols on him and dared him to fight, and then they told him that Tutt was a-goin ter pack that watch across the squar next day at noon.

I heard of this, for every body was talking about it on the street, and

[7] *Missouri Weekly Patriot*, July 20, 1865.

so I went after Bill, and found him in his room cleaning and greasing and loading his revolvers.

"Now, Bill," says I, "you're goin ter git inter a fight."

"Don't you bother yerself, Captain," says he. "It's not the first time I have been in a fight; and these d——d hounds have put on me long enough. You don't want me ter give up my honor, do yer?"

"No, Bill," says I, "yer must keep yer honor."

Next day, about noon, Bill went down to the squar. He had said that Dave Tutt shouldn't pack that watch across the squar unless dead men could walk.

Sure enough, Tutt appeared on the square wearing the watch. Hickok warned him not to cross the square, but Tutt ignored him and started across, at the same time pulling his pistol. Wild Bill immediately drew his and both shots sounded as one. Tutt fell, shot through the heart.

Said Honesty:

The instant Bill fired, without waitin ter see ef he had hit Tutt, he wheeled on his heels and pointed his pistol at Tutt's friends, who had already drawn their weapons.

"Aren't yer satisfied, gentlemen?" cried Bill, as cool as an alligator. "Put up your shootin-irons, or there'll be more dead men here." And they put 'em up, and said it war a far fight.

Captain Honesty concluded his story with the significant remark: *"The fact is, thar was an undercurrent of a woman in that fight."*[8]

Women and gambling never mix, as Hickok and many of his contemporaries found when they fought and died over one or the other. Provided both antagonists were armed and facing each other when the pistols exploded, the result was usually accepted as "self-defense" or "justifiable homicide." Such outcomes, however, did not prevent the local law from taking an interest. So it was that Wild Bill was arrested shortly after the killing.

On July 22 the coroner of Green County rendered his report on Tutt's death and a bench warrant was issued for Hickok's arrest on a "charge of killing," but on July 24 it was reduced to "manslaughter." On the same day Hickok was granted bail in the sum of $2,000 put up by R. B. Owen, Isaac Hoff, and John H. Jenkins.[9]

Following his release on bail, Hickok's next problem was his defense. It seems evident that Owen once more came to his aid. It is not certain whether he personally approached John S. Phelps or

[8] Nichols, "Wild Bill," *loc. cit.*, 275–77.

[9] Circuit Court Record, Greene County, Missouri, Book G (1865), 302. Copy supplied by William B. Secrest.

recommended that Hickok try; in any event, Phelps agreed to defend Hickok at his trial.

Colonel Robert W. Fyan, state attorney of the Fourteenth Judicial District, appeared for the prosecution, and the court was presided over by Judge C. B. M'Afee, who had been commander of the Union post at Springfield at the close of the war.[10]

Wild Bill and his attorney appeared in court on August 3, when he pleaded "not guilty" to the charge. The court then elected a jury: J. W. Langston, A. H. Murphy, J. P. Julian, John Foster, W. B. Gregory, A. Morrison, T. Rushim, A. Cargile, E. S. Bray, C. C. Howell, G. M. Lacey, and W. M. Morris. The first session was brief and the court was adjourned until the following morning, the jury being permitted to "retire in charge of the sheriff until tomorrow morning at 9 o'clock."

On August 4 the indictment against "William Haycock" for the killing of "Dave Tutt" was amended to read "James Hickcock" and "Davis Tutt," to "denote the real name[s] of the parties." The court then heard testimony from the witnesses and adjourned until the morning of August 5.[11]

The witnesses all claimed that Tutt had fired first and his revolver, with one chamber empty (picked up beside the body), was exhibited. Having heard the witnesses' statements, the judge summed up and gave his instructions to the jury:

1st. If they believe from the evidence that the defendant intentionally shot at the deceased, Davis Tutt, and the death of said Tutt was caused thereby, they will find defendant guilty, unless they are satisfied from the evidence that he acted in self-defense.

2d. That defendant is presumed to have intended the nature and probable consequences of his own acts.

3d. The defendant cannot set up justification that he acted in self-defense if he was willing to engage in a fight with deceased.

4th. To be entitled to acquital on the ground of self-defense, he must have been anxious to avoid a conflict, and must have used all reasonable means to avoid it.

5th. If the deceased and defendant engaged in a fight or conflict willingly on the part of each, and the defendant killed the deceased, he is guilty of the offense charged, although the deceased may have fired the first shot.

6th. If it appear that the conflict was in any way premeditated by the defendant, he is not justifiable.

[10] "Historical News And Comments," *Missouri Historical Review*, Vol. X (Oct., 1915–July, 1916), 314.
[11] Circuit Court Record, Greene County, Missouri, *loc. cit.*, 377, 387–88.

7th. The crime charged in the indictment is complete, whether there was malice or not.

8th. If the Jury have any reasonable doubt as to the defendant's guilt, they will give him the benefit of such doubt, and acquit him.

9th. But such doubt must be reasonable doubt, not mere possibility. It must be such a doubt as leaves the mind disatisfied with a conclusion of guilt.

10th. This rule, as to a reasonable doubt, does not apply as to matters set up in justification.

11th. If the defendant claims to have acted in self-defense it is his duty to satisfy you that he so acted, and it is not sufficient to create a doubt in your minds whether he so acted or not.

12th. The jury will disregard evidence as to the moral character of deceased, and as to his character for loyalty, as the character of the deceased could afford no excuse for killing him.

13th. Every murder includes in it the crime of man-slaughter, and if the jury believe that the defendant has committed the crime of murder in the first or second degree, they will find him guilty under this indictment of man-slaughter, the crime charged in this indictment.

14th. The Court instructs the jury that they may disregard all that part of the evidence of Tutt's declaration to Lieut. Warner.

15th. The Court instructs to disregard all Werner's testimony.

16th. That the jury will disregard any threats made by Tutt against Haycock prior to the meeting at the Lyon House in Haycock's room.[12]

The jury retired and soon rendered their verdict: "We the Jury find the Deft not guilty in manner and form charged."[13]

The fact that Wild Bill was acquitted by the jury was not welcomed by the local press:

The trial of Wm. Haycock for the killing of Davis Tutt, in the streets in this city week before last, was concluded on Saturday last, by a verdict of *not guilty*, rendered by the jury in about ten minutes after they retired to the jury room.

The general dissatisfaction felt by the citizens of this place with the verdict in no way attaches to our able and efficient Circuit attorney, nor to the Court. It is universally conceded that the prosecution was conducted in an able, efficient and vigorous manner, and that Col. Fyan is entitled to much credit for the ability, earnestness and candor exhibited by him during the whole trial. He appeared to be a full match for the very able Counsel who conducted the defense.—Neither can any fault be found with the Judge, who conducted himself impartially throughout the trial, and whose rulings, we believe, gave general satisfaction. . . .

Those who so severely censure the jury for what they regard as a disre-

---

[12] *Missouri Weekly Patriot*, Aug. 10, 1865.
[13] Circuit Court Record, Greene County, Missouri, *loc. cit.*, 392.

gard of their obligations to the public interest, and a proper respect for their oaths, should remember that they are partly to blame themselves. The citizens of this city were shocked and terrified at the idea that a man could arm himself and take a position at a corner of the public square, in the centre of the city, and await the approach of his victim for an hour or two, and then willingly engage in a conflict with him which resulted in his instant death; and this, too, with the knowledge of several persons who seem to have posted themselves in safe places where they could see the tragedy enacted. But they failed to express the horror and disgust they felt, not from indifference, but from fear and timidity.

Public opinion has much to do with the administration of justice, and when those whose sense of justice and respect for law should prompt them to speak out and control public sentiment, fail to do so, whether from fear or from indifference, we think they should not complain of others. That the defendant engaged in a fight willingly it seems is not disputed, and lawyers say—and the Court instructed the jury to the same effect—that he was not entitled to an acquital on the ground of self-defense unless he was anxious to avoid the fight, and used all reasonable means to do so; but the jury seems to have thought differently.[14]

Hickok escaped jail but he did not escape a divided public opinion. Then as now the controversy raged. In 1883 an anonymous writer declared:

Hickok . . . being by nature a ruffian he soon became a desperado—a drunken, swaggering fellow, who delighted when "on a spree" to frighten nervous men and timid women. After settling in Springfield a favorite diversion of his was to ride his horse on sidewalks and into saloons, hotels, stores, and other public places, and make the animal lie down and perform other tricks, to the infinite delight, no doubt, of the proprietors, none of whom, unfortunately, had grit enough to blow the bully's head off.[15]

The same writer had little good to say of Dave Tutt either:

A man after Wild Bill's own heart was . . . David Tutt, an ex-Confederate soldier. . . . Tutt was a ruffian and a crack pistol shot. He was said to have "gotten in his work," not only on Federal soldiers, but on citizens who had crossed his path against his protest. Both Tutt and Hickok were gamblers, and good ones, although the ex-Confederate was the more proficient of the two. The two men were boon companions for a time; the one touch of ruffianism made them both akin. They walked the streets together, they drank together, they gambled together—and in the latter pastime Tutt effectually "cleaned out" Bill.[16]

[14] *Missouri Weekly Patriot*, Aug. 10, 1865.
[15] *History of Greene County*, 763–64.
[16] *Ibid.*, 764.

79

What was claimed to be the "truth" about the Hickok-Tutt fight was published in 1920 by E. C. M'Afee, son of the judge. He wrote:

Wild Bill's Springfield career was before I was born, but I have an intimate knowledge of it from my father, who was first commander of the post at Springfield, in which he came in contact with him as a so-called "scout." . . . It was from my father that details of the killing and real cause of it [the fight] came to me and some of it has never before been published. . . . Although but three witnesses testified at the preliminary trial, within that generation several thousand persons could be found who "saw" the killing and of course corroborated the prevailing "duel" story. . . .

As to the killing of Tutt here are the facts. As Wild Bill's lawyer John S. Phelps knew them. As Judge advocate my father knew them, and got them from participants of the card game, and so they have come to me. I refer now . . . to the act itself. . . .

In the top story of the old Lyon House . . . Dave Tutt ran a gambling room. A few days before the killing Wild Bill played there and lost all his money. He pawned his watch for more money and then lost that. A half dozen or more men were playing. Angered at Tutt's refusal to lend him still more money, Bill declared that if he couldn't play, nobody should play, and threw the deck of cards out an open window into the backyard below. At the muzzle of a pistol, Tutt forced Wild Bill to go down the stairs, pick up every card, carry them back to the card room and place them back where he found them. This was pretty tough on Bill. Here at least in the presence of his cronies he was "wild" no longer, his reputation as a "bad man" with them was gone. Humiliated and crushed he was thrown out.

M'Afee alleges that Hickok used the story of the watch to boost his ego with those of his cronies who had not witnessed his degredation. He further claims that Wild Bill ambushed Tutt, drawing and firing before Dave had a chance to defend himself.[17]

However, another early version asserts that when Hickok ordered Tutt not to come "any farther and carry my watch," the

men walked to within forty steps of each other, both drawing their pistols and firing simultaneously, the reports sounding so near together that bystanders could not tell which man shot first. Tutt was encumbered with a long linen duster and his pistol caught in his coat, it is believed he fired before he was ready, and he received Wild Bill's ball

[17] E. C. M'Afee, "Wild Bill's Reputation as 'Bad Man' Overrated," *Springfield Leader*, Feb. 1, 1920. M'Afee was severely criticized by old-timers in Springfield, and the Connelley Collection in Denver contains several contradictions. Connelley himself claimed that M'Afee's father, the judge, actually spoke well of Hickok when he discussed the subject in 1884.

through the body near the heart. He retreated to the court house and fell dead near one of the pillars.[18]

Obviously, somewhere between the pro- and anti-Hickok stories lies the truth. It is apparent that there was fault on both sides, but it is also evident that the contemporary view of Hickok was not as unfavorable as is made out by later generations. Apart from the initial disagreement over the verdict, the *Patriot* carried no further attacks on Hickok's character, even when the Nichols article was published. M'Afee also made the claim that John S. Phelps (who joined with his father to form a law partnership a year after the trial) was ashamed of only one thing in his life—his defense of Wild Bill. But he offers no documentation.

In his summation for the jury, the judge mentioned a Lieutenant Warner. Who was this man and what did he say that was so prejudicial to the prosecution's case? In attempting to locate a copy of the original court transcript, I learned: "The clerk of the county circuit courts said that the transcript was missing after being displayed to a group of writers some years ago. Efforts to retrieve the records have been unsuccessful."[19]

Perhaps Hickok was right when he is reported to have said to Nichols: ". . . there was a cause of a quarrel between us which people round here don't know about. One of us had to die; and the secret died with him."[20]

So the controversy continues. But one man did not think Hickok was a murderer. Richard Bentley Owen was to be instrumental in furthering Wild Bill's fame when, a few weeks after the trial, he introduced him to the man who more than anyone else spread the Hickok legend far and wide—Colonel George Ward Nichols.

It was about September 13, 1865,[21] that James Butler Hickok met Colonel George Ward Nichols. As a result of his interview "Wild Bill" was blazed across the nation's press. Nichols' pen picture of Wild Bill was the synthesis of a host of stories of the scout's prowess which he had heard. Wrote Nichols:

Whenever I had met an officer or soldier who had served in the Southwest, I heard of Wild Bill and his exploits, until these stories became so frequent and of such an extraordinary character as quite to outstrip per-

[18] *Pictorial and Genealogical Record of Greene County,* 290.

[19] Mildred M. Roblee, reference librarian, Springfield Public Library, to the author, Nov. 13, 1969.

[20] Nichols, "Wild Bill," *loc. cit.,* 280.

[21] "The Case of James Butler Hickok, *alias* 'Wild Bill,' " Westerners' *Brand Book* (Chicago), Vol. III, Nos. 2–3 (Apr.–May, 1946), 1–7.

sonal knowledge of adventure by camp and field; and the hero of these strange tales took shape in my mind as did Jack the Giant Killer or Sinbad the Sailor in childhood's days.[22]

In his flattering description of Hickok, Nichols said:

As I looked at him I thought his the handsomest *physique* I had ever seen. . . . Bill stood six feet and an inch in his bright yellow moccasins. A deer-skin shirt, or frock it might be called, hung jauntily over his shoulders, revealed a chest whose breadth and depth were remarkable . . . his small round waist was girthed by a belt which held two of Colt's navy revolvers. . . . There was a singular grace and dignity of carriage about that figure which would have called your attention meet it where you would. The head which crowned it was now covered by a large sombrero, underneath which there shone out a quiet, manly face; so gentle is its expression as he greets you as utterly to belie the history of its owner, yet it is not a face to be trifled with. The lips thin and sensitive, the jaw not too square, the cheek bones slightly prominent, a mass of fine dark hair falls below the neck to the shoulders. The eyes, now that you are in friendly intercourse, are as gentle as a woman's. In truth, the woman nature seems prominent throughout, and you would not believe that you were looking into the eyes that have pointed the way to death to hundreds of men. Yes, Wild Bill with his own hands has killed hundreds of men. Of that I have not a doubt. "He shoots to kill," as they say on the border.[23]

Once this remarkable article was published, it caused a great deal of comment in Springfield and parts of Kansas. To quote once more from the *Patriot* for January 31, 1867:

A good many of our people—those especially who frequent the bar rooms and lager-beer saloons, will remember the author of the article, when we mention one "Colonel" G. W. Nichols, who was here for a few days in the summer of 1865, splurging around among our "strange, half-civilized people," seriously endangering the supply of lager and corn whisky, and putting on more airs than a spotted stud-horse in the ring of a county fair. *He's the author!* And if the illustrious holder of one of the "Brevet" commissions[24] which *Fremont* issued his wagonmasters, will

22 "Wild Bill," *loc. cit.*, 275.
23 *Ibid.*, 274.
24 F. B. Heitman's *Historical Register of the United States Army* (1890) states that Nichols was born in Maine. He entered the service from New York. He was made captain assistant aide-de-camp, April 26, 1862; brevet major Volunteers, January 12, 1865; lieutenant colonel Volunteers, March 13, 1865 (for meritorious service in the campaigns of Atlanta and Savannah, Georgia, and the Carolinas). It has been claimed that Nichols was an aide-de-camp to General Sherman during his march from "Atlanta to the sea." He was honorably mustered out on October 23, 1865, and died in Cincinnati, Ohio, on September 15, 1885.

come back to Springfield, two-thirds of all the people he meets will invite him to "pis'n hisself with suth'n" for the fun he unwittingly furnished them in his article—the remaining one third will kick him wherever met, for lying like a dog upon the city and people of Springfield.

James B. Hickok, (not "William Hitchcock," as the "Colonel" misnames his hero,) *is* a remarkable man, and is as well known here as Horace Greely in New York, or Henry Wilson in "the Hub." The portrait of him on the first page of *Harper* for February, is a most faithful and striking likeness—features, shape, posture and dress—in all it is a faithful reproduction of one of Charley Scholten's photographs[25] of "Wild Bill," as he is generally called. No finer *physique*, no greater strength, no more personal courage, no steadier nerves, no superior skill with the pistol, no better horsemanship than his, could any man of the million Federal soldiers of the war, boast of; and few did better or more loyal service as soldier throughout the war. But Nichols "cuts it very fat" when he describes Bill's feats in arms. We think his hero only claims to have sent a few dozen rebs to the farther side of Jordan; and we never, before reading the "Colonel's" article, suspected he had dispatched "*several hundreds* with his own hands." But it must be so, for the "Colonel" asserts it with a parenthesis of genuine flavorous Bostonian piety, to assure us of his incapacity to utter an untruth.

We dare say that Captain Kelso, our present member of Congress, did double the execution "with his own hands," on the Johnnies, during the war, that Bill did. This is no disparagement to Bill. . . . Bill was the best scout, by far in the Southwest.

A number of Kansas papers criticized the article and its author. Yet George Ward Nichols will always be remembered as the creator of the legend of "Wild Bill." Perhaps the oft-quoted denial of the interview, as Nichols told it, by Hickok can be traced back to the *Patriot*'s closing remarks:

In reading the romantic and pathetic parts of the article, "the undercurrent about a woman" in his quarrel and fatal fight with Dave Tutts; and his remarks with "quivering lipts and tearful eyes" about his old mother in Illinois, we tried to fancy Bill's familiar face while listening to the passage being read. We could almost hear his certain remark, "O! hell! what a d——n fool that Nichols is." We agree with "Wild Bill" on that point.

25 Charles W. Scholten's "Photographic Palace of Art," (at the corner of College and Public Square) combined photography and painting in oils or water colors. Nichols' description of Hickok tallies with Wild Bill's most famous photograph— that taken in buckskins. It is this writer's belief that Scholten made the original about 1865. An examination of an album of his portraits in the possession of two granddaughters by Mildred Roblee failed to uncover any other portraits of Hickok or other frontier personalities. The tintype used by *Harper's* (and copied in reverse like the original, by the noted Civil War artist, A. R. Waud) has also disappeared.

On the same day that Nichols is believed to have met Wild Bill, an election for town marshal took place. Public opinion, or political pull, was probably responsible for the result: Charles C. Moss, 107 votes; J. B. Hickok, 63; James R. Mays, 57; Thomas O'Neil, 3; and ——— Gott, 1.[26]

For the next four months Hickok remained in Springfield, during which time his friend Owen prepared to close down the quartermaster's post, disposing of all the goods by public auction in October. In December, Owen left Springfield, much to the sorrow of the residents who had formed quite an attachment for him, and went to Fort Riley, Kansas, where he had been appointed assistant post quartermaster.

Late in January, 1866, a young man named Coleman was killed by city policeman John Orr. A description of the shooting stated:

On the 25th of January one James Coleman, a young man living in the country was shot and killed in Springfield, by a policeman named John Orr. The circumstances were that James Coleman, his brother Samuel, and another man named Bingham, rode into town that day and got on a spree. As they were riding out on South street Bingham, who was very drunk, began whooping and yelling. A policeman arrested him. Sam Coleman followed and seemed to be trying to effect Bingham's release. James Coleman, who had been left with the horses, came up, a scuffle ensued and he was killed.[27]

Among the witnesses who testified before a coroner's jury was Wild Bill:

J. B. Hickock, being duly sworn, says: When I got where the fuss was, the police took a man [Bingham] off a horse; after they had got him off the horse, Charles Moss came and took hold of him; he did not appear to want to come with the police; kept talking, and when they got opposite Jacob's store, he commenced scrambling, and they threw him down the second time; then they took him along to where Ladd keeps grocery, and by that time one of his comrads came up; those they stopped; Samuel Coleman commenced talking, and the one who was killed had tied the horses at the blacksmith shop and came up and joined them at Ladd's, or near Ladd's grocery; the two Colemans wanted to stop the police and have a talk with the police; from that they got to jarring worse and worse until the[y] commenced shooting; the first I saw of the shooting I saw John Orr jerk his pistol and put it up against the man and shot; did not see whether James Coleman had a pistol in his hand or not; his back was to me; and Samuel Coleman grabbed a stick and struck, but

26 *History of Greene County*, 763.
27 *Ibid.*, 766.

did not know whether he struck John Orr or Charles Moss, and as soon as the first shoting was done, Orr turned and shot Samuel Coleman; the crowd scattered around, and some person or persons grabbed the first man arrested [Bingham] and ran off down town this way; we pulled the man [James Coleman] upon the platform and intended taking him into Ladd's but he was locked up, and he was then carried to the drug store of N. P. Murphy & Co.; affray commenced first opposite the Lyon House and closed opposite Ladd's grocery, on South street, Springfield, Missouri.[28]

The aftermath of the shooting aroused much feeling:

There was much excitement over the killing of Coleman, and a great deal of ill-feeling on the part of the country people toward the Springfield police, who, it was alleged, arrested country people for trivial offences, and allowed town gentry to go unmolested for grave ones. The excitement culminated in a public meeting, which was held on the Monday following. The meeting was presided over by Capt. See, Col. Marcus Boyd, and other prominent citizens. A resolution calling on the city authorities to discharge the police was unanimously adopted, and then the meeting adjourned, the country people being apparently satisfied.

Orr was arrested, but managed to be released on bail. He fled the country, and was never afterward brought to trial. It is said that on one occasion this same Orr, in Springfield, made Wild Bill "take water," and put up with a gross insult.[29]

The account of the shooting of Coleman is interesting—no doubt among the witnesses were some of the "outraged citizens" referred to by the local press following the Tutt killing. Hickok's testimony may have been requested or volunteered. Never a man to let slip any opportunity, his defeat in the election may have prompted his testimony. Or perhaps he may have wanted to re-establish himself with the citizens in the hope of getting Moss's job. Certainly the allegations made by the writer of the sketch that Orr had made Hickok back down are not substantiated.

Wild Bill soon tired of Springfield, and at the first opportunity took his departure. The Tutt family had returned to Yellville, and whatever attractions Dave's sister may have had for him were severed when she left. Whether Hickok was influenced in his decision to leave by the offer of employment from a party of excursionists or by Uncle Sam is not certain, but whatever the cause, James Butler Hickok made all haste to answer it.

[28] *Missouri Weekly Patriot*, Feb. 1, 1866.
[29] *History of Greene County*, 766–67.

---&{ 5 }&---

Deputy United States Marshal

EARLY IN 1866, Wild Bill Hickok was summoned to Fort Riley, Kansas. Upon reporting to his friend Captain R. B. Owen, assistant post quartermaster, he was recommended for appointment to the post of deputy United States marshal. George W. Hance, whom records disclose was a messenger at the post, recalled:

In the winter of 1865–66, the commissary and quartermaster's storehouses at Fort Riley, Kansas, were burnt—it was common talk to balance some army officer's books. Captain Owens was ordered there and sent to Springfield, Mo., for Wild Bill to come to Fort Riley, and on the recommendation of General Easton, who was chief quartermaster at Fort Leavenworth, and Captain Owens at Fort Riley, Wild Bill was appointed a deputy United States marshal.[1]

Hickok's appointment had nothing to do with the disastrous fire at the fort on January 24, 1866. First reports claimed that a million dollars' worth of equipment had been destroyed when the fire broke out in the commissary at the fort, destroying the building and its contents. At great risk to themselves the clerks managed to save most of the books and papers. The fire was "supposed to have caught in the second story of the ceiling between the first and second, from a stove pipe or chimney."[2]

The high estimate of the loss was quickly refuted by Captain O. J. Hopkins, post commissary, who declared that the Board of Officers convened to inquire into the origin and cause of the fire reached the conclusion that the losses were valued at only "twenty-

[1] "The Truth About Wild Bill," *loc. cit.* Owen served as post quartermaster (although he was officially only assistant) of Fort Riley from January 17, 1866, until October 21 of that year. Langdon C. Easton was quartermaster of Fort Leavenworth. Easton held the rank of captain as early as 1848; but on July 29, 1866, he was appointed lieutenant colonel, staff (deputy quartermaster general), and served in that capacity in the military Division of the Missouri until September 5, 1866, when he was appointed chief quartermaster of the Department of the Missouri. The headquarters of the Division were in St. Louis and of the Department at Fort Leavenworth (Victor Gondos Jr., to the author, Sept. 14, 1960; KSHS *Quarterly*, Vol. XXVI [Winter, 1960], 366).
[2] Junction City *Union*, Jan. 27, 1866.

three thousand, three hundred and sixty-six dollars and sixty-four cents."[3] The damaged buildings were quickly rebuilt and the fort was probably back to normal when Hickok arrived, though the date of his arrival at the post is not known.

Since there has been a good deal of misconception about United States marshals and their deputies, a little clarification might be in order. In popular legend a United States marshal is regarded in the same romantic light as a Texas Ranger or a member of the Northwest Mounted Police—an awesome being vested with the powers of judge, jury, and executioner. He was no such thing in reality. His appointment was often political, and he was not necessarily even a peace officer.

Under the Judiciary Act of 1789, United States marshals were appointed by the President of the United States, subject to confirmation by the Senate. The act stated their duties, gave them authority to command all necessary assistance, and empowered them to appoint deputies. They were mainly concerned with federal offenses. They were expected to attend court, to take charge of prisoners before and after trial, to arrange and attend executions.[4]

Only crimes committed against the government or on government property were their responsibility. If one of them witnessed a murder or other crimes, he could make a "citizen's arrest," a term loosely applied when on occasion a marshal brought in wanted men and lodged them with civil or military authorities.[5]

The old-time marshal could not perform by himself all the duties entrusted to him, which is why he appointed field deputies. To keep these men on their toes, he also had a head deputy who worked in his office. The field deputies were scattered all over his particular state or territory, and in the early days received their instructions by mail or telegraph. Once having received his orders, a deputy had to rely on his own initiative and resources to carry them out.

Until 1896 deputies were paid under the fee system but were given allowances for travel. They were not given commissions but usually could present a letter of authority. Many of these men were already serving local city or county peace officers. Possemen could be recruited if necessary, but most of their work was done

3 *Ibid.*, Feb. 17, 1866.

4 Thad Page, chief archivist, General Records Division, National Archives, to the author, Jan. 28, 1958. Zoe A. Tilghman, *Spotlight—Bat Masterson and Wyatt Earp as U.S. Deputy Marshals*, 1–3. (Deputies are correctly referred to as "deputy United States marshals" and not "U.S. or United States deputy marshals.")

5 See Chapter Eight and the arrest of Bob Connors.

under cover. They were the ones who performed the legendary deeds for which the United States marshal gets credit in fiction.

All this is different now. Since 1896 they have been paid salaries and given regular commissions. They are now members of the Civil Service system and their appointment as deputies must be approved by the Department of Justice. Their detective work has been taken over almost entirely by the Federal Bureau of Investigation.

In the early days appointments as deputy United States marshals were mostly by recommendation. Each marshal was responsible for the appointment of his deputies. He gained authorization from the Attorney General of the United States, and the appointments were usually made from the political party of the President, Attorney General, and Marshal. These appointments continued at the pleasure of the Marshal, who was often a major party power in the district.[6]

Owen evidently considered that Hickok was the man for the job to be undertaken at Fort Riley, although there is no record of any service on Wild Bill's part for the then United States Marshal for Kansas, Thomas A. Osborne. A search of the Post Returns of Fort Riley has revealed a number of interesting facts. At least two "detectives" are shown to have been on the Post's strength, but their duties were not defined. Later, a man claiming to be a "detective" was apprehended at the post and, according to the Junction City *Union* of May 12, 1866, his authority signed by Quartermaster Owen was confiscated and sent to the captain for his comments. Owen pronounced it a forgery and hastened over to charge the man, but found he had escaped.

The same records disclose that Wild Bill's brother, Lorenzo, was employed as a wagon master for $75 per month at Fort Riley from October, 1865, until December, 1866, when he was posted to Fort Lyon, Colorado. Also mentioned in the reports is J. B. Hickok, contracted by Captain R. B. Owen on March 11, 1866, to "hunt up public property" at a salary of $125 per month. However, Owen's reports between April and September show his salary as $75 per month, and from May onward Hickok is listed as a "guide."

This latter information is very significant, and suggests that Hickok was not employed as a deputy United States marshal while

---

[6] Mark G. Eckhoff, director, Legislative, Judicial, and Diplomatic Records Division, National Archives, to the author, Feb. 25, 1970.

at the fort. If the "public property" referred to was government horses and mules, then George W. Hance's recollections have some value. He asserts that Owen's first task for Hickok came when he was detailed to hunt up and bring in a lot of big government mules

that had been stolen and traded off. On one trip over in the Council Grove and Little Arkansas River country, he brought in nine big mules and one big and two small men, army deserters. He did all this alone and was gone about three weeks. I saw him when he came in with them. The largest man was riding on a mule by Wild Bill's side. I asked Wild Bill if he was not afraid to take such chances, as that big man could reach and draw one of the six-shooters, and then they would then be on equal terms. He replied he could equally draw the other and shoot every one of them dead before they could fire a shot.

I have seen him draw a pistol and hit a spot, not larger than a silver dollar, at 20 to 30 steps, before an ordinary man could fire a shot into the air or into the ground.[7]

It must also be remembered that had Wild Bill been employed as a deputy United States marshal it is unlikely it would show up on the Post Returns unless he had been responsible for some specific job that was considered of sufficient importance to merit official recognition. In this connection we come to an episode that has been the cause of great controversy among historians for years —did Wild Bill receive orders to "clean up" Fort Riley and tame the unruly teamsters and soldiers who allegedly populated it?

Unfortunately, the available records are not very helpful. Fort Riley early in 1866 was the jumping-off place for emigrant trains, and was also the home station of a brawling, dissatisfied, underpaid, and poorly fed subdivision of the United States Army—a bad combination on the frontier. The end of the Civil War had depleted the army in number and lowered its morale. General unemployment in the postwar years brought in irresponsible and sometimes undesirable recruits, whose only reason for enlisting was a chance to move west. A great number of them deserted within months of enlistment. Many of those who were not rounded up and punished (some of them were shot) fell foul of roving bands of Indians, or died of thirst and starvation out in the desert. Some

---

[7] "The Truth About Wild Bill," *loc. cit.* William E. Connelley's *published* book cites this incident without credit to Hance and indicates that it was Wild Bill's brother Lorenzo who met him. But this may be bad editing (*Wild Bill and his Era*, 89–90).

were lucky and returned to civilization, but they were the exceptions.

It has been claimed that when Wild Bill arrived at the post, the scene was one of chaos. There was open hostility between the scouts and the troopers. And on the side of the scouts were the teamsters and laborers, prepared to fight the "blue-bellies" at the drop of a hat. The situation looked grim. Unable to summon enough troops to form a regular provost marshal patrol, it is alleged that Owen recommended that Hickok get the place under control.

If this is true then it is curious that no official record has been found verifying his actions, or any reports in the local press (the Junction City *Union* paid particular attention to the events at the fort). It is also significant that Lorenzo Butler Hickok's recollections of his younger brother on the plains did not include any reference to peace-keeping activities at Fort Riley. The late Horace A. Hickok told the writer that his uncle Lorenzo often spoke of his own services as a wagonmaster out west, and his brief period with his brother James at Fort Riley, where "James was a government scout." The logical conclusion must be that Wild Bill's activities at Fort Riley in 1866 were confined to the recovery of stolen horses and mules, rather than the restoration of law and order among the inhabitants.

Among the people Hickok got to know at Fort Riley, was the family of Dr. William Finlaw of the 5th U.S. Volunteer Infantry, acting as post surgeon. The post returns indicate that Dr. Finlaw was to be transferred to Fort Lyon, Colorado Territory, but this was changed and in the April he was transferred to Fort McPherson, Nebraska Territory, where he is shown on the post's strength as of April 14, 1866. However, his family was still at Fort Riley in May when William Tecumseh Sherman came through en route for Omaha before continuing on to St. Paul, Minnesota.[8] Sherman wanted a reliable scout and Owen suggested Hickok, to which the general agreed and Wild Bill was detached from the post to act for him. The Finlaw family then joined the command.

Some confusion exists concerning Sherman's guide on this occasion (Buffalo Bill Cody is also credited with this honor). In later years Sherman wrote to Cody and said: "You guided me honestly and faithfully, in 1865–66, from Fort Riley to Kearny, in Kansas

---

[8] Robert G. Athearn, *William Tecumseh Sherman and the Settlement of the West.* 46–47. Post Returns, Fort Riley, Kansas (Microfilm copy, Manuscripts Division, KSHS).

and Nebraska."[9] Cody himself recalled that in the fall of 1865 he was employed as a scout and dispatch bearer for General Sherman and some peace commissioners on their way from Fort Zarah to council grounds on the Little Arkansas River, where they met Kiowas and Comanches. During the trip the chief scout, Dick Curtis, lost his way and Cody took over. Under his direction the party reached council grounds safely. Here they were welcomed by Colonel Jesse H. Leavenworth (after whose father Fort Leavenworth had been named), agent for the Kiowas and Comanches with headquarters at Fort Larned. With Leavenworth were such notables as John B. Sanborn, William S. Harney, Thomas Murphy, Kit Carson, William W. Bent, and James Steel. Treaties with the Indians were signed on October 14, 17, and 18, 1865. Following the council, Cody claimed he guided Sherman to Fort Kearny and then on to Leavenworth.[10]

However, Sherman did not reach Fort Riley until May, 1866, and Cody, who had been married in St. Louis on March 6, was then in Leavenworth with his bride, so it must be concluded that Hickok was the scout.[11]

When the command stopped at Marysville, Kansas, Wild Bill took Dr. Finlaw's small daughter bullfrog-hunting along the Blue River. Scrambling around on the riverbank, spurred on by the little girl's laughter, Wild Bill eagerly chased after the frogs and soon, to the little girl's further delight, they had enough for a meal. All small children took James Butler Hickok to their hearts, and for his part he liked nothing better than to forget everyday cares and engage in their games—to spend a carefree hour or so fishing with them, or discussing, in all seriousness, the merits of a small boy's puppy. He was as much at home sitting on a sidewalk among a crowd of children eating an apple pie which some kind mother had supplied as he was dining with generals and their ladies.

---

[9] Wetmore, *The Last of the Great Scouts*, 255. Fort Kearny was established in 1847 to protect overland emigrants. Originally called Fort Childs, it was renamed in 1848 after General Stephen W. Kearny (1794–1848). Confusion over the spelling was caused by the inclusion of an *e* in "Kearney City" (sometimes called "Doby Town") which was on the western edge of the Fort Kearny military reservation. The county was also spelled with an *e*. The fort was abandoned in 1871 (Luther North, *Man of the Plains*, 8n.).

[10] Russell, *Lives and Legends of Buffalo Bill*, 74–75.

[11] *Ibid.*, 74. In his book Athearn states that Sherman went from Fort Riley to Fort Kearny in 1866, but in a letter to Don Russell (*Lives and Legends of Buffalo Bill* 75n.) he contradicts himself and gives the year as "65." Don Russell expressed the opinion that Sherman "might have confused Wild Bill and Buffalo Bill, as many did even that early." (Don Russell to the author, July 2, 1971.)

One old-timer has left on record Hickok's concern for a sick child. Writing about 1910, Theophilus Little recalled:

He was a great lover of children and tender hearted. My little boy Will, then nine years old, had the misfortune to cut off two of his fingers. As Dr. McCollam was dressing his hand one day, Wild Bill stepped in. "Ah," said he, "that is too bad, too bad and such a fine manly little fellow too," patting him on the head. Dear glorious Will.[12]

Leaving Marysville, the troops proceeded along the Blue River and camped near Rock Creek. Once again Wild Bill looked upon the scene of his fight with McCanles. Few recognized him. One who did was Frank Helvey, who had been near the scene of the fight when it took place. He always recalled that Hickok was a deadly shot, a very reticent man, and difficult to get acquainted with. He noted that in "1866 or 1867, when he was with General Sherman as a guide or escort . . . They encamped for the night on the Little Sandy near our Station. Before they had got fairly settled, General Sherman with Wild Bill accompanying him, rode up to the Station and warned us not to let the soldiers have any whisky."[13]

Hickok left the command at Fort Kearny to act as a civilian guide for a party of excursionists. He lavished his full attention on them, even to the extent of legpulling, as he and his contemporaries delighted to do to most greenhorns. Under the date of June 11, at Fort Kearny, James F. Meline noted:

By the way, I forgot to tell you about our guide—the most striking object in camp. Six feet, lithe, active, sinewy, daring rider, dead shot with pistol and rifle, long locks, fine features and mustache, buckskin leggins, red shirt, broad-brim hat, two pistols in belt, rifle in hand—he is a picture. Has lived since he was eleven on the prairies; when a boy, rode Pony Express on the California route, and during the war was scout and spy. He goes by the name of Wild Bill, and tells wonderful stories of his horsemanship, fighting and hair-breadth escapes. We do not, however, feel under any obligation to believe them all.[14]

Following the Meline excursion (Hickok probably only served as their guide in Nebraska), Wild Bill returned to Fort Riley where he noticed a distinct change. Gone was the boredom of the earlier months. A new regiment of cavalry was being formed—the Seventh. Wild Bill found that his time would be spent hunting horse thieves

[12] "Early Days in Abilene," typescript supplied by Stewart Verckler, Abilene Kansas.
[13] Connelley, *Wild Bill and His Era*, 91.
[14] *Two Thousand Miles on Horseback: Santa Fe and Back: A Summer Tour Through Kansas, Nebraska, Colorado and New Mexico, in the Year 1866*, 17.

and illegal timber-cutters. But he was around long enough to make the acquaintance of the regiment's new Lieutenant Colonel, George Armstrong Custer.[15]

History does not recall any particular friendship between these two at this time, but the following year Custer was to know much of Wild Bill. For the remainder of 1866, Hickok stayed in or around the post, but in the fall he again crossed the path of the Finlaw family. Dr. Finlaw was transferred back to Fort Riley. The late Mrs. Julia Snyder Rockwell recalled that her mother, who had been staying with another daughter, "whose husband, Dr. Finlaw, was an army surgeon at Ft. McPherson, Neb., arrived at Fort Riley under guard of Wild Bill Hickok, who with ten men had escorted her, her daughter and son, from Marysville, Kans., urging them not [to] fear the Indians as he would sleep close to the ambulance."[16]

Shortly afterward, Hickok was in Junction City where he met Will Cody, not yet generally called Buffalo Bill. Having realized that he was not cut out for running a hotel (a venture which had been a financial disaster), Cody and his wife Louisa had the first of their many partings, and he had gone west where he believed he would make more money. Cody states that Hickok was employed as a scout at Fort Ellsworth (later renamed Fort Harker), but the records have not verified this. However, Hickok did use his influence and Cody obtained employment as a scout, and when the work slackened during the winter months he spent some of his time living in a dugout with a man named Northrup.[17]

Wild Bill's activities as a deputy United States marshal during 1867 are obscure and lack any real documentation. As will be seen, he spent the first seven months of that year actively engaged as a scout for the United States Army. In December he appeared in Hays City in company with the new United States Marshal, Charles Whiting. There is documentary evidence of Hickok's service as a deputy United States marshal during Whiting's tenure in office.

Charles C. Whiting was born in Fryeburg, Maine, on February

[15] George Armstrong Custer's true lineal rank was that of lieutenant colonel; but he also held the brevet rank of major general, U.S.A., which, unlike his Civil War volunteer rank of major general, was never revoked, and he was entitled to be called "General." Because of difficulties in connection with the Belknap scandal with President Grant, in 1876, the President ordered that Custer should not invoke his brevet rank when he went on the ill-fated trip to the Little Big Horn. Thus it was that "Lieutenant Colonel" Custer led some of his beloved Seventh Cavalry to their deaths on June 25, 1876.

[16] "Julia Rockwell's Story," Kansas City Star, Dec. 14, 1947.

[17] Russell, Lives and Legends of Buffalo Bill, 77–78.

26, 1837, and came to Kansas in 1855, where he worked for some time as a carpenter in his father's business. In August, 1858, he was elected a constable of Topeka township. In 1860 or 1861 he went to St. Mary's mission as a trader for the Pottawattomie Indians, but kept his residence in Topeka. He was elected sheriff of Shawnee County in 1863 and re-elected in 1865. Still a young man, he had earned a great respect in and around Topeka.[18]

In 1861 a letter dated April 1 and signed "C. Whiting" was addressed to William H. Seward, reminding him of services rendered and asking "for a single crum of your patronage—I am fifty—I have served long and faithfully & do beg a crumb." Evidently this was from Whiting's father. Perhaps this had the desired effect and William H. Seward returned the favor, for on March 7, 1867, Charles C. Whiting received his commission as "Marshal of the United States, in and for the District of Kansas," signed by Seward on behalf of President Andrew Johnson. Whiting's predecessor, Thomas A. Osborne, continued his duties until April.[19]

Whiting took his job seriously, and a report in the Junction City Union of August 24, 1867, noted that he had arrested at Ellsworth three men charged with stealing government mules.

According to Connelley, early in January, 1867, Hickok and a chosen band of scouts pursued some horse thieves in the Solomon Valley. On their return two weeks later they had about two hundred horses and mules but no prisoners. On making his report, Hickok stated that they had met some opposition with no loss to themselves. Connelley added that Hickok had pursued one John Hobbs and twenty-eight others and arrested them for illegally cutting timber on government land. Connelley based this latter information on the following report published thirty years later:

John Hobbs and twenty-eight other workmen, were arrested over on the Paradise Creek in 1867 for cutting railroad ties on government land. The arrest was made by Deputy U.S. Marshal William Hickok (Wild Bill) and posse, and the prisoners were all taken to Topeka where they were acquited by the U.S. Court. Hobbs afterward owned a large drug store in Hays.[20]

18 Topeka State Record, Jan. 5, 1870.
19 Topeka Daily Commonwealth, Jan. 4, 1870. Department of State Permanent Marshal's Commissions, Vol. III, 51. Applications and Recommendations for Public Office, 1861–1869 (Records of the Department of State, Washington, D.C.). Mark G. Eckhoff to the author, Jan. 18, 1970.
20 Connelley, Wild Bill and His Era, 96. An intensive search into the U.S. Circuit and District Courts of Kansas and Colorado Territory for the period has failed to find any reference to Hobbs or the others (R. Reed Whittaker, archivist, Federal

Adolph Roenigk reports a similar incident at Fossil Creek, which was halfway between Hays and Ellsworth. During the building of the railroad more illegal timber-cutters were at work, and Wild Bill, then a deputy United States marshal at Hays City, came down to arrest them:

When he arrived on the train he wore a broad brimmed hat and a brand new buckskin suit with fringes on his elbow sleeves and trouser legs. A pair of sixshooters strapped to his sides, he made the appearance of just such a picture as one could see on the cover of a dime novel. While I was working at Fort Harker I had seen both Wild Bill and Buffalo Bill, who, with a number of others were carrying dispatches from one post to another. At the sight of them going and coming no more attention was paid than we do now to people in every day life. But on this occasion Wild Bill was dressed up for a purpose other than every day scout duty. He went to the wood camps on Paradise Creek and arrested five wood choppers for cutting wood on government land. With his five prisoners he took the train at Fossil Creek Station to Topeka where he turned them over to the United States court, who discharged them, no doubt for want of evidence.[21]

Evidently the *Republican's* report and the recollection of Adolph Roenigk are not related, but the latter incident and its reference to Hays City suggests that it took place late in 1867 or early 1868 because Hays City was not founded until September, 1867.

In March, 1868, the Post Commander of Fort Hays received the following letter:

DISTRICT OF KANSAS
UNITED STATES MARSHAL'S OFFICE,
TOPEKA, March 19th 1868

SIR

I understand that you have in custody one or more parties, confined for offences for which they should be tried by the civil authority. If you have any such at present or should have any in the future please notify Mr J. B. Hickok of Hays city who will promptly respond to your notice.

Very Respectfully
Your Obt Servant
(Signed) C. C. WHITING
U.S. Marshal

Commander of the Post
  Fort Hays Kans.[22]

Records Center, Kansas City, Mo., to the author, Jan. 18, 1971; Delbert A. Bishop, center manager, Federal Records Center, Denver, Colo., to the author, Feb. 1, 1971). Hays City (Kan.) *Republican*, Apr. 10, 1897.

21 *Pioneer History of Kansas*, 182.

22 Fort Hays Letter File, Letters Received (1867–69), Microfilm Copy, Manuscripts Division, KSHS.

Some days later the Post Commander received another letter:

HAYS CITY, KANSAS

March 28th 1868

Capt. Sam Ovenshine,
Comdg. Post of Fort Hays, Kans.
CAPT:
I have the honor to request that a guard of a Corpl. and five men may be detached to assist me in conveying the prisoners of the U.S. Marshal now in the Post Guard House to Topeka Kans. I would respectfully call your attention to the number and character of these prisoners and the feeling in their behalf in this community which renders a guard of U.S. soldiers absolutely necessary.
I am Captain, very respectfully

Your obd't servt.
(Signed) J. B. HICKOK
Dept. U.S. Marshal[23]

This letter is written in faultless copperplate, not in the hand of Hickok. He probably had it written out for him in the official manner in the adjutant's office at Fort Hays and merely signed it. In response to his request the following order was issued:

SPECIAL ORDER HEADQUARTERS FORT HAYS KANS
No. 51 March 28th 1868
III. Sergt William Alloways Co. "H" 5th Inft and five (5) Privates of Co. "G" & "H" 5th Inft. will proceed to Topeka Ks as guard to a number of citizen prisoners, accused of stealing Government property, who are about to be taken to that place for trial. Having turned over the prisoners Sergt Alloways with his party will return at once to this post. The A. A. Qr. Mr. will furnish transportation for the guard.

By Order of
CAPT SAM'L OVENSHINE
[J. A. SOUDERS]
2nd Lieut 38th Inft & Brvt
Capt USA
Post Adjt

Copies
Forwarded to
Dept & Dist HdQrs
April 3" 1868[24]

The movements of these prisoners were noted in the press, and Buffalo Bill accompanied Hickok in an unusual capacity:

[23] *Ibid.*
[24] *Ibid.*, "Special Order Book, October 15, 1866–May 26, 1868."

BAND OF ROAD MEN CAPTURED—

W. F. Cody Government detective, and Wm. Haycock—Wild Bill—deputy U.S. Marshal brought eleven prisoners and lodged them in our calaboose on Monday last [March 30]. These prisoners belonged to a band of robbers having their headquarters on the Solomon and near Trinidad, and were headed by one Major Smith, once connected with the Kansas 7th. They are charged with stealing and secreting government property, and desertion from the army.

Seventeen men, belonging to this same band, were captured eleven miles from Trinidad, on the 13th of March, and sent to Denver, Colorado Territory, for trial.[25]

No further details of this affair have been uncovered. Unfortunately, sometime after Colorado became a state in 1876, the records of the territorial district court were divided between the state and the federal government, and research has not yet revealed which department has the relative documents.[26]

During the summer of 1868, Wild Bill rode into Atchison, Kansas, in pursuit of a horse thief. On his way in he met a small boy and his sisters. He probably soon forgot the incident, but not so the small boy. His name was Bill Tilghman.

The late Mrs. Zoe A. Tilghman kindly copied her late husband's recollections of this meeting:

It was on a blackberry excursion that young Bill Tilghman, 12 years old, unwittingly met with Destiny. With his sisters and Frank and some neighbor children, lunch and pails and baskets in the wagon, they set out for the river [Missouri] brakes where the long canes bent with their weight of juicy berries. Their way lay for some distance along the main road West from Atchison and on it came another traveler who pulled up and greeted them. The children stared, round-eyed, and Bill especially noted every detail of the stranger's appearance.

He was mounted indeed upon no prancing charger, only on a sturdy government mule. But he rode with the easy grace of a Plainsman. His buckskin jacket and broad hat were strange to their eyes, and savored of far regions. Two pistols hung from his belt. His boots were of fine tanned leather.

Tall, he was over six feet, splendidly built, and his face as handsome as his form, with strong, clear-cut features and keen dark blue eyes, long drooping mustache and hair curling upon his shoulders. Distinction sat upon him as a garment. He spoke in a slow, assured manner.

"Good morning boys; and young ladies." The girls' eyes sparked as

[25] Topeka *Weekly Leader*, Apr. 2, 1868.

[26] Delbert A. Bishop to the author, Feb. 1, 1971. Dolores C. Renze, state archivist of Colorado, to the author, June 17, 1971.

they strove to keep down embarrassed giggles. It was flattering to be
called young ladies, especially by such a handsome stranger.

"Did you happen to see a man driving a span of mules to a covered
wagon?" he asked.

Bill, from his position as driver, answered "Yes sir, we did. About two
miles back."

"Uh. And does this road lead straight to Atchison? No turning off anywhere?"

"Yes, sir. It goes straight up to town."

"Thank you. Good day." He swung off his hat gracefully and rode on.

"He certainly is handsome." "He must be somebody important." "That
was a real deerskin shirt."

Bill's remark was, "I'd like to have a pair of pistols like his."

Mrs. Tilghman then quoted a newspaper report which her late
husband had written in his notebook from memory. It reads in part:

Atchison had a distinguished visitor this week. Mr. William B. Hickok
. . . known as "Wild Bill," the most expert pistol shot in the West. He is
now a Deputy U.S. Marshal and scout at Fort Hays, and came here following for four hundred miles a stolen team of mules and a wagon. The
thief had just sold them, but Wild Bill nabbed him before he left town,
and took back the stolen property.

This newspaper story of Wild Bill, complete with references to
his ability to shoot well with either hand, enthralled the young Bill
Tilghman. Mrs. Tilghman went on:

Wild Bill became the hero and pattern for adventure for young Bill
Tilghman. He clipped the story from the paper, read and re-read it, and
showed it to his boy companions. For weeks he talked of Wild Bill, even
dreamed of him.

He had a pair of cap-and-ball pistols, and now all the money he could
get hold of, he spent for caps, powder and lead. He practised shooting
pop-shots from the hip, with both hands in emulation of Wild Bill. Left-
hand shooting was extremely hard at first; and the quick draw, and
shooting as soon as the gun was leveled, aiming, in fact, in the very motion of drawing it, by judgment rather than actual sighting, was a re-
finement of skill that sometimes seemed almost impossible. But he kept
determinedly at it, and the practice of a thousand shots told. The time
came when he could hit a rabbit or a prairie chicken sitting in the grass
thirty feet away, with a quick pop-shot.[27]

[27] Mrs. Zoe A. Tilghman to the author, undated (April?), 1959. A search of the
available Atchison papers for the period has failed to reveal the date of this interesting quote. The alleged accomplishments of Bill Tilghman as a pistol shot are
possibly magnified. But until his murder in 1924, he enjoyed a tremendous reputation as a peace officer.

No further references to Wild Bill's services as a deputy United States marshal during 1868 have been found, but in May, 1869, he was sent to Fort Wallace in an official capacity. The following letter was dispatched to the United States Marshal:

HEADQUARTERS FORT WALLACE KAS.
May 8th 1869

The United States Marshal
    Topeka Ks.
SIR:
    I have the honor to inform you that I have arrested two men (citizens) for stealing Government mules. Please send a Deputy Marshal to this post and I will turn them over to you.

I am, Sir,
Very Respectfully,
Your Obdt. Servant
(Signed) CHAS. R. WOODS
Lieut. Col. 5th Infty
Bt. Maj Genl USA
Comdg Post[28]

On May 16 a deputy United States marshal arrived at the post to collect the prisoners:

HEAD QRS. FORT WALLACE, KANSAS,
May 16, 1869

United States Marshal
    Topeka, Kas.
SIR,
    The Commanding Officer directs me to inform you that he has this day turned over to Mr. Hickox, Deputy U.S. Marshal, Baker and Carter, two citizen prisoners charged with stealing public mules, also Edward Lane and James Dwyer witnesses in these cases having been sent to Topeka.

I am Sir, Very Respectfully,
Your Obdt. Servant
(Signed) GRANVILLE LEWIS
1st Lieut 5th Infy
Post Hqs.[29]

On the same day the post acting assistant quartermaster was ordered to furnish transport by rail from Sheridan to Topeka for Lane and Dwyer, in order that they could attend the court then in session

---

[28] Fort Wallace Letter File (Letters Dispatched, 1869), Microfilm Copy, Manuscripts Division, KSHS.
[29] *Ibid.*

at Topeka. Two days later another letter was sent to the United States marshal:

HEAD QRS., FORT WALLACE, KANSAS
May 18th 1869

U.S. Marshal
Topeka
Kas.

SIR,

I yesterday turned over to Deputy Marshal Hickock the two prisoners detained at this post for stealing Government mules. I also sent down two witnesses, Edward Lane and James Dwyer for whom I furnished Government transportation and as the amount of this transportation will be charged to me I would respectfully request that the amount may be refunded to the Quartermaster at this Post.

The witnesses were sent down at the request of the Deputy Marshal, and their transportation should be paid from the civil appropriation.

I am, Sir,
Very Respectfully,
Your Obdt Servant
(Signed) CHAS R. WOODS
Lt. Col. 5th Infy &
Bvt. Maj. Genl. U.S.A.[30]

When Hickok arrived in Topeka with his prisoners, he learned that United States Marshal Whiting had been in trouble with the government over the killing of friendly Pawnee Indians.

Early in March a number of Pawnees appeared in Kansas. Some were arrested and taken to Fort Harker, while others were reported to be stealing property and terrorizing civilians in outlying areas. On March 9, Marshal Whiting was in Ellsworth, and telegraphed Brevet Lieutenant Colonel E. H. Leib at Fort Harker: "Twenty (20) Indians are in town send squad of soldiers." This was followed by another telegram from M. H. Henry, alleging that "they are not arrested and are making themselves generally free." On the twelfth a number of the Indians came to the outskirts of Ellsworth, and were victims of an unprovoked attack by citizens of the town. Thomas A. Atkins[31] wrote to the Secretary of War declaring "there has bin the most horable outrage perpittrated on the Pawneei In-

---

[30] Ibid.

[31] No relation to Wild Bill's scouting friend. This man was a freighter who had been involved with the army over a Springfield rifle believed stolen (at Fort Hays on December 21, 1868). A few weeks after writing to the Secretary of War, he was killed in a saloon brawl in Ellsworth on April 6, 1869.

dians, at this place that ever [illegible] sight of man."[32] Whether Whiting was still in Ellsworth when the killing took place is not certain,[33] but great concern was felt by the settlers in and around the town and numerous letters were directed to the governor and to Washington. On March 31, by Special Order No. 63, Colonel Leib ordered Major Jno. W. Craig to proceed at once to Ellsworth to report on the incident. In his report he said:

> After parleying a short [time the Indians] came to the main street whe[re] the acting sheriff Whitney [and] [deputy] U.S. Marshal P[arker] [told] the Chief of the party that he must [a]rest him until the authorities at Fort Harker were informed the presence of his party in the town. This Indian then made signs of an intention to use his bow & arrow and said to his [party] what caused them to disperse [rapidly.] On this occurring the Chief was fired on and killed by [several persons] and many citizens [joined] in pursuit of those who had run away, one of whom was killed about [a] quarter of a mile from the town.[34]

It was concluded that no criminal proceedings would follow the incident because the attack had been provoked by the Indians' resistance to arrest and by the state of excitement that existed in the area due to their presence in large numbers. After some investigation at government level, a letter was dispatched on April 26 from the Department of the Interior to the Attorney General, which referred to "the murder of friendly Pawnee Indians, alleged to have been committed by certain Deputy U.S. Marshals."[35]

No trace has been found of a Deputy United States Marshal Parker, but a deputy named John S. Parks was operating out of Hays City in 1868. For Whiting, the allegation against "certain Deputy U.S. Marshals" was damning. He was summoned before his superiors and suspended from office as of May 13 and succeeded by D. W. Houston.[36]

Whiting's dismissal probably came as a great shock to his many friends, but it made no difference in his political activities. He continued to be a prominent figure in and around Topeka, and was a member of several committees and organizations.

---

[32] Roll 660, *Pawnee Agency, 1863–69, Letters Received, Office of Indian Affairs, 1824–81*, Group W204, National Archives, Washington, D.C.

[33] He probably went to Washington on routine business. The Topeka *Weekly Leader* of March 18, 1869, noted that Whiting "has returned from Washington looking well and hearty."

[34] Roll 660, *Pawnee Agency, 1863–69, loc. cit.*

[35] *Records of the Secretary of the Interior, Indian Division, Letters Sent* Vol. 8, 294 (M606, Roll 8), National Archives, Washington, D.C.

[36] Mark G. Eckhoff to the author, June 18, 1970.

It is also evident that Whiting's sudden removal from office did not necessarily affect his deputies, because some of them, including Wild Bill, continued to be employed by his successor. As late as January 30, 1870, Colonel George Gibson, post commander of Fort Hays, was writing to the Department of the Missouri, concerning the disposition of a Private William Gleason, of Company I Third Infantry, charged with "murder committed in the state of Kansas." Gleason had been lodged in the guardhouse at Fort Hays pending a trial by the "proper civil authorities." When the local authorities (Sheriff Peter Lanihan?) refused to receive him, Colonel Gibson wrote: "I have held him until Hickock Deputy U.S. Marshal should arrive."[37] When Wild Bill did not appear (he was actually in Topeka at the time), Colonel Gibson arranged for a military escort to take Gleason to Topeka. However, three months later Wild Bill was again active in an official capacity.

In the records of the United States District Court at Topeka, in the case of the United States *versus* Manly B. Gilman and James Stitt for Larceny and misappropriation of U.S. property (a number of horses and mules), a subpoena issued for John Schooler and John Tucker to testify for the defendants, was shown on the return as having been served at Junction City on May 2, 1870, and was signed "J. B. Hickok, Deputy U.S. Marshal."[38]

At this date, no further references have been found to Wild Bill's employment as a deputy United States marshal after May, 1870, but his services in other capacities were still much in demand.

[37] Major George Gibson, commanding Fort Hays, to Colonel W. G. Mitchell, Acting Assistant Adjutant General, Department of the Missouri, Jan. 30, 1870, Letters Sent, Fort Hays, Kan., Vol. X (Jan. 5, 1869–June 14, 1870), Microcopy No. T–713, Records of Fort Hays, Kan., Roll 1, National Archives, Washington, D.C.

[38] Records of the U.S. District Court, Topeka, Kansas, case No. 828. General Services Administration, Federal Records Center, Kansas City, Missouri (Waldo E. Koop to the author, September 23, 1973).

--᎒ 6 ᎒--

Scouting for the Cavalry

WHILE OFFICIAL DUTIES as a deputy United States marshal occupied much of his time during the period 1867–69, Wild Bill was also engaged in activities equally exciting, and possibly more hazardous—as a scout with the army in the field against hostile Indians.

At the end of the Civil War the frontier West was threatened by an Indian war. During the late hostilities the Indians had taken full advantage of the situation and undone much of the work which the army had done to preserve the peaceful and reasonably safe frontier. Sioux warriors from Minnesota and the Dakotas, aided by the Cheyennes and the Kiowas, were waging war with the settlers on the Plains. In New Mexico and Arizona the Apaches increased their depredations, and the country was full of reports of Indian outbreaks, massacres, and burned-out property. This situation was not new. There had always been trouble between red man and white, for obvious reasons. The land belonged to the Indian but the white man wanted it, and he was not particularly worried about how he got it. On both sides there were those who realized the futility of bloodshed, and they strove to attain some sort of peace. But treaties signed by both sides were quickly broken. Between the factions was the army, whose sole purpose was to protect the citizens of the United States—the immigrants who settled on land granted by the government in its bid for Western expansion. The army at first rarely adopted a warlike policy toward the Indian— its actions were determined solely by the needs of the moment. Later, rightly or wrongly, it was forced to take the part of the whites against the Indians, who considered the army their enemy also.

In the land south of the Platte, Black Kettle and other chiefs of the Cheyennes, still fearful of a repetition of the Sand Creek Massacre (when over 150 of their people under White Antelope had been killed in a dawn ambush by Colonel John W. Chivington and part of the Colorado militia in 1864), signed a treaty in 1865. They agreed to move their people to a reservation at a point which is

103

now on the border of Kansas and Oklahoma. But the treaty was never ratified by the Senate, and until 1867 they had no home.

By 1867 most of the tribes wanted peace, but among them there were still warmongers, some of whom were the Dog Soldiers, a military organization of the Cheyennes. Although an uneasy truce prevailed, there were outbreaks on both sides. In Washington the situation was viewed with alarm. To get a definite settlement, Lieutenant General William Tecumseh Sherman, in command of the Division of the Missouri, ordered Major General Winfield Scott Hancock, commander of the Department of the Missouri, into the field in Kansas to organize a force to march into Indian country. His purpose was to proceed at once to the Cheyennes and Kiowas, in the country below the Arkansas, and to confer with them, to try to make peace.

Far from creating an impression of peaceful motives, Hancock's force was positively warlike. His command was made up of six companies of the Seventh Cavalry, seven companies of the Thirty-seventh Infantry, and a battery of the Fourth Artillery Battalion, a total of about 1,400 men. As his field commander Hancock had Brevet Major General A. J. Smith, who, besides holding the position of command of the Upper Arkansas District, was also colonel of the Seventh Cavalry. Custer was placed in command of the mounted troops.

With them were a number of Delaware Indians and some noted plainsmen as scouts and trailers. Among these were, besides Wild Bill, Jack Harvey, William "Buffalo Bill" Comstock, Edmund Guerrier (known as Ed Geary), Thomas H. Kincaid, and several others.

The presence of this large force frightened the Indians. Despite the efforts of their agent, E. W. Wynkoop, to convince them of the peaceful purpose of the expedition, they remained suspicious. Then Hancock received word from his scouts that the Indians, who had excused themselves on the pretext of hunting, had finally left their villages in fear of attack. Furious, Hancock ordered Custer in pursuit. In a panic now, the fleeing Indians attacked everything in their path and burned several settlements. Hancock ordered their villages burned in reprisal.

Several weeks of marching and countermarching achieved nothing but frayed tempers among Hancock's officers, including the fiery Custer, who made no secret of the fact that he considered Hancock had blundered. One last meeting with the Indians was held at Fort Dodge, where a semblance of peace was restored. Custer was then ordered to take command of the Smoky Hill Region, to reopen the mail routes as soon as possible, and to see all that the mails were adequately protected.

The importance of the part which Hickok and his fellow scouts and guides played during the Hancock campaign and others during the next two years has never been given full acknowledgment. It was their responsibility to keep the lines of communication open; to act as dispatch riders, and scout ahead of the main columns; to keep the troops up to date on the Indians' whereabouts. Their task was hazardous and meant risking their lives daily. On fast-moving, hardy ponies the scouts rode during the darkness, and rested where possible during daylight. Many of them owed their lives to their mounts, to their ability to outshoot the hostiles, and to their own knowledge of the country through which they raced for life. Many of these brave men were killed, the manner of their deaths a mystery—unless, as sometimes happened, their scalped and mutilated bodies were found by a patrol or a fellow scout. Sometimes, too, their fate could be guessed at by the return of a riderless horse to the home fort, the saddle blood-spattered and the animal wounded by bullet or arrow. All along the mail routes it was common for people to receive letters stained with the blood of the luckless stagecoach drivers and messengers who had sacrificed their lives in order that the mail might go through.

Such were the hazards to be faced when Wild Bill signed on as a scout for the Seventh Cavalry at Fort Riley on January 1, 1867, in the office of Captain G. W. Bradley, acting quartermaster at the post.[1] The duties of a deputy United States marshal kept him busy only part of the time; the remainder was spent with the cavalry, or trapping in Nebraska and other places. Sometimes, too, he sat for hours under the glare of a smoky lamp in the company of the officers and men at Fort Sidney, gambling. The Leavenworth *Conservative* on February 1, 1867, noted that Wild Bill "is now a gambler at Junction City, which statement we have no reason to doubt." Some confirmation of this is found in the Junction City *Union* of August 19, 1876, which stated that Hickok "formerly lived in this city and kept a saloon and gambling hell on Seventh street, about where Mrs. Kiehl's millinery store now stands." However, whatever connection Wild Bill may have had with a gambling establishment, he did not allow it to interfere with his other activities.

[1] Records of the Quartermaster General, Reports of Persons Hired (May–July, 1867), National Archives, Washington, D.C. Bradley replaced Captain Owen, who had retired from the army and returned to Springfield, Missouri, to live.

In Junction City, close by Fort Riley, a copy of *Harper's* aroused some comment in the press:

The February number of Harper's Monthly is of unusual local interest, because of a long sketch of adventures of our townsman Wild Bill. The usual number of our periodical dealers was rapidly exhausted. Wild Bill is on duty at Riley, but makes Junction his home. Send for a number, and you will enjoy one of the most interesting sketches ever in print.[2]

A couple of weeks later Hickok was in Leavenworth:

"Wild Bill".—This somewhat noted individual was in the city yesterday, having recently arrived from Riley with a lot of furs and skins. He was the observed of a good many observers.[3]

A few days earlier a rival newspaper had reported on Hickok:

. . . recently arrived from the Far West with trains loaded with furs, peltries, and buffalo robes. Wild Bill brings his wife along, and is resting at the Brevoort. The value of the furs and robes he brings with him is said to exceed $20,000.[4]

The identity of the lady discreetly referred to as his "wife" is a matter for conjecture, but perhaps it was a woman named by some as "Indian Annie," about whom we shall learn more.[5] Two weeks later Hickok was in Atchison, where this comment was published:

PERSONAL.—Yesterday we had a call from Major James Butler Hickok, the "Wild Bill" of Harper's Magazine. The Major is in good health and fine spirits, and enjoys himself in the very best manner. He is stopping a few days in our place, on business entirely his own, and seems to be the observed of all observers. "Wild Bill" did good service during the war for the Union cause, although he is as fierce as a lion when aroused on the side of right, yet ordinarily he is as gentle as a lamb. If we are the judge of human nature, "Wild Bill" has a heart as big as an ox, and would scorn to do a mean act.[6]

This reference to a rank held by Hickok is inexplicable, unless it was meant as a courtesy or a compliment.

Less than a month later Hickok appeared at Fort Zarah to join the Hancock expedition against the hostiles. While at the fort he met two journalists who left behind conflicting impressions. One was Theodore R. Davis, an artist for *Harper's Weekly*, and the other

---

2 Junction City *Weekly Union*, Feb. 2, 1867.
3 Leavenworth *Daily Conservative*, Feb. 19, 1867.
4 Leavenworth *Daily Bulletin*, Feb. 13, 1867.
5 See Chapter Twelve.
6 Atchison *Weekly Free Press*, Mar. 2, 1867.

This rare tintype of Wild Bill was made by an unknown photographer about 1858. Reproduced here for the first time, the print has been reversed to correct the mirror-image of the original, which was hand colored. This may be the "likeness" which Hickok mentioned in his letter home of August 14, 1858.

Reproduced for the first time, this tintype was made about 1863–64 when Wild Bill was a Union Army scout. Framed without glass, this photograph has suffered the ravages of time. It has also been reversed to obtain the correct image.

COURTESY ETHEL HICKOK

This rare photograph, made by Alexander Gardner, was titled "The Quartermaster's Staff, Fort Harker, Kansas, 1867." It was included among the 10" x 20" prints sold in portfolio form of his series *Across the Continent on the Union Pacific Railway, Eastern Division.* Wild Bill, the giant figure at the left, carries his Colt's Navy revolvers in the "butts forward" position in open-top and open-bottom holsters.

COURTESY ANTHONY GARNETT

In buckskins, Wild Bill fits the description of him given in 1867 by
Colonel George Ward Nichols, who immortalized him in *Harper's New
Monthly Magazine.* "Kernel," Hickok said to Nichols, "I have a mother
back there in Illinois who is old and feeble. . . . I'm not a cut-throat and a
vagabond, and I'd like the old woman to know what'll make her proud."

The first published illustration of Wild Bill. Engraved by A. R. Waud from a photograph made by Charles W. Scholten of Springfield, Missouri, the picture accompanied Nichols' article "Wild Bill" in *Harper's New Monthly Magazine* (February, 1867). Evidently the original was a tintype, because the picture seems to be reproduced in reverse.

Wild Bill as he is best remembered—in a Prince Albert frock coat, checkered trousers, and cape. From a plate made about 1868.

Wild Bill about 1873–74.

George Rockwood of New York made several plates of Wild Bill. Badly retouched copies of this full-face portrait were sold in the 1890's, but this version (a) is from an original print. Another (b) of Rockwood's plates; and the most widely publicized (c) of Rockwood's three plates.

Henry M. Stanley, a special correspondent for the *Weekly Missouri Democrat*. Stanley's recollections are well known, but Davis' comments have not received the same publicity. They were written many years afterward and first appeared in print in 1946.[7]

Davis met Stanley at Fort Zarah. He does not give a date, but it must have been toward the end of March, 1867. There had been a blizzard and everyone was feeling uncomfortable:

This was the situation, when toward dusk one afternoon I was seated on the ground wrapped in a blanket for warmth, and just by the opening of the tent to catch enough of the waning light to finish a drawing over which I was shivering—and my then especial aversion, "Wild Bill" sauntered up. Seeing that he was not welcome, the Scouts stay was short and starting off remarked with some irony, "Ther's another dodgasted sardine of a newspaper cuss bunken in the sutlers shack what wants my wind, I see you dont!" A fellow worker and sufferer in camp: This was news, and I was not long in starting, for the sod structure toward which the festive "Bill" who's right name was "Jim" had swaggered away in a miff.

It was thus I found Stanley and promptly effected his rescue from the deluge of romance with which the voluble plains man was flooding him[.] The trip was Stanleys first experience of the Great American Desert—located by school geographers on their maps—It was not mine—And in characters novel to him Stanley was searching for the "Leather stocking" element of which as he said not even a shaddow materialized[.] Both garments and character of honest old Natty Bumpo seemed a shocking misfit, for the self named "Wild Bills" and Texas Jacks.

Stanley awoke one morning to find that some deserters had stolen part of his equipment, including his saddle blanket, so it was decided to organize a deserter hunt. Davis went on:

It is here worth while to describe "Wild Bill" whom we determined upon as the most available individual for chief operator, although our confidence in the critter was slim. This man was by nature a dandy, sufficiently vain of his personal appearance, phisique and constitution—gifts of nature which had thus far—proved armor for his mad gallop, amid irregularities the end of which only: has connection with the word moral[.] Even his countenance was then unmarked by dissipation; In his usual array "Wild Bill" could have gained unquestioned admittance to the floor—of most fancy dress balls in metropolitan cities[.] When we ordinary mortals were hustling for a clean pair of socks, as prospective

[7] Elmo Scott Watson (ed.) and Theodore R. Davis, "Henry M. Stanley's Indian Campaign in 1867," Westerners' *Brand Book*, Bound Volume II (1945–46), 103. Watson obtained the manuscripts from the late Dr. Robert Taft, who had a number of Davis's writings which had not been published.

limit of change in wearing apparel, I have seen "Wild Bill" appear in an immaculate boiled shirt, with much collar and cuffs to match—a sleeveless Zouave jacket of startling scarlet, slashed with black velvet[.] The entire garment being over ornamented with buttons which if not silver seemed to be. The trousers might be either black velvet or buck skin and like his jacket fitted with buttons quite beyond useful requirement. The french calf skin boots worn with this costume fitted admirably, and were polished as if the individual wearing them had recently vacated an Italians arm chair throne on a side street near Broadway. The long wavey hair that fell in masses from beneath a conventional sombrero was glossy from a recent anointment of some heavily perfumed mixture.[8] As far as dress went only[,] "Wild Bill" was to border plainsmen what "Beau" Neil was to the Army of the Potomac—faultlessly clad under surprising circumstances. In fact I dont believe that it would have occasioned comment had the scout produced and deliberately fitted on, kid gloves matching perfectly his expansive neck tie[.] Contrasted with this figure[,] the usual useful scout or guide, clad in such garments as his last opportunity for a ready made outfit afforded[,] the gallus Wild Bill was a feature in the landscape to attract attention[.] Uncertainty was created as to Wild Bills legal name after it had been printed as Wm Hitchcock[,] Wm Hancock[,] and Wm Hickock[,] also Wm Haycock, and you were told that "Jim" Hicock was correct. This unique being, now the object of our quest, was with but little difficulty made favorably inclined to Stanleys proposition to go on a deserter hunt.

Having exaggerated Hickok's personal appearance to alarming proportions, Davis grudgingly admitted that Wild Bill successfully guided the expedition some ten or twelve miles from camp to the deserters' hideout:

. . . when the Ranch was surrounded, "Wild Bill" upon his own suggestion stole noislessly and alone to the door, gaining admittance after a short parley. . . . An element of danger ample to interest every participant pervaded the movement and "Wild Bills" action dispelled something of the vail of doubt which in our minds clouded the title to genuineness of personal incidents narrated as fact by that gay party.[9]

Davis' personal references to Stanley can also stand some examination; a careful perusal of his comments reveals an odor of sour grapes. When commenting upon Stanley's finding of Livingstone and bringing back letters, he makes a pointed reference to the

---

[8] It was common for scouts and others with long hair on the Plains to use an ointment of a perfumed nature to make their locks glossy (Agnes Wright Spring, *Colorado Charley, Wild Bill's Pard*, 46).

[9] Watson and Davis, "Henry M. Stanley's Indian Campaign in 1867," *loc. cit.*, 105–106.

doubts concerning their authenticity: "Few persons, knew as well as myself, Stanleys remarkable facility in imitating any ones hand writing, even when he was afforded only a few moments to study its characteristics."[10]

Stanley did not share Davis' view of Wild Bill. The following is part of a dispatch to the *Weekly Missouri Democrat* dated April 4, and published on April 16, 1867:

James Butler Hickok, commonly called "Wild Bill," is one of the finest examples of that peculiar class now extant, known as Frontiersmen, ranger, hunter and Indian scout. He is now thirtyeight years old [twentynine], and since he was thirteen the prairie has been his home. He stands six feet one inch in his moccasins, and is as handsome a specimen of a man as could be found. *Harper's* correspondent recently gave a sketch of the career of this remarkable man, which excepting a slight exaggeration, was correct. We were prepared, on hearing of "Wild Bill's" presence in the camp, to see a person who would prove a coarse, illiterate, quarrelsome, obtrusive, obstinate, bully; in fact, one of those ruffians to be found South and West, who delight in shedding blood. We confess to being agreeably disappointed when, on being introduced to him, we looked on a person who was the very reverse of all we had imagined. He was dressed in a black-sacque coat, brown pants, fancy shirt, leather leggings, and had on his head a beaver cap. Tall, straight, broad compact shoulders, herculean chest, narrow waist, and well-formed muscular limbs. A fine handsome face, free from any blemish, a light moustach, a thin pointed nose, bluish-grey eyes, with a calm, quiet, benignant look, yet seemingly possessing some mysterious latent power, a magnificent forehead, hair parted from the center of the forehead and hanging down behind the ears in long, wavy, silk curls. He is brave, there can be no doubt; that fact is impressed on you at once before he utters a syllable. He is neither as coarse and illiterate as *Harper's Monthly* portrays him....

The following *verbatim* dialogue took place between us: "I say, Bill, or Mr. Hickok, how many white men have you killed to your certain knowledge?" After a little deliberation, he replied, "I would be willing to take my oath on the Bible tomorrow that I have killed over a hundred, a long ways off." "What made you kill all those men; did you kill them without cause or provocation?" "No, by Heaven! I never killed one man without good cause." "How old were you when you killed the first white man, and for what cause?" "I was twentyeight years old when I killed the first white man, and if ever a man deserved killing he did. He was a gambler and counterfeiter, and I was in a hotel in Leavenworth City then, and seeing some loose characters around, I ordered a room, and as I had some money about me, I thought I would go to it. I had

10 *Ibid.*, 101.

lain some thirty minutes on the bed, when I heard some men at my door. I pulled out my revolver and bowie-knife and held them ready, but half concealed, still pretending to be asleep. The door was opened, and five men entered the room. They whispered together 'let us kill the son of a b——h; I'll bet he has got money.'" "Gentleman," said he further, "that was a time—an awful time. I kept perfectly still until just as the knife touched my breast; I sprang aside and buried mine in his heart, and then used my revolvers on the others right and left. Only one was wounded, besides the one killed; and, then gentlemen, I dashed through the room and rushed to the fort, procured a lot of soldiers, came to the hotel and captured the whole gang of them, fifteen in all. We searched the cellar and found eleven bodies buried there—men who were murdered by those villains." Turning to us, he asked "Would you have not done the same? That was the first man I killed, and I never was sorry for that yet."

The first half of Stanley's account has an authentic ring, but in his account of the alleged fight in a Leavenworth hotel, either he was guilty of fabrication or he was a genuine victim of Hickok's acknowledged sense of humor. Wild Bill, according to Stanley, was twenty-eight years of age when the "massacre" occurred—yet he was only a few weeks from his thirtieth birthday when Stanley met him. The deplorable marksmanship displayed by Wild Bill suggests that whatever he told Stanley was later embellished. But perhaps only Hickok could supply the truth of this amazing interview. Nevertheless, he had added another notable hero-worshiper to his credit. Even when he had achieved immortality by saying, "Dr. Livingstone, I presume?" Stanley never met anyone quite like Wild Bill Hickok; and to the end of his days he delighted in telling stories about him. Stanley claimed that once when a man insulted him, Wild Bill reached out with his long arms, picked the fellow up, and threw him over a billiard table.

Despite legendary accounts of his exploits with Custer, there is no evidence to support the statement that Hickok was Custer's chief of scouts. At General Hancock's request, Wild Bill (along with Tom Atkins, Ed Geary, and Kincaid) was paid one hundred dollars a month from May 1, 1867, as a scout with the Seventh Cavalry in the field.[11] Custer in later years recalled Hickok's value

[11] Records of the Quartermaster General, loc. cit.; Hickok's services as a scout were interspersed with employment as a wagon master, in which capacity he is listed for March and April. After May 1 he was listed as a scout. Thomas H. Kincaid served as a scout at Forts Harker and Hays, and at Fort Union, New Mexico, in 1867. Tom Atkins was chief of scouts at Fort Smith, Arkansas, and at Omaha, Nebraska Territory, during 1863–65. He served as a scout at Fort Gibson, Indian Territory, in 1865, and as a guide at Forts Harker and Hays in 1867. During 1874–75 he was at Fort Concho, Texas (Victor Gondos, Jr., to the author, Sept. 21, 1960).

as a scout and left behind him an excellent pen picture. Originally published in the *Galaxy Magazine* in 1872, his recollections were later published in book form in 1874 as *My Life on the Plains*. He wrote:

Among the white scouts [in the Hancock expedition] were numbered some of the most noted in their class. The most prominent man among them was "Wild Bill" . . . a strange character, just the one which a novelist might gloat over. He was a Plainsman in every sense of the word, yet unlike any other of his class. . . . Whether on foot or on horseback, he was one of the most perfect types of physical manhood I ever saw. Of his courage there could be no question: it had been brought to the test on too many occasions to admit of a doubt. His skill in the use of the rifle and pistol was unerring; while his deportment was exactly the opposite of what might be expected from a man of his surroundings. It was entirely free from all bluster and bravado. He seldom spoke of himself unless requested to do so. His conversation, strange to say, never bordered either on the vulgar or blasphemous. His influence among the frontiersmen was unbounded; his word was law, and many are the personal quarrels and disturbances which he has checked among his comrades by his simple announcement that "This has gone far enough," if need be followed by the ominous warning that when persisted in or renewed the quarreler "must settle it with me."

Wild Bill is anything but a quarrelsome man; yet no one but himself can enumerate the many conflicts in which he has been engaged, and which have almost invariably resulted in the death of his adversary. I have a personal knowledge of at least half-a-dozen men whom he has at various times killed, one of these being at the time a member of my command.[12] Others have been severely wounded, yet he always escaped unhurt. On the plains every man openly carries his belt with its invariable appendages, knife and revolver, often two of the latter. Wild Bill always carried two handsome ivory-handled revolvers of the large size; he was never seen without them.[13]

By May the Indian situation was settling down. The Junction City paper noted: "Jack Harvey returned to town last night. We are now looking for Wild Bill, and when he appears we will conclude the Indian war is over."[14] And a few days later: "Wild Bill came in from the West the other day. He reports all quiet at the front. Jack Harvey has also returned. Hancock will be in in a day or so. Custar will be the only notable left behind."[15] Less complimentary was the comment from Marysville, Kansas: "Wild Bill is out after the In-

12 Private John Kile. See Chapter Eight.
13 Pages 33–34.
14 Junction City *Union*, May 4, 1867.
15 *Ibid.*, May 11, 1867.

dians. If his history as published in 'Harper' is correct, we suppose he will eat three or four of the red prairie birds every day before breakfast! Ugh!"[16]

Stanley continued to make the exploits of Wild Bill news. He arrived in Junction City where he once more met up with Hickok, and in his dispatch dated the eleventh mentioned the bravery of Thomas Atkins, the express rider, who managed to convince some Indians of his peaceful intentions (by producing a Dragoon Colt) and without bloodshed persuaded them to allow him to continue with his dispatches to Fort Hays. Of Hickok he wrote:

"WILD BILL,"

who is an inveterate hater of the Indians, was also chased by six Indians lately, and had quite a little adventure with them. Taught by long practice with Indians to be always on his guard, he never walks out of the house without a brace of fine revolvers slung to his waist, but on an important errand he goes armed to the teeth, and woe to the Indians who cross his path. Riding about in the late field of operations, he was seen by a group of the red men, who immediately gave chase. Too soon they found whom they were pursuing, and then commenced to retrace their steps, but not before two of them fell dead before the weapons of Wild Bill. A horse was also killed and one wounded, after which Wild Bill rode unconcernedly on his way to camp, and in a very modest manner related the little adventure, which report was verified by a scout named Kincaid who shot an Indian on his way with dispatches for General Custar.[17]

When Stanley attended the Medicine Lodge Peace Councils later in the year, and met some of the Indians the troops and scouts had fought, he noticed in particular Satanta (or White Bear) the noted Kiowa. Looking at the Indian, the words of Wild Bill were still ringing in his ear: "That man has killed more white men than any other Indian on the plains, and he boasts of it."[18]

Hancock's primary mission against the Indians had failed, and though the presence of the troops kept the Indians in check, the military were in a state of readiness all through the summer. Stories of the exploits of the various scouts still cropped up in print, and Hickok received a good portion of the publicity. The following gives some idea of how even then legends were started:

[16] Marysville Enterprise, May 18, 1867.

[17] Weekly Missouri Democrat, May 21, 1867. In his My Early Travels and Adventures in America and Asia, 97, Stanley has made subtle changes in this report. Hickok's "fine revolvers" are described as "ivory-handled," and there are other differences.

[18] Daily Missouri Democrat, Oct. 21, 1867.

FROM THE PLAINS . . .
(From our Special Correspondent)
FORT HARKER, July 8, 1867.
. . . I noticed in the Commercial of Saturday morning the following interesting paragraphs relative to Fort Harker and the Indian matters:
"A gentleman, just from Fort Harker, says the town is full of vague and indefinite rumors of Indian depredations, outrages etc.

On the 2nd inst. it was reported that four men had been killed and scalped some eight miles West of Fort Harker. Troops were immediately put in readiness, and, under the direction or guidance of Wild Bill, started in pursuit of the bloody depredators. The next day Wild Bill and his party returned, bringing five red skins with them, and having killed some eight or ten Indians on the trip.

As the train left Fort Harker on the morning of the fourth, pickets firing was heard in various directions around the Fort, indicating the presence of skulking Indians."

If there is such a town as Fort Harker "your own" has failed to discover it. If it has an existence, it is in the imagination of the author of the paragraphs above quoted.

As to the second paragraph it is true in part. Four men were reported killed on the 2nd inst. and a scouting party was sent out to investigate. The party returned on Friday, but with nary a dead Indian; neither had they seen a live one.

A reference to this Indian scare is to be found in the memoirs of Colonel Augustus Armes, whose exploits and escapades (in 1869, when under close arrest at Fort Hays, he was reprimanded for taking his meals in Hays City) have fascinated military historians for years. In his journal for 1867, he wrote:

CAMP NEAR BUNKER HILL, KAN., July 9, 1867
Just as I sat down to breakfast this morning General Smith sent orders for me to take thirty men and scout up the Smoky Hill river to Wilson creek to capture and punish a war party of Indians reported to be depredating in that vicinity. Wild Bill, my guide, reports fresh signs of Indians this evening.[19]

What may also have some bearing on this incident was later recalled by Charles H. Sternberg, a seventeen-year-old in 1867. With his twin brother Edward he came to live on a homestead about two and one-half miles from Fort Harker. He wrote:

In July, 1867, owing to the fear of an Indian outrage, General A. J. Smith gave us at the ranch a guard of ten colored soldiers under a colored

19 Leavenworth *Daily Conservative*, July 10, 1867. Col. George A. Armes, *Ups and Downs of an Army Officer*, 232.

sergeant, and all the settlers gathered in the stockade, a structure about twenty feet long and fourteen wide, built by settling a row of cottonwood logs in a trench and roofing them over with split logs, brush, and earth. During the height of the excitement, the women and children slept on one side of the building in a long bed on the floor, and the men on the other side.

The night of the third of July was so sultry that I concluded to sleep outside on the hay-covered shed. At the first streak of dawn I was awakened by the report of a Winchester, and springing up, heard the sergeant call to his men, who were scattered in rifle pits around the building, to fall in line.

As soon as he had them lined up, he ordered them to fire across the river in the direction of some cottonwoods, to which a band of Indians had retreated. The whites came forward with guns in their hands and offered to join the fight, but the sergeant commanded: "Let the citizens keep to the rear." This, indeed, they were very willing to do when the order was given, "Fire at will!" and the soldiers began sending leaden balls whizzing through the air in every conceivable arc, but never in a straight line, toward the enemy, who were supposed to be lying on the ground.

As soon as it was light my brother and I explored the river and found a place where seven braves, in their moccasined feet, had run across a wet sandbar in the direction of the cottonwoods, as the sergeant had said. Their pony trails could be easily seen in the high wet grass.

The party in the stockade were not reassured to hear the tramp of a large body of horsemen, especially as the soldiers had fired away all their ammunition; but the welcome clank of sabers and the jingle of spurs laid their fears to rest, and soon a couple of troops of cavalry, with an officer in command, rode up through the gloom.

After the sergeant had been severely reprimanded for wasting his ammunition, the scout Wild Bill was ordered to explore the country for Indian signs. But although the tracks could not have been plainer, his report was so reassuring that the whole command returned to the Fort.

Some hours later I spied this famous scout at the sutler's store, his chair tilted back against the stone wall, his two ivory-mounted revolvers hanging at his belt, the target of all eyes among the garrison loafers. As I came up this gallant called out "Well Sternberg, your boys were pretty well frightened this morning by some buffalo that came down to water."

"Buffalo!" I said; "that trail was made by our old cows two weeks ago."

Later the general in command told me that they had prepared for a big hop at the Fort on the night of the fourth, and that Bill did not report the Indian tracks because he did not want to be sent off on a long scout just then.[20]

[20] *Life of a Fossil Hunter*, 11–13.

The legends built around Wild Bill's scouting days would fill volumes. What truth there is in a majority of instances has been lost, and important dates and other information have been carelessly discarded in favor of the sensational. One of Hickok's most constant companions was Jack Harvey. Although not a great deal of information is available on this man, something of his exploits can be gleaned from the press of the time.

Jack Harvey was born in 1836 in New York state, where his parents were still living in 1868. He came west at an early age, and in 1862 was already earning a name for courage among the guerrillas and scouts on the Kansas frontier. As "Captain" Jack Harvey he was one of Tough's Buckskin Scouts, and was reported to have been present in the battles of Newtonia, Cane Hill, Honey Springs, Van Buren, and the capture of Fort Smith. He was badly wounded at Cane Hill, and was captured by the rebels in 1864, but was released through their ignorance. During Hancock's Indian War he further distinguished himself as a scout.[21] It is not certain just when he and Wild Bill first met.

A recently discovered clipping in the possession of Ethel Hickok, from an undated but contemporary newspaper, gives this amusing anecdote about the two scouts:

> The celebrated scout, Wild Bill, and his pardner Jack Harvey are both here [Fort Harker?]. The other day an amusing characteristic little scene occurred between these two, somewhat as follows:—Wild Bill had a brand new gold watch worth $200 which he was sporting about and showing to Jack. The latter took it by the end of the chain, held it at arms length, and bet a trifling sum that he could put a pistol ball through the ring without hurting the watch. Bill thought he would bet him a ten he couldn't. Jack fired and shattered the timepiece into a thousand fragments. With impurturable coolness Bill put the chain into his pocket, together with Jack's note and said simply, "Remember Jack Harvey, I own you for one month and if you don't do just what I tell you, I'll shoot you, by G——." Jack showed his white teeth, twinkled his blue eyes and said, "all right Bill." The next day as Jack was walking over the parade ground Bill saw him, called him to stop, told him to hold his hat over his head, and then drawing his pistol put a ball between his hat and Jack's head ploughing a long furrow through the latter's hair, just above his forehead. The latter never winced but put his hat on and walked away as though nothing had happened.

So runs the story.

Wild Bill and Jack Harvey were frequent visitors to Colonel

21 Leavenworth *Daily Conservative*, Mar. 17, 1868.

Jennison's gambling rooms on Delaware Street, Leavenworth. The erstwhile colonel of the Seventh Kansas still had around him many of his former friends of the war, numbering many of the old Red Legs and Buckskin Scouts. Among the many who frequented the establishment was Theodore Bartles, the man who gave Connelley so much information on Hickok's war experiences. Bartles claimed in later years that he and Hickok used to shoot at targets when the latter visited his home, the Six-Mile House, on the Leavenworth road. Bartles claimed that he always beat Wild Bill at targets, but readily admitted that as a fast shot at a living, shooting target, Hickok had no equal during his time. It has yet to be established how much of what Bartles told Connelley was fact and how much was fiction.

On July 31, 1867, Wild Bill's current engagement with the cavalry came to an end, and the government acknowledged a debt to him of three months' back pay ($300).[22] He then moved on to Ellsworth which was to hold its first election. It was reported in the press that "on the 10th of August, next, they hold a special election in Ellsworth county, for the county and town officers. Kingsbury wants to be sheriff . . . and Wild Bill wants to be marshal of Ellsworth City."[23] But it was Chauncey B. Whitney who was elected township constable, and Captain E. W. Kingsbury was elected county sheriff.[24]

Wild Bill was one of the five contenders for the post of sheriff in the November elections for Ellsworth County, and although he polled the largest number of votes within the city of Ellsworth, (155) he received little support in the rest of the county, and Kingsbury was re-elected.[25]

On the day of the election one old-timer recalled that Wild Bill, dressed in a buckskin suit, raced a train from Fort Harker to Ellsworth in a feat of horsemanship that aroused the admiration of all. He beat the train to town simply because he could keep a fairly straight course, whereas the train had gradients and curves to contend with. Later during the preliminaries that led to the voting, Hickok accused M. R. Lane, another candidate for sheriff, of mak-

[22] Records of the Quartermaster General, *loc. cit.* It is noteworthy that the top pay for most scouts was only $75, but Hickok never received less than $100 for a full month's work.

[23] Junction City *Union*, July 27, 1867.

[24] Nyle H. Miller and Joseph W. Snell, *Why the West Was Wild*, 630.

[25] *Ibid.*, 630. This same Kingsbury is alleged to have told Buel about the McCanles battle. Buel also credits him with a prominent position in government service some years later, but this could not be verified (Victor Gondos, Jr., to the author, Sept. 14, 1960).

ing a remark that would prejudice Wild Bill's chances of success. Lane denied the accusation, and the crowd fully expected the two men to shoot it out as neither would back down. Fortunately, friends of both men stepped in and prevented what would have been a gory battle.[26]

On October 21, some days before the election, the editor of the Manhattan *Independent* took a train ride to Leavenworth and in his issue of October 26, 1867, reported on his fellow passengers:

WILD BILL

the celebrated scout, with Jack Harvey and some dozen of their companions were upon the train, having just come in from a scouting expedition under Gen. Sherman. All the party were more or less affected by frequent potations from their bottles, and Wild Bill himself was tipsy enough to be quite belligerent.

He is naturally a fine looking fellow, not much over 30 years of age, over 6 feet in height, muscular and athletic, possessing a fine figure, as lithe and agile as the Borneo Boys. His complexion is very clear, cheek bones high, and his fine auburn hair, which he parts in the middle hangs in ringlets down upon his shoulders, giving him a girlish look in spite of his great stature. He wore a richly embroydered sash with a pair of ivory hilted and silver-mounted pistols stuck in it. Doubtless this man and his companions have killed more men than any other persons who took part in the late war. What a pity that young men so brave and daring should lack the discretion to sheath their daggers forever when the war terminated! But such is the demoralizing effect of war upon those who engage in it and certainly upon all who love the vocation.

We learn from a gentleman who has frequently met these wild and reckless young men, that they live in a constant state of excitement, one continual round of gambling, drinking and swearing, interspersed at brief intervals with pistol practice upon each other.

At a word any of the gang draws his pistol and blazes away as freely as if all mankind were Arkansas Rebels, and had a bounty offered for their scalps.

How long these Athletes will be able to stand such a mode of life; eating, drinking, sleeping (if they can be said to sleep) and playing cards with their pistols at half cock, remains to be seen. For ourself, we are willing to risk them in an Indian campaign for which their cruelty and utter recklessness of life particularly fit them.

A strange item appeared in the St. Louis *Weekly Missouri Democrat* on November 6, 1867: a report from Springfield, Illinois, mentioned a robbery of a bank in a local county. The man charged was named Henry O'Connor. It was stated that this man was the

26 Cyrus Edwards to J. B. Edwards, Apr. 8, 1926, Manuscripts Division, KSHS.

Wild Bill of *Harper's* fame. But the article brought an immediate denial, and on November 11 the following letter was published:

CONCERNING WILD BILL.

ELLSWORTH, KAS., November 9, 1867.

Editors Missouri Democrat:

I notice a communication in your edition of date the 6th instant, from Springfield, Ill., wherein it is stated "it may be interesting to the curious to know that O'Connor was a somewhat distinguished Union scout during the rebellion, and is no other than the Wild Bill of *Harper's Monthly*."

Please remove this stain from the character of Wild Bill by a contradiction of this most unjust and false report.

"Wild Bill" is respected by his fellow citizens as a true friend and perfect gentleman. He was in this town at the time stated by your correspondent, and further may it be said to his credit, was the radical candidate for sheriff of Ellsworth county, and received the full support of the party—was only destined to suffer the fate of his ticket which was defeated by only a very small majority, but to bloom and blossom again at an early day.

Please give the foregoing a place in your columns, and oblige the friends of Wild Bill.

Yours very truly, JAS. B. COMSTOCK.[27]

In Hays City the local press also sprang to Wild Bill's defense, stating that "He is Deputy U.S. Marshal. . . . We set the Democrat right in justice to Mr. Haycock, the original Wild Bill." It was later reported that Wild Bill was in Hays and that "U.S. Marshal Whiting, Wild Bill, Jack Harvey, Surcey and others called in at our quarters Tuesday. They were all welcome. William is still around, probably engaged in preparing his LIFE for DeWitt."[28]

This mention of DeWitt no doubt referred to the publication in July, 1867, of the first dime novel story of Wild Bill's adventures. Titled "Wild Bill, the Indian-Slayer," its front cover shows Wild Bill battling for his life with the McCanles gang—the magazine had used the same cut which had appeared in *Harper's* five months before. This issue was followed by one in December entitled "Wild Bill's First Trail."[29]

[27] No trace of a J. B. Comstock has been found, and it is apparent it was not Hickok's scouting friend William A. "Buffalo Bill" Comstock.

[28] *Railway Advance*, Nov. 9, 1867; Leavenworth *Daily Conservative*, Dec. 14, 1867.

[29] Paul Preston, "Wild Bill, the Indian-Slayer," *De Witt's Ten Cent Romances*, No. 3. One source gives the date of publication as September 27, 1867, but a copy held by the Library of Congress has "July 17 67" written in ink on the front. "Wild Bill's First Trail," edited by Col. Cris. Forrest, No. 10 in the series, is dated December 27, 1867. I am indebted to Frederick R. Goff, chief of the Rare Book Division,

Early in January, 1868, Wild Bill was still in Hays, where he met Frank A. Root, editor of the Atchison *Daily Free Press*, who wrote of his meeting: "In Hays I formed the acquaintance of Wm. Haycock, better known as 'Wild Bill.' . . . He is in the employ of the Government as a detective and is probably better acquainted with the plains than any other man living, of his age."[30]

On March 13, 1868, one of Wild Bill's best friends died in tragic circumstances, the victim of tuberculosis. Whether Hickok was with him at the time is not known, but he could have been, and probably was. On March 17 the Leavenworth *Daily Conservative* carried the following obituary:

DEATH OF JACK HARVEY

Captain Jack Harvey died at Ellsworth on Friday last, of consumption, with which he had been afflicted for several months. [The paper then gives the details of his career as previously related]. . . .

No man in the army did his duty more faithfully and willingly than Captain Jack Harvey, and few as effectively. Brave, cool in the hour of danger, and one of the best shots on the western border, Jack was always ready for a bold ride or a fight with the enemy. He was as generous and true-hearted as he was brave, and no man hereabouts had more friends.

Another report added: "For several years past, he was the companion and partner of Wild Bill. His parents are living at present in Dunkirk, New York."[31]

Following the delivery of the United States marshal's prisoners previously related, it is reported that Wild Bill caused a disturbance in Lawrence, which was publicized in Leavenworth:

It seems that on Thursday, says the Daily Lawrence Republican, "Wild Bill went into tantrums," (which we presume to be the Lawrence expression of indicating that the ancient Henry has been elevated) "and with an axe, chopped down the door of Mary Ann Winfrey's cabin, and threw the axe at the afore said Mary." This survival of the battle axe practice which was quite popular in the days of the Crusaders, must have been interesting to the spectators, and agreeable to the irate William, if indeed, not pleasant to Mary Ann, but in view of the warlike repute of the performer, we congratulate that outraged female upon her escape from the further manifestations of gentle Bill.[32]

for additional information on these publications which would otherwise have been unobtainable.

[30] January 6, 1868. Root later coauthored *The Overland Stage to California* with William E. Connelley in 1901.

[31] Burlingame (Kan.) *Chronicle*, Mar. 28, 1868.

[32] Leavenworth *Daily Commercial*, Apr. 5, 1868.

It is doubtful that this "Wild Bill" was Hickok, for the Lawrence *Daily Tribune* of March 18, 1868, makes reference to a Negro thief named Bill Smith, "*alias* Wild Bill," who was making a nuisance of himself at the time. The same newspaper on September 28 remarked, following a report that Smith had been arrested in Leavenworth on a charge of horse-stealing, but released for want of evidence, that "the black Wild Bill" was wanted in Lawrence. "It would be a satisfaction to some people here to know whether he is *our* Wild Bill or not. If he is, it is a pity that he was not kept a little longer. The bona fide 'black Wild Bill' is badly 'wanted' here."

Hickok arrived in Leavenworth on April 29,[33] yet four days later the same paper reported the arrest of a "Wild Bill" in Omaha on April 29. He was "taken to the Police Court and fined. He remarked that it was the only town in the west where he couldn't do as he had a mind to without being interferred with by the 'd——d policemen.' Guess he forgot Leavenworth."[34]

At this date it would be difficult to establish the truth in such stories, but at least it is established that there was much confusion and misreporting on Hickok's movements in the contemporary press. "Numerous friends" of Hickok's, "the fiery, untamed William —familiarly styled by the vulgar—'Wild Bill,' will be pleased to learn that this distinguished personage is now sojourning in this city," announced the Leavenworth *Daily Commercial* on July 18. But by August, Wild Bill Hickok had moved on to Hays.

In Hays he was on hand when a party of about two hundred tourists arrived from Topeka early in the month. The Topeka press remarked: "The first man we saw was 'Wild Bill.' He was ready, waiting to give welcome to the excursionists. Gentle William said he had brought two hundred of the nastiest, meanest, Cheyennes to Hays that we might get a sight of the red men who did most of the murdering and scalping during the troubles of the past two years."[35]

John H. Putnam, one of the tourists, in a letter dated August 22, 1868, recalled meeting Hickok when they arrived:

Here we met some acquaintances—among them "Wild Bill" the great scout, a romantic but not o'er true history of whom you may find in *Harper's Monthly* about a year ago. He said there were some hundreds of Cheyenne Warriors camped a few miles out.

33 *Ibid.*, Apr. 30, 1868.
34 *Ibid.*, May 3, 1868.
35 Topeka *Weekly Leader*, Aug. 13, 1868.

Later in the evening some of the tour's ladies were invited to accept beds "*at a nice house in town*. And against our advice, *gently offered*, concluded to accept." In the search for this haven (the home of M. E. Joyce, justice of the peace), between the Eldorado Club rooms and Pat Murphy's Saloon (opposite the Prairie Flower Dance House), they were advised to "Find it with the help of 'Wild Bill.' "[36]

With tourists and other attractions to interest him, Wild Bill lingered around Hays and Fort Hays most of the summer of 1868. In August the Indians were once again on the warpath, attacking settlers and running off stock. This time the military leaders were determined to settle the issue once and for all, although as it turned out, it was many years before they finally did so. All available scouts and guides were engaged. On August 18, Hickok was signed on as a guide at Fort Hays to act for Captain G. W. Graham of the Tenth Cavalry during an expedition to the Republican River. At the conclusion of the trek, on August 31, he was discharged, and was paid $43.43 for the thirteen days' service.[37]

The following day, September 1, Hickok was again hired as a guide for the Tenth Cavalry at $100 a month. He was signed on at the "Headquarters Detachment Tenth Cavalry near Skimmerhorn's Ranche," which was somewhere near Elkhorn Creek, Lincoln County, Kansas. The record shows that he was listed at camps in the field and near Fort Dodge in September, and at Fort Lyon from October to December. During this trek, Hickok again served with George A. Armes, who was at that time a captain with Company F, Tenth Cavalry. Armes's journal contains this interesting entry:

> Camp above Headwaters
> of Walnut Creek, September 2, 1868
> We started out at seven o'clock this morning with Wild Bill as our scout, and while resting a few moments and allowing the horses to graze he came rushing in with fifteen of his scouts to inform me that a fresh Indian trail had been discovered.[38]

Wild Bill's brother Lorenzo is listed as an assistant wagon master at a depot at Fort Union for the months of January, February, and

[36] John H. Putnam, "A Trip to the End of the Union Pacific, in 1868," KSHS *Quarterly*, Vol. XIII, No. 3 (Aug., 1944), 199–200.

[37] Records of the Quartermaster General, Reports of Persons Hired (Aug.–Dec., 1868, and Jan.–Feb., 1869), *loc. cit.*

[38] *Ibid.* Armes, *Ups and Downs of an Army Officer*, 273.

May, 1868, but there is no indication that the brothers met during this campaign.

General Phil Sheridan, in command of the Division of the Missouri, dispatched the Seventh Cavalry to Fort Larned in August and went there himself to hold council with the Indians. The lodges of the Arapahoes, Cheyennes, Comanches, and Kiowas were within a few miles of the fort, and for a time cordial relations were established between the army and the Indians, with frequent councils taking place in each other's camps. Sheridan had been quick to avail himself of the opportunity to become acquainted with his future enemies. One of Sheridan's aides at this time was Arthur MacArthur, father of the famous World War II general Douglas MacArthur. He told his son a story which has all the elements of fiction, but is worth repeating because the younger MacArthur used it to reprimand boastful young officers who never liked to admit losses.

At one of the meetings between Sheridan and the Indians, Wild Bill was the interpreter. To impress them, the General ordered Hickok to tell the Indians about the iron horse that could haul all the buffalo meat they could eat in a month, and was twice as fast as a horse could run. They were not impressed. Sheridan then ordered him to tell them about the steamboat that could move across the water without sails or paddles and could carry the whole Sioux nation up and down all the rivers. They were still unimpressed. "They don't believe you general," reported Hickok. Exasperated, Sheridan demanded that he tell them about the telegraph, and that with the aid of a little black box he could talk to the great White Father in Washington. This time Hickok remained silent. "Well?" Sheridan was impatient, "go ahead, Bill, tell them about the telegraph." Hickok shook his head, "General, now I don't believe you!"[39]

A classic Hickok legend asserts that he was involved in a battle with a number of Cheyennes who had attacked the settlement of Gomerville on September 10, 1868. With some thirty-five armed men he had set off on a hunt for the hostiles, but they were themselves attacked by the Indians who pinned them down on the Big Sandy, some ten miles from the Sand Creek battlefield. In a desperate bid to obtain assistance, "a daring man called 'Wild Bill' [was selected, and they] put him on their fleetest horse and started him for the [Bijou] Basin for relief. He ran the gauntlet through

[39] Maj. Gen. Courtney Whitney, *MacArthur—His Rendezvous with History,* 96–97.

the enemy's line, receiving only a slight wound in the foot, and reached the Basin at 8 o'clock."[40] An armed force of men was quickly mounted and set out to rescue the beseiged men, arriving about three o'clock the next morning.

For years this story has remained unquestioned, and even this present writer repeated it, but with reservations, without uncovering any further information. The mystery was solved by the Englishman, R. B. Townshend, who was introduced to the hero of the ride in Colorado. Townshend, upon hearing that the man's name was "Wild Bill," assumed it was Hickok, but was told:

No it ain't Bill Hickok; he's another Wild Bill they've got over there in Kansas, and a mighty fine man too, so they say; but he don't live here in Colorado. This Wild Bill of ours lives down here on the Arkansaw mostly, or on the Fountain or thereabouts; he works on a ranch usually, or at any job he can get. He's called Wild Bill for several things he's done, including killing various men at various times. But I've always understood as most of 'em was men that wanted killing.[41]

Sheridan's winter campaign against the Indians was in full preparation by the end of September. General E. A. Carr,[42] in command of the Fifth Cavalry, left Fort Wallace early in October. He had with him as chief of scouts Buffalo Bill Cody. The Fifth and Tenth Cavalry regiments were involved with Tall Bull's Cheyennes and Whistler's band of Oglala Sioux in three battles on October 11, 18, and 26.[43] Meantime, Custer had gone to Fort Dodge to join his regiment, the Seventh, following his year's suspension. At the conclusion of Hancock's campaign in July, 1867, he had charged Custer with absenting himself without leave. Custer had gone to be with his wife during a cholera outbreak at Fort Harker. He was court-martialed and deprived of his rank and pay for one year, but at Sheridan's request he was recalled to active duty before the year was up. Now he was back in harness and anxious for action.

[40] Central City *Daily Register* (Sept. 8, 1868). The actual incident took place several days before the legendary version. Writing in the *Rocky Mountain News*, Sept. 14, 1868, from Enterprise Mill on September 10, Will A. Johnson stated that the rider's name was actually William Carrolton, "known as Texas Bill."

[41] *A Tenderfoot in Colorado*, 73.

[42] Carr's lineal rank at this time was major, but he was using his brevet rank of major general. Penrose was a captain, but he too was using his brevet rank of brigadier general—as was Brevet Lieutenant Colonel A. W. Evans: he was a major!

[43] A telegram to Fort Hays on December 27 stated that Sharp Grover, the scout, had met with Black Crow, Cheyenne Chief, Black Bull, or Cut Arm, Oglala, and Whistler, with 110 lodges of Sioux and Cheyenne Indians on the Arikaree Creek (Fort Hays Correspondence, Telegrams Received, 1868–68, Microfilm copy, Manuscripts Division, KSHS).

On November 13, General Carr and seven troops of the Fifth Cavalry left by road for Fort Lyon. They were on their way to join forces with General W. H. Penrose of the Third Infantry, who was in command of four companies of the Tenth Cavalry and one of the Seventh. Penrose's column had left on a march to the Canadian River. Wild Bill was his guide, but not his chief of scouts. This honor went to Charles B. Autubees, who had been transferred from Fort Lyon for the purpose—apparently he was a regular scout for the regiment. His eldest son, Mariano, was also listed as a scout.[44]

Sheridan's plan was simple. The tribes would not expect an attack during the winter, so he relied on the element of surprise. Custer and Sheridan would converge on the Cheyennes under Black Kettle on the Washita, and a second command, under Brevet Lieutenant Colonel A. W. Evans, would come up from Fort Bascom. The third column, under Carr, would move in from Fort Lyon. The troops would then mount an all-out offensive on the tribes camped as far as the headwaters of the Red River.

But things did not go according to plan—at least for Penrose and Carr. Custer attacked Black Kettle on November 27, killed an estimated 103 Indians including women and children, and captured the pony herd. Fifty-three women and children were captured. Hickok and Penrose, in the vanguard of Carr's command, were snowed up on Palo Duro Creek, where they remained until an advance guard sent ahead by Carr found them about the middle of December. Buffalo Bill led the advance guard, and one of the first people he saw as they came into Penrose's camp was Wild Bill. Cold and hungry though he was, Hickok was busily massaging his hands in a desperate bid to keep them supple and keep the circulation going. Come what might, he was determined that his hands should not suffer.

On December 30, Carr established a supply camp on the creek, and soon the half-starved men of Penrose's command were able to feel alive again. During the time they had been stranded awaiting rescue, most of their mules had died of fatigue and starvation. Carr sent his wagons back for more supplies. He then picked five hundred of his fittest men and horses to be sent south into the Texas Panhandle toward the Canadian River to join Colonel Evans' Third Cavalry from Fort Bascom. Evans had established a supply camp, which was named Fort Evans in his honor, some twelve miles from the South Fork of the Canadian River. Carr's column made camp on the Fork, and were soon joined by a number of scouts from the

[44] Records of the Quartermaster General (1868–69), loc. cit.

Evans camp. Wild Bill and Cody had been detailed to join Carr, and both were interested to learn from the new arrivals that a Mexican bull train carrying beer all the way from Fort Union was expected at Fort Evans. Wild Bill and Cody decided that they would hijack the beer. This seems to have suited the Mexican wagon master, because he sold the beer to the scouts twelve miles short of its destination. Just how much they paid for it is not certain, but a profit was made in their favor, as can be gathered from Cody's own recollections: "It was sold to our boys in pint cups, and as the weather was very cold we warmed the beer by putting the ends of our picket-pins heated red-hot into the cups. The result was one of the biggest beer jollifications I ever had the misfortune to attend."[45]

But it was not all "jollifications" for the boys that winter. Anxious for outside news, Carr dispatched Cody and Hickok, and such other scouts as were willing to risk it, to Camp Supply and other points with messages for General Sheridan. Both Hickok and Cody are credited with carrying news to Sheridan at this time, and it could well be that both did so by riding at different times. Meanwhile Carr organized a trip with a scouting party along the Canadian without any results, and returned to Palo Duro Creek.

On one occasion when Carr needed someone to ride to Camp Supply for provisions, he could get no volunteers. He lined up all the military scouts but none volunteered:

Finally Wild Bill, for whom Carr had no special regard, arose from his blankets, where he lay watching the proceedings, and said: "Well, General, it seems that you haven't got any men in your crowd. I guess I'll have to make the trip." The offer was gratefully accepted, and Wild Bill, accompanied by an English teamster, started on the perilous journey. As Bill was well acquainted with the country, by taking a course along the base of a range of hills, he avoided a great many difficulties that would have opposed him had he taken the regular trail. Just as he arrived within sight of the fort, the Englishman fell from his horse. He was taken to camp, more dead than alive, and although he survived, one of his arms had to be amputated. Bill, after resting a short time, during which he was rubbed with whiskey, both inside and out, as he termed it, started on the return trip, passed the provision sleds and reached the . . . [camp] just ten days from the time of his departure.[46]

A number of Penrose's scouts were Mexicans, and added to an

---

[45] *The Life of the Honorable William Frederick Cody, Known as Buffalo Bill*, 226.

[46] Hiram Robbins, "Wild Bill's Humors," undated clipping from the *Arkansaw Traveler*, supplied by Don Russell.

already existent rivalry was the belief by them that Hickok had not made the ride at all. The story is a little confused, but apparently Cody got involved in a fight with them and hearing the noise, and its cause, Wild Bill "seized his pistols, ran to the scene and killed three Mexicans, remarking when he returned . . . that Bill Cody would get hurt if he didn't stop fooling around."[47] No one else has suggested that Hickok killed anyone in that fight, but the story persists that there was a fracas between the Americans and Mexicans.

Carr is reported to have been furious. He suggested that Hickok and Cody use up their excess energy in a hunt for meat, and the scouts readily agreed. The camp badly needed meat anyway, and thus Carr disposed of two problems in one move.

Hiram Robbins tells of an amusing interview between Hickok and Carr. He says that an orderly was sent to Hickok with an order expressing appreciation of his services, but that he must leave camp within six hours:

"All right," remarked Bill. "Tell the General I'll see him pretty soon." Shortly afterwards he went to Carr's quarters, a kind of tent, and handing him the order, said:
"You writ that, did you."
"Yes," said Carr, turning from a table where he had been writing.
"Well, General, it looks pretty hard to send me out in this weather. After making that long trip for you, risking my life in the cold, I don't feel that I can stand another such pull. If I leave this camp I'll die, and if I stay you'll have me bayonetted out. So I have come to the conclusion to take you along," and drawing two pistols he leveled them at Carr and explained:
"Take back that order."
"The order is rescinded," said the general.
"That's right, General," replied Bill. "I knew that there were good spots about you."[48]

On one of his trips to Camp Supply, Wild Bill had heard the news of the Battle of the Washita, and the part played in it by his old friend California Joe. Custer had appointed Joe chief of scouts just before the battle, but within hours he heard that Joe was drunk and promptly demoted him. Yet Custer and Joe remained the best of friends, frequently exchanging letters after they finally separated. Joe's spelling was a constant source of amusement to Custer.[49]

[47] Ibid.
[48] Ibid.
[49] Hickok's association with California Joe is not easily defined. It is possible that they first met at Fort Riley in the autumn of 1866 or the early part of 1867. Born

Although Wild Bill had been nowhere near the Battle of the Washita, his original biographer, Buel, alleged that he had been, and his account was reprinted in Buffalo Bill's Wild West program for years. According to Buel, Wild Bill and Cody fought their way through about fifty Indians, until Hickok got close enough to kill Black Kettle with his knife. Then, in the struggle to get away, Wild Bill was wounded, and Cody saved his life. Buffalo Bill's press agents must have thought this a good story, and for that no one can blame them.

The Fifth Cavalry returned to Fort Lyon on February 19, 1869, but it is not certain that Wild Bill was still with them. Possibly he rejoined the Tenth, and in turn was detailed to carry dispatches between Fort Lyon and Wallace. It is fairly well established that toward the end of February, while making the return trip to Fort Lyon, Hickok got into a fight with some Cheyennes. In a running battle he was wounded in the thigh, high up, by a warrior who got close enough to deliver a lance thrust. He eluded the Indians finally, and set course for Lyon. He was found the next morning about a mile from the fort by an early-morning wood detail. His horse had strayed, or been killed, and he was dragging himself along, hindered by his wounded leg. He still had the lance, which he used to walk with. Half-frozen and suffering from loss of blood, he was rushed to the fort. Buffalo Bill heard the commotion and at once hunted up the surgeon. Wild Bill later gave Cody the lance, which he still had as late as 1914.[50]

With his leg still paining him, Hickok could do little work. At the end of the month he allowed his enlistment as a scout to expire. As of February 28, 1869, another chapter in his life was closed. Never again would he take up scouting.[51]

Debating what to do, Wild Bill received a letter from his sister Lydia. It had been addressed to him at Fort Leavenworth, but had been forwarded through army channels. He opened it to read

Moses Embree Milner, on May 8, 1829, he went west in 1864, during which year he is believed to have gained the name "California Joe" in Montana. He was no relation to Berdan's sharpshooter of that name. From 1867 until 1871, Joe served as a scout for the United States Army. At Fort Hays and Hays City during 1869 he and Wild Bill were a familiar sight together. He was perhaps Hickok's best friend after Jack Harvey died—yet they only met about half a dozen times in ten years. A great rifle shot, Joe was killed at Fort Robinson, Nebraska, on October 29, 1876. A man named Newcomb shot him in the back with a Winchester rifle as he stood talking to friends. Newcomb was never brought to justice, so far as is known. California Joe was buried in the post cemetery.

[50] Connelley, *Wild Bill and His Era*, 220.
[51] Records of the Quartermaster General (1868–69), *loc. cit.*

that his mother was seriously ill and wanted to see him. It was many years since he had last seen his family, and that was far too long. Thus it was that the most noted man-killer then alive made his way back to the one person in the world to whom all men are always little boys, and Polly Butler Hickok was glad to see him.

-✦ 7 ✦-

A Visit Home and Back to the Plains

WILD BILL'S JOURNEY to his mother's home took him through Mendota, Illinois, and his brief appearance was recorded in the local press: "Last week Wild Bill was stopping at the Passenger House and was visited by many of our citizens. He was the center of attraction."[1] Later that month or early in April he arrived in Troy Grove to find his mother standing at her door with tears streaming down her face. She flung her arms around his neck, embraced him, and led him inside. The gangling youth who had left home so long ago was now a man fully grown, and approaching his thirty-second year—a man whose name was second to none on the frontier. Of all her sons, her youngest was the man of destiny. What fame the others achieved was nothing compared to his. Before her stood the cause of a hundred conflicting stories: a reincarnation of D'Artagnan, a hero to his fingertips, or, some said, a killer every bit as bad as Slade. But the important thing was that her son James was home again. For how long she did not know, and in her heart she did not care. He was here and she was happy; that was all that mattered.

His brother Horace was there to greet him with his wife Martha —the Martha Edwards of his youth whom James had told to wait for him. His sisters Celinda and Lydia, both married now and living in the village, were there too. Oliver was still in California where he had settled, while Lorenzo was out west in his capacity as a wagon master and superintendent of transportation. He came home a year or so later. "He had spent ten years in Government service," wrote Howard. "Ten long years of weary trail with supply wagons. Strenuous work with little glory and less appreciation. He went back to Illinois and engaged in farming with Dad. I remember the old McClellan saddle, and the cavalry saber and scabbard he brought back from the West. They laid around and were finally thrown away. How I would treasure them now."[2] Lorenzo

[1] Mendota *Bulletin*, Mar. 18, 1869.
[2] "The Hickok Legend," *loc. cit.*, 30.

129

never married and spent the remainder of his life as a respected member of the local community. He died in 1913.

When James came home in 1869, "he brought with him many presents for his mother and the family," recalled Horace A. Hickok. "I believe somewhere in the family—probably in California—there is still one of the dresses he brought for my grandmother."[3] Mr. Hickok also said: "There was never anything said, but it was felt that James should have given her money or something more practical, for although my dad [Horace] and my mother took care of her, they felt he should have contributed something for her welfare. But I guess his presence at home was all *she* cared about."

Years later Wild Bill's sister Lydia recalled that he had visited home several times, but does not give dates:

The longest time he ever remained was three weeks, and that was when he was wounded up in Minnesota by an Indian spear. It struck him in the hip, the point bending when it struck the bone so that he had to stop and get off his horse to pull it out. He paid little attention to the wound and rode to Fort Leavenworth, where there was a letter from me to him telling him that mother was not well and asking him to come home. He came but said nothing of his wound for several days, although he had Dr. Thomas,[4] of Mendota, Ill., to dress it and care for it. We learned of it only when he asked for some lint to put a fresh bandage on it. Later, it became necessary to lance the wound and scrape the bone....

The doctor came one evening to perform the operation, but Bill would not take chloroform. The doctor made four cuts outward from the wound, making a perfect cross with the lance. Then he drew the flesh back and began to scrape the bone. I was holding the lamp and felt myself getting faint. "Here, give it to me," said Bill. He took the lamp and held it while the doctor scraped away, never flinching once during the operation.[5]

Homer, Wild Bill soon learned, was very dull. For a time he tolerated the enthusiastic approaches of his family and their neighbors. Lydia recalled that her young son Marshall, then only five years old, was a favorite of her brother's: "Bill thought Marshall was a pretty nice little boy and used to let him shoot his big re-

---

[3] Interview with Horace A. Hickok, Troy Grove, Ill., Oct., 1965.

[4] Dr. Edward Thomas is buried in the Northville Cemetery along with his family. Northville is about twenty miles from Troy Grove. It is doubted that he actually practiced in Mendota. The inscription on the tombstone of the twice-married doctor reads: "Dr. Edward Thomas, b. Feb. 14, 1822, d. Feb. 28, 1895" (W. M. Thomas, Ottawa, Ill., to the author, Dec. 12, 1959).

[5] Chicago *Daily Record*, Dec. 26, 1896.

volvers, and Marshall thought it was fine sport."[6] Among the neighbors who came around to see Wild Bill was the now-grown-up youngster Wylie, whom Hickok had saved from drowning many years before. Howard noted the event:

Wylie drove to Homer to renew his acquaintence with his boyhood hero. During an afternoon of reminiscences he asked Uncle whether he would do some shooting for them. He agreed to do so if someone would furnish six dimes. He placed the dimes on the top rail of a fence. He aligned them three inches apart with the edges of the dimes toward the shooter. He stepped back ten paces, pulled his revolver and fired. He did not fan the hammer, but the reports came so rapidly that they seemed as one. And every dime was a direct hit. The same afternoon he did some shooting from horseback, using both guns, shooting marks on posts on either side of the road using both right and left hands. Wylie called it wizardry. His testimony confirmed other tales I had heard during my boyhood from less reliable sources. No one could question Wylie's word for he was a man of unimpeachable character and honesty.[7]

If the shooting from horseback is strictly accurate, it is not surprising that Wild Bill's leg pained him, and he probably regretted his eagerness to impress the locals.

Paul McDonald (of Noola, Illinois, when Howard knew him) was a boy in Homer when Wild Bill visited his mother, and told Howard that the boys of the village used to watch for Hickok to come uptown to visit the post office or store and would follow him around, "eager and anxious to hear him talk of the West. He witnessed the exhibition of shooting, told about by Mr. Wylie and was greatly impressed by what he witnessed."[8]

It is alleged that during those few weeks spent at his mother's home Hickok received the following letter:

WASHINGTON, D.C.,
May 17th, 1869.

James B. Hickok, Esq.,
DEAR SIR:

A party consisting of several gentlemen, ladies and myself, desire to spend a few weeks in the far West during the warm season, and I hope it will be our fortune to secure your excellent services as our guide. I have heard much concerning your wonderful exploits in the West, and of such a character, too, as commend you highly for efficiency in the scouting service of the government. If it be possible for you to accompany

[6] *Ibid.* Lydia's reference to her brother as "Bill" was probably the work of the writer for the newspaper. To the family he was always James or "Uncle James."

[7] "The Hickok Legend," *loc. cit.*, 10, 26.

[8] *Ibid.*, 26.

our party as guide some time during the following month, please write me at once at Willard's Hotel, Washington, indicating what compensation you will expect, and also from what point in Kansas we had best start on the tour. I shall leave to you the selection of a pleasant route, as your general acquaintance with the places of interest between the Missouri river and the Rocky Mountains better qualifies you for deciding the trip that promises the most attractions.

Hoping to hear from you at your earliest convenience,

I am, yours truly,

HENRY WILSON.[9]

It is said that Hickok fixed his fee at five hundred dollars and arranged to organize the tour starting from Hays City in June. Following a successful trip, he was presented with a pair of engraved Colt's revolvers in appreciation of his services. While a revolver bearing the engraving "J. B. HICKOCK 1869" on the backstrap exists,[10] there is no evidence that the trip ever took place. The date on the letter indicates that even if it had been forwarded to Wild Bill at Homer, it would not have reached him. He was at Fort Wallace in his official capacity as a deputy United States marshal. What then is the answer? Did Buel make up the story, and if so, why? Or is it possible that such a letter did exist but was *not* from Wilson but from some lesser-known individual? Remember, Wilson was dead when Buel's book was published and unable to refute it. Only the appearance of the original letter and Buel's notes could clarify the issue; as of now, this writer believes the whole story to be a hoax.

Sometime toward the end of April or early May, Hickok left Homer and returned to keep his appointment at Fort Wallace, and then he was back in Hays City. Like most of the residents, he was

---

[9] Buel, *Heroes of the Plains*, 107. Both Wilstach and Connelley copied this letter from Buel without any attempt at verification. Henry Wilson was an interesting person. Born on February 16, 1812, and christened Jeremiah, he was the son of Winthrop and Abigail Colbath (or Colbraith). When he was twenty-one he changed his name to Henry Wilson with parental consent. A largely self-educated man, his antislavery views brought him into prominence, and in 1855 he was elected United States senator from Massachusetts. He was re-elected three times. In 1872 he was elected Vice-President under Grant, and died after a stroke on November 22, 1875. No mention of Hickok has ever been found in his papers, personal or public.

[10] The weapon is a .36-caliber Colt Navy, model of 1851, engraved and fitted with ivory grips. A photograph of it was sent to the Colt Company in the 1950's for comment; the name of the present owner is not known. One writer suggests that the weapon was actually one of a pair presented to Hickok by the Union Pacific for cleaning up Hays City, but offers no evidence (J. L. Beardsley, "The West's Top Triggerman," *Guns*, Vol. II, Nos. 4–16 [Apr., 1956], 52).

probably surprised to read the following in the Leavenworth *Times and Conservative*, copied from the St. Joseph *Union*:

Wild Bill, of Harper notoriety, was shot three times in Colorado the other day. Wounds not mortal. If the enthusiastic admirers of this old plainsman could see him on one of his periodical drunks, they would have considerable romance knocked out of them.[11]

Two months later the mystery was resolved. The Topeka press reported:

"Wild Bill" got into a difficulty on election day at Colorado City, and while being taken to jail was fired upon from the brush and killed.

In another column there appeared a hurried denial:

"WILD BILL"

Among our afternoon dispatches summarized elsewhere, is one from Pueblo, Colorado, announcing the killing of "Wild Bill." "Those who have tears to shed" need *not* "prepare to shed them now," for it is evidently a bogus "Wild Bill" who has thus handed in his checks. We have the best reason for believing that the great original "still lives," and that at this present moment, in the character of a peace officer, he is keeping in tolerable subjection the turbulent spirits of Hays City. We know not what was the specific offence of the deceased, but we doubt not that the public will mourn his loss less keenly than if he had frankly said "Ladies and Gentlemen:—I am not *the* "Wild Bill" concerning whom so many fine magazine and newspaper articles have been written, but a humble imitation, striving for an honest living in this rude frontier country."[12]

The man killed in Colorado was evidently the hero of Gomerville who had been immortalized by Townshend. Apparently he was killed in Central City, and Townshend's version of "Wild Bill of Colorado's" death differs somewhat from the newspaper report:

I never saw him again, but I heard of his finish three years later when I was ranching on Black Squirrel Creek. This was the story as it reached me.

Bill was working for Mr. John Jones, a married man, and one day when Mr. Jones came home Mrs. Jones complained to him that Bill had insulted her. Mr. Jones was a resolute man; he went straight to where Bill was, said not a word, but pulled his gun, and got the drop. Bill, recognizing the magic of the drop, knew the uselessness of trying to reach for his gun, and instead tore open the front of his shirt with both hands showing his bare brest over his beating heart. "Shoot, shoot," he cried. It was an off chance. They do say that some men have found themselves

[11] July 17, 1869.
[12] Topeka *Daily Commonwealth*, Sept. 18, 1869.

unable to shoot thus into a naked breast; but Mr. Jones was not one of them; the next second his bullet was through Bill's heart.

The jury cleared Mr. John Jones. When there was a woman in the case a Colorado jury in those days would clear almost anybody.[13]

But the real Wild Bill was very much alive when a party of Eastern excursionists arrived in Hays in the middle of July:

EXCURSION TO SHERIDAN.

On Monday last, a party, consisting of Richard Bowne, Esq., a prominent member of the New York bar; Mrs. Bowne; Misses Eliza and Annie Bowne; Mr. T. C. Bowne; Mr. E. W. Parsons of New York City; Mr. Charles E. Alioth of Lausaune, Switzerland; and Mr. and Mrs. Boller of this place, started on a trip to Sheridan, the present terminus of the Kansas Pacific railway. . . .

At Hays City, the excursionists had the pleasure of meeting "Wild Bill," of Harper's Magazine notoriety, and were besides greatly impressed with the air of respectability which characterized all the inhabitants of that wealthy and flourishing metropolis.[14]

Unfortunately, the "air of respectability" surrounding the residents of Hays City was only on the surface; beneath it there lurked a wave of violence that threatened at any time to break over the whole town. And as happened at other times in his life, Wild Bill Hickok was on hand to help.

[13] A Tenderfoot in Colorado, 85–86.
[14] Junction City Weekly Union, July 31, 1869.

⟶⟨ 8 ⟩⟵

Peace Officer in Hays

HAYS, KANSAS, by the fall of 1869, was a rapidly growing city. It was the headquarters of the buffalo hunters, skinners, and others connected with the hide-hunting business, as well as the haunt of gamblers, pimps, and prostitutes, inevitable followers of the ever-expanding railroad. The town was born in September, 1867, and was about a mile from Fort Hays. In October of that year the Union Pacific Railway Company, Eastern Division, pushed its tracks into town, and for a short time Hays was the terminus.

In its earliest days it had a bad reputation, justified in part but promoted to some extent by outside newspapers who delighted in scare-head allegations against the town and its citizens. One tongue-in-cheek writer declared: "There is a row of saloons on the Kansas Pacific Railway called Hays City; having visited the place, we should call it the Sodom of the Plains."[1] Another reporter declared that "it was Wild Bill who said there was 'no Sunday west of Junction City, no law west of Hays City, and no God west of Carson City;' and his remark bids fair to go into history as thoroughly representative of an epoch."[2]

Among the many early settlers who arrived in 1867 and lived through the good and bad times was Mrs. Josephine Middlekauff. In later years she described what Hays looked like in its hectic days as a railroad boom town:

It had big freighting facilities, the government had an immense warehouse where the Farmers' Elevator now is. The government freighted all their supplies from this to Fort Larned, Fort Dodge, Camp Supply, Fort Sill and other small forts and had in its employ a thousand or more civilian employees as "Mule Whackers" and clerks in the different departments at Fort Hays, a mile south of Hays. It being the terminus of the railroad the round house, the turn table and all of the other buildings

[1] Junction City *Weekly Union*, July 8, 1871.
[2] Wichita *Weekly Beacon*, Oct. 28, 1874, citing an undated issue of the Boston *Journal*.

that go to make a railroad town were located just east of the Schwaller Lumber Yard.

The Othero and Sellars warehouse was where the P. V. Elevator later stood. They did a big freighting business and employed Mexicans exclusively. North and South Main streets were built solidly on either side of the track from Chestnut to about one half block west of Fort Street. In my mind's eye I can see Old North Main street in all its former glory; from east to west from Chestnut street were the Capless and Ryan Outfitting store, the "Leavenworth Restaurant," "Hound Saloon and Faro House, "Hound Kelly's Saloon," the office of M. E. Joyce, our first justice of the peace, a jewelry store, Mrs. Gowdy's little sod hut, Ed Godard's Saloon and Dance Hall, Tommy Drum's saloon, Kate Coffee's Saloon, Mose Water's Saloon, R. W. Evans' Grocery store and Post Office, Ol Cohen's Clothing store, Paddy Welshes' Saloon and gambling house, the Perry Hotel, M. J. R. Treat's Candy and Peanut Stand, Cy Godard's Saloon and dance hall and in the corner "Nigger Whites" barber shop—and all the saloons were not on North Main either. It was conceded that places where one could quench his thirst with liquor all the way from "whiskey straight" at twenty-five cents a drink to Madam Cliquid at five dollars the pint.

Fort street was likewise built from Normal Avenue north as far as the courthouse square; true most [of] the buildings were of flimsy construction and were taken down and put up again where ever the railroad made its next stop. Tents and dugouts were also numerous. And while all was "hustle and bustle and go" and thousands of feet had tramped the streets they were still paved with buffalo sod.[3]

Saloonkeeping was perhaps the most profitable business in the town. Next to this were gambling and prostitution. The permanent residents soon began to be seriously alarmed at the increasing violence. Added to the menace of the drunken buffalo hunters was the presence of the troops at Fort Hays; so the citizens' first consideration was for law and order.

Ellis County was organized on October 28, 1867, by Governor Samuel J. Crawford, and Hays City was declared the temporary county seat. Marcellus E. Joyce, an Irishman from Ennis, County Clare, was appointed notary public. He had been sent out as a reporter for the Leavenworth *Commercial* but remained in Hays where he later became a justice of the peace. A short, sandy-haired man with a large red handle-bar mustache, Joyce had a great sense of humor, and seems to have been a forerunner of the noted Judge Roy Bean, "The Law West of the Pecos." His office on Main Street

[3] Hays *Daily News*, Nov. 11, 1929. The name of the saloon-keeper Welsh also appears in various accounts as Welche and Walsh.

was quite a meeting place. There the innocent and the guilty were judged and fined according to how much they had in their pockets. Protests were met with the remark: "Appeal Hell! There is no appeal from Judge Joyce's Court!" So they paid. Local legend asserts that on one occasion Joyce signed himself "M. E. Joyce, Notorious Public."[4]

But law enforcement in the township of Hays was a slow starter. Matt Clarkson recalled that when he and his brother George arrived in Hays in July, 1867, "there were twenty-two saloons, three dance halls, one little grocery and one clothing store. We did not think anything of having one or two dead men on the streets nearly every morning. Some of them were soldiers from the Fort. There was no law except the law of the six shooter."[5]

On December 5, 1867, Thomas Gannon was elected first sheriff of Ellis County, and William L. Totten and Peter Carroll, constables of Big Creek Township.[6] Gannon, who made Hays his headquarters, took his job very seriously. The records of Fort Hays contain a number of letters from him requesting military assistance in chasing horse-thieves and outlaws. On one occasion a private in the Thirty-eighth Infantry was bound over for grand larceny by M. W. Soule, justice of the peace, and ordered to appear before the district court. "We have no place to keep him at present," wrote Gannon on January 7, 1868, "but will have a jail erected in a few days, so I would respectfully request that you keep him until then."[7]

Gannon's reign was short. By early April, 1868, he had disappeared, believed by many to have been murdered from ambush to prevent his giving evidence as a witness in a criminal case.[8]

Some weeks earlier, the citizens of Hays petitioned Probate Judge Pliney Moore to incorporate Hays, and the petition was granted on February 6, 1868. The new city trustees, headed by chairman M. W. Soule, hired W. T. Butler, Isaac Thayer, and Peter Lanihan as the new city's law enforcement officers. Rufus Edwards later joined

[4] Mrs. J. H. Middlekauff, Paul King, H. R. Pollock, and Nick Ruder, *Ellis County Courthouses and Officers*, (1867-1942) (n.p., n.d.). Typed copy headed "The Court House and Officers of Ellis County (1867-1942)" located in the Ellis County papers Part A, Manuscripts Division, KSHS, hereinafter cited as "The Court House and Officers of Ellis County."

[5] *Ibid.* Mr. Clarkson apparently gave several interviews, and his recollections are quoted in both the past and present tense. His date of "July, 1867" may be an error on the interviewer's part.

[6] "The Court House and Officers of Ellis County," *loc. cit.*

[7] Records of Fort Hays, Letters Received (1867-69), microfilm copy, Manuscripts Division, KSHS.

[8] "The Court House and Officers of Ellis County," *loc. cit.*

them, but by August two of the men had resigned for reasons not given.[9]

Tom Gannon's successor was J. V. Macintosh, who kept a drugstore on South Fort Street. He was appointed sheriff by the District Judge on April 14, 1868, and served until January, 1869, when Isaac Thayer is shown in the records as sheriff.[10]

The duties of sheriff at this time were adequately performed by the men appointed when it came to court duties and serving papers, but they were unable to keep the peace of the community at a reasonable level. What there was of the city police force seemed equally incapable of keeping the lid on Hays. In January, 1869, word reached the Governor that the town had been placed under martial law. Governor Harvey immediately requested an explanation and was advised by Lieutenant Colonel Anderson D. Nelson, commanding the post, that:

Fort Hays (about a mile from Hays City) has been the Depot of supplies for Gen'l Sheridan's forces in the field and consequently it sometimes happens that three or four hundred, Wagonmasters, teamsters, &c are congregated here at one time. While here numbers of these men have been in the habit of visiting Hays City, after night-fall and what with the use of whisky and their revolvers the town was rendered very uncomfortable for the better class of citizens.

It was upon the representation of such citizens that I sent a patrol a few nights since to stop the dangerous rowdyism then going on. Nearly fifty arrests were made and of that number there may have been five or six citizens, the balance were government employees. It can well be imagined that a few citizens might be arrested under such circumstances as much from accident as design, albeit if they were in rather bad company as I am told nearly all the arrests were made in a bawdy dance house.

I feel assured my Dear Sir, that you will justify me in any arrest I may deem it my duty to make in Hays City, for I shall interfere with such a stretch of authority on the part of the military, only for the protection of life and property, and at such times when I am satisfied that the better class of citizens are unable to protect them selves.

I presume also that you have been informed that three colored soldiers were very recently taken out of jail at Hays City at midnight and hung by the inhabitants of that town.

Martial law has never been declared in Hays City—should such a necessity arise I should certainly notify you immediately, believing that

9 *Ibid.*
10 *Ibid.*

the circumstances which would call forth such an order would also in your estimation justify the declaration.[11]

In May, 1869, there was another fight between citizens and colored troopers from Fort Hays, and by July the citizens were desperate. On July 7 the following petition, signed by a number of them, was dispatched to the Governor:

DEAR SIR,

We the undersigned citizens of Hays City most respectfully solicit you to affirm the wishes of the law abiding citizens of this place by appointing R. A. Eccles Sheriff of this county as we know him to be an honest and law abiding man and well qualified for the position and we greatly feel the need of an honest officer.

By complying with the above you will confer a favor on Ellis County and the undersigned . . .

Eccles was not appointed. In a recently discovered letter written by the Governor some three months later, he declared that no one had legal authority whatever to "act as Sheriff of Ellis county, nor under the circumstances through which the vacancy occurred can any sheriff be chosen until the regular election in November next." The Governor was evidently referring to Isaac Thayer, but he did not explain why the vacancy occurred, and an examination of available records has not revealed what happened to Thayer, or who had authorized his election in January, 1869.

A search of the revised statute books for 1868 has revealed a confusing situation. One article ruled that whenever a vacancy occurred for the office of sheriff of any county, the undersheriff assumed the duties until a new sheriff was elected and qualified. If there was no undersheriff, then the provisions of a statute relating to elections authorized the governor to appoint an officer until an election was held, "unless otherwise provided for by law." In its ambiguity, this ruling made no provision for special elections; therefore the Governor believed it meant a regular election. Thus he could not officially recognize any "elections" held outside the time prescribed by law, namely, "the Tuesday succeeding the first Monday in November, A.D. 1869."

Evidently some confusion arose between the Governor and the citizens. They based their petition on the law which allowed him to fill a vacancy by appointment, but they were unaware of the re-

[11] Records of Fort Hays, Letters Dispatched (1867–69), microfilm copy, Manuscripts Division, KSHS.

139

vised statute of 1868 which ruled: "unless otherwise provided for by law." The Governor took no action because he did not have the authority, and a perusal of the statutes failed to reveal who, apart from the governor, was empowered to call special elections. An eminent historian, who kindly reviewed the evidence, reached the logical conclusion that there were "two interpretations of the law, one by the county and one by the governor."[12]

Few copies of the Governor's correspondence for 1869 exist, so what reply, if any, he sent in answer to the petition is not known. But some urgent action was called for, and this was taken by the County Commissioners with the following result:

HAYS CITY ITEMS.

HAYS CITY, Aug. 31, 1869.
EDITOR *Times and Conservative*:
At the election held here a few days ago . . . J. B. Hickok, familiarly known as "Wild Bill" [was] elected Sheriff of the county.[13]

Writing in the Hays *Sentinel* on January 28, 1878, Martin Allen stated that the special election took place on August 23, when the "County Commissioners canvassed the vote" and together with Hickok as sheriff, "M. E. Joyce was elected Justice of the Peace over A. D. Gilkeson." However, a curious news item suggests that this election was earlier in the month. A special correspondent for the Leavenworth *Times and Conservative*, who visited Hays and was considerably impressed by its business potential, expressed concern at the lack of law enforcement. He wrote from Hays on August 18:

The greatest need of Sheridan is a magistrate. If Wild Bill arrests an offender [for judicial purposes, Sheridan was attached to Ellis county] there is a log jail to receive him, but no justice to try the case. Justices of the Peace have before been appointed, but they resign so fast that the Governor has become disgusted and gone off to New York.[14]

Hickok's election caused some comment among the barflies and

12 Records of Ellis County, Governor's Correspondence, Manuscripts Division, KSHS; Records of the United States Army, Continental Commands, 1821–1921, Department of the Missouri, Letters Received, Letter No. G143/1869, October 27, 1869, National Archives, Washington, D.C.; *The General Statutes of the State of Kansas*, revised by John M. Price, Samuel A. Riggs, and James McCahon, Commissioners Appointed by the Governor, Under an Act Approved February 18, 1867; Joseph W. Snell to the author, Apr. 28, 1972.
13 Leavenworth *Times and Conservative*, Sept. 2, 1869.
14 *Ibid.*, Aug. 22, 1869.

gambling men, for up to now Wild Bill's presence in the town had caused no speculation. As a deputy United States marshal and an Army scout, he had been a common sight at Fort Hays and in the city, and some even recalled that he had also been mixed up in the saloon business in late 1867. But men now looked at him with a new kind of respect, and Wild Bill was not slow to take advantage of it.

His buckskin suits were discarded in favor of a Prince Albert coat and all the trimmings, although during the day he was frequently seen meandering around the place in shirt sleeves. Even his passion for taking a bath, at first frowned upon by the wild men of Hays, soon started a tradition, and many of them made regular trips to the bathhouse.

Wild Bill's acknowledged supremacy in Hays was viewed with jealous disfavor by many of the "gambling elite." One in particular is said to have expressed a grudge against him. This was the notorious Jim Curry, the Irish-born former locomotive engineer, who became restauranteur, gambler, saloonkeeper, and gunfighter, and is alleged by some to have been a scout at Beecher's Island with Forsyth.[15] C. J. Bascom, who worked for the railroad, knew Wild Bill in the early days and claimed, in a manuscript prepared about 1915, that once when he visited Hays and went for a walk with Jim Curry:

> . . . we went into Tommy Drums saloon, Wild Bill and some others was playing cards, Bill was setting with his back towards the door, a thing he was not in the habit of doing, Jim walked up and put his six shooter against Bills head saying, "Now you Son of a Gun, I've got you[!]" Bill did not bat an eye, but said, "Jim you would not murder a man without giving him a show." "I will give you the same show you would give me, you long haired tough." Tommy Drum was more excited than either Bill or Jim and was jumping around cussing, "by the boot, by the boot, Jim let us settle this feud, how would a bottle of champagne do all round[?]" It seemed so ridiculous, that all hands burst out in a laugh[.] Tommy put up a Pint bottle for every one in the place, Jim and Bill shook hands and the war was over[.] it seemed the trouble arose over Ida May, and these men had been on the outlook for each other.

---

15 Mrs. Frank C. Montgomery, "Fort Wallace and Its Relation to the Frontier," KSHS *Collections*, Vol. XVII (1926–28), 234. She states that Curry arrived too late to join Forsyth. But Sigmund Schlesenger in a letter to E. A. Brininstool dated Aug. 4, 1917, reproduced in *The Beecher Island Annual*, Vol. V (Forty-Ninth Anniversary Edition, 1917), 45, states that Curry was there and that he was well acquainted with him.

I knew nothing of this or the chances are I would not have taken the walk with Curry.[16]

It was in Hays that Wild Bill faced for the first time the reality of his reputation. At first mildly amused by the awed glances he received from all manner of people when he entered a town, room, train, or store, he was now forced to take the whole thing with deadly seriousness. No more was he just a "living legend"—he was a target of flesh and blood, a man with a reputation at the call of all comers who thought they could take it.

The realization of his position came to him early. Once his appointment became known, he set out to enforce what law he could. People who watched him go about his duties did so with mixed feelings, but most were favorably impressed. The late Frank Motz, publisher of the Hays *Daily News*, wrote:

My father [Simon Motz], first mayor of the town, was one of a group of citizens who hired Wild Bill for marshal. . . . The old-timers with one or two exceptions, spoke favorably of Hickok. That was many years before both eulogizers and deflaters went to work on his reputation. One woman who helped care for me when I was a small boy, was his fast friend. She told me many stories of his courage and courteousness.[17]

"It was not his desire to bring on trouble or kill anyone," wrote Root and Connelley. "One of his favorite ways in bringing a fellow to terms was clubbing with his guns. When the occasion required, he could pound with ease an unruly cowboy or lawless thug until his face resembled a raw beefsteak."[18]

"To the people of Hays he was a valuable officer," wrote W. E. Webb, "making arrests when and where none other dare attempt it. His power lies in the wonderful quickness with which he draws a pistol and takes his aim." Webb predicted Wild Bill's violent end, and before he and his companions left Hays, one of them "took occasion, before parting with Wild William, to administer some excellent advice, urging him especially, if he wished to die in his bed, to abandon the pistol and seize upon the plow-share. His reputation as Union scout, guide for the Indian country, and Sheriff of frontier towns . . . was sufficient competency of fame to justify his

---

[16] Undated manuscripts prepared by C. J. Bascom, Manuscripts Division, KSHS. Extracts from this appeared in the Kansas City *Star*, June 13, 1915. Connelley's published book on Hickok has an edited version of the *Star* feature which is misleading. Bascom asserts that Curry and Ida May, a noted prostitute in the early cattle towns, ran his restaurant together.

[17] Frank Motz to the author, June 27, 1956.

[18] *The Overland Stage to California*, 145.

retirement upon it. In this opinion the public will certainly coincide."[19]

As in other places, Hickok attracted the attention of the youngsters, and had a regular audience as he went about his business. One of these was Miguel Otero, son of the partner in Otero and Sellar's "Groceries and Provisions" wholesale house in Hays. He recalled that Hickok spent a lot of time in the store speaking to his father, who was a member of the vigilante committee. On occasion Hickok used to take Miguel and his brother buffalo-hunting, and went out of his way to teach the boys many things about the animals and prairie lore. Buffalo Bill Cody sometimes joined them, and Miguel's impression of both men was quite different in many respects:

Wild Bill was by far the more likable man: he was always kind and considerate toward others. Indeed, it was a real joy to meet him, and when we were under his care on a buffalo hunt, his entire time and attention were centered on us. In a chase he would cut out a cow and maneuver the animal so that either my brother or I could get an easy shot and down the buffalo. After we had one apiece, he seemed perfectly satisfied, no doubt feeling that he had filled his contract. He would then take us with him into the herd, killing two or three with his pistol on the run, but invariably keeping his eye on us. Wild Bill was genuinely brave; I never met his equal for courage on the frontier. I believe, if necessary, he would have tackled a buzzsaw. The word fear was not in his vocabulary. Wild Bill cared nothing for show or glamour, neither did he care for money, except so far as it paid his bills and amused him at the gambling table.

Buffalo Bill, on the other hand, was rather selfish and wanted all the pomp and grandeur for himself. I would not call him a brave man; he was much too cautious. He was smart enough to arrange matters so he would always be in the clear. On these little hunts when we were together, he would leave us and dash off to the herd by himself, killing buffalo to the right and left of him and never once seeming to care whether we got a shot or not. He was always spectacular and in the first row on parade day. I never heard of his killing anybody, or getting into any personal difficulty. He was quite a success as a Pony Express rider. . . . As a scout and Indian fighter he had many superiors. Buffalo Bill was in no sense a bad man; he was a perfect gentleman and a good business man. He believed long hair and buckskin garments attracted attention and brought in the dollars. . . . Buffalo Bill was a fine horseman and a commanding figure in the saddle. His associates were mostly officers in the United States Army. He never mingled with the common

[19] *Buffalo Land*, 145–49.

herd and was neither a gambler nor a frequenter of the saloon or dance hall. He was a good buffalo hunter and made a great business success in that line.[20]

Around the town Wild Bill posted anti-firearm notices, which in general were obeyed. Occasionally someone preferred to step out of line and then there was trouble. He had hardly been in office more than a few days when he killed a man. Local legend says his name was Bill Mulvey. A press report dated Hays City, August 23, stated:

Last night Bill Hitchcock, better known as "Wild Bill," acting sheriff of the county, while attempting to preserve peace among a party of intoxicated roughs, or "wolves," shot a man named Bill Melvin through the neck and lungs. Melvin is still living, but the doctors say, with no hopes of recovery. He attempted to shoot several citizens, and was determined to quarrel with every one whom he met, using his revolver freely, but fortunately injuring no one.[21]

The same report also stated that two Negroes, both deserters from the Tenth Cavalry or Thirty-eighth Infantry, "were arrested by Conductor Jim Williams, and turned over to the military at Ft. Hays. They deserted from near Wichita last spring." A search of the Fort Hays records produced the following:

HEAD QRS FORT HAYS KAS
August 26th 1869

To the Asst Adt Genl
Department of the Mo
Fort Leavenworth, Kas

SIR,

I have the honor to report that J. B. Hickok delivered at this Post on the 21st a Mulatto and a negro whom he claims to be deserters from the 10th U.S. Cav. Troop "C". I have ascertained since the men have been confined at this Post, that they came from Sheridan, Ks. where they have been living for some time past, that they there acknowledged that they were deserters, and left precipitately, when Capt Circy[22] U.S. Marshall, attempted to arrest them the name of the Mulatto is given as Ed. Fry and of the Negro as George ——— [Allen] his last name being unknown.

They are reported to have deserted at some time during the last winter, in Indian Territory, Fry being Sergeant of the Guard at the time and have taken a number of horses with them. I have the honor, to request to

[20] *My Life on the Frontier*, I, 14, 32–33.

[21] Kansas City *Daily Journal of Commerce*, Aug. 25, 1869, citing the Leavenworth *Daily Commercial*.

[22] Circey or Surcey is something of a mystery man, for there is little information on him in the record.

be informed whether information of any such deserters has been received at Dept Head'qrs, also what disposition be made of these prisoners.

I am Sir Very Respectfully
Your Obdt. Servt.
(Signed) GEO GIBSON
Maj. 5ʰ Infantry
Brvt. Lt. Col. U.S.A.
Commanding[23]

In response to this letter the following was received at Fort Hays:

HEADQUARTERS DEPARTMENT OF THE MISSOURI
FORT LEAVENWORTH, KANSAS
September 1st, 1869

Bvt. Lt. Col. Geo. Gibson
Major 5th Infantry
Commanding Fort Hays, Kans.

SIR,
In reply to your letter of the 26th Ult. referring to the cases of Ed. Fry and George ——— [Allen] who were delivered at your post by J. B. Hickok, as deserters from "C" Troop, 10th Cavalry; I am directed by the Major General Commanding to say that you will send them to Fort Dodge under a suitable guard, from which point they will be forwarded to Camp Supply, I.T., with a view of their being sent from that Post to the company or companies to which they belong, at the first opportunity.

"C" Troop, 10th Cavalry is stationed at Fort Sill, I.T.

Copies of this letter have been sent to the commanding Officers at Fort Dodge, Camp Supply, and Fort Sill.

Very Respectfully,
Yr Obt Servant
W. G. MITCHELL,
Bvt. Col. U.S.A.
A A A General[24]

Colonel Gibson complied with the request, and the two men were sent under escort to Fort Dodge to be sent to their respective companies. He enclosed photographs of the men and requested that should the men be identified, "notification of the fact be sent me in order that legal reward may be paid to the civil authorities of Hays City by whom the prisoners were apprehended." The military were slow in responding, and Colonel Gibson wrote once more in October, as "the claimant of the reward has been to see me several times in relation to its non payment." It was not until Decem-

[23] Records of Fort Hays, Letters Dispatched (1867–69), *loc. cit.*
[24] Records of Fort Hays, Letters Received (1867–69), *loc. cit.*

ber 12 that the Post Adjutant at Fort Hays wrote to Wild Bill, stating: "Enclosed please find vouchers prepared for your signature for the apprehension and delivery of Butler Tillman who called himself Allen, Pvt. 'H' Troop 10th U.S. Cavalry. Please acknowledge receipt at your earliest convenience."[25] It is not known if Hickok got the reward money for the other deserter.

During all this time Hickok had been keeping a vigilant watch on the situation in Hays. Late in September he was forced once more into a fight. Samuel Strawhun was the next to go up against Wild Bill's pistols. It is alleged that Wild Bill first crossed swords with him in Ellsworth some time before when he went to the assistance of Ellsworth's sheriff, E. W. Kingsbury,[26] and his deputy Chauncey B. Whitney,[27] and helped them round up Strawhun and some of his cronies. All the toughs were drunk and armed. Strawhun and his companions were tied to fence posts to cool off. While no contemporary records reveal any truth in this, old-timers point out that it was because of this incident that Strawhun fought Hickok.[28]

Strawhun was well known in Hays as a ruffian. In July, 1869, he was mixed up in a scrape in the Hays Post Office. With a companion named Joe Weiss,[29] he attacked A. B. Webster,[30] the clerk, because

[25] Records of Fort Hays, Letters Dispatched (1867–69), *loc. cit.*

[26] Kingsbury disappeared from Ellsworth early in 1869, and Whitney carried on as acting sheriff until E. A. Kesler was appointed sheriff on March 1, 1869. Kingsbury was plaintiff in a unique court action in November, 1869, when he sued Shoemaker, Miller & Co., for negligence, alleging that in October, 1867, while a passenger on the defendants' construction train, "it was thrown from the track by running over a steer a little after sundown." After great deliberation the jury returned a verdict in his favor and he was awarded $16,041.66. The defendants gave notice for a new trial (Topeka *Daily Commonwealth*, Nov. 28, 1869).

[27] In 1873, Whitney was sheriff of Ellsworth County. On Friday, August 15, he was fatally wounded by Billy Thompson, Ben's hotheaded younger brother. Billy used his brother's English shotgun (made by George Gibbs of Bristol), and Whitney died on August 18. Ben then used the shotgun to hold off the townsfolk while his brother escaped. Years later Wyatt Earp's biographer claimed he arrested Ben, but this is not substantiated by the record. Billy was brought back to Ellsworth three years later and put on trial for murder, but was acquitted on September 14, 1877. The shotgun, with six inches sawed off the barrels, is now on view in the Beeson Museum in Dodge City. George Gibbs and Company are still in business in Bristol.

[28] Paul King, "Wild Bill—Peace Officer in Hays," *The Aerend*, Vol. V, No. 2 (Spring, 1934), 116.

[29] Joseph Weiss was twenty-six years old, of Leavenworth County, and is said to have served a brief term as a deputy United States marshal. On February 26, 1866, he was convicted of grand larceny and sentenced to one year and six months in the state penitentiary. He was "a carpenter by trade, 6 feet 3½" tall, dark complexion, black hair, blue eyes, born in Kansas, pardoned August 23, 1867." (Records of the Kansas State Penitentiary, Archives Division, KSHS.)

[30] In 1883, as mayor of Dodge City, Webster headed the movement that drove Luke Short out of town. But with the help of Wyatt Earp and friends, Luke was "reinstated." (Rosa, *The Gunfighter: Man or Myth?* 78.)

he had served notice on them to leave town by order of the vigilance committee. "They entered the Post Office at about 3 p.m., abused, slapped and finally drew a revolver upon Webster, who was too quick for them."[31] Weiss was shot through the bowels and died soon afterward. His death was recorded in the 1870 census. But Strawhun made his escape until things quieted down.

Wild Bill had his showdown with Strawhun on September 27. There are many conflicting stories, especially about where the shooting took place. John Hobbs stated that it was in Odenfeld's Saloon on Fort Street,[32] while another source stated that it was in "the house of John Bittles."[33] Hickok was called when Strawhun and his companions tried to clean the place out. Accompanied by his assistant, Peter Lanihan,[34] Hickok moved in to stop the row. "Strangham was on a spree, and tried to clean out a beer saloon," declared one report. "In quieting the disturbance Wild Bill shot him, which quieted the disturbance, so far as Strangham was concerned."[35] Sam made remarks against Wild Bill, and "in his efforts to preserve order, Samuel Stringham was shot through the head by him, and instantly killed. Justice Joyce held an inquest on the body today, six well-known citizens being selected for the jurymen. The evidence in one or two instances was very contradictory. The jury returned a verdict to the effect that Samuel Stringham came to his death from a pistol wound at the hands of J. B. Hickok, and that the shooting of said Stringham was justifiable."[36] The fight took place at 1:00 A.M., the coroner's court convened soon after 9:00 A.M., and Strawhun was buried in the afternoon.

An eyewitness report provides an interesting insight into the events which led up to the shooting:

PARTICULARS OF THE KILLING OF STRANHAN
AT HAYS CITY.

HAYS CITY, September 30, 1869.

Eds. Commercial:—Allow me, an eye witness, to relate to you the details of the shooting affair last Sunday night, during which a certain Sam Stranhan was killed.

It seems that there was on the part of this Stranhan and some of his

31 Junction City *Weekly Union*, July 31, 1869.
32 Hays City *Sentinel*, Aug. 16, 1876.
33 Lawrence *Daily Tribune*, Sept. 30, 1869. The actual scene of the fight was John Bitter and Company's Leavenworth Beer Saloon on South Fort Street.
34 Lanihan's (sometimes spelled Lanahan) position is not clear. Evidently he was still a police constable, but some sources suggest that he was a deputy or undersheriff to Hickok.
35 Junction City *Weekly Union*, Oct. 2, 1869.
36 Lawrence *Daily Tribune*, Sept. 30, 1869.

associates bad feeling against certain citizens of this town, and members of the Vigilance committee. To satisfy their hatred they mobbed together and went on Sunday night, about half-past 11 o'clock to the saloon of Mr. John Bitter, with the intent to break up the establishment. The crowd, numbering about fourteen to eighteen persons, called for beer in a frantic manner. The glasses had to be filled up continually. Meanwhile the men were passing in and out of the saloon, and as it afterwards appeared carried the glasses to an adjoining vacant lot. Mr. Bitter remarked that the number of glasses was diminishing, and saw that Stranhan carried out some of them. The noise was fearful, all the men crying at the top of their voices, beer! beer! and using the most obscene language. This went on for a short time, when they began throwing the beer at each other. During all the noise one could hear threats as: "I shall kill someone to-night just for luck," or "some one will have to go up to-night," etc.

Mr. Bitter finally called the policeman, Mr. Wm Hickock, known as "Wild Bill," asking him to go out and fetch the missing glasses back. Wild Bill shortly returned with both hands full of glasses, when Stranhan remarked that he would shoot anyone that should try to interfere with his fun. Wild Bill set the glasses on the counter, Stranhan took hold of one and took it up in a threatening manner. He had no time to execute his design for a shot fired by Mr. Hickock killed him. He dropped down dead. The inquest was held next morning at 9 o'clock. The verdict of the jury was that deceased was shot by Mr. Hickock, and that the homicide was justifiable, the same being in self-defense.

Too much credit cannot be given to Wild Bill for his endeavor to rid this town of such dangerous characters as this Stranhan was.[37]

In 1876 a friend of Wild Bill's claimed that when Hickok carried the glasses back into the saloon the conversation went as follows: "Boys," Hickok remarked, "you hadn't ought to treat a poor old man in this way." Strawhun said he would throw them out again. "Do," retorted Wild Bill, "and they will carry you out."[38]

[37] Leavenworth *Daily Commercial*, Oct. 3, 1869.
[38] John Malone quoted by the Wichita *Eagle*, Sept. 14, 1876. Strawhun was confirmed as the correct spelling of Sam's name by his great grand niece, and it is written this way on the citizens' petition to the Governor in July, 1869, asking him to appoint R. A. Eccles as sheriff. The family Bible records that Samuel O. Strawhun was born on October 10, 1845, and spent his early years in Southern Missouri, but may have accompanied his parents and sisters when the family moved to Illinois. Official records confirm that Strawhun was hired as a teamster on Nov. 1, 1868, and promoted on December 14 to courier riding between Forts Hays and Dodge, possibly remaining in Government service until 1869. According to the Ellis County Probate Court records, on Feb. 8, 1869, Judge John V. Macintosh ordered Sam to serve papers on the commanding officer of Fort Hays, requesting the latter to bring before the court a prisoner held in the guardhouse. However, on March 28 Strawhun was himself detained at the fort as a prisoner of Deputy United States Marshal John S. Park (or Parks), on a Federal warrant issued by U.S. Com-

The killings of Mulvey and Strawhun are the only known civilian lives Hickok took while in Hays. Although there are many stories of his killing bad men by the score, nothing in the official record backs them up. But there were many attempts on his life. Several times he narrowly escaped death when a bullet buzzed past him in the darkness to smack against a wall, and the distant sound of running feet was the only clue to the identity of his attacker. Wild Bill naturally became cautious. He avoided strong lights, dark alleys, and sidewalks. He paced down the street—right in the center. No one was allowed to get too close, especially behind him. Down North Main Street he would stalk, eyes darting right and left. When he reached a saloon which gave forth more than the usual sounds of revelry, he turned sharply from his path and pushed the doors back against the wall (batwing doors were not so common then). Advancing into the room, he would face the crowd, push his back against the bar, say his piece, and get out. As always when Wild Bill had anything to say, men listened. He rarely raised his voice, speaking in an even tone so that all could hear and understand. Few failed to heed him.

One incident during October, 1869, serves to indicate how much importance was placed in official papers, and suggests a lack of cooperation between the peace officers and the military. Wild Bill received quite a setback when he presented a warrant before the post commander of Fort Hays for the delivery of Bob Connors, who had murdered a drover near Pond City. His request was refused because the post commander, Colonel George Gibson, regarded his warrant as illegal.

Connors' trouble began on September 15, when he killed his employer, a man named Hammy. Apparently, Hammy awoke to find Connors with his hand under his pillow, and in the morning Hammy dismissed him. As Hammy paid him off, Connors pulled a pistol and shot him dead, at the same time saying; "I will show you how to accuse me of stealing!" Three days later as he mingled with the crowds of loafers and hide men in Hays, Connors tried to get aboard a train and was arrested by Deputy United States Marshal Jack Bridges,[39] who lodged him with the commanding officer of

missioner Milton W. Soule, but on what charge is at present unknown (Mrs. Jean Fisherkeller to the author, Jan. 7, 1974; Waldo E. Koop to the author, January 1, 1974; Rev. Blaine Burkey, *Wild Bill Hickok, The Law in Hays City*, 11).

[39] John L. "Jack" Bridges was a controversial character. Believed to have been "born at sea," he was the celebrated "Beauregard" of the Red Legs, whose leader, George E. Hoyt, later appointed him as his deputy among the "detectives" attached to the Military District of the Border, Department of the Border. However, Jack's

Fort Hays for safe-keeping, fearful that a lynch mob might try to take him. It was expected that he would be taken to Sheridan or Topeka for trial.

However, on September 20, Colonel Gibson wrote to Bridges, who was staying in Hays, and informed him that news had come in from a Leavenworth merchant that if Connors were taken to Sheridan he would be lynched:

Under the circumstances then I earnestly appeal to you as an officer of the law that you convey the prisoner to Topeka and confer with the Governor of Kansas in regard to what disposition shall be made of him.

I am aware of the natural jealousy that attaches to any interference on the part of the military and the civil authorities. Being powerless to act in the matter I can only earnestly appeal to you to pursue what I believe to be the proper course. Of course I can have no earthly interest in the matter not having known either of the parties. I have every reason to believe that by doing this the ends of justice would be best subserved and that the man will swing if he is guilty as alleged.[40]

Bridges did not appear willing or able to make the decision, so Gibson telegraphed the Governor for instructions, who replied on September 25: "I know nothing of the case deliver Connors only to the proper legal authorities. JAS. M. HARVEY."[41]

To add to Colonel Gibson's difficulties, on September 28 there was a mass escape from the Fort Hays guardhouse and Connors was with them, but he was recaptured within hours.[42] So when Hickok walked into Gibson's office on October 3 with a warrant for Connors, the interview resulted in the following letter:

FT. HAYS. KANS.
October 3rd—69

To His Excellency
    The Governor of Kansas
    Jas. M. Harvey
DEAR SIR:
If you will be pleased to recollect I telegraphed you on the 24th day of Sept last asking you whether I should deliver a certain Bob Connors to any one but the parties who had placed him in my Guard House for safe keeping.

---

reputation suffered a setback in 1871 following the killing of John Ledford (Elmer O. Parker, assistant chief, Old Military Branch, National Archives, Washington, D.C., to the author, Nov. 17, 1971; Miller and Snell, *Why The West Was Wild*, 43–45; Rosa, *The Gunfighter: Man or Myth?* 104–105).

[40] Records of Fort Hays, Letters Dispatched (1867–69), *loc. cit.*
[41] *Ibid.* Telegrams Received.
[42] Leavenworth *Times and Conservative*, Sept. 30, 1869.

Bob Connors is charged with being the murderer of a Drover near Pond City several weeks since, and was arrested by Deputy U S Marshal Bridges & Ass of Hays City. They claiming the use of my Guard House in order to protect him as they alledged from threatened violence at the hands of some of the citizens of Hays.

It having been represented to me that in all probability Connors would be lynched, were he taken back to Sheridan I deemed it to be my duty to urge upon his Captors (by letter, a copy of which I have carefully preserved on file) that justice demanded that they should take him to Topeka and confer with your excellency in regard to the proper disposition to be made of him under the circumstances.

Up to the present moment they have made no formal demand for him.

In reply to my telegram you directed that Connors should only be given up to the proper legal authorities.

This morning about 10 o'clock Mr. J. B. Hickok (commonly known as Wild Bill) presented himself at my office accompanied by an Asst whom he called Pete [Lanihan], and made a formal demand for Connors, handing me what he claimed to be a Warrant for the arrest of said Connors signed by John Whitteford claiming to be a Justice of the Peace for the County of Wallace, Kansas. The document in question did not bear upon its face any seal.

Inasmuch as the Warrant directed Mr. Hickok *as Sheriff* of Ellis County to make the arrest I demanded to see his Commission which was not produced, he acknowledging that he had never been Commissioned by you. Under the circumstances I deemed it to be my duty to decline turning him over. Further I had no evidence that there was any regularly constituted Justice of the Peace for Wallace County.

Acting then purely agreeable to your instructions I have the honor to request that should any State Official endeavour to interfere with me in regard to my non Compliance in this case that you will at once interpose your strong arms in my behalf.

> With Sincere respect
> Yr Excellency's Obedt Servant
> (Signed) GEO GIBSON
> *Maj 5" Inf*
> *Bvt Lieut Col U.S.A.*
> *Comdg Post*[43]

In his recently discovered reply, the Governor clarified Hickok's position and the legal situation in Ellis County:

> STATE OF KANSAS
> EXECUTIVE DEPARTMENT.
> TOPEKA, Oct. 5, 1869

[43] Governor's Correspondence, Archives Division, KSHS.

Col. George Gibson,
Comd'g Fort Hays,
Fort Hays, Kas.

COLONEL:

I have the honor to acknowledge the receipt of your favor of the 3rd inst. with reference to the case of one Bob Conners, now confined in your guard house on a charge of murder in Wallace County, Kas.

Your refusal to deliver Conners on the demand of Mr. J. B. Hickok meets with my full approval. That person has no legal authority whatever to act as Sheriff of Ellis county, nor under the circumstances through which the vacancy occurred can any Sheriff be chosen until the regular election in November next.

Mr. Whiteford is, I believe, a Justice of the Peace for Wallace county, and Justice's warrants are not attested by seal. However, I am at a loss to know why a warrant should have been addressed to Hickok, or what purpose is to be served by removing Conners from your custody now.

Wallace county is attached to Ellis for judicial purposes, and as Conners cannot be tried until the meeting of the District Court in the last named county, which will occur, I am informed, very soon, I see no object to be gained in moving in the matter at present.

The execution of accused parties without trial must be stopped, and while I have no positive assurance that such is the design in this instance, I can see no hardship, no hindrance of justice, in safely retaining Conners until he can have a legal trial at the next term of the court of the Eighth Judicial District for Ellis County.

Renewing my approval of your action in this matter, I beg to request that you will continue to retain Conners in your custody. I am obliged to leave the State to-morrow, to be absent some three weeks, and should any action be initiated hostile to your authority, I trust that its final determination may be withheld until my return.

I have the honor to be, Colonel,

Very Respectfully,
Your obedient Servant,
(Signed) JAMES M. HARVEY,
Governor.[44]

[44] John Whiteford (believed to be the correct spelling) was appointed first justice of the peace in Wallace County on August 25, 1868, by the then Governor of Kansas, S. J. Crawford, who had decided that Pond City should be the temporary county seat. A colorful character, Whiteford administered the law with an old Enfield rifle. On October 30, 1868, he killed Private Joseph Foster, of Company "M," Second United States Cavalry, at Pond City. He was handed over to Deputy United States Marshal George Ferguson of Sheridan, and as there were several witnesses in his behalf, Whiteford was acquitted on his plea of self-defense (Montgomery, "Fort Wallace and Its Relation to the Frontier," *loc. cit.*, 227; Records of Fort Wallace, Letters Dispatched (1868–69), Microfilm copy on file, Manuscripts Division, KSHS; Elmer O. Parker, assistant chief, Old Military Branch, Military Archives Division, National Archives, Washington, D.C., to the author, March 9,

The Governor's comments clearly indicate that while he did not recognize Hickok as sheriff of the county, so far as the local citizens and county commissioners were concerned, Wild Bill was the law. Perhaps Jack Bridges' dilemma could have been resolved earlier had he requested Hickok's assistance, in his capacity as a deputy United States marshal, to join him in escorting Connors to Sheridan, but he did not. Later, and prior to the receipt by Colonel Gibson of the Governor's letter, Bridges finally made his move; on the morn-of October 5, Connors was handed over to his assistant, Deputy United States Marshal C. J. Cox, who took him to Sheridan where he was examined and acquitted.

Another disturbance in Hays soon occupied Wild Bill's attention. The residents of the city heard five quick pistol shots about half-past eleven on the night of October 8, and an investigation revealed that:

A man, a mason boss at the Fort, was caught unscrewing the nuts from a wagon standing opposite the depot. The driver of the team, named Allmeyer, told him to stop, at which he pulled his revolver and fired two shots, one of which entered the right breast of Allmeyer. He then ran, Allmeyer firing three shots after him, but none of them taking effect. He was then taken into Tom Drum's saloon, and afterwards removed to the Commercial Hotel for medical treatment. The man who shot Allmeyer came into Drum's saloon after the wounded man had been removed, and asked for his hat, saying it had been shot off his head. He was recognized as the man who shot Allmeyer, and they attempted to capture him. He made a motion to draw a revolver, when one of the citizens shot him through the right breast. He then made his escape to the Fort, where he was captured this morning and brought to town. Both parties are now laying very low, at the Commercial Hotel, and it is doubtful whether either man will ever recover.[45]

In his version of the incident, in a letter to Colonel W. G. Mitchell, acting assistant adjutant general, Department of the Missouri, Major Gibson wrote, on October 27:

Several Saturdays Since, during the evening, a discharged Qr. Mr. Employe from Camp Supply, Shot a German Employed by Messrs Caplice and Ryan (Traders in Hayes) through the liver injuring an intestine. The would be murderer (named Cole) was placed in charge of a Vigilant Committee man in a drinking Saloon and it is alledged attempted to draw his pistol a Second time, when the party having him in charge

1972; Records of the United States Army, Continental Commands, 1821–1921, loc. cit.).
[45] Leavenworth *Times and Conservative*, Oct. 13, 1869.

fired at him, Shooting him through the lung. It being reported to me the next morning (Sunday) that some of the people in the town had gone So far as to put a rope around Coles neck for the purpose of dragging him out and hanging him (which I must say was prevented by Wild Bill)[.] I drove over unattended and demanded That he be Surendered to me which was done promptly. With a desire to Conciliate all parties, I brought him over and put him in my Hospital under Guard together with the man whom he had shot through the liver. Strange to say (through the admirable Skill of our Post Surgeon who I believe introduced a new Combination of remedies in their treatment, namely Carbolic Acid & Morphia) The German is This day walking about the Streets of Hayes nearly well, and has requested me to withdraw the guard over Cole (also rapidly recovering) it being his intention not to prosecute him. They having become reconciled to Each other in Hospital Through the intervention of a Catholic Priest. It will be perceived by the Major General Commanding That my policy has been to avoid making unnecessary display of military force in what I Conceived to be a proper discharge of my duty as a Conservator of the Peace.[46]

In the same letter Major Gibson mentioned the forthcoming election in Hays and the concern felt by some that there might be trouble. But the election, which took place on November 2, passed off quietly. Peter Lanihan, Democrat (as were most of the voters), defeated Wild Bill. The result was: J. B. Hickok, Independent, 89; Peter Lanihan, Democrat, 114.[47] But Hickok would remain in office until his term expired on December 31.

Early in November it was rumored that Hickok and Major Gibson had been killed, but this was quickly denied:

A HOAX.

The story of the shooting of Col. Gibson and Wild Bill is a hoax. It was started yesterday in the down train by a waggish Leavenworth boy, as a sensational report.[48]

Hickok's actual activities during this time were better reported: "'Wild Bill', whom they have attempted to kill, but who has the inexorable will to perambulate the earth still, and who is always ready for a 'mill,' save when he may chance to be ill, yesterday came up the Topeka Hill to get a stomach fill," remarked one paper.

---

[46] Records of Fort Hays, Letters Dispatched (1867–69), loc. cit.

[47] Leavenworth Times and Conservative, Nov. 5, 1869, a report dated Hays City, Nov. 3. Sheriff Lanihan was killed in a saloon brawl in Hays in July, 1871. The fight took place on the sixteenth and he died on the eighteenth. Lanihan had interfered to break it up (Topeka State Record, July 26, 1871; Oxford [Kan.] Times, July 27, 1871; Neodesha Citizen, July 28, 1871).

[48] Topeka Daily Commonwealth, Nov. 3, 1869.

And in another column: "Sheriff Hickok, of Ellis county—yclept, in many a well-known story of border-life, 'Wild Bill,' is in town, registered at the Topeka House. Long may he be at Hays,

> 'Shake his ambrosial locks and give the nod,
> the stamp of fate, the sanction of a god!' "

On December 9 the same newspaper remarked that "Hays City under the guardian care of 'Wild Bill' is quiet and doing well."[49]
December 9 was also the date on which Wild Bill, as sheriff of the county, was obliged to serve legal papers on J. V. Macintosh, the duly elected representative for Ellis County. Macintosh's defeated opponent accused him of irregularities of conduct. Through his deputy, Wild Bill certified the deliverance of the papers, as is shown by the following excerpt from the *House Journal* for 1870:

Served the within notice at Hays City, Kansas, on the 9th day of December, A.D., 1869, by delivering a certified copy of the same, at the usual place of residence of the within named J. V. Macintosh.

J. B. HICKOK,
Sheriff.
By PETER LANIHAN
Deputy Sheriff.[50]

News of the election in Ellis County received some strange publicity. From New York state the Kansas press learned, according to the Rochester *Chronicle*, that "Wild Bill has been elected sheriff of Ellis county, Texas," and promptly took the paper to task:

There are so many reasons why "Wild Bill" has not been elected sheriff of Ellis county, Texas, that we are at a loss which to give first. However, here are a few to be arranged to suit the reader: He didn't get votes enough. The people of Texas didn't like him for sheriff. He did not get the nomination. There is no such county in Texas. Wild Bill is Deputy Sheriff of Ellis county, Kansas. There are other reasons but it is not necessary to give them. We may state, however, that he is very busy just now in geography, to fit himself for the solitorship of an eastern paper.[51]

One final mention of Wild Bill in Hays is found in the Topeka press, and this shows him performing a seasonal good-will act: "Jas. B. Hickok, *alias* Wild Bill sent a whole buffalo to McMeekin

---

[49] *Ibid.,* Nov. 18 and Dec. 9, 1869.
[50] Governor's Correspondence, *loc. cit.*
[51] Leavenworth *Times and Conservative*, Dec. 10, 1869.

yesterday from Hays City. Mac serves up buffalo roasts and steak today with the usual etcetras."[52]

His official duties just about completed, Wild Bill prepared to look for new employment. At about this time he is believed to have submitted the following undated account of services rendered:

ELLIS COUNTY

   To J. B. Hickok Dr.

   To services as policeman 1 month and 19 days at $75.00 per month $22.50

   I certify that the above account is correct and remains due and unpaid.

(Signed) J. B. HICKOK.[53]

The departure of Wild Bill from Hays has been a much-disputed episode in his colorful career. The popular legends indicate that he left after a fight with several troopers of the Seventh Cavalry. Local tradition supports this story, and even Mrs. Custer hinted at it, but she could not or would not add any details. There was a fight with some soldiers, but it was not in the manner of the legend. When Hickok left Hays, about January, 1870, he did so without incident. It was only when he returned to Hays on a visit the following July that he fell out with the army.

On the evening of July 17, 1870, Wild Bill was in a saloon in Hays City. No one is certain which one it was, but opinion is about divided between Drum's or Paddy Welche's place. During the evening he got into a row with several troopers of the Seventh Cavalry. The following press reports give some idea of how the incident was magnified even at the time:

On Monday last "Wild Bill" killed a soldier and seriously wounded another, at Hays City. Five soldiers attacked Bill, and two got used up as mentioned above. The sentiment of the community is with "Bill," as it is claimed he but acted in self-defence.[54]

Another paper said there was only one soldier involved, and it was a "friendly scuffle" which "ended in a row. Bill shot and mortally wounded another soldier who had a hand in the muss and left for parts unknown."[55] But another thought otherwise and added a few more details:

---

[52] Topeka *Daily Commonwealth*, Dec. 21, 1869.

[53] This sheet of paper was presented to the KSHS in 1882. It is all written by the same hand, and doubt has been expressed that Hickok actually wrote it because it bears little resemblance to his normal handwriting.

[54] Topeka *Daily Commonwealth*, July 22, 1870.

[55] Clyde *Republican Valley Empire*, Aug. 2, 1870.

Two soldiers of the Seventh cavalry were shot at Hays City last Tuesday night by Wild Bill. The names of the men were Langan and Kelly. The greatest excitement prevails in the town owing to the outrage. After the shooting was over Wild Bill made for the prairie and has not been heard of since. The citizens were out *en masse* looking for Bill so that he might be summarily dealt with. The parties were all under the influence of liquor at the time.[56]

From details supplied by old-timers, even if fictionalized, it seems evident that Hickok was provoked—even he would not willingly go up against five armed men. But it will be seen from these accounts that no date for the incident is agreed upon. The three papers each give different dates—July 18, 19, and 20. A search of the records of the War Department revealed a muster roll of the Seventh Cavalry dated July and August, 1870, which reported that Private John Kile of Company I, Seventh United States Cavalry, died on July 18, 1870, at Fort Hays, Kansas, of a "pistol shot wound received July 17th 1870 at Hays City, Kansas in [a] drunken row and not in the line of duty." The "Register of Sick and Wounded at Fort Hays, Kansas, During the Month of July, 1870," was also checked and confirmed that Privates Jerry Lonergan[57] and John Kile[58] of Company M (both I and M were stationed at Fort Hays at the time), Seventh United States Cavalry, were admitted to the post hospital for treatment of gunshot wounds. Lonergan recovered and was returned to duty on August 25, 1870.[59]

It has been alleged that General Phil Sheridan issued a "dead or alive" order for Hickok. But this is unlikely, for such brawls were common in frontier towns between soldiers and civilians.

Recollections of old-timers are often suspect, and Captain John Ryan was no exception. But as he was a sergeant in the Seventh

---

[56] Junction City *Union*, July 23, 1870.

[57] Jerry Lonergan was born about 1841 in Cork, Ireland, and enlisted in Company M, Seventh United States Cavalry, on December 26, 1867, at New York, for five years. He was discharged on October 17, 1871, at Fort Leavenworth. It was almost a century before the real names of these two luckless individuals were properly publicized. In 1904, Alfred Henry Lewis, in his inimitable style, remarked that "in an evil hour a trio of soldiers . . . led by one Lanigan . . . took drunken umbrage at Mr. Hickok's hair." ("How Mr. Hickok Came to Cheyenne: An Epic of an Unsung Ulysses," *The Saturday Evening Post*, Vol. CLXXVI, No. 37 [Mar. 12, 1904], 6.)

[58] John Kile was born about 1846 at Troy, New York. He enlisted in Company C, Thirty-Seventh Infantry, in 1867, and was discharged in 1868. In May, 1870, at Chicago, he enlisted in the Seventh United States Cavalry, Company I, and was posted to Fort Hays.

[59] Elmer O. Parker, Army and Air Corps Branch, National Archives, to the author, Apr. 15, 1963. Joseph W. Snell, KSHS, to the author, July 31, 1963.

Cavalry at Fort Hays at the time of the fight with Lonergan and Kile, his comments are worthy of repetition. He stated in 1909 that Kile was known as Kelley or Kelly, and held the rank of corporal in Company M. He deserted but later re-enlisted in Company I. He was recognized and taken before General Custer who, having listened to Ryan's plea on his behalf, ordered him returned to duty with Company M from which he had deserted. This information conflicts with the official records cited elsewhere, but here follows Ryan's description of what happened in Hays that hot July day:

One beautiful moonlight night, after tattoo roll call, Kelly and a friend of his in the company named Lonergan, left camp to visit Hayes City, which was about two miles west from our camp. I think they left without permission. A certain barroom, kept by Thomas Drum, was frequented by the men of our camp, and the two men visited this saloon. Lonergan was a powerful man, and although he had been in the company only a short time he was considered one of the pugilists of M troop. When they arrived at the saloon Wild Bill, whom I have spoken of before, was standing at the bar having a sociable chat with the bar tender. Lonergan walked up behind Wild Bill without being discovered, and as quick as a flash he threw both arms around Wild Bill's neck, from the rear, and pulled him over backwards on to the floor, and held his arms out at full length. Lonergan and Wild Bill had had some words before that caused this action. In the meantime Wild Bill got his right hand free and slipped one of his pistols out of his holster. Some of the men in visiting this city were in the habit of carrying their pistols stuck down inside the waistband of their pants, with the hilt protruding, but covered up by their blouse, and a man could whip out one of those pistols in an instant. Kelly had his in this position, and he immediately whipped it out and put the muzzle into Wild Bill's ear, and snapped it. The pistol missed fire, or it would have ended his career then and there. Lonergan was holding Wild Bill's right wrist, but Bill turned his hand far enough to one side to enable him to fire his pistol, and the first shot went through the right wrist of Kelly. He fired a second time, and the bullet entered Kelly's side, went through his body, and could be felt on the other side. Of course Kelly was knocked out of service in a few seconds. Wild Bill did his best to kill Lonergan, who was holding him down, but Lonergan held his wrist in such a position that it was impossible for him to get a shot at his body. He finally fired again, and shot Lonergan through the knee cap. That caused Lonergan to release his hold on Wild Bill, who jumped up from the floor and made tracks for the back of the saloon, jumped through a window, taking the glass and sash with him, and made his escape. I was on the scene a few moments after Kelly breathed his last. A doctor was sent for. He asked me if Kelly was a friend of mine. I said that he was, and that both men were members of my company. He exam-

ined him thoroughly, and then removed a gold ring from Kelly's finger
and handed it to me. I kept the ring for a few years, but I never could
find any of Kelly's relations, though I tried diligently to do so. I was
informed later that his name was Kyle, and that he belonged either in
Chicago, Illinois, or Cincinatti, Ohio. Finally I gave the ring to a friend
of mine, John Murphy, who was a trumpeter in my company and was
wounded in the battle of the Wichita.

The news of this affair very quickly reached camp, and a number of the
men seized their guns and started for Hayes City, where I joined the
party, and we visited all the saloons and dives in the place, but we could
not find Wild Bill. If we had found him we will leave it to the reader to
imagine what would have happened to him. In the mean time Kelly's
body was taken to our camp and Lonergan was sent to the post hospital
at Fort Hayes.

I saw Wild Bill about a year later, about 30 miles from Fort Harker,
on the line of the Kansas Pacific railroad, either at the little town of
Aberdeen or Salina, Kansas, I have forgotten which, while going south
in May, 1871. Some of the officers and myself and a number of the men
had a talk with him. He told us that after leaving Drum's saloon he went
to the room that he occupied and took his Winchester rifle and 100
rounds of ammunition and preceeded to a cemetery a little west of that
town. There he laid until daylight the next morning, as he expected the
soldiers would round him up and end his career. He declared that he
never intended to be taken alive in that cemetery, and would make many
of those soldiers bite the dust before he would be taken. After daylight
he left there and started for Big Creek station, on the line of the Kansas
Pacific railroad, about eight miles east of this city, and boarded a train.
. . . Wild Bill told me once that he never ran up against a man that he was
afraid of in a square pistol duel, but that he did expect sometime some
desperado would come up and shoot him from the rear. . . .

Kelly was buried from our camp and I had charge of the funeral ceremonies. We marched with the body and it was interred in the Fort Hayes
cemetery. Lonergan recovered from his wounds and joined the company again, from which he deserted some time afterward, and I understood was killed a little later in Kansas by a man named Kelly belonging
to an infantry regiment.[60]

But Hickok's actual movements after the shooting are obscure.
One old-timer claimed:

He realized what he had done and thought he had better leave. His
horse was tied behind the saloon. He jumped on him and started north.
In thirty minutes a bunch of soldiers started in persuit. When Bill got to
North Fork he turned down the creek. The soldiers tho[ugh]t he had

[60] Newton (Mass.) *Circuit*, Aug. 20 and Sept. 3, 1909, copy supplied by John
S. Manion, Jr.

gone north to Stockton. Bill went on down to a wood choppers camp, where he had his wounds bound, and stayed in camp about a week.[61]

C. J. Bascom, after referring to the killing of two soldiers by Wild Bill, makes this interesting comment:

I was at North Fork, (Victoria now) this place was just a section house and water tank[.] . . . Wild Bill came there and wanted to know if there had been any strangers there that day[.] I told him "no"[,] he said he was looking for two horse thieves[.] I asked him if he had had any dinner, if not to come into the Section house and I would get him a lunch, he said, "no," he did not care to do that and requested I should bring him a hand out[.] I went in and brought him some Corn Beef and Cabbage, bread and butter and Coffee, after eating what he wanted, he gave me a dollar to give the Missie, and said he would go up the Creek a ways[.] Inside of an hour an ambulance from Fort Hays drove up with a Lieutenant and four Soldiers[,] this Snob I had seen his kind in the Civil war, got out and come bluntering up to me saying, "who are you[?]" I replied none of your damn Business[.] He wanted to know, did I live there, I replied, "no, I live at Ellsworth" and was an officer of the road. "Do you know Wild Bill?" "No I don't know Wild Bill." He got in his wagon and told his men, ["]that man knows more than he cares to tell["] and they drove down the Creek in the Direction of Old Fort Fletcher.[62]

Rumors that Hickok had been wounded in the fight were current at the time, and one newspaper remarked that he had "fled, and wounded, found his way to Abilene. Is he dead? Some say yes; but we cannot rely on people's *on dits*, for he has already died many times, and risen again as many."[63]

Just where Hickok went is not known; he could have gone to any number of places. His brief term as a peace officer in Hays, where he had established law and order, and had taught the citizens to respect it, had brought home to him that he had a reputation second to none, and whether he sought it or not, notoriety was his.

[61] A typed copy of an interview with Matt Clarkson by W. D. Philip, Manuscripts Division, KSHS.
[62] *Loc. cit.*
[63] Ottawa (Kan.) *Journal*, Sept. 29, 1870.

---≈{ 9 }≈---

A Wild West Show

AFTER LEAVING HAYS in January, 1870, Wild Bill next appeared in
Topeka, where he was the guest of his old friend Captain H. C.
Lindsay. Hickok is believed to have known Lindsay during the war,
and was probably associated with him during the Indian campaigns when Lindsay served in the Eighteenth Kansas Battalion.
Lindsay owned a livery stable and at one time was a deputy sheriff.
For several days the pair were seen together frequenting the fashionable saloons, or leaning on a corral rail discussing horseflesh. Life
for Wild Bill at this time was almost carefree.

But at Topeka during January there occurred a tragic incident
that probably did not escape Hickok's attention. Following his dismissal as United States marshal for Kansas, Charles C. Whiting
busied himself with local politics and was active as chairman of
the State Republican Committee. In November, 1869, Whiting
came down with an illness that was not discussed at any length in
the press, but during his last days he was "not once in his right
mind." He died soon after noon on January 2, and was buried on
January 4. The funeral was attended by a great many people, but
no mention was made of Wild Bill's being among the mourners.[1]

Early in February, Hickok was in trouble. Details are not clear,
but evidently he was involved in a fist fight on the corner of Sixth
and Kansas Avenue. A man walked up to him and started to insult
him. Wild Bill wasted no time and promptly knocked him down,
for which he was arrested and fined "five dollars for striking straight
out from the shoulder and consequently hitting a man."[2]

Anxious to avoid more trouble, Wild Bill accompanied Lindsay
when he took a drove of horses and mules to Kansas City. In recounting the incident to William E. Connelley, Lindsay mentioned
that Hickok pointed out various landmarks of the pre-Civil War
days. Passing through the ruined town of Old Franklin, east of

---

[1] Topeka *State Record*, Jan. 5, 1870; Topeka *Daily Commonwealth*, Jan. 4, 1870.
[2] Topeka *Daily Commonwealth*, Feb. 8, 1870.

Lawrence, Wild Bill remarked that he had seen a thousand Border Ruffians camped there in the summer of 1856.

Leaving Lindsay, Hickok visited Missouri:

"Wild Bill," *alias* Sheriff Wm. Hickock, has recently been "lionising" at Jefferson City. Here is what the St. Louis *Democrat* correspondent says about it: "Quite a sensation was created on the floor of the House by a visit from Wm. Hicock, Sheriff of Ellis county, Kansas, better known as 'Wild Bill of the Prairies," a cognomen secured by his hair-breadth escapes, his personal encounters, and his services as a scout in the Union army. He has had great experience among the Indians, and as a trapper and hunter, and meets many old friends among the members.[3]

" 'Wild Bill' is in the city again," it was reported[4] as Hickok once more appeared on the streets of Topeka in April, and during the next few weeks he was a familiar sight. Old residents recall that he gave several shooting exhibitions before leaving once more to reappear in a Wild West show.

Some authorities have gone so far as to state that the Wild West show, now firmly established in American folklore, was the brain child of Wild Bill Hickok. Several people, including Buffalo Bill and Doc Carver, had a hand in publicizing it on a world-wide basis, but perhaps the earliest attempt was made by Phineas T. Barnum.

In June, 1843, Barnum was fascinated to discover about fifteen starved and weary buffalo calves, all about one year old, which had been driven from the Far West by C. D. French, an expert rider and lasso artist who presumably intended to exhibit them. Barnum made a hasty decision, offered $700 for the lot, and promptly hired French to look after them. An elaborate publicity scheme, which hinted at a trip to Europe with the animals, soon provoked great interest. A show was held at Hoboken, New Jersey, on August 31 of that year, and although it attracted 24,000 people, it was a shambles. The buffaloes escaped from the arena and disappeared into a swamp, and few were recaptured. Their escape caused some panic in the crowd, and one man was reported killed when he fell from a tree into which he had climbed when the animals broke through the barriers and ran into the crowd. However, despite such setbacks, Barnum made a profit and attracted more visitors to his "American Museum."[5]

There is a much-repeated story that in the spring of 1870, Hickok, assisted by a number of drovers, or cowboys, roped six buffaloes,

[3] Topeka *State Record*, Mar. 22, 1870.
[4] Topeka *Daily Commonwealth*, Apr. 29, 1870.
[5] Irving Wallace, *The Fabulous Showman*, 96–98.

and with great difficulty, got them to Niagara Falls. There on July 20, before a Canadian audience, he put on the first "Buffalo Show."

Unfortunately, the facts do not support this story. As has been previously pointed out, Hickok was involved in a shooting scrape in Hays at the time of this alleged show. (It has also been claimed that during the summer of 1870 he was performing in Colonel Ginger's Circus at Sherman, Texas.[6]) Investigations conducted in Niagara Falls finally unearthed the truth. There was such a show and Wild Bill was in it; but he was not the organizer. In actual fact it took place not in 1870 but in 1872.

The promoter was Colonel Sidney Barnett, son of Thomas Barnett, a Niagara Falls museum owner and a man dedicated to publicizing the Falls to the world. Thomas Barnett instituted his museum in 1827, and he and his son roamed the world to find suitable exhibits and relics to impress the public and attract tourists. It is evident that great rivalry existed between the American and Canadian authorities, who vied with each other to make their side of the Falls more attractive to the innumerable visitors. There were stories of swindling and extortion among the tourists, and to counteract this the Barnetts kept their admission prices low, even admitting school children free.

In 1872, Colonel Barnett decided upon his greatest venture—a grand buffalo hunt. Elaborate preparations were made, and Barnett and others visited the United States to engage drovers (or cowboys) and Indians for the show. One agent got as far as Wichita: "One of the parties connected with the promised big buffalo hunt at Niagara Falls was in Wichita last week hiring Mexican greasers and buying Indian ponies and Texas cattle for the great sell."[7]

Early in June, Colonel Barnett reached Fort McPherson, where he made the acquaintance of John B. Omohundro, better known as "Texas Jack." A correspondent for an Omaha paper, writing from the fort on June 3, remarked:

A novel undertaking is on foot here, and is of gigantic proportions. Colonel Sidney Barnett, of Niagara Falls, is getting up a grand Buffalo hunt at Niagara Falls, from the 1st to the 4th of July. He is now here for the purpose of completing arrangements and superintending the starting of the enterprise, and shipping the buffaloes East.

He has secured the services of the celebrated scout and hunter, Mr. J. B. Omohundro, better known as "Texas Jack," the hero of the Loup

[6] J. Marvin Hunter, Sr., "Reminiscences of Colonel Lewis Ginger," *Frontier Times* (Original Series), Vol. XXX, No. 2 (April–June, 1953), 221.

[7] Wichita *Weekly Eagle*, Aug. 9, 1872.

Fork. "Texas Jack" is a partner of "Buffalo Bill," and nothing that skill and foresight can accomplish will be spared to make this hunt a perfect success.

Through the kindness of Major North, the commander of the Pawnee scouts, arrangements are being made for a party of Pawnee Indians—the deadly and bitter enemies of the Sioux—to go to Niagara with their fleet ponies and lodges, and full war and hunting equipment.

The buffaloes will pass through Omaha the latter part of this, or early part of next month.

We here think this is a grand affair, and believe there can be no question of success from the reputation of the parties engaged in it. The spectacle that will present itself to the scores of thousands who will be spectators at Niagara will be the most novel and thrilling ever seen east of the great plains, and will give our eastern friends an idea of what buffalo hunting is in Nebraska.[8]

W. D. Wildman, a correspondent for another newspaper, described how Texas Jack set about obtaining the buffaloes for the show:

I will relate an incident heretofore unheard of in Buffalo Hunting. A gentleman from Saratoga, N.Y., came to Fort Mcpherson and hired three of the Western scouts to capture eight full grown Buffalo, to astonish the town of Saratoga, on the 4th of July, at a grand celebration on that day, and I understand a party of Pawnee Indians were to be taken along to shew the uninitiated how Lo could do the Buffalo on a hunt. Three gentleman well known to Western men for daring were chosen as the leaders, viz., Dashing Charley, Texas Jack, and a man by the name of Barrett [Barnett?] (his initials I did not know, as my informant did not know them). They started from Red Willow early Sunday morning, 9th June, crossed the Republican, and proceeded to Beaver Creek, 15 miles away, and before noon the eight bulls were prisoners, and loaded on wagons. The mode of capture was as follows: One would throw a lasso over the animal's neck, and follow with a slack rope, until another could lasso the foot. Then they proceeded to down the "baste." Once down he was quickly tied, and ready for loading on the wagons, and so the fun went on with one variation. After Texas Jack had lassoed an uncomm[on] large ugly old bull, and before any one could secure his leg, he turned short, and charged, caught the horse, and pitched both into a gully. Here the grit and action of a true western hunter became apparent; his well trained horse waited for its rider, and my informant stated that the rope was not even dropped, but man and horse were together, again following the buffalo, until he was finally captured. To read of such things is all very well; but to do them is quite a different thing.

8 Omaha *Weekly Herald*, June 12, 1872.

For my part I believe rather than be one to capture one of those fellows, I had rather go through the Battle of Chickamauga again.[9]

This incident of Texas Jack and the buffaloes had curious repercussions. Doc Carver (of whom more will be said later) informed his biographer that as early as 1867 he had signed a contract to deliver "a hundred" live buffaloes to the railroad yards in Kansas City for shipment to Niagara Falls for a great exhibition and buffalo hunt to be held there the following year. It is further related that Hickok was persuaded to join the hunting party, which included John Nelson (the squaw man), Hank and Monty Clifford, a couple of half-bloods, and several Sioux Indians. What would happen when a buffalo was roped—would he choke or fight?—caused some speculation:

They learned the next day that a buffalo would do both. The first rope was thrown onto an old bull by Wild Bill, who used too large a loop. The rope slipped back on the buffalo's hump; this gave the animal all the advantage and with a surge he turned Bill's horse head over heels. The greatest pistol-man the West ever knew described an ungraceful arc in the air and landed head-first on the prairie. Getting to his feet, Bill spat grass and buffalo dung from his mouth and watched his horse, still fast to the buffalo, disappear toward the horizon. It did not help his feelings when one of the Oglala braves rode up and commiserated with him: "You ketchem, dam tonka heap gone," at the same time pointing in the direction where the buffalo and horse had disappeared. None of them got a buffalo that day, and all they had to show for their work were broken ropes, torn saddles and crippled horses.[10]

Evidently Carver heard the story about Texas Jack, but for reasons best known to himself, distorted the facts and changed the characters.

Even as Texas Jack and his companions were discovering the difficulties to be experienced in capturing buffaloes, other troubles cropped up. Omohundro wrote to Jacob M. Troth, the Pawnee Indian agent at Genoa, Nebraska, requesting permission to take the Indians to Niagara Falls. Troth then informed Barclay White, superintendent of Indian affairs at Omaha, that he would refuse permission, and on June 13 wrote to Texas Jack:

Your letter was rec[eived] and I have had an interview with the Superintendent on the subject and we unite in our view in reference to our

[9] Lincoln *Daily State Journal*, July 2, 1872.
[10] Raymond W. Thorp, *Spirit Gun of the West*, 46.

Indians going off [on] an expedition of the kind you propose. It is also prohibited by the Department.[11]

Back in Niagara Falls, Barnett was getting anxious. On June 20 he telegraphed the Commissioner of Indian Affairs in Washington:

I made arrangements with Major North of Columbus, Nebraska, for five Pawnee Indians to come here for a Buffalo Hunt Exhibition first July. Their tickets were bought and great expense incurred by advertisements &c. The Agent on Reserve now refuses to let them come will you direct that they be allowed come. Can refer you to any person here. Will be most serious loss to me & disappoint thousands if Indians not allowed to come.

SIDNEY BARNETT.[12]

The following day Barnett again telegraphed the Commissioner:

I have incurred expenditure of five thousand dollars. This disappointment will utterly ruin me. Can refer you as to my character to Col. Parker ex Comm. to Mr. Chilton ex Consult at Clifton or any person at Niagara will give any amount of security. Please reconsider.

SIDNEY BARNETT
Ans[wer] quick.[13]

F. A. Walker, the commissioner of Indian affairs, sent the following terse reply: "Matter cannot be reconsidered."[14]

Barnett was bitterly disappointed, but having invested so much money into the project, he was determined to put on some sort of show. He could no longer count on the support of Texas Jack, who had backed out once his Pawnees had been refused permission to go to Niagara Falls. On top of this new setback came the news that most of the buffaloes he had captured had died—as many of them did in captivity. What happened next was described by an obscure newspaper report published some years later:

This upset Colonel Barnett's arrangements for the buffalo hunt, and it was postponed. Colonel Barnett then went to the Indian territory, where he engaged some Sac and Fox indians and mexican cowboys, and secured a fresh lot of buffaloes for his show. It was in Kansas City that he met Bill Hickok, one of the most daring and dashing scouts in the

---

[11] Pawnee Agency Documents, Vol. II, 19–20 (microfilm copy, NSHS).

[12] Records of the Social and Economic Records Division, Group 75, M234, Roll 661, Washington, D.C.

[13] Ibid.

[14] Records of the Social and Economic Records Division, Group 75, M21, Roll 108, Washington, D.C.

west, and he engaged him to go east and manage the Niagara Falls buffalo hunt.[15]

The many delays had an adverse effect on the interest in the show:

The performance actually took place on August 28th and 30th, 1872, in an enclosure of possibly 80 acres or more in which the Hydro transformer building and the Falls View school now stand. The attendance fell far short of expectations. Many were delighted and considered the event highly satisfactory and entertaining.

The program consisted of lassoing wild Texas steers by cowboys and Indians. Wild Bill, Wm. Hickok, a famous Western scout, had charge of the ceremonies. Buffaloes were loosened and attacked by the Indians who charged on fleet mustangs, shooting with blunt arrows and finally capturing them by lassos. There were some war dances and the final event was an interesting, exciting and well-contested game of lacross between two Indian tribes for the championship. The band of the 44th regiment from St. Catharines provided the music. Stephen Peer of Lundy's Lane gave exhibitions of rope-walking on ropes stretched across the street.

There were spectators, however, who were disappointed, claiming the show was too tame and the animals were disposed to be docile and inactive and showed very little fight and spirit. Nevertheless, Mr. Barnett had spared no expense. The travelling expenses, engaging the Indians and cowboys, capturing and transporting the buffaloes and steers, constructing the high board fences and grandstands all cost an enormous sum of money with very little prospect of corresponding returns, the result of which was a heavy financial loss to the Barnetts, and was one of the contributory causes leading to their relinquishment of the museum business at the Falls.

The two postponements had a tendency to blight the prospects and dampen the confidence and enthusiasm of the public.[16]

How much outside publicity the show received is uncertain, but the following advertisement appeared in the Niagara Falls (New York) *Gazette* of August 28:

GRAND BUFFALO HUNT
AT NIAGARA FALLS
28 & 30 August, 1872

This novel and most exciting affair will positively take place on the days mentioned and will be under the management and direction of "Wild Bill" (Mr. William Hickok), the most celebrated Scout and Hunter

[15] Denver *Field and Farm*, June 1, 1895, copy supplied by Clifford P. Westermeier.
[16] J. C. Morden, *Historic Niagara*, 105–106.

167

of the Plains. No expense has been spared to make it the most interesting, the most exciting, and the most thrilling spectacle ever witnessed east of the Missouri River.

On the same date appeared the following news item:

The Grand Buffalo Hunt over the river opens today at 3 o'clock P.M. Sidney Barnett has spared neither pains nor expense to make the undertaking a perfect success, and a most novel and exciting time may confidently be expected. Seats have been prepared to accommodate 50,000 spectators. The hunt will be under the direction of the celebrated William Hickok, or "Wild Bill" as he is familiarly called. A number of the Sacs and Fox Tribes of Indians will appear in full war costume, mounted on fleet ponies brought from the plains. A Mexican Vaquero Troupe will also participate. Altogether there will be over fifty Indians and mounted men taking part in the chase. The second day of the hunt will be equally interesting and exciting. Excursion trains are being run on all the principal railroads, and it is expected that a large concourse of people will witness the hunt.

An account of the performance was given in the *Gazette* for September 4, 1872:

The great Buffalo Hunt over the river came off last week according to the programme. The managers of the enterprise used every endeavour to make the exhibition one of interest and amusement to the spectators, and to meet the expectations of all concerned. No doubt some were disappointed in not seeing a herd of wild buffaloes instead of 3. Some 3,000 people were present the first day and a large number on Friday. "Wild Bill" was on hand with several Indians and Mexicans accustomed to the western plains, and exhibited what they knew about lassooing wild cattle and buffaloes.

The large race course gave ample room for an exciting chase and the whole field was traversed. The skill of these men in riding and lassooing is remarkable. A large number of Cayuga and Tuscarora Indians played a game of "La Crosse" which was novel to a good many and quite exciting.

In fact, the whole show was such as every person would like to see.

The show proved a financial disaster to the Barnetts. The traveling expenses, cost of engaging the cowboys, Mexicans, Indians, and Wild Bill's fee (which is not known) far exceeded the gate receipts. Barnett understandably blamed the two delays, which caused the show to be held right at the end of the tourist season. The family never recovered from the loss, and five years later, in 1877, their museum changed hands. As one writer remarked:

The Buffalo hunt and rodeo may not have been a happy event in the lives of the Barnett family but it gave many a local lad his first glimpse of a real wild West show and a chance to see that hero of the old West, Wild Bill Hickock. Clifton and Drummondville had witnessed something that was to be the talk of the town for many days to come, the like of which is still yet to be seen by today's generation.[17]

Certainly, Hickok had played his part well. It was reported that he "wore a buckskin suit—leggins and all—at this provincial wild west show. It was just another such suit as Colonel Cody wears now." However, it was carefully noted:

On the street he dressed like any other man, save that he always wore the picturesque sombrero of the cowboy. It was his custom before starting a walk to take a brace of pistols from his pockets and raise the hammers to see if they were all right. As he always walked with his hands in his pockets they were necessarily constantly on his derringers. That was the only indication of his fighting propensities he showed. He was peaceful enough when left alone, but ready for emergencies.[18]

It was also claimed that during his brief stay at the Falls, Wild Bill indulged in one of his favorite pastimes—practical joking. One of his friends at the hotel was a young man named Woodruff who lived close by:

One day Woodruff fell asleep in an arm chair in the bar room of the little hotel where Wild Bill was stopping. He had tipped back his chair and put his feet on the bar in front of him. Hickok came in, and when he saw Woodruff sound asleep he drew a derringer and fired at the floor between Woodruff's legs. He expected that Woodruff would jump about ten feet. Instead, Woodruff never moved, except to lazily open his eyes and blink like a sleepy dog at Wild Bill.

This delighted Hickok, who brought down his fist with a thump, crying: "You're game! I wish I had you out west."[19]

So ended Wild Bill's "Wild West Show." Back in 1870, Wild Bill's appearance in the Ginger Circus at Sherman, Texas, was short-lived, because he left the company at the end of the performance, but no reason is given. Following his sudden exit from Hays after the shoot-out with the soldiers, his movements are in doubt. Whether he did got to Abilene or some other place has not yet been clarified, but by October he was back in Topeka, where

---

[17] Francis J. Petrie, "Buffalo Hunt, Wild West Show Was Staged Here in 1872," [Niagara Falls?] *Evening Review*, Sept. 17, 1966. Copy supplied by Stanley J. Smith.

[18] Denver *Field and Farm*, June 1, 1895.

[19] *Ibid.*

it was reported: "Wild Bill, he of the protracted hair, the aquiline nose, the shiny rainment and the bloody reputation, is in town."[20]

No further reference has been found to the shooting scrape in Hays, so it must be assumed that the army authorities had satisfied themselves that Hickok did act in self-defense, and no charges were preferred.

Back once more in familiar surroundings, Hickok probably decided to spend the whole winter in Topeka—at least that appears to have been his intention. Buffalo Bill Cody was at this time at Fort McPherson, and legend has it that he brought his wife to Topeka that winter. Actually, there is some doubt just where she did meet Hickok. Accounts differ. Some say it happened at Hays City, Cheyenne, or Topeka. Louisa Frederici Cody named no place but recalled that she first met Wild Bill at a dance and expressed amazement at his apparent lack of pistols and other weapons. She described him as a "mild-appearing, somewhat sadfaced man bent low in a courtly bow" before her, and she found him "a Sir Walter Raleigh." Later she confided, "We danced, and I must confess that we danced and danced again."[21]

Commented Don Russell:

I do not trust much in Mrs. Cody's book, on Courtney Ryley Cooper's advice, and he wrote it, but she may have met Hickok in the winter of 1870–71. I know no occasion for Cody going to Topeka, but it runs in my mind that Mae or Helen (his sisters) might have lived there. He was on the payroll at Fort McPherson that winter, but might have been sent there on some occasion, or have taken a few days off. Also she was running back and forth to St. Louis. I'd say a bit improbable, but possible.[22]

A number of women probably concerned Wild Bill that winter. One in particular was a lady of Ellsworth named Emma Williams. Legend tells that he had a rival for her affections, one Bill Thompson (not Ben Thompson's homicidal brother). There is no evidence to suggest Hickok spent any time in Ellsworth that winter, but it is alleged that Thompson made up his mind to put Hickok out of the way. His attempt at assassination met with failure. A warning look from the waiter of a restaurant which he was patronizing enabled Wild Bill to take care of Mr. Thompson between the soup

[20] Topeka *State Record*, Oct. 21, 1870.
[21] "Memories of Buffalo Bill," *Ladies' Home Journal*, Vol. XXXVI, No. 7 (July, 1919), 19. This was later published as a book in collaboration with Courtney Ryley Cooper.
[22] Don Russell to the author, Nov. 3, 1960.

and the main course. Stories of this type are rarely documented and must be considered hearsay.

The remainder of the winter of 1870–71 seems to have passed uneventfully for there are no references to Wild Bill in the press. No doubt he continued to gamble to his heart's content, but his winnings rarely covered his losses, and he was the first to admit that his dexterity with the cards was inferior to his dexterity with a pair of pistols. As Hickok was by nature a wanderer, a man of action, a complete change was the answer. Early in January he changed his base and appeared once more in his old haunt, Junction City, where the Englishman Percy G. Ebbutt met him.

Ebbutt had recently emigrated to Kansas, and was still somewhat awed by the country and its people. Having been brought up in a country whose civilized way of life and culture was the envy of the world, he was puzzled by Hickok's status in the community as a man-killer, and his comments indicate that he had been hearing many stories about the man:

"Wild Bill" was a fine-looking fellow with long curly hair hanging down his back and was dressed in a rather dandified fashion. He was said to have twenty-seven nicks cut on the handle of his revolver, each signifying a man whose life had been taken by him. And yet he walked the streets as free as any man, and perhaps with more security than a less desperate criminal would, for he would have to be a plucky man to arrest "Wild Bill."[23]

Ebbutt also noted that he watched Hickok shoot quail in the stable yard of the Empire Hotel. Other residents have recalled similar events. Henry Thiele claimed he had seen Wild Bill stand on the corner of Sixth and Washington Streets, and with a six-shooter, shoot silver half-dollars out of a cleft of a stick in the grass in the park. And Jack Ebbutt, believed to be a relative of Percy (who returned to England), recalled seeing Hickok shoot rats in Callen's livery stable with a six-shooter.[24]

By March or early April, 1871, Wild Bill was at Fort Harker, where he was confronted by a messenger of fate with tidings that were to enhance his already snowballing legend—he was offered the job of marshal of Abilene.

---

23 *Emigrant Life in Kansas*, 12–13.
24 Major General James A. Weir, M.C., Commanding, Department of the Army, Fitzsimons General Hospital, Denver, Colorado, to the author, Apr. 27, 1970, citing Captain W. F. Pride's book, *History of Fort Riley*.

--◦✦ 10 ✦◦--

Marshal of Abilene

ABILENE WAS THE FIRST of the famous cowtowns[1] of Kansas. Named after the Biblical city "The Tetrarch of Abilene—City of the Plains" in the third chapter of Luke, it was little more than a frontier village in 1867 when Joseph G. McCoy came upon it in his search for a place suitable for shipping Texas cattle east from Kansas on the railroad. Baxter Springs, Kansas, was then in use but was not suitable, partly because of trouble with Jayhawkers and other mobs anxious to prevent the cattle crossing their land. Of primary importance to the buyers and sellers alike was the establishment of a permanent point on the railroad from which the cattle could be shipped directly east.

During the Civil War cattle had run wild, and with the cessation of hostilities it became an enormous task to round up the many thousands adrift in the scrub and brush country of the Texas plains. Having joined forces with his brothers in the firm of William K. McCoy and Brothers to round up these cattle, Joseph G. McCoy set out to find a suitable shipping point east. Kansas, with its good grazing and water, was the ideal location, but quarantine laws barred Texas cattle from most parts of the state for most of the year. McCoy decided that he must find a place with all these facilities and access to the railroad. Eventually he found it—Abilene.

It was, he recalled, "a very small, dead place, consisting of about one dozen log huts, low, small, rude affairs, four-fifths of which were covered with dirt for roofing; indeed, but one shingle roof could be seen in the whole city. The business of the burg was conducted in two small rooms mere log huts, and of course, the inevitable saloon, also a log hut, was to be found."[2] Situated as it was in the middle of rich grassland and water, Abilene was ideal

---

[1] The contemporary word was "cattle town" but the single word "cowtown" has since become popularized. When first used, in the 1880's, "cowtown" was "mildly derogatory." (Robert R. Dykstra, *The Cattle Towns*, 5n.).

[2] Joseph G. McCoy, *Historic Sketches of the Cattle Trade of the West and Southwest*, 44.

for the purpose. The cattle could be put to graze while waiting their turn at the loading pens.

On June 18, 1867, McCoy purchased 250 acres of land at the northeastern edge of the village. Within three months he had built a shipping yard large enough to hold one thousand head of cattle. He also constructed a barn, a livery stable, an office, and the later-celebrated three-story Drover's Cottage[3] hotel, together with a bank. The shipping pens (later known as the Great Western Stockyard) were enormous, and could load forty railroad cars in two hours. All he needed now was access to the railroad. Following lengthy negotiations with the Union Pacific Railway Company, Eastern Division,[4] a one-hundred-car switch was constructed at Abilene, and transfer pens and feed yards were built at Leavenworth.

Men were dispatched to Texas and other places with orders to persuade cattle buyers and drovers to drive their herds north via the Chisholm Trail, named after Jesse Chisholm, a half-blood trader. It was a long route which ran up from the Rio Grande River, through Indian Territory as far as Wichita, where it officially ended. From there on it was known as "McCoy's Extension" or the "Abilene Trail." Slowly the herds moved toward the new shipping center; after a few setbacks, the first shipment of cattle was dispatched from Abilene to Chicago on September 5, and the town was in business.

The layout of the town was typical of the pattern followed by Abilene's successors. Running east-west and parallel to the railroad was Texas Street (later renamed South First Street). At its main intersection was Cedar Street, which ran south from the railroad some five blocks east of Mud Creek. East from Cedar Street was a small street known simply as "A"—at the end of which was McCoy's famous Drover's Cottage and the Shane and Henry real-estate office. A collection of shacks north of the railroad housed the dance halls and brothels.

The Drover's Cottage served two purposes. Built three stories high, it had one hundred rooms, serving as both a hotel and a meeting place for the cattlemen and buyers who contracted their busi-

[3] The placing of the apostrophe has long been in doubt. However, some contemporary newspapers have expressed it as I have it.

[4] Many writers (including this one) have been confused by the name of this railroad. From 1855–63 it was the Leavenworth, Pawnee and Western; from 1863–69 it was the Union Pacific Railway Company, Eastern Division; from 1869–80 it was the Kansas Pacific; and from that date to the present it has been known as the Union Pacific (Joseph W. Snell to the author, Mar. 7, 1972).

ness there. It also boasted a laundry, and was regarded as one of the finest hotels of its type in the West.

Cedar and Texas Streets were in reality the heart of the "Texan" Abilene, and on Cedar Street was located the most palatial of the high-class saloons, The Alamo.

George L. Cushman gives this graphic description:

The Alamo was the most elaborate of the saloons, and a description of it will give an idea of the plan of them all. It was housed in a long room with a forty-foot frontage on Cedar street, facing west. There was an entrance at either end. At the west entrance were three double glass doors. Inside and along the front of the south side was the bar with its array of carefully polished brass fixtures and rails. From the back bar arose a large mirror, which reflected the brightly sealed bottles of liquor. At various places over the walls were huge paintings in cheaply done imitations of the nude masterpieces of the Venetian Renaissance painters. Covering the entire floor space were gaming tables, at which practically any game of chance could be indulged. The Alamo boasted an orchestra, which played forenoons, afternoons, and nights. In the height of the season the saloons were the scene of constant activity. At night the noises that were emitted from them were a combination of badly rendered popular music, coarse voices, ribald laughter and Texas "whoops," punctuated at times by gun shots.[5]

It was, of course, the Texas cowboy who helped make Abilene, and all the other cowtowns. His antics and exploits in these places have become part of American folklore. In his way the cowboy played a genuine part in the building of the nation.

His arrival in town, sometimes after spending some three months on the trail, was heralded by a chorus of shouts and pistol shots, and by the sound of galloping horses. The first chance he got to "let her rip" he did so, and once he had drink inside him, he often became almost a maddened creature. In the early days, the arrival of the cowboys (or "drovers" as they were then called) was quite an event. One old-timer recalled:

My lumber yard and office were located on Texas Street, northwest corner of Mulberry and Texas, now called First. The grazing grounds of these immense herds of cattle were west of town and Mud Creek and every cowboy from Texas had to pass my office as he came in to town to get a drink of whiskey or lose his money at poker or roulette. They came in by twenties, fifties and hundreds. Their ponies having been strung along the sidewalks, the bridle reins having been slung over the pony's head on the ground and that pony hitched and stood there till his rider

---

[5] "Abilene, First of the Kansas Cow Towns," KSHS *Quarterly*, Vol. IX, No. 3 (Aug., 1940), 244.

came. The signal for leaving town at about 3 P.M. was a few pistol shots into the air, their ponies mounted, a general fusilade all along the line, every pony on the dead run and as they passed my office, it was crack, bang, boom, of fifty or a hundred six shooters into the air. The air, blue with smoke as it curled upward in spiral wreaths. The boys whooping and yelling like Comanches and then they would whoop down into Mud Creek and up the west bank and then scatter to their different herds. Oh! it was a soul-inspiring or rather, soul perspiring [sight]. At first I would rush to the door to see the show, but I soon learned to dodge behind a pile of lumber, as soon as I heard the signal crack for their leaving town.[6]

Rotgut whisky combined with lead poisoning was responsible for much of the cowboy's trouble. J. B. Edwards noted:

When a man from Texas in those days, especially those who were connected with the cattle business, got too much tanglefoot aboard, he was extremely liable under the least provocation to use his navies [six-shooters], of which not less than one or two were always hanging to their belts. In fact if their fancy told them to shoot they did so, in the air, at anything they saw and a plug hat would bring a volley at any time from them, drunk or sober.[7]

The cowboy was a natural prey for the gamblers, pimps, and prostitutes, who fleeced him at the first opportunity. Once he was paid, the cowboy headed for the nearest bathhouse, and then for a store. There he was fitted in a new suit, spending as much as seventy-five dollars on it. As extras he demanded fancy waistcoats, tight-fitting trousers, new high-heeled boots, and the inevitable ten-gallon Stetson. If he still had any money left (and the boss had not claimed it for debts), he permitted himself a fling at cards—and women. Many a Texas cowboy returned home broke and disillusioned by a trip across the tracks to the houses of doubtful pleasure. Broke he may have been, but he was a little wiser—or so he thought. But next time he returned, history had a bad habit of repeating itself.

By 1869 the cattle trade in Abilene was increasing at a terrific rate. A special correspondent for a Leavenworth paper visited the town in June, ignored the lawless element, and spoke favorably of the town's business. He added that "Abilene . . . might be called a Texan town, so much of the Texan being apparent on the surface. In the busy season thousands of Texan steers are the principal in-

---

[6] Roenigk (ed.), *Pioneer History of Kansas* (an article by Theophilus Little, "Early Days of Abilene and Dickinson County"), 36.
[7] *Early Days in Abilene*, 3.

habitants, but at present the Texan drovers take a prominent position."[8]

Among the Texans there were some who shared local concern over the increasing violence. One wrote: "We found the town was full of all sorts of desperate characters, and I remember one day one of these bad men rode his horse into a saloon, pulled his gun on the bartenders, and all quit business. When he came out several others began to shoot up the town."[9] A resident recalled: "When you heard one or two shots, you waited breathlessly for a third. A third shot meant a death on Texas Street."[10]

To counteract the violence, a number of responsible citizens appeared before Cyrus Kilgore, probate judge of Dickinson County, on September 3, 1869, and presented a petition "praying for incorporation" of Abilene. The judge examined the document, signed by forty-three citizens, and granted the request, and Abilene became a third-class city. Until an election could be held, he appointed as trustees K. B. Shane, Theodore C. Henry, Thomas Sheran, T. F. Hersey (one of the earliest settlers), and Joseph G. McCoy. This group selected Henry as acting mayor, and he remained in this position until 1871.[11]

In the spring of 1870 the office of town marshal was created, in an attempt to enforce law and order and curb the activities of the town's thirty-two saloons[12] and to prohibit brothels within city limits. An ordinance against the carrying of firearms was passed, but proved almost unenforceable. Posters were put up and were promptly torn down or riddled with bullets, and a similar disrespect was shown for the city's first jail. The drovers tore it down and it was only reconstructed under strong guard. The first prisoner, a Negro cook, was "rescued" by some drovers who chased off the guards. And there were other problems: the town was shot up, and businessmen were threatened. In retaliation the citizens organized a vigilante posse and pursued some of the drovers, capturing them and imprisoning them. But the Texans continued to terrorize the inhabitants.[13]

[8] Leavenworth *Times and Conservative*, June 25, 1869.

[9] John Marvin Hunter (ed.), *The Trail Drivers of Texas*, 503.

[10] Stuart Henry, *Conquering Our Great American Plains*, 82.

[11] Cushman, "Abilene, First of the Kansas Cow Towns," *loc. cit.*, 249.

[12] By the spring of 1871, according to one writer, "Abilene boasted ten saloons, five general stores and four hotels," which indicates that the saloon business had suffered a decline (Stewart P. Verckler, *Cowtown Abilene*, 51).

[13] Cushman, "Abilene, First of the Kansas Cow Towns," *loc. cit.*, 250.

Law and order had been the rule in Dickinson County long before Abilene became the center of the cattle trade, but until that time there had been little need for more than one officer. In March, 1867, William Chapman was elected constable for Grant Township, and in April, 1869, a man named Benson was elected to the position.[14] But by May, 1870, the situation in Abilene was serious, and on May 2 the position of marshal was created by a city ordinance. Yet it was not until June 4 that this position was successfully filled, when Thomas J. Smith offered to act as chief of police for $150 a month. His offer was accepted and he was appointed the same day, and allowed to choose his own assistant. The old police force (the only one named was James A. Gauthie) were asked to resign.[15]

It was claimed by T. C. Henry in 1904 that Thomas J. Smith was the celebrated "Bear River" Tom Smith who led the riot at Bear River, or Bear Town, Wyoming Territory, in November, 1868, while acting as a troubleshooter for the Union Pacific Railroad. According to the Utah Deseret News of December 24, 1868, "Tom Smith, the leader of the riot was sent to the Salt Lake Penitentiary." At this writing, it has not been established when he was released or if in fact Abilene's Tom Smith was the same man. Certainly, Smith's origin prior to his arrival in Abilene is obscure. Henry claimed that he had been born in New York about 1849, where he had served as a policeman and later as town marshal of Kit Carson, Colorado, before moving to Kansas.

Having once taken up his appointment, Smith chose as his deputies a young Canadian named James H. McDonald, and shortly afterward a man named Robbins was recruited to assist. Just how long Robbins actually served is uncertain because the municipal records are incomplete.

Tom Smith proved himself a good officer, and his handling of the lawless element in Abilene met with approval among the permanent citizens of the town. For the first time firearms were banned within city limits, and the few that chose to ignore the order usually changed their mind when Smith helped persuade them with his huge fists. Rarely did he have to resort to pulling the two silver-plated Colts he wore at his waist.

Realizing that he would be an easy target on foot, Smith took to riding his horse (a silver-gray called "Silverheels") up and down Texas Street, always on the move, and sure in the knowledge that

14 Dickinson County, Proceedings of the County Commissioners, Vol. A (not paged), Manuscripts Division, KSHS.
15 Minute Book of the City Council of Abilene, Kansas, 1871, KSHS, 29, 34.

he would thus be harder to hit if some drunken drover tried to line him up in his sights.

In Tom Smith the Texans found themselves outclassed. Baffled and bewildered, they could not understand a man who used fists to assert his authority when everyone else, if he were a man, used weapons. Perhaps his approach had been deliberate, for although his two silver-plated Colts were very much in evidence, his lack of a reputation in their use may have been partly responsible for the way he held his own. So far as the citizens of Abilene were concerned, Tom Smith was the ideal policeman, and as a gesture of their faith, on August 9 they increased his salary from $150 to $225 a month, retroactive to July 4. He was also appointed a deputy and undersheriff of the county.[16]

Ironically, Smith's downfall was not caused by a Texan but by a homesteader. On November 2, at the request of the County Sheriff, Joseph Cramer, who was seriously ill,[17] Smith and McDonald went out to arrest a man named Andrew McConnell, charged with the murder of John Shea, near Chapman Creek. McConnell, backed by his neighbor, Moses Miles, had pleaded self-defense, but it was soon learned that both men had lied. When Smith and McDonald arrived at McConnell's dugout, McDonald stood by their horses while Smith walked over to tell him he was under arrest. McConnell produced a rifle and as they struggled for it, Smith was shot in the chest. Immediately Tom Smith fired back, wounding McConnell. Despite his wound, Smith began to gain the upper hand when Miles came up behind him and struck him over the head with a gun. As the marshal fell, Miles grabbed an axe and all but decapitated him. It has been claimed that during this affray, McDonald stood rooted to the spot, too frightened to help, and when the two men turned their attention to him he mounted his horse and fled to Abilene for assistance.

In Abilene news of the fight was met with disbelief, and according to one resident, McDonald bolstered his courage in a saloon, where, "leaning against the bar, with a drink of whiskey in his hand, he blubbered out his yarn. There being nobody to dispute him, his story had to go. But I can still recall the looks that passed between men who had been raised from birth to eat six-shooters. It was so rank that no one could say a word."[18]

[16] Miller and Snell, *Why the West Was Wild*, 576.

[17] Sheriff Cramer was taken ill in September, 1870, and died on December 26.

[18] Abilene *Chronicle*, Nov. 3, 1870; Charles F. Gross to J. B. Edwards, Aug. 23, 1922, Manuscripts Division, KSHS.

The Junction City *Union* of November 5, 1870, gives another version of what happened. After describing the arrival of Smith and McDonald at the dugout, the paper stated:

They arrived at McConnell's claim, and found himself a man named Miles and another individual in the "dug-out." Smith inquired for Mc-Connel, [*sic*] who answered promptly. McConnel was sitting down and had a gun between his knees. Upon Smith's telling him that he was a prisoner McConnel fired at Smith, a scuffle ensued, the man Miles and his companion taking part. This action called McDonald to the field and he interferred shooting Miles' companion, name unknown. McDonald's attention was next given to Miles, who was a person of great physical strength. When McConnel saw that Smith was killed, the combined efforts of [both] men turned toward McDonald, who using his weapon succeeded in wounding Miles in three places, himself being shot through his hat and receiving a ball in his vest, which fortunately struck a pocket book and then stopped. The two men, McConnel and Miles succeeded in getting hold of the horses Smith and Deputy McDonald had and started off. McDonald roused the neighbors as soon as possible and pursuit was given. The two men exchanged horses in some way, and returned again to the dug-out, where their fiendish work was completed by severing Smith's head entirely from his body. Wednesday night about ten o'clock they arrived at this place when their wounds were dressed. Miles had two fingers on one hand shot off, which was noticeable. The absence at that hour of any of the particulars of the murder, did not cause a lookout for parties committing the same; but as soon as the midnight train came down the facts became noised around and parties are now out scouring the country . . . .

Deputy McDonald went by us last night and we hope he will get upon their track and succeed in his efforts.

When Smith's death was confirmed, a furious posse set out after the killers. Way ahead of the posse rode James Gainsford, a butcher, and C. C. Kuney, a magistrate. The *Union* on November 12 reported that the pair captured the murderers at a house on the Republican twenty miles from Clay Center, and took them to Abilene. On the 19th the paper reported that at the Dickinson County District Court three special venues were exhausted without securing the full number of jurors. Feeling in the area was very high and the authorities feared attempts at lynching, so the prisoners were removed to Riley county to await trial at the next term of the District Court. In March, 1871, they went on trial.

The Jury rendered a verdict of guilty and both men were sentenced to hard labor in the state penitentiary, Miles for sixteen years, McConnell for twelve. The comparatively lenient sentences aroused much anger in Abilene, where it was generally agreed that they should have been hanged. The verdict prompted the comment:

Twelve and sixteen years in the penitentiary seem long periods, but the condemned ought to be thankful that they got off with even such sentences. Never during their natural lives can they atone for their great crime.[19]

Despite McDonald's evident courage in attempting to arrest the murderers, his reputation has suffered down the years, and it is reflected in the records of the Abilene City Council. Following Tom Smith's murder, gunsmith Patrick Hand was appointed to serve as the town policeman until a strong man could be found to succeed the marshal. The council minutes show that Hand did not last long and that James H. McDonald remained on the police force, perhaps as acting marshal, during the remainder of the Henry Administration, for on April 1, 1871, it was recorded that: "On Motion J. H. McDonald was allowed one hundred and fifty Dollars ($150) for services as policeman."[20]

On April 3, 1871, Joseph G. McCoy, was elected mayor in the first municipal election, and his primary problem was to find a new marshal. He was aided in his search by Charles Gross, an old friend who had originally told McCoy of the herds of cattle running loose in Texas during the war. His tales of the half-wild longhorns had inspired McCoy and strengthened his ambition.[21] Gross kept McCoy's books and also worked as a room clerk at the Drover's Cottage. He spoke to McCoy about a man he had known in his home state of Illinois, James B. Hickok. McCoy was aware of Wild Bill's reputation and was impressed by Gross's recommendation. He wasted no time and dispatched him to find the scout and bring him to see him. Gross made a few enquiries and the next day took the train to Fort Harker.[22]

---

[19] Abilene *Chronicle*, Mar. 23, 1871. Miles was convicted of first-degree murder, but only served six years of his sentence. He was pardoned by the Governor and discharged on January 2, 1877. McConnell was convicted of first-degree manslaughter but was not so fortunate. It was January 12, 1881, before he was discharged and allowed 791 days remission (Records of the Kansas State Penitentiary, Archives Division, KSHS). Gainsford and Kuney each received $100 from the Abilene City Council as a reward for capturing the murderers.

[20] Minute Book of the City Council of Abilene, *loc. cit.*, 49.

[21] Charles Gross to J. B. Edwards, Apr. 13, 1922, Manuscripts Division, KSHS.

[22] Gross seems very certain that Hickok was at Fort Harker, but J. B. Edwards asserted that Wild Bill himself sought the position (Edwards, *Early Days in Abilene*, 6).

About April 11, Gross walked into McCoy's office, accompanied by Hickok. No definite negotiations were conducted during those first few days; Wild Bill made sure that he got a good look at the town first. Evidently what he saw impressed him. His love of gambling would be well catered for, but on the debit side he noted the number of gambling houses and saloons owned or operated by the Texans. He sensed the friction between them and the townspeople, particularly the shopkeepers. Nevertheless it was regular employment, so he accepted the job; but he went into it with both eyes open—completely aware that his reputation might bring him trouble, possibly death.

At a special meeting of the Council, Mayor McCoy's choice was "unanimously confirmed," and James Butler Hickok became the marshal of Abilene on April 15, 1871. His salary of $150 per month was to be supplemented by 25 per cent of all fines imposed in court.[23]

Many years later Joseph G. McCoy wrote of his choice of Hickok: "For my preserver of the Peace, I had 'Wild Bill' Hickok, and he was the squarest man I ever saw. He broke up all unfair gambling, made professional gamblers move their tables into the light, and when they became drunk stopped the game."[24]

It was agreed that Wild Bill would be answerable to the Council on matters of policy, but he would be allowed to use his own methods to keep the peace, provided he

. . . be industrious and vigilant, not only in preventing any infraction of the ordinances of said city and bring offenders against them to justice, but also in causing the prosecution or punishment of offences against the penal laws of the State of Kansas, committed within said City and in suffering disturbances, affrays, riots and other breaches of peace therein. He shall keep an account of all moneys received by him for the use of the said City, and pay the same to the treasurer thereof on the first Saturday of every month and take his receipt therefore, and do and perform all such other duties as are now or hereafter may be required of him by said Council.[25]

Hickok's appointment caused quite a stir, not only in the town and the state, but on the trail back to Texas, where the drovers were preparing to point their herds north. Around campfires, it was said, men talked about it and wondered. Hickok was different from Smith, they argued. He used his pistols to fight with, and he

23 Minute Book of the City Council of Abilene, *loc. cit.*, 55.
24 Topeka *Capital*, Aug. 30, 1908.
25 Abilene *Chronicle*, June 1, 1871.

had never lost a fight. Any cursory researcher into the newspapers of the time will find that great attention was paid to the fact that Hickok was marshal, and visitors and others who wrote about the place made a point of mentioning him. So it is logical to assume that when the Texans pointed their herds north that season, he was included in the sights they should see in Abilene.

In the month before the cattlemen began to arrive, Wild Bill was kept busy strengthening the jail. Later he was given the privilege of shooting stray dogs for the princely sum of fifty cents a dog.

News of the pending arrival of a cattle herd in the town was greeted with mixed feelings. Those anxious to make money from the drovers or potential buyers welcomed it. Others viewed the appearance of the dust haze that signaled a herd's approach with fear and alarm. These were the small homesteaders and settlers who had the misfortune to be close by the cattle trail. Few of them had much to fear from the drovers, provided they did not interfere with them or their cattle, but an old Irish-born lady, living in Salina, Kansas, in 1936, recalled an incident in her childhood which suggests that her family had reason to fear the Texans:

My father took a claim on the Trail, a few miles south of Abilene, and we lived there in a soddy. Marshal Hickok would often ride out to spend Sunday afternoon with us, always with a sack of candy in his pocket for us children. I was very little then and he would trot me on his knee and curl my hair around his finger. He dearly loved children, did Marshal Hickok.

One day we were busy around the place when we saw a big cloud of dust to the south. It frightened us terribly for we knew a herd was coming up the Trail and the cowboys with these herds would kill any settlers they found. Usually riders were sent out from Abilene when a herd was coming, and the settlers taken to town for safety, but this time there had been no warning.

We huddled around my father and then we saw a rider coming from the north.

"'Tis someone coming to meet them with whiskey," said my father. "That finishes it."

"What can we do?"

"Nothing. There's no way to get away or any place to hide on this prairie. We'll just have to take it."

He gathered us close and we waited. Then suddenly he cried, "Children, we're safe! I can see the rider's long yellow hair. 'Tis Marshal Hickok, and they'll not harm us now."

Nor did they. Oh, I tell you [there were tears in her eyes as she finished] I tell you he was a grand man was Marshal Hickok, a grand man![26]

The arrival early in May of Columbus Carrol's herd of 1,600 head (the first herd of the season, according to the Topeka *Commonwealth* of May 11) was overshadowed by another event. This was an incident which involved Hickok with members of the Council. According to the Minute Book:

At an adjourned meeting of the Mayor & Councilmen of the City of Abilene [on May 8] all members were present. On Motion of G. L. Brinkman the order of business was suspended and the resignations of members discussed. Moved by G. L. Brinkman that both resignations of councilmen be considered at once motion unanimously carried. Moved by G. L. Brinkman that the resignations of Messrs. L. Boudinot and Carpenter be accepted, carried. S. A. Burroughs voting against. S. A. Burroughs left the council without permission and on motion of Mr. Brinkman the Marshal was instructed to compell his attendance. Mr. Burroughs brought in by the Marshal and immediately left the council. On motion of G. L. Brinkman the Marshal was instructed to again bring Mr. Burroughs back which order was executed.

Wild Bill's actions caused an uproar—especially as he carried the unfortunate Mr. Burroughs over his shoulder the last time he brought him back, and for the remainder of the meeting sat inside the door to prevent any further escapes. V. P. Wilson, editor of the town's only newspaper, the *Chronicle*, hotly attacked Mayor McCoy in his issue of May 18, adding:

Of course the Marshal simply obeyed orders—whether legal or not— and is not to blame. But our silly mayor goes down to Topeka, publishes his exploit in the papers, gets up a picture which pretends to represent the transaction, carves upon it in big letters, "Who's Mayor now?" and sends them all over the country to be hawked about and laughed at as a standing disgrace to his own town.

The same issue carried a report that McCoy was in dispute with two councilmen over the amount which saloons were to be taxed. McCoy favored a low tax, and embarrassed Hickok by suggesting that any loss of revenue could be made up by the marshal, who would collect fines from all incoming gamblers and prostitutes, and "no one would be the wiser for it." Wilson took McCoy to task for the scheme but expressed no opinion about Hickok's alleged connection with it.

By June 1 the cattle were pouring into the territory, and Wild Bill had his work cut out to keep order. The saloons and gambling houses were doing a roaring trade—as were the houses across the

[26] Lucile Stevens to the author, Sept. 10, 1964.

tracks. One old-timer noted that the population of Abilene was no more than five hundred in April, but by June 1 it had about seven thousand, "eating wherever they could and sleeping everywhere, some in houses, some in tents, but the greater number under blankets spread upon the prairie. As to drink, there was probably more whisky drank than water, and of a quality that would make rabbits fight a bull dog."[27]

A visitor to Abilene in August noted that the town was split in two by the railroad. On the north lay the residential area, shops, banks, and churches, but on the south side "you are in Texas, and talk about cattle, varied by occasional remarks on 'beeves' and 'stock.'" He also made a point of the fact that the prostitutes ("vice in one of its forms") were "sternly driven forth from the city limits for the space of at least a quarter of a mile, where its 'local habitation' is courteously and modestly, but rather indefinitely designated as the 'Beer Garden.'"[28]

This re-locating of the red-light district had been prompted by many things. In July the decent citizens had risen up in protest of the bawdyhouses and loose women. A recent writer summed up their feelings:

There were now several children of school age in the town, and the school house was just a few blocks away from the hell-hole of Texas Street. They [the citizens] protested. Not all of the children would have to walk through Texas Street, but some would. Others would, as they did errands for their parents. Most parents would not send a child on this type of errand, but sometimes it was absolutely necessary; perhaps a child was sick and the mother would have to stay instead of going to the store herself. Before, in previous years, Texas Street was quiet and deserted by the time school started, but it was not the case this year. The drovers had flooded the market, and many had planned to winter their herd near Abilene. The respectable people could see that Texas Street would flourish as it never had before. The steady income from the Texans would keep it rolling throughout the winter, too.

The plan of moving the women of Texas Street was a daring scheme. Could a small group of honest and upright citizens oppose the hard-fighting and short-tempered Texans? The citizens were determined to try at least. The spot chosen was a quarter to a half mile south and east of Texas Street. Oddly, because this is the present site of a recreated Texas Street. The entire community of the women of Texas Street were moved into a fenced area. This location was to be known as the Devil's Addition and later Fisher's Addition, as the name Texas Town did not

[27] Roenigk (ed.), *Pioneer History of Kansas*, 35.
[28] Topeka *State Record*, Aug. 5, 1871.

last long. Surprisingly, the Texans did not object to the mass movement. They accepted the changes almost joyfully, realizing the many advantages. Now the marshal and the school were no longer to worry them, especially those who wished female sociability. The women could come to town on legitimate errands, but otherwise they stayed in their own bailiwick. In their quarter, shooting and raising hell in general could be indulged in full blast.[29]

For Wild Bill, the movement of the women from Texas Street must have been a relief. He had enough problems with the Texans themselves without additional complications.

Some weeks before, on June 8, the *Chronicle* published the following ordinance against carrying of pistols in town:

Fire Arms.—The Chief of Police has posted up printed notices, informing all persons that the ordinance against carrying fire arms or other weapons in Abilene, will be enforced. That's right. There's no bravery in carrying revolvers in a civilized community. Such a practice is well enough and perhaps necessary when among Indians or other barbarians, but among white people it ought to be discountenanced.

The law was certainly disregarded by some. On June 22 the *Chronicle* reported a shoot-out between two men. Each was wounded but not fatally, and the police (Hickok?) soon arrived and arrested them.

Such incidents did not sit well with the council, and on June 24 they took the unprecedented step of passing an ordinance invoking the Kansas state law, passed in 1868, which prohibited vagrants, drunks, or former Confederate soldiers from carrying "a pistol, bowie-knife, dirk or other deadly weapon," for which the penalty was up to $100 fine or three months in jail.[30]

By now Hickok's police force consisted of three deputies—Tom Carson, James Gainsford, and, surprisingly, Tom Smith's deputy, James H. McDonald. The latter's appointment brought a protest from McCoy.[31] Perhaps he had a personal dislike of the man or, like others in the town, believed that McDonald had deserted Smith. Even Hickok had his difficulties with McDonald. In August the Minute Book records a dispute between them over the sum of twenty dollars.

Flagrant disregard for the anti-firearms law was shown by John Wesley Hardin, at that time an eighteen-year-old drover who had fled from Texas. He was wanted by the Texas police, and was al-

29 Verckler, *Cowtown Abilene*, 62.
30 Kansas Statutes, 1868, 378.
31 Minute Book of the City Council of Abilene, *loc. cit.* 71.

ready carving himself a niche in history. He had come up the Chisholm Trail with the Columbus Carrol outfit in May (although he later claimed that he did not arrive until about June 1). On the way in he killed a couple of Mexican herders in a "duel" on horseback. Both sides displayed a remarkable lack of accuracy, but Wes emerged the victor. He met Ben Thompson when he visited the Bull's Head, and Ben discussed the question of Wild Bill. He claimed Hickok was down on Southern boys, and made it his business to supervise the saloon men, and was responsible for starting the stories about the Texans being fleeced by their own kind.

To these stories Hardin paid little heed. He had found out early that there was no love lost between Ben and the Marshal. Ben was obviously trying to influence the youngster and get him to pick a quarrel with Wild Bill, and Hardin was angered: "I am not doing anybody's fighting just now except my own, but I know how to stick to a friend. If Bill needs killing, why don't you kill him yourself?" Ben backed down and replied: "I would rather get someone else to do it." Hardin told Ben he had struck the wrong man for that kind of work and walked out.[32]

Actually, Hardin's version of his exploits in Abilene, although they contain glimmers of truth, are for the most part at variance with the facts. The recent discovery of some missing issues of the Abilene *Chronicle* help to explain a number of things.

On July 5 a young Texan named William M. Cohron was shot and killed by a Mexican herder. The *Chronicle* reported on July 13 that the Mexican had been followed by two Texans and shot as he rose from dinner in a restaurant. Hardin in his book claims that he killed one Juan Bideno, for the murder of his friend "Billy Coran." He alleges that he pursued the murderer after being approached by prominent cowmen to do so. They secured a warrant for the man's arrest, and Wes was appointed "a deputy sheriff and was given letters of introduction to cattlemen whom I should meet." He asserts that he set out on June 27 (eight days before Cohron was killed!), accompanied by Cohron's brother and a man named Anderson. Bideno was eventually caught at a place called Bluff and shot in a restaurant as he tried to rise from the table. However, an obscure Oxford, Kansas, paper gives a different story:

TERRIBLE MURDER.

A man was shot dead while sitting at the table in the dining room of the Southwestern Hotel, at Sumner City, at noon last Friday [July 7],

[32] John Wesley Hardin, *The Life of John Wesley Hardin*, 44.

by a man who called himself Conway [Cohron], from Cottonwood river. Conway claimed that the man whom he shot without warning killed his brother a short time before, and that he (Conway) had followed him until he overtook him at Sumner, where he had stopped to take dinner. The murdered man was supposed to be a Mexican. His name was not ascertained by those who witnessed the tragedy, nor but few of the particulars of the incentives Conway had in thus taking the law into his own hands—if, indeed, he had any other motive than the obtaining [of] a fine horse ridden by the murdered man, which he asserted belonged to his brother. The Mexican being instantly killed, of course could not give his side of the story.

The shot took effect in the forehead, passing through the head and the partition, barely missing a lady in the next room, and was flattened against the stove. The so-called Mexican was totally unconscious of danger seemingly, and though facing the door fairly in which the assassin stood, was struck down while drinking coffee, with the cup to his lips.

Conway apologized for the confusion the shooting occasioned, handed the proprietors of the hotel five dollars, remarking that that would pay for cleaning up, and left, taking with him the horse before mentioned. No arrest.[33]

A tombstone for Cohron arrived in Abilene in August. The *Chronicle*, in noting its arrival, reported that the man who killed the Mexican also "killed Charles Couger on the 6th inst., in this place."[34]

This particular incident is described by Hardin as having taken place in the American Hotel on July 7. He claimed that a man came into his room with a dirk in his hand, so Wes put four shots into him, and then fled the town for fear that Hickok would be after him. The press gave a different version, which explains why Hardin was known as "Arkansaw" at the time:

MURDER.—A most fiendish murder was perpetrated at the American House, in this place, on the night of the 6th inst. The murdered man's name was Charles Couger, and that of the murderer Wesley Clemens, *alias* "Arkansaw." Couger was a boss cattle herder, and said to be a gentleman; Clemens is from Mississippi. Couger was in his room sitting upon the bed reading a newspaper. Four shots were fired at him through a board partition, one of which struck him in the fleshy part of the left arm, passing through the third rib and entering the heart, cutting a piece of it entirely off, and killing Couger almost instantly. The murderer

---

[33] Oxford *Times*, July 13, 1871. This newspaper was discovered by Waldo E. Koop, who saved it from oblivion by having it microfilmed by the KSHS.

[34] Abilene *Chronicle*, Aug. 17, 1871.

escaped and has thus far eluded his pursuers. If caught he will probably be killed on sight.[35]

Another report stated: "This was his sixth murder."[36]

Perhaps Hardin is best remembered in Abilene for his alleged backing down of Hickok with a "road-agent's spin," or something similar. Hickok came upon Wes and some companions playing tenpins in a bowling alley, wearing pistols in defiance of the ordinance. Wild Bill ordered him to take them off, at the same time pulling his own pistol.

I said all right and pulled them out of the scabbard, but while he was reaching for them, I reversed them and whirled them over on him with the muzzles in his face, springing back at the same time. I told him to put his pistols up, which he did. I cursed him for a long-haired scoundrel that would shoot a boy with his back to him (as I had been told he intended to do me). He said, "Little Arkansaw, you have been wrongly informed."

I shouted, "This is my fight and I'll kill the first man that fires a gun."

Bill said, "You are the gamest and quickest boy I ever saw. Let us compromise this matter and I will be your friend. Let us go in here and take a drink, as I want to talk to you and give you some advice."[37]

Hardin does not explain how Hickok was supposed to put down his own pistols in order to relieve him of his—far more likely Wild Bill would have shot him at the first move. Until Hardin's *Life* was published in the 1890's the incident was unknown. Certainly none of the old-timers in Abilene ever credited Hardin (or "Arkansaw") with any such feat. The only sensible conclusion is that the showdown never happened—and if it did, it was not as described. Wild Bill had been dead a long time when Hardin wrote his book.

It is alleged that during Hardin's stay in town he was forced to ask a favor of Wild Bill which concerned his cousin Manning Clemments. Manning and his brother Jim had shot it out with the Shadden brothers, Joe and Ad. Both were killed. Although, so Wes claimed, the killing was justifiable, Manning came in ahead of the herd, leaving Jim in charge, to try and fix it with Hickok. Texas tradition has it that Hickok arrested Manning on a charge made by the Shadden faction, but Hardin interposed on his behalf and Wild Bill released him for want of evidence. No records of any arrests

---

35 *Ibid.*, Aug. 10, 1871.

36 Saline County *Journal*, Aug. 10, 1871.

37 Hardin, *Life of John Wesley Hardin*, 44.

could be found in the Abilene city records, many of which were destroyed in a fire in 1882.[38]

It has long been believed that Hardin's book was an attempt to vindicate himself and boost a rapidly fading ego, and this impression is strengthened by a perusal of some of the voluminous correspondence he wrote to his first wife while he was serving his sentence in Huntsville Prison. In a letter dated June 24, 1888, he makes the following interesting statement:

It has been said of me . . . that I had invaded a foreign state [Kansas] and released from prison a relative[,] a dear true friend[,] whose custodian was Wild Bill the Notorious[,] the redoutable Bill Heycox of Abaline of whom no braver man ever drew breath[.] as to the truth or falsity of these assersion I have nothing to say[,] except that I have ever been ready to stand trial on any or all of these charges.[39]

After Hardin finally left Abilene he and Hickok never met again, except in fiction.

During June and July the flow of gamblers and prostitutes had continued unabated, and each time Hickok strolled down to the depot it was to witness the arrival of a few more. The councilmen were quick to take note of the situation. On July 19 the Minute Book records that Hickok was "instructed to stop dance houses and the vending of Whiskeys Brandies, &c., in McCoy's addition[40] to the town of Abilene," and on July 22, "to close up all dead & Brace Gambling Games and to arrest all Cappers for the aforesaid game."

Wild Bill instructed his deputies accordingly, and they went about their work with zest. Across the tracks the Marshal and his men were openly cursed.

Ben Thompson had left town about the beginning of July. He had returned to Texas to bring his wife and family back, but a buggy accident upset his plans and he never returned that season. His wife lost an arm, and Ben suffered several injuries. Phil Coe, thinking ahead to his own return to Texas at the end of the season,

---

[38] Verckler, *Cowtown Abilene*, 33. George L. Cushman to the author, Nov. 12, 1964, remarked that early in the 1930's he had seen many of the Abilene records in an Abilene suburban fire station, "earmarked for the incinerator," and he wondered if they were destroyed or preserved.

[39] Copies of these letters are on file at the University of Texas and the San Marcos, Texas, Library. I am indebted to Charles Parsons of Racine, Wis., for the above extract.

[40] George Fisher owned the site on which these places were built. Because McCoy was mayor in 1871 when efforts were made to get rid of them, his name was associated with them, but his property was in another part of town (Cushman, "Abilene, First of the Kansas Cow Towns," *loc. cit.*, 248).

transferred the Bull's Head license to Tom Sheran on August 2, but remained as a house gambler.[41]

Meantime Wild Bill continued his supervision of Abilene. Unlike his predecessor, Tom Smith, he kept up no ceaseless town patrol. He left much of the menial work to his deputies. But at least once during the day, he meandered along Texas Street, and every night, at varying times, he did the same. And he was frequently found walking or riding through the "Devil's Addition." Residents who were worried by the violence of the Texans soon learned that they had nothing to fear so long as Wild Bill was on Texas Street. His headquarters became The Alamo, where he was frequently to be seen gambling, or he retired to his office and attended to the paper work which had to be kept up to date. When the need arose, he appeared in court.

In time the strain of being Abilene's marshal began to tell. He was constantly aware of the feeling against him among the Texans and saloonkeepers, and fearing assassination, was ever on his guard. His independent nature extended to his official position. There were some who objected to his methods. He was not always prepared to arrest wrongdoers. "He often took justice in his own hands," declared one writer, "contrary to all the conception of our courts. As he was not trained as a peace officer, he saw no harm in running a man out of town, instead of locking him in the small jail. . . : he had many enemies and many admitted they were out to get him in any possible way."[42]

Wild Bill always walked down the middle of the street, a precaution he had learned in Hays, and rarely used the sidewalk. "It was a very common sight in Abilene in those days," wrote John Conkie, city jailor of Abilene, "to see Wild Bill sitting in a barber's chair getting shaved, with his shotgun in hand and his eyes open."[43] The barber accepted all this as part of a day's work. Hickok avoided open doorways and windows, and he always had a wall at his back. This all hints at nervous tension—but with only three deputies to control an estimated five thousand Texans and others, Wild Bill had cause to worry![44]

[41] Minute Book of the City Council of Abilene, loc. cit., 83.

[42] Verckler, Cowtown Abilene, 61.

[43] Wilbert E. Eisele, The Real Wild Bill Hickok, 186. Conkie led quite an eventful life. Besides working as a jailer in Abilene during the cattle days, he had served with distinction in the Civil War as a Secret Service agent, and was much respected in Colorado. He died in August, 1931, aged eighty-seven (Denver Post, Aug. 13, 1931).

[44] It has been disputed that such a number were ever in Abilene at any one time, but Theophilus Little noted: "One of our citizens had the curiosity to count

Hickok's distrust of the Texans was equaled by his wary approach to women friends. Although Susannah Moore, the mystery girl from the Ozarks, is reputed to have lived with him during this time, there is no record of it. Charles Gross recalled that when Hickok first came to town, he stayed at the Drover's Cottage, where Gross was room clerk. Wild Bill shared a room with him since he would not sleep with a stranger. For a month or so this arrangement lasted; then Hickok moved to a cottage, or two-story wooden cabin, at the south end of town. There various ladies of his choice stayed with him from time to time. On the subject of women, Gross said:

The many talks I had with Bill I do not now recall any remark, or refference to any Woman other than those he made to the One he lived with in the Small house & he did not Ever show bifore me any Especial affection for her—What he called her I do not recall but *I do Know he was on Guard Even against her*[.] I was there alone with the two Many times but I was Very careful never to go unless I knew Bill was Home & always there was good reason for my going. Having to go Early one morning Bill was still in Bed & when I went to the door and the woman came to let me in she saw through the window who I was.—she was only just up & was still in night dress[.] Bill said "let him in; you dont give a Dam for Gross seeing you"; but she did and showed it in looks. she went into the next room & Bill got up leasurely and as he sat side ways on the Bed I saw he had his 6 shooter in his right hand and on the Bed spread lay a sawed off shot Gun (Double Barreled) with a strap on it so he could swing it over his shoulder and Carry it under his Coat out of sight[.] I dont think the Barrell was More than a 1-1/2 feet long. . . . He always had a Mistress[.] I knew two or three of them[.] one[,] a former mistress of his was an inmate of a cottage in McCoys addition. Bill asked me to go with him to see her to be a witness in an interview. I believe she was a Red Head but am not sure. She came to Abilene to try & make up with Bill. He gave her $25.00 & made her move on. There was no Row but Bill told her he was through with her. She moved On.[45]

Wild Bill met his future wife, Agnes Lake Thatcher, at this time. Mrs. Lake's "Hippo-Olympiad and Mammoth Circus" played in Abilene on July 13, 1871. The *Chronicle* for August 3 reported: "The attendance was large at each performance." But on this occasion he fobbed off her advances with excuses, and she, too, left town.

The removal of the brothels from Texas Street prompted some

the people [on Texas Street], there were 2,500 on the south side and 1,500 on the north side." (Roenigk (ed.), *Pioneer History of Kansas*, 36.)
[45] Charles Gross to J. B. Edwards, June 15, 1925.

Council members to suggest that the city police force be reduced by half, but the vote was equally divided. Finally, on September 2, it was decided to dismiss J. H. McDonald and James Gainsford from the force, "by reason that their services are no longer needed."[46] This left Hickok with Tom Carson and "Brocky Jack" Norton, both hired during June to help cover the brothel district. On this same date it was ordered that "the Marshall be directed to suppress all Dance Houses and to arrest the proprietors if they persist after the notification."[47]

Wild Bill was by now probably fed up with Abilene politics. Following the dismissal of Gainsford and McDonald and the suppression of the dance halls, the Council set him against the prostitutes, and on September 6 he was ordered to "inform the proprietor of the Abilene House to expell the prostitutes from his premises, under the pain and penalties of prosecution."[48]

The editor of the *Chronicle* in an article headed "Reformation in Abilene," on September 14, made some pointed remarks about the exit of the undesirables:

We are happy to announce . . . that within the last fortnight wholesome and magnificent changes have been wrought in the moral *status* of Abilene. For the last ten or twelve days almost every train eastward bound has carried away and relieved this community of vast numbers of sinful humanity. Prostitutes, "pimps," gamblers, "cappers," and others of like ilk, finding their several nefarious avocations no longer remunerative or appreciated in this neighborhood, are embracing their earliest possible convenience, by hook (mostly by *hook*) and by crook, to obtain the necessary wherewithal with which to procure passage to Newton, Kansas City, or St. Louis, where in all probability most of them will end their miserable lives in dens of shame—unless the better angel in their nature leads them to forsake the paths of sin.

Editor Wilson went on to allege that such characters had been

---

[46] Minute Book of the City Council of Abilene, *loc. cit.*, 83–85. McDonald moved on to Newton where he was appointed city marshal. It was alleged that he left town in a hurry to avoid arrest for stealing $400, but this was untrue. Early in October McDonald appeared in Humboldt, Kansas, where he arrested a man named John Williams for horse-stealing and a fellow named Wallace for stealing "four hundred dollars in cash, and a fine watch from Newtonians. McDonald appears to be a wide awake, efficient marshal." Shortly afterward he went to Kansas City where he provided the *Times* with a copy of the *Chronicle's* report of the Hickok-Coe shoot-out in Abilene. The *Times* described McDonald as "ex-Deputy Marshal McDonald," (Waldo E. Koop to the author, Nov. 28, 1961; Oxford (Kansas) *Times*, Oct. 28, 1871; Kansas City (Missouri) *Times*, Oct. 15, 1871.)

[47] Minute Book of the City Council of Abilene, *loc. cit.*, 86.

[48] *Ibid.*, 88.

"invited here by those in official position, and protected by officers whose sworn duty it is to see that the laws and ordinances are enforced." Gambling, he went on, was on the decrease because the "hells" were closed mostly for want of "business." He next attacked the City Council, but not by name, saying: "In the future, true men will be elected to office—men who will see that the ordinances are properly enforced." He then made the following statement: "It affords us no pleasure to write a word of censure against a sworn officer of the law—but when officers themselves violate, and permit its violation, it becomes the duty of the press to stand up for law and the rights of the people."

It is not clear who the "sworn officer of the law" was, but some have concluded that he meant Hickok. In view of his later praise of Wild Bill's police work, it is also possible that his remarks were directed at Carson and Norton, both dubious characters—the former a particularly obnoxious individual.

As a special policeman, Tom Carson seems to have been able to come and go as he pleased, for he appeared in Newton and served a brief period as a policeman, where he was actively disliked by the Texans. His reputation in Abilene, too, was bad, and he once threatened a man with a shotgun.[49]

Clashes between the permanent citizens of Abilene and the Texans were rare. The tracks of the Kansas Pacific served as a boundary that was respected by both sides. But there were still difficulties. The erection on the north side of a large barnlike structure to serve as a place of entertainment caused friction. An end-of-term school program was held there and the public were invited. To the consternation of many citizens, a number of Texans appeared in the audience. For a time they remained quiet, but eventually some of them became quite noisy, and Theophilus Little decided he must take a hand:

Mrs. Little and I and the two little boys, Eddie and Willie, were seated together in chairs[.] immediately in front of us were two big Texans. Each one big enough to have swallowed me whole. They became very noisy and offensive and I remonstrated with them quietly, plead[ed] with them to keep quiet. They turned and laughed at me, asking what in "h–ll" I was going to do about it anyhow. I quit talking and began to get mad, madder yet. I was young then, if not handsome. I began to think I could just whip 20 wild cats right there with a lot of Texans thrown in. They were standing up right in front of me, swearing and laughing,

49 Charles F. Gross to J. B. Edwards, Apr. 20, 1922, Manuscripts Division, KSHS.

having the biggest time in town. I lost sight and sense of everything but mad and fight[.]

I jumped up and caught one of them by the throat jammed him into his chair and choke him till he gurgled[.] In a flash I had the other huck by the throat. *You too* I yelled and choked him until his Texas tongue ran out of his mouth, jammed him into his chair and hissed into their ears, another word out of you tonight and I'll smash every bone in your bodies.

It is a wonder that I was not shot to pieces, but I just thought then that I could smash every cowboy in that big shanty. I think they thought so too for I tell you that silence reigned profound the balance of that evening.

They were so utterly astounded at the audacity and foolhardiness of the act that they were cowed and helpless. Just as the exercises closed, Wild Bill strode swiftly toward us with his wilk [silk?] hat in his left hand, his right thrown across the left breast and with a low and courtly bow to Mrs. Little, in most gracious tones said, "Mr. Little if you will allow me, I will walk home with you and your family this evening." I thanked him saying, "We would deem it an honor but not a necessity." Said he, "I think I understand this case better than you do, Mr. Little" and he went to our home with us.[50]

By the end of September the cattle season was drawing to a close, and the prostitutes, cappers, gamblers, and others began to move on to spend the fall and winter elsewhere. Many of the Texans also left town, and the few that were left decided to visit the Dickinson County Fair. The weather was bad, and many of the men were in a mood for some excitement. Among those still in town was Philip Coe, Ben Thompson's former partner in the Bull's Head Tavern. For some reason he and Hickok were bitter enemies. Some claimed it was because of the affections of a prostitute named Jessie Hazell (of whom there has been found no trace in contemporary records) or because Hickok had claimed Coe's game was crooked. Coe, it was stated, had threatened to kill Wild Bill "before the frost."[51] But the real reason for ill-feeling between these two will probably never be known.

Little information is available on Philip Coe. He was the son of Philip and Elizabeth Coe, and according to the family Bible, he was born on July 17, 1839 (his tombstone says July 18), in what was known as Coe Valley, Gonzales County, Texas, possibly ten or twelve miles from the city of Gonzales. Phil's father came from

[50] "Early Days in Abilene," typed manuscript, *ca.* 1910, copy supplied by Stewart P. Verckler.
[51] Junction City *Union*, Oct. 7, 1871.

Georgia and his real name has led to some family confusion. Documentary evidence suggests that it was originally Hattox, Haldox, or Haddox and was changed when the elder Philip left the state in a hurry for Texas, with a $750 reward on his head for murder. Part of the reward was offered by the relatives of the victim, and part by the governor of Georgia. To avoid attention or arrest, Philip changed his name to his mother's maiden name—Coe, and from then on was known as Philip Alex H. Coe.

In Texas, Philip senior became a "colonist of the Empresario Stephen F. Austin; and was awarded 4,446 acres of land in Washington County, Texas, in 1831. He was also a fast-living man."[52] During the war with Mexico in 1836, Coe is reputed to have been in command of one of the baggage trains at San Jacinto. On December 6, 1852, Philip Coe (described as "captain") was murdered by a man named John Oliver. Family sources say it was in a poker game, but the local press merely stated that Oliver "inflicted upon him four pistol shots. Coe was unarmed and could make no resistance." Ironically, his wife Elizabeth offered a reward of $1,000, to which was added $300 by the governor of Texas, for Oliver's capture and delivery to the sheriff of Gonzales County, but it is not known if she was successful.[53]

Coe's son Phil joined the Confederate Army as a young man, but after only one day of discipline (during which time he struck an officer) he deserted and made his way to Mexico. There, during the fight to help Maximilian, he met up with Ben Thompson, and the two became friends. Back in the United States he became noted as a gambler, and in 1871 he came to Abilene with Thompson.

According to family sources, in appearance he was a large man, 6 feet 4 inches tall, and weighed between 220 and 225 pounds. He had black hair which he wore in a pompadour, a mustache, but no sideburns. Men who knew Coe said he had the coldest gray eyes they had ever seen. His visits home were infrequent, and the family noted that he was not disposed to make himself sociable, and was known to lock himself away in his room and play the violin for days upon end.

Opinion of Phil Coe is mixed. During the summer of 1871 he moved to Salina for a short time and was "regarded by those who knew him as a quiet and inoffensive man."[54] To Theophilus Little

52 Mrs. Betty Plummer to the author, July 15, 1971. For additional information on the Coe family origin, I am indebted to William Peacock, Jr., who in October, 1971, interviewed Mrs. P. J. Lewis of Gonzales, Texas, on my behalf.

53 Texas State Gazette, Dec. 25, 1852.

54 The Saline County Journal, Oct. 12, 1871.

he was "a red mouthed, bawling 'thug—'plug' Ugly—a very dangerous beast," who owed him forty dollars for a bill of lumber. "I had asked him to pay and he was very abusive and I was always afraid that he would burn me out."[55]

On the night of October 5 trouble arose, ending in violence and tragedy. The town was full of Texans making the most of their last few days in the city, and they were in the mood for excitement. Little wrote

I remember the evening so well. About dusk I left my office to go to the Gulf House on my way home. I saw this band of crazy men. They went up and down the street with a wild swish and rush and roar, totally oblivious to anything in their path. It was a drunken mob. I hurried home and got my family into the house, locked the doors and told my folks not to step outside, that the town was liable to be burned down and the people killed before morning.[56]

When the mob reached The Alamo, Phil Coe drew a pistol and fired it into the air. At the Novelty bar Wild Bill heard the sound, as did others present. With him was his friend Mike Williams.[57] Telling Williams to remain where he was, Hickok hurried across the street. Making his way through the rear of The Alamo, Wild Bill pushed his way through the glass doors out front and surveyed the mob from the veranda.

He demanded to know who had fired the shot. Coe admitted that he had shot at a stray dog. Hickok cut him short and told the assembled drunks and hangers-on exactly what he thought of them. The June ordinance against firearms still applied, and he ordered them to disarm and leave town. Continued Little:

The howling mob gathered around, but Wild Bill had singled out Phil Coe, who had his gun out, but the Marshall had his two deadly guns leveled on Coe and pulled a trigger of each gun and just at that instant a policeman [Mike Williams] rushed around the corner of the building right between the guns and Coe and he received both bullets and fell dead. The Marshall instantly pulled two triggers again and two lead balls entered Coe's abdomen. Whirling on the mob his two .44 six shooters drawn on them, he calmly said, "If any of you want the balance of these pills, come and get them." Not a word was uttered, they were sobered and paralyzed. "Now every one of you mount his pony

---

[55] Roenigk (ed.), *Pioneer History of Kansas*, 36–37.
[56] *Ibid.*, 37–38.
[57] Williams has been incorrectly described as one of Hickok's deputies, but he was in fact a special deputy hired by the Novelty Theater to curb the amorous advances of the Texans toward the chorus via the stage door.

and ride for his camp and do it damn quick." In less than five minutes every man of them was on the west side of Mud Creek. Coe did not die that night, and this son of a Presbyterian Elder, Wild Bill, got a preacher out of bed and had him go to the dying gambler, Phil Coe, and pray with him and for him. . . .

The policeman [sic] whom the Marshall killed was the son of a widow of Kansas City, Missouri. He sent money to the mother to come to Abilene procured a fine burial casket, had a large funeral and shipped the body to Kansas City for burial, paying all expenses.[58]

There is no doubt that the killing of Mike Williams had a profound effect on Wild Bill. For once the *real* Wild Bill Hickok emulated his legend. Like a man possessed, he swept into the few saloons and gambling houses still in business and in no uncertain manner kicked everybody out. Those who resisted he knocked aside. Others took one look at the death in his eyes and fled. Carson and Norton did little to assist; there was no need. They merely tagged along, interested and much-impressed observers of Wild Bill's fury.

It is claimed that Williams was actually due to leave that evening for Kansas City where his wife was unwell; instead, he was shipped home in a casket for burial. "Mike Williams, the policeman who was accidentally shot at Abilene by Wild Bill," it was reported, "was buried at Kansas City last Sunday afternoon [October 14?] Wild Bill paid the funeral expenses."[59]

For Phil Coe death was not so quick. He was taken to his cottage near the schoolhouse, in the southwest part of town. As the children gathered for school next morning, they quietly though excitedly discussed the events of the tragedy, for they knew that desperate efforts were being made to save Coe's life. But it was to no avail. Late on the evening of the eighth, or early hours of the ninth, he died in great agony. His family were notified of his death and arrangements were made to have his body shipped back to Texas. The body went by rail to "Houston which was the end of the line at that time," wrote his nephew. "By the time it arrived in Houston it was in such a condition it could not be brought to Gonzales for burial."[60] The family met the train and the body was taken to Brenham for burial. The local paper remarked:

[58] Roenigk (ed.), *Pioneer History of Kansas*, 37–38.
[59] Topeka *State Record*, Oct. 16, 1871. The Kansas City directories were checked, and the 1871 edition lists an M. W. Williams as a bar-keeper (Miss Marjorie Kinney, Kansas City Public Library, to the author, Jan. 13, 1970).
[60] Claude D. Coe to the author, Jan. 11, 1971.

The remains of Mr. Phil. Coe, who was murdered at Abilene, Kansas, by a notorious character known as "Wild Bill," arrived on Monday evening last, and was intered at our city Cemetery on Tuesday morning, by his relatives and friends, with whom we deeply sympathise.[61]

As with other incidents in Hickok's career, there are two versions of what happened that night. The Texas version asserts that Wild Bill pulled two derringers on Coe and shot him in the back, whereas the Kansas story tallies with Little's and other accounts and was widely publicized. It would be remiss not to repeat the following contemporary reports of both versions. On October 12 the *Chronicle* reported:

SHOOTING AFFRAY.

TWO MEN KILLED.

On last Thursday evening a number of men got on a "spree," and compelled several citizens and others to "stand treat," catching them on the street and carrying them upon their shoulders into the saloons. The crowd served the Marshal, commonly called "Wild Bill," in this manner. He treated, but told them that they must keep within the bounds of order or he would stop them. They kept on, until finally one of the crowd, named Phil. Coe, fired a revolver. The Marshal heard the report and knew at once the leading spirits in the crowd, numbering probably fifty men, intended to get up a "fight." He immediately started to quell the affair and when he reached the Alamo saloon, in front of which the crowd had gathered, he was confronted by Coe, who said that he had fired the shot at a dog. Coe had his revolver in his hand, as had also other parties in the crowd. As quick as thought the Marshal drew two revolvers and both men fired almost simultaneously. Several shots were fired, during which Mike Williams, a policeman, came around the corner for the purpose of assisting the Marshal, and rushing between him and Coe received two of the shots intended for Coe. The whole affair was the work of an instant. The Marshal, surrounded by the crowd, and standing in the light, did not recognize Williams whose death he deeply regrets. Coe was shot through the stomach, the ball coming out through his back; he lived in great agony until Sunday evening; he was a gambler; but a man of natural good impulses in his better moments. It is said that he had a spite at Wild Bill and had threatened to kill him—which Bill believed he would do if he gave him the opportunity. One of Coe's shots went through Bill's coat and another passed between his legs striking the floor behind him. The fact is Wild Bill's escape was truly marvelous.

[61] Brenham *Banner*, Oct. 19, 1871. Phil was buried in what is now the Prairie Sea Cemetery, and his inscription, surmounted by a pair of clasped hands, reads: "Gone but Not Forgotten. Philip H. Coe, Jr., Born July 18, 1839, Died October 9, 1871." (Mrs. Betty Plummer to the author, Aug. 25, 1971.)

The two men were not over eight feet apart, and both of them large, stout men. One or two others in the crowd were hit, but none seriously. We had hoped that the season would pass without any row. The Marshal has, with his assistants, maintained quietness and good order—and this in face of the fact that at one time during the season there was a larger number of cut-throats and desperadoes in Abilene than in any other town of its size on the continent. Most of them were from Kansas City, St. Louis, New Orleans, Chicago, and from the Mountains.

We hope no further disturbances will take place. There is no use in trying to override Wild Bill, the Marshal. His arrangements for policing the city are complete, and attempts to kill police officers or in any way create disturbance, must result in loss of life on the part of violators of the law. We hope that all, strangers as well as citizens, will aid by word and deed in maintaining peace and quietness.

Another paper declared that "As a reply to the Marshal's demand that order should be preserved, some of the party fired upon him, when drawing his pistols 'he fired with marvelous rapidity and characteristic accuracy,' as our informant expressed it, shooting a Texan, named Coe, the keeper of the saloon, we believe, through the abdomen, and grazing one or two more. . . . The verdict of the citizens seemed to be unanimously in support of the Marshal, who bravely did his duty."[62]

A comparison of the foregoing and the following reports will show some remarkable differences. In Oxford, Kansas, it was alleged that "At Abilene, the untamed William, city marshal, amused himself by shooting two of his policemen." In a long report a week later the same paper declared:

THE ABILENE MURDERS.
WILD BILL KILLS TWO MEN!

We this week present to our readers the particulars of the shooting affray in Abilene briefly mentioned last week. It is stated that on the night of the fifth instant, a large party of men were drinking together in the Alamo saloon, Wild Bill and other city officials among the number, and that Philip H. Wilson [sic], one of the murdered men and the marshal seemed to be on the most friendly terms, and took a drink together just before the firing. A young man named Harding [apparently no relation to John Wesley Hardin], one of the party, was getting rather drunk, and for fear of accidents, Coe took his revolver from him, holding it in his hand. A short time after this, a pistol shot was heard, and Wild Bill went to the door and asked who fired it, when Coe said he had fired at a dog. Bill asked him what he was doing with the pistol in his hand, but before Coe could answer, a friend to one side called to him and while

[62] Junction City *Union*, Oct. 7, 1871.

his head was turned, Bill drew a pistol and fired. Coe instantly fired three shots at the Marshal from the pistol he had in his hand, but the latter dodged behind a door and escaped. Coe then fell into the arms of his friends. With a revolver in each hand, Bill then started to run down the stairs from the saloon which is in the second storey, and meeting Mike Williams at the bottom, fired a shot from each revolver, both balls passing through his body. It is said that the above are the facts in the case, and that there was no other provocation for the shooting. Coe is said to have been a kind and generous hearted man well thought of by all who knew him. He had many friends among the Texans and cattle dealers about Abilene. It is darkly hinted that avengers are on the trail and we will probably soon hear of another tragedy in Abilene.[63]

Understandably this version was popular in Texas, where Hickok was much reviled, and some reports described him as "Wild Bill, the terror of the West," a "notorious gambler and desperado."[64] One report even alleged that " 'Wild Bill,' marshal of Abilene, shot and instantly killed two of his policemen on the night of the 4th inst. This is the same man that killed Phil Coe, of this city, a few weeks ago. The gallows and penitentiary are the places to tame such blood thirsty wretches as 'Wild Bill.' "[65] An examination of all available evidence (which regrettably does not include the records of the coroner's court) indicates that Hickok's actions in quelling a mob were justified. Perhaps time will reveal evidence of the reason for the bitterness between both men that culminated in violence and tragedy. One man who believes that the Kansas version is closer to the truth than that spread over Texas is the owner of a recently discovered watch, which suggests that there were many in Abilene who supported Hickok's actions and respected him as a policeman. On the back of the watch is inscribed: "J. B. Hickok from His Friends, October 26, 1871." In the center of this inscription is engraved a six-pointed star with the legend "Marshal Abilene Kansas."[66]

The double tragedy sounded the death knell of Abilene, so far

---

[63] Oxford *Times*, Oct. 14 and 21, 1871.

[64] Austin *Democratic Statesman*, Oct. 12, 1871.

[65] Austin *Weekly State Journal*, Oct. 26, 1871.

[66] The present owner is Lou R. Mahnic, of La Salle, Illinois, who kindly allowed me to examine this watch in October, 1967. It is a key-winder with a one-quarter-carat ruby in the stem. The coin-silver case, numbered 6429, bears the name Western Watch Company Chicago, Illinois, and the movement the number 15926. The only "Western Watch Case Company" found in the city directories was listed first in 1887 and last in 1956 (Larry A. Viskochil, reference librarian, Chicago Historical Society, to the author, Mar. 22, 1968). When I asked the Hickok family about this watch, they doubted its authenticity.

as the Texans were concerned. For some time the cattlemen had been experiencing difficulties, and after the killings they became more aware of a feeling of animosity toward them from the surrounding farming population. Hickok began to receive threatening letters from Texas, informing him that his life was forfeit. Never a man to take unnecessary risks, he reinforced his armament with a shotgun (possibly the one to which Gross referred). Otherwise, he carried on as usual, making himself a familiar sight on the streets of the now quiet town.

On November 4, according to the Minute Book, Wild Bill was instructed to arrange payment of railroad fares for R. E. McLeay and his family, paupers, from Abilene to Kansas City. The same entry records that Tom Carson and "Brocky Jack" Norton were allowed fifty dollars each for police work. But a couple of weeks later Carson was in serious trouble.

It was reported that "A shooting affair occurred at Abilene, during the fore part of the week, which resulted in the wounding of John Man, a bar tender, at the hands of Tom. Carson, who was acting as policeman at the time. It is said the shot was fired without provocation. Man was struck somewhere about the hip, and is slowly recovering."[67] A special meeting of the Council was called on November 27, and "On Motion City Marshall be instructed to discharge Thomas Carson & Brocky Jack from off Police force from & after this 27th day of Nov. 1871 (carried)."[68]

Whether or not Hickok was actually in Abilene when the shooting took place and the subsequent order for him to fire his policemen was given is not known; it is reported that he was in Topeka at about this time. Much in need of a rest, the Marshal decided to have a few days off and took a train ride to the capitol. What happened during the journey is best described by the Abilene *Chronicle* of November 30:

ATTEMPT TO KILL MARSHAL HICKOK
HE CIRCUMVENTS THE PARTIES

Previous to the inauguration of the present municipal authorities of Abilene, every principle of right and justice was at a discount. No man's life or property was safe from the murderous intent and lawless invasions of Texans. The state of affairs was very similar to that of Newton during the last season. The law-abiding citizens decided upon a change, and it was thought best to fight the devil with his own weapons. Accordingly Marshal Hickok, popularly known as "Wild Bill," was elected

[67] Junction City *Union*, Nov. 25, 1871.
[68] Minute Book of the City Council of Abilene, *loc. cit.*, 105.

marshal. He appointed his men, tried and true, as his assistants. Without tracing the history of the great cattle market, it will suffice to say that during the past season there has been order in Abilene. The Texans have kept remarkably quiet, and, as we learn from several citizens of the place, simply for fear of Marshal Hickok and his *posse.* The Texans, however, viewed him with a jealous eye. Several attempts have been made to kill him, but all in vain. He has from time to time during the last summer received letters from Austin, Texas, warning him of a combination of rangers who had sworn to kill him. Lately, a letter came saying that a purse of $11,000 had been made up and five men were on their way to Abilene to take his life. They arrived in Abilene, but for five days they kept hid, and the marshal, although knowing their presence, was unable to find them. At last wearied with watching and sleepless nights and having some business in Topeka, he concluded to come here and take a rest. As he stood on the platform of the depot at Abilene he noticed four desperate looking fellows headed by a desperado about six feet four inches high. They made no special demonstrations, but when the marshal was about to get on the train, a friend who was with him overheard the big Texan say, "Wild Bill is going on the train." He was informed of this remark and kept a watch upon the party. They got on the same train and took seats immediately behind the marshal. In a short time, he got up and took his seat behind them. One of the party glanced around and saw the situation, whereupon they left the car and went into the forward car. The marshal and his friend, then, to be sure that they were after him, went into the rear end of the rear car. The marshal being very tried, sought rest in sleep, while his friend kept watch. Soon the Texans came into the car, and while four of them stood in the aisle, the leader took a position behind the marshal, and a lady who was sitting near, and knew the marshal, saw the Texan grasping a revolver between his overcoat and dress coat. The marshal's friend, who had been a close observer of the party, went to him and told him not to go to sleep. This occurred about ten miles west of Topeka. When the train arrived at Topeka, the marshal saw his friend safely on the bus and re-entered the car. The party of Texans were just coming out of the door, when the marshal asked them where they were going. They replied, "We propose to stop in Topeka." The marshal then said, "I am satisfied that you are hounding me, and as I intend to stop in Topeka, you can't stop here." They began to object to his restrictions, but a pair of 'em convinced the murderous Texans that they had better go on, which they did. While we cannot justify lawlessness or recklessness of any kind, yet we think the marshal wholly justifiable in his conduct toward such a party. Furthermore, we think he is entitled to the thanks of law-abiding citizens throughout the State for the safety of life and property at Abilene, which has been secured, more through his daring, than any other agency.[69]

The Junction City *Union's* brief account of the incident published on December 2, noted that:

Wild Bill, the Marshal of Abilene, who preserved order so admirably this year, has been dogged by Desperados from Texas for the purpose of taking his life, and but recently five of them followed him to Topeka for that purpose. But being aware of their intentions he faced them with a couple of repeaters and bade them go on their way to Kansas City rejoicing. They did so, and he still lives and moves, a terror to evil doers.

After this episode the Texans gave up their scheme to rid themselves of Wild Bill. He was getting too much publicity for one thing, and assassination was becoming a risky undertaking.

It was claimed by Charles Gross that during the summer of 1871, Jesse and Frank James and the Youngers hid out in Abilene. Hickok's price for his silence was his life, for one word from him and he would have been shot down by their many friends. Students of Jesse James have refuted the incident, which if it is fiction is odd, for Gross is usually very reliable.[70]

Early in December the friction that had been building up among the Council members reached a head. Former mayor Theodore C. Henry, at the head of a substantial number of citizens and farmers, finally persuaded the city fathers to ban the cattle trade. Henry[71] and his friends had long been against the cattle business, for they believed the future of Kansas lay not in cattle but in farming. Following experiments carried out in secret in Abilene, he developed a strain of wheat which eventually established him—he even became known as the "Wheat King of Kansas."

But Joseph G. McCoy did not fare so well. He had no written contract with the Union Pacific, who had agreed orally to construct a one-hundred-car switch and pay him up to five dollars a carload for all cattle shipped over their line. McCoy bought out his brothers in 1870, promising to pay them when he received his money from the railroad. They did not pay up and he filed suit against their

---

[69] Despite a search of the Topeka press, I have been unable to find any other reference to this incident. However, this story seems to be the basis of the legendary account which claims that eight men attacked Wild Bill on a train, that he forced them at gun point to jump off, and that several of them were killed as they hit the ground.

[70] Charles F. Gross to J. B. Edwards, Apr. 20, 1922, Manuscripts Division, KSHS.

[71] Despite the disagreements that Henry and McCoy had over the cattle trade, they were good friends. It had been McCoy who had suggested that Henry come to Abilene. Henry had been an unsuccessful cotton grower and unwilling law student before he finally found his destiny in the Kansas cowtown. (Verckler, *Cowtown Abilene*, 14.)

successors, the Kansas Pacific; in July, 1871, the Kansas Supreme Court ruled in his favor. But it was too late; McCoy was broke. He had spent vast sums of money engaging attorneys, and to meet his expenses he had had to sell his Abilene home and his interests in the Great Western Stockyards and the Drover's Cottage.[72]

Long arguments raged among the Council members over the cattle trade during that winter of 1871. Finally the following notice was approved, and copies of it were sent to Texas in February, 1872:

We the undersigned, members of the Farmers' Protective Association, and officers and citizens of Dickinson County, Kansas, most respectfully request all who had contemplated driving Texas cattle to Abilene the coming season, to seek some other point for shipment, as the inhabitants of Dickinson County will no longer submit to the evils of the trade.

Then followed a long list of signatures. The Texans took note and turned their cattle toward Newton, and later Ellsworth, Wichita, and eventually Dodge City. But nearly two months before this notice appeared, Wild Bill's position as town marshal was vacant.

The end of the cattle trade also meant the end of a need for the expensive services of a marshal of Wild Bill's caliber. On December 13 a special meeting of the City Council was called, and as Mayor McCoy was absent, J. A. Gauthie, president of the council, ordered that the meeting should be held. During the discussion a bill from Tom Carson was presented for $175 (presumably for services as a policeman) and ordered "tabled." Then came the important item on the agenda. According to the Minute Book:

Be it resolved by Mayor & Council of City of Abilene that J B Hickok be discharged from his official position as City Marshall for the reason that the City is no longer in need of his services and that the date of his discharge Take place from and after this 13th day of December A D 1871. Also that all of his Deputies be stopped from doing duty.

This brief period as marshal of Abilene was Hickok's last official act, although an item in the press stated that Wild Bill was soon to accept the position of marshal of Newton at a salary of $200 a month.[73] He never took the job and no other information is available. Several other references to his movements appeared, includ-

---

[72] Wayne Gard, The Chisholm Trail, 63. Verckler, Cowtown Abilene, 10, 51–52. McCoy later became involved in the cattle business of Newton and Ellsworth, but never repeated his early Abilene success. At various times he was a grocer, commission livestock dealer, and real-estate salesman. For many years his home was Kansas City, where he died in 1915, but he was buried in Wichita.

[73] Topeka Daily Commonwealth, Dec. 6, 1871.

ing the amusing comment that "The Ellsworth *Reporter* says it is negotiating with 'Wild Bill,' to take the position of fighting editor on its staff."[74] But Wild Bill remained in Abilene until at least the end of the year, for he was still negotiating with the Council for his last month's salary.

In Hickok's place in Abilene they hired a man for one-third his salary. The man who had, on December 12, called a special meeting to discharge Hickok, James A. Gauthie, was on motion "appointed City Marshal of the City of Abilene for the period of one month commencing this 13th day of December A D 1871, at a Salary of $50.00. On motion the same be put to vote, carried by unanimous vote of Council."[75]

That entry wrote the finale to cowtown Abilene, and was typical. Townspeople on the cattle trails made a practice of hiring a "specialist" to clean up their community; then when the job was done, they kicked them out and hired another man for less than half the salary. But in fairness to the council, they were doing what was best for the town. Wild Bill had been hired to control the Texans, and with no Texans left to control he was no longer needed.

How successful Hickok was as marshal of Abilene is a controversy in itself. He was not a professional peace officer, but he did the job he was paid for. It was his responsibility to keep the peace in a community that was largely composed of transients anxious for a good time and a little hell-raising. He put a stop to much of the rowdyism and gunplay that had marked the town's early years, and most of the Texans complied with the rules because they knew he never bluffed.

Wild Bill did not concern himself with the town's morals. The suggestion that he "cleaned up" Abilene is nonsense. He was responsible only for the protection of the citizens and their property and for seeing that the city's and state's laws were not broken—a fact fully appreciated by editor Wilson in his *Chronicle*.

However, the editor, like his readers, really knew little of what had gone on across the tracks. The respectable citizens were never well acquainted with Marshal Hickok. All they had was an impression of a very strong, conscientious man who almost single-handedly maintained law and order in an unstable, criminal-infested part of town. His methods may have pleased or irritated individuals, but by containing the violence across the tracks, he

[74] *Ibid.*, Dec. 10, 1871.
[75] Minute Book of the City Council of Abilene, *loc. cit.*, 107–108.

ensured those individuals' continued existence in reasonable peace and security.

With few exceptions the citizens of Abilene who survived the trail-driving era continued to remember Hickok in a near-heroic role, which a century later still survives. Where Abilene's star went into a decline, its cowtown era a memory, Wild Bill's was on the ascent. Abilene did much for Hickok. His brief period as the city's marshal had spread his legend down the trail to Texas and to other places. Come what may, his fame was now assured.

----◆{ 11 }◆----

The Murder of Chief Whistler

IN THE FALL OF 1872 three leaders of the Cut-off band of Oglala Sioux were shot to death. Some historians say that Wild Bill Hickok did it.

The murder of Whistler, Badger, and Handsmeller somewhere near the Republican River brought fear to the settlers. At first it was thought to be the result of a dispute between the Sioux and Pawnees over stolen ponies. As more details of the killing were revealed, and evidence piled up that white men were responsible, the army was called in to prevent a serious threat of war.

At Fort McPherson, Nebraska, Captain Charles Meinhold, commanding Company B, Third United States Cavalry, was ordered into the field to investigate the incident. He left the fort on the morning of January 7, 1873. His command consisted of two commissioned officers and fifty-one enlisted men. One of the officers was Lieutenant Frederick Schwatka.[1]

In his official report of the trek dated January 21, which also included a map, Captain Meinhold described his arrival at a Pawnee camp:

On the fourth day I reached Beaver Creek, where I found a camp of about 60 Pawnee Lodges. It appeared as if the Indians had left it a few days ago.

Following the trail, I found, on the 13th instant, Peter, the head chief of the Pawnees, in a camp near the mouth of Beaver Creek, at a place on the Republican River known as the Stockade, with about 200 of his people, the rest being in camp in different places in the vicinity. On the same evening, Peter, his son and five of his principal men, at my request, visited my camp. I told them that I had been sent out to enquire into the troubles between the Pawnees and Sioux. Peter replied that the Sioux had killed one of his men, and stolen 20 of his horses. He did not desire war, but was far from fearing it. If the Sioux would return the stolen

---

[1] Frederick Schwatka was later well known as an explorer in the Yukon and Alaska. In 1891 his book *A Summer in Alaska* was published. He was the first man to explore the Yukon River for its full length. He died at Portland, Oregon, in 1892.

horses and were willing to make peace, he on his part was anxious to live in peace with everybody. He denied that Whistler, Badger and Handsmeller had been killed by his men, and in a manner that convinced me of the truth of his statements. I told him that he must go to his reservation, and urge his claim for the recovery of the stolen horses through his proper Agent, adding, however, that I thought General Reynolds would use his best endeavors to induce the Sioux to return the horses. He replied that he would start on the 3rd day, and I believe he has kept his word. I had been informed that he intended to send his squaws home, gather all his men, and take revenge on the Sioux. They had been unsuccessful in their hunt, and were actually starving. I gave them all the provisions I could spare.

Peter asked me to allow 4 of his men to go along with me to get the stolen ponies, if the Sioux could be induced to return them. I granted his request. Having been informed by settlers on the Beaver, and more accurately by a Mr. Byon, who keeps a store at the stockade, as to the manner in which, and the parties by whom Whistler, Badger [and Handsmeller] were killed, I sent Lieut. Schwatka to the house of a Mr. Gast, on Oyster Creek, a tributary of the Republican, with instructions to obtain from him a statement, under oath, in regard to this matter, and to obtain all the evidence he could, as well as certain articles belonging to the murdered Indians, said to be in the possession of Mr. Gast. Lieut. Schwatka obtained a medal bearing the date of 1801, arm and hair rings and a bow, which were recognized by a Mr. Emmett, who accompanied my command, as the property of Whistler, and the following statement under oath:—

Personally appeared before me 2d Lieut. Fredk. Schwatka, 3d Cavalry, Saml. C. Gast, who, being duly sworn according to law, deposes and says:

I am a farmer living in Harlam County (P. O. Watson), State of Nebraska.

While hunting for buffalo at or near Whiteman's Fork on December 3d 1872, I discovered the dead bodies of three Indians apparently murdered, and under the following circumstances:

While hunting for water, I was directed by one of two men camped there hunting wolves, to a certain place toward the river, and seemed very anxious for me to follow his directions, which would have taken me about one-half mile from where the dead bodies were found. I took the course he advised me not to take, which I believe, was the best course, and after traveling about one-half mile, came upon the bodies of the Indians referred to.

There was one rather small Indian and one big Indian had his head split open, apparently by an axe—one was shot close to the heart.

I found and took from them certain articles which, with the exception of one buffalo robe, a cartridge box and an Indian saddle, are now in the possession of Lieut. Schwatka.

There were also two dead ponies. I am satisfied they were shot on the spot where found lying. One was a bay horse with a white face, and the other a roan horse. The bay was shot through the head.

I believe the bodies were brought where they were found by me, and not killed on the spot for the following reasons: There was a wagon track leading to the spot and the bodies looked as if they had been dumped there, they being stretched across each other and one was directly on his face. One of the two men watched us very intently for some time, and even went back to a higher bluff to watch us. From the direction he took when I last saw him, I inferred he went back toward the bodies. I also found some papers which I brought home and burnt. One paper commenced "The bearer," 'Whistler,' " etc., and further stated that he wanted to be peaceable with the whites etc. The Indians, I should judge, were killed about two weeks.

One of the men's name is, I believe, Jack Ralston, and belongs to what is called "Wild Bill's Outfit." He was the man who gave me the directions referred to. There was no revolvers about them when found, but a gentleman by the name of E. A. Cress took a rifle from their bodies. It was a long rifle, stocked clear up to the muzzle, large bore,—when found, I believe it was loaded.

(Signed) S. S. Gast

Subscribed and sworn before me this 15th day of January, 1873, at Watson P. O. Harlam County, State of Nebraska.

(Signed) Fred. Schwatka,
2d Lieut. 3d Cavalry.

I am convinced that Whistler and the other two Indians were killed by "Wild Bill" and his men, as stated in the above affidavit.

I regret that I was unable to go to the Sioux Camp on Whiteman's for to ascertain how the killing of Whistler by white men affected the Indians, but the epizootic disease amongst my horses crippled me so much that I only could make short marches,—I had to leave one horse at Clifford's ranche.

The settlers on Red Willow, Beaver and Republican are seriously alarmed. They certainly are without any protection, and should the Sioux turn hostile, they will be in great danger.

I respectfully enclose the map of the country I have traveled over, also my Journal.

I am, Sir,
Very respectfully,
Your obedient servant,
(Signed) Chas. Meinhold,
Capt. 3d Cavalry.
Comd'g Co. 'B'[2]

This report was then dispatched through the usual army chan-

[2] Red Cloud Documents W885, Washington, D.C.

nels to the various departments. The army admitted that there was insufficient evidence to attach the blame to anyone, but agreed that the murderers were white men. General Sheridan, after reading the report, passed it to General Sherman, with the remark: "I have frequently protested against permitting the Indians going into the country between the Platte and Arkansas Rivers, and have repeatedly called the attention of the authorities to the danger that might come from it."[3]

The "Wild Bill's Outfit" referred to by Gast was that of Mortimer N. Kress (the similarity between his name and that of E. A. Cress in the army report is interesting). A newspaper account in the early 1950's reported:

In the early spring of 1873 the country was aroused by a report that the Indians were coming to take the life of Wild Bill who was at his claim in Little Blue Township, for shooting "Whistler," chief of the Sioux. So excited were the settlers that some threatened to hang Wild Bill Kress if he could be found. All this time Bill was on friendly terms with the Indians and was in no danger although circumstances did point toward him. The story, in effect, was as follows:

In the spring of 1873, Bill was camped on the Republican River when he fell in with a man named Jack Ralston. The latter was a man with a good education who had been on the successful side of life at one time, but he had become too familiar with the bottle and had chosen to move to the wild west to reform. Bill took the man in and shared his gains with him. One day the latter part of March, Bill and his companion crossed the river while hunting in the timber. They came upon a dead mule. Shortly after that two Indians were found and they took them over the river to camp. A few days later, the weather being cold and wet, the two companions, after finishing their evening meal, saw three Indians coming into their camp. They asked for food and lodging. But Ralston, being of a somewhat kind nature, wanted to entertain them more royally and gave them a hot supper. Bill knew that the supply of coffee, sugar and salt would not last but only a few days long and, not wishing to run short, finally differed with him. The difficulty ended with Ralston being kicked out of camp. He took one of the ponies and went to some of the small trading places in the upper part of the country and there traded the pony for a plug of tobacco, a square meal and a half-gallon of good whiskey which was too freely imbibed. The result was that he told a sordid story of Bill and himself killing the three Indians who had come into their camp. At about this time Whistler was killed and one of the ponies proved to be his. Suspicion was naturally attached to Kress. Ralston could not be found. Kress was not arrested and the Indians did not attempt to kill him. In fact, Snow Flake, who took

[3] *Ibid.*

Whistler's place, thanked him for the favor he supposed Bill had done for him.[4]

The chronology of the above account is bad, but it fits in with the information given the army by Gast. It is evident that Jack Ralston sold the pony to a man named Newt Moreland. Luther North wrote to Frank M. Lockard:

I don't remember the man Kress but the story I heard of the killing of Whistler and two more Indians that were with him, was that Newt Moreland killed all of them. Mr. A. E. Allen of Freedom, Nebraska, wrote me that Moreland killed Whistler. He said, "I knew Moreland when he was a boy. He lived on the Pawnee." John Williamson . . . said when he camped at Plum Creek that Moreland came to his camp. He was riding a spotted pony which was recognized as Whistler's and he told John that he had killed Whistler, Fat Badger, and another Indian. He was nearly starved and John gave him something to eat. He said he was going to Kearney and that the spotted horse he was riding was the same horse Whistler was riding when he came to his camp on the Arickaree. Moreland lived at Kearney at that time.[5]

"Wild Bill" Kress was an interesting character. In appearance he was described as handsome, well-proportioned, graceful, and almost six feet tall, with keen blue eyes and raven-black hair, which by the time of his death had turned snow white. How he came by the name "Wild Bill" is a mystery. Born near Williamsport, Pennsylvania, on August 31, 1841, he served during the Civil War in the First Pennsylvania Cavalry. Following the war he migrated to Nebraska, where he eventually settled on the Blue River in 1870, remaining until his death on July 4, 1914. He was a controversial character. E. E. Allen, in attempting to point out that the "Wild Bill" of Nebraska was not Hickok, said he was:

. . . a man named Kress, and I believe his name was Bill . . . [who] lived in Arapahoe, before that between Arapahoe and Cambridge, and before that in Frontier County for a short time. He went around with two revolvers and a very fierce look and was called Wild Bill, and thoroughly enjoyed [it], but [when] speaking about him [he] was usually called "Wild Bill of the Blue" to distinguish him from Hickok. "Wild Bill of the Blue" had a very depressing experience on the Medicine before this. He put on a white shirt and two revolvers and rode up to the Medicine to exhibit himself to the cowboys, one revolver or none, was rulable, two announced a grandstander.

[4] Blue Hill (Neb.) *Leader*, June 20, 1952.
[5] Collection of Everett S. Sutton, Benkelman, Nebraska. Copy supplied by Paul D. Riley.

After some time, when they stopped work to eat, the cowboys lay hands on the "Wild" man and plastered his shirt, revolvers and holsters with nice fresh digested grass, and Wild William was too Wild to go on the Medicine any more.

W. B. of the B. was considered a thorough coward and finally left and I believe went back to the Little Blue somewhere south of Hastings. Ask the old timers of [if] this Wild Bill was not dark complected. There also used to be a real grandstander here, called "Texas Jack" but he was not Jack Omohundro.[6]

During the autumn of 1873 the name "Wild Bill" cropped up again in the Republican country. On August 5 the Pawnees and the Sioux had what was virtually the last battle in America between hostile Indian tribes. It went down in history as the "Battle of Massacre Canyon." J. W. Williamson, the subagent for the Pawnees at Genoa, Nebraska, who was himself in the battle, had the task of burying the dead. He wrote:

Sometime during the fall I was sent by the government to the battlefield to bury the dead. At Plum Creek station I hired a livery man named Coles to help me. We drove to Arapahoe, where I hired four more men. I recall the names of only two of them. One was the famous Wild Bill, who was murdered a few years later by Jack McCall at Deadwood. The other was Frank Martin.[7]

This "Wild Bill" was probably Kress. So far as is known, James Butler Hickok was on his way to or in New York in the autumn of 1873, to join Cody's Combination.

In more recent years, some writers have suggested that the Battle of Massacre Canyon was a reprisal on the part of the Sioux against the Pawnees for Whistler's murder. As early as February, 1873, it was reported that the Sioux were gathering in a warlike manner to avenge the deaths of Whistler and his companions at the hands of white men. Contemporary and historical records do not associate the name Whistler at all with the Battle of Massacre Canyon.[8]

Confusion caused by the mention of a "Wild Bill" in connection with the death of Whistler has led many to believe it was Hickok. One Kansas paper, endeavoring to establish Hickok's whereabouts early in 1873, remarked that the Omaha papers alleged that "he is far out on the Union Pacific railroad, where, the other morning, in a fit of pleasantry, and because they objected to drinking cold cof-

[6] E. E. Allen to Addison E. Sheldon, Nov. 7, 1929, copy supplied by Arthur Carmody.
[7] *The Battle of Massacre Canyon* (not paged).
[8] Beatrice (Neb.) *Express*, Feb. 13, 1873.

fee with him, insisting that it should be hot, he shot and killed three Indians."[9]

Perhaps the most important error was made by the late Mari Sandoz in her novel *The Buffalo Hunters*. She described how during the year 1867, Hickok and his buffalo skinner, a man named Coke, were surrounded by a Sioux war party while hunting buffalo, and but for the intervention of Whistler, a "peace" chief, both would have been killed. So humiliated by this rescue at the hands of an Indian was Wild Bill that he bore Whistler a grudge. His chance at revenge came one day when the three Indians came to his camp on the Republican and asked for coffee. When Hickok and his companions ignored them, they uncovered the tins and helped themselves. Thereupon Wild Bill opened up with his revolver and killed all three Indians. Newt Moreland was seen several days later riding Whistler's horse. Miss Sandoz makes no reference to Jack Ralston's part in the affair.

Later, on the subject of the army report, she wrote:

Folded in . . . the . . . report was a penciled account signed by Hank Clifford, trader to Whistler's band, telling of going to Hickok's deserted buffalo camp on the wagon tracks from where the bodies of Whistler and his companions were found. This has no date and no number. That Clifford was the trader with Whistler's band and had been for the past year is verified by a letter of Nov. 1, 1872, from Jno. E. Smith, C.O. Ft. Laramie, Red Cloud Document Files, 1872, Indian Bureau Records, National Archives.

In my childhood up near the Pine Ridge, S. Dak., Sioux reservation I heard the Cliffords tell the story of the news that Whistler and his companions had been found dead, and the keening and crying while men rode out to get the bodies, and others to discover what had been done. According to old Mrs. Clifford and Charles, a son, the Indians traced the wagon tracks from the bodies to Hickok's camp and reconstructed what had happened there from the blood patches and the dragging signs of the bodies, etc., much as Newt Moreland, Hickok's partner in the buffalo camp at the time, told it, and much as my father wrote it in a letter to an Albie McCormack of Brownlee, Nebr., Jan 1, 1910, from the story that the Sioux told him back in 1884. There are always rumors that Wild Bill told the story himself once up in Cheyenne to a party of guests at the home of his wife's friend, a former actress. The Hickok version is the same as Moreland's except that it made Moreland out pretty much a coward, which could be true. Nothing known of Moreland is very good.

There are a dozen accounts at least of Newt Moreland telling the

9 Topeka (Kan.) *Daily Commonwealth*, Mar. 1, 1873.

story of the killing of Whistler and his companions in their buffalo camp. All those that I traced came from the Platte region of 1873. Such old timers as Capt. Luther North and Alexander, who used to come up from the Kansas border to the Nebraska State Historical Society when I was on the staff there, said that Moreland always gave the story of the Whistler killing as the reason that he gave up buffalo hunting in Sioux country. Luther North saw Moreland riding Whistler's spotted horse up on the Platte some time after the chief was shot. . . . I asked Capt. North about Moreland and the horse, back in 1933. He verified this and the whole Wild Bill story as it works out for the serious researcher. He knew Hickok from 1861 on. Much of the life story he told me of Hickok was, of course, from hearsay. North was never much of a saloon man.[10]

If Luther North did suggest that Hickok had any connection with the Whistler killing, then this conflicts with a statement he made in 1929, when he wrote:

. . . here is the true story of the killing. there was quite a few Sioux Indians camped on the Medicine and other streams at that time and with them were several Squaw men old John Nelson the two Cliffords Hank & Monty and perhaps Al Gay. Newton Moreland and a man named Logan were camped on the Medicine somewhere near the head. I guess the three Indians Whistler Fat Badger and Handsmeller were going to Fort Mc Pherson and they sto[p]ed at Morelands camp for supper—and Moreland and Logan killed them. Morelands story was that while the Indians were eating he heard Whistler tell the other two that when they got through eating they kill the white men (Newt couldnt talk Sioux). Newt told Logan what they said and he pulled his Revolver[,] Logan did likewise. they were behind the Indians. Newt Shot Whistler in the back and Logan shot one of the other two, the third one Ran for his Gun which was leaning against a tree but Newt killed him before he got to it.[11]

There is room for considerable investigation into the alleged Clifford story, because even his own nephew was ignorant of any information connecting Hickok with the killing. He wrote:

I have herd my uncle Hank and my Father Mortimer Clifford disgus the killing of Chief Whistler and two other Indians while enroute to Fort Mcferson[.] they did all they could to find out who did the killing But to [t]heir diring [sic] days it was a mistry to them and to all of the Whites that were living in the visenity of the Medison at that time. My uncle Hank was in Charge of those Indians at that time, and it was his

[10] Mari Sandoz to the author, Nov. 3, 1956.
[11] Luther North to Dr. Richard Tanner, Mar. 3, 1929 (reproduced in *Man of the Plains*, 317).

Duity to investigate the killing[.] that is all I can tell you about it. all I have to say is that Some one made a falts [false] Report in Washington.[12]

There is some evidence to suggest that Ralston and Kress were the men responsible for the killing of Whistler and his companions. Barclay White, superintendent of Indian affairs, took the following description of the killing "from the lips of Mr. John C. Ralston":

Two Lances, the head soldier of Whistler's band, who had charge of the band while Whistler was in Washington, accompanied by two companions, came into our camp about dark. They remained until midnight. We gave them their suppers and endeavored to trade for some robes, but could not trade, and Bill said to me, "Let's freeze them out."

The fire was allowed to die out and the Indians left on two ponies— one was a white pony.

Bill says to me, "I will watch half way to morning and then wake you."

About 3 o'clock Bill caught hold of my foot and called, "Jack, get up; I don't like the looks of things." I had just got out of the blanket and got my belt on when we found that the Indians had cut the hobbles of our ponies, and we saw three on horse back, on a bank ahead of us. We dropped on our knees and fired at an Indian on a white pony, when they all hallooed, "Don't shoot any more, white man; we won't take the mules."

We followed them up, they driving the mules, for about six miles, and fired at all the noise we could hear. We couldn't see them, at all. We gave up at last, and went back to camp.

In the morning Bill says to me, "Jack, we'll go to Broadmouth's camp, and get even or die." I baked some bread while Bill rolled up the blankets. We took a pair of blankets apiece, a loaf of bread, yeast powder, can of coffee, our belts with forty rounds, and our guns.

Before we started, I left a note on a twig for Weaver [presumably a companion], if he came that way, to bring down what things we had left. We then started down the road. About three miles below camp we struck the trail of the mules, they having got away from the Indians, followed the trail for two or three miles, into the sand hills south of the road where we found the mules. We then returned to camp. Mr. Search and two sons, from Arapahoe, Mr. Smith and two sons, from Republican City, camped with us that night. In the morning we proposed to go up the river after Weaver and Graves. They would not agree, and Bill and I determined to cross the river on to Rock Creek and try our luck there for four or five days. While there [we] had sixtyfive wolf hides stolen and our dog killed. Seeing no further use in staying there, we went twenty-five miles down the river. The first night we were here (at the mouth of White Man's Fork) Whistler, Fat Badger and a warrior came into camp with

[12] Orlando H. Clifford to Arthur Carmody, Oct. 18, 1954, copy supplied by Mr. Carmody.

four ponies and a mule, called for black medicine (coffee). Bill set the coffee pot on the fire to make it for them, and put in some coffee. They wanted him to put in more. Bill then set the pot off the fire. Whistler then undertook to open the mess box and help himself to the coffe. Bill jumped onto the lid of it. The Indians then commenced talking in Sioux, not thinking we understood the language, and laid plans of how to get away with us.

Bill says:—"Jack, we have got to waltz those fellows or they will waltz us, tonight." Seeing no other remedy I told Bill, "You're running this ship, I'll obey orders if I break owners." Bill told me to sit down in the end of the wagon, take his gun in one hand and mine in the other; "when I give the signal, turn loose at the two sitting down, I'll go for the one on foot." He snapped his fingers. I turned loose at the two sitting down, and killed them in their tracks. Never made a motion. Bill turned loose at the one standing alone with his six shooter, shot him through the right shoulder. The Indian commenced pulling the cover off his gun, crying out "No good! No good!" when Bill waltzed it to him with his hatchet, and silenced him.[13]

A few days later the same newspaper reported that Superintendent White was satisfied that the killings were committed by white men, and then quoted from a statement made by J. D. Calhoun of the Franklin County *Guard* which indicated that he had little sympathy for either side:

The latest diabolical murder in Nebraska was committed by Wild Bill and a companion named Ralston, when they coolly shot three unsuspecting Indians a few weeks ago. They happened to be three leading chiefs, and now people are mad and surprised because the Indians want revenge. As long as public sentiment allows that it is no crime to kill a Sioux, just as long will there be trouble on the border.

We have little sympathy for the worthless brute of an Indian, and still less for the white man who knows no higher amusement than to brag of the number of "Indians he has lifted." One should be put on a reserve and the other in the penitentiary, and both kept within bounds on penalty of death.[14]

The most irresponsible claim to have killed Whistler came from William F. "Doc" Carver, who no doubt read the details of the killing in the press of the time and thought it good for his later show publicity. Had Carver really been involved, Ena Ballentine would have known. In her papers she makes mention of Carver (of whom more will be said later), and several references are made to

[13] Omaha *Weekly Herald*, February [not dated], 1873, Governor Robert W. Furnes scrapbooks, MS–2051, NSHS.
[14] *Ibid.*

Whistler before and after his killing. On October 8, 1872, she says that "Whistler and some of the Pawnees are apt to have a little unpleasantness 'over the River' tonight. Believe Texas Jack has gone over to see something about it." Following the murder of the three Indians, she expressed contempt for the cowardly way they were murdered, but Carver's name did not get one mention—and neither, for that matter, did Hickok's.[15]

Whistler, the Sioux chief at the center of the controversy, was not the paragon of virtue Miss Sandoz and others liked to think. As previously related, he was involved in fights with the Cavalry in 1869, and one account published in the 1890's stated that Whistler's

... name was a terror to the soldiers as well as the trappers. It is related of him that he murdered a band of emigrants near Julesburg in 1869 while holding a council under a flag of truce. This is only one of the many incidents that are recorded of his cruelty and treachury. . . . The stories of rapine and murder committed by him and his band in this country from 1865 to 1872 would if written, fill a book. He never lost an oppertunity to kill a white man and would practice any kind of deception to gain their confidence and watch for an oppertunity to shoot them unawares.[16]

It was claimed that Whistler was also responsible for the massacre of the Nelson Buck surveying party in 1869. But from about 1870, Whistler's Cut-off band of Oglala Sioux lived on the Medicine in what is now Frontier County. In the fall of 1872 the band moved to a hunting camp on the Stinking Water, where the women and children remained, while the men went buffalo-hunting on the Upper Republican.[17]

To establish or disprove any possible connection between James Butler Hickok and the Whistler killing, it is necessary to trace his movements during the year 1872.

When his job as marshal of Abilene literally collapsed, Wild Bill collected his last month's pay late in December or early in January, 1872, and moved on. According to Charles Gross, Wild Bill was on the Royal Buffalo Hunt which took place in January, 1872, held in honor of Grand Duke Alexis of Russia. But he was probably con-

15 Diary of Ena Palmer Raymonde, The Ena Palmer Raymonde Ballentine McLeary papers, NSHS. For Carver's alleged implication in the Whistler killing, see Dr. Charles R. Nordin, "Doc W. F. Carver, 'Evil Spirit of the Plains,'" NHM, Vol. X, No. 4 (Oct.–Dec., 1927), 344–51; Thorp, Spirit Gun of the West, 54–56.

16 F. M. Lockard, The History of the Early Settlement of Norton County, Kansas, 125.

17 Paul D. Riley, "Red Willow County Letters of Royal Buck, 1872–1873," Nebraska History, Vol. XLVII, No. 4 (Dec., 1966), 382; NHM, loc. cit., 350n.

fusing Hickok with Cody, who acted as scout. Among the celebrities who attended the hunt were Generals Sheridan and Custer. And noted among the Indians who accompanied the expedition were Spotted Tail and Whistler.[18] No contemporary record places Wild Bill in or near the hunt.

The first reference to Wild Bill in 1872 stated that he was in Boston:

It is said that Hacock, the scout, known in this country as "Wild Bill," is exhibiting himself to the inhabitants of Boston. Ever since his achievements were narrated in Harper's Magazine, three or four years ago, Wild Bill's star has been ascending, and now the credulous New Englanders have an opportunity to interview in person the man who has shot men down in cold blood by the scores and is as big a criminal as walks the earth. If it is a pleasure for those down-easters to welcome a gambler, a libertine and rowdy, we can furnish those of the same ilk, just as deserving, by the hundreds, from our "wicked plains." Bill is making money, showing himself, so they say. "A prophet is not without honor save in his own country."[19]

Whatever Wild Bill's activities were in the east, he soon returned west, and despite such adverse comments, was back among friends. In March he was in Colorado, where he stayed at his friend Charley Utter's[20] rooming house in Georgetown.

"Colorado Charley," as he was popularly called, had joined with Wild Bill in a freighting business in Hays in 1868 or 1869, but there are no details available, and the venture must have been short-lived. Now Charley was running a fairly profitable business, most of his customers being miners from the O. K. Mine. During March, 1872, A. D. McCanless of Wymore, Nebraska, a distant relative of David C. McCanles of Rock Creek fame, went to work in the mine and stayed at Utter's place. "Wild Bill," he recalled, "was there for six or eight weeks after I got there. He was out of work, and put in

---

[18] Charles F. Gross to J. B. Edwards, Jan. 20, 1926. The American correspondent for the London *Times* mentioned Whistler in his reports published during January and February, 1872. The Records of Fort Wallace contain a letter written by the Commanding Officer on July 8, 1873, to the Adjutant General, Department of the Missouri, stating that Spotted Tail and Two Lances were hunting and found Whistler's body. Through their interpreter they demanded "50 head of horses, $2,000 & Subsistence for one year—or Buffalo Bill (Cody) who they say killed their chief & if this demand is not conceded they will take white scalps." (Copy supplied by Arthur Carmody.)

[19] Saline County *Journal*, Jan. 18, 1872.

[20] Agnes Wright Spring, his biographer, told this writer that he spelled his name Charley and not Charlie.

most of his time playing poker. He was very pleasant, and agreeable, and never had any trouble while there."[21]

Hickok soon decided that life was too dull in a mining town and resolved to employ his talents elsewhere. "Madame Rumor," it was reported, "has it that Wild Bill is to return to Ellsworth in a few weeks, and will make this his future home. Black your boots."[22]

But he did not go there; instead he went to Kansas City, perhaps to gamble for his own profit or to work for someone else. It is believed that he stayed there with his friend the redoubtable Dr. Joshua Thorne, a prominent surgeon and well-known Wild Bill legend-builder.[23]

In 1910, Bat Masterson made the claim that when Hickok visited Kansas City, town Marshal Speers used to make him disarm, and that when the news got around

. . . every bum in town began taking pot shots at him from unsuspected places, and Bill had to go skipping past alleys and street corners, especially on dark nights, till you'd have taken him for a ballet dancer. Finally he began to feel the annoyance. In response to his protests to the authorities he was allowed to carry two derringers. Being a man of peace, he advertised the fact that he had two shots coming on the next ambitious marksman, and I never heard that any one went gunning for him any more. If he had said he had one shot ready it would have served equally well.[24]

However, it is unlikely that Bat Masterson ever met Wild Bill Hickok. His comments, although amusing, disguise a situation that is hinted at in the press of the time—that Wild Bill did have difficulties in Kansas City but not from would-be assassins. It was stated in 1876 by the Kansas City *Times*:

William spent many months in this city after he left Hays City, where he spent a season with the lamented Custer. . . . While in Kansas City he made his headquarters about the saloons on Main Street, between 4th and Missouri avenue. But becoming obnoxious to the police, and having no visible means of support, he was arrested by Marshal Speers as a vagrant. He left here and went to Clinton and Springfield, Mo., where he met with some trouble, got away with his life.[25]

[21] A. D. McCanless to William E. Connelley, Dec. 19, 1925. Original in the George Hart Collection.

[22] Ellsworth *Reporter*, Mar. 28, 1872.

[23] Dr. Thorne was an emeritus professor of medicine in the Homoeopathic Medical College, Kansas City, and lived in the city for many years. He died on June 9, 1893 (Miss Marjorie Kinney, Kansas City Public Library, to the author, Mar. 10, 1970).

[24] "A Few Scrapes," Denver *Republican*, July 17, 1910.

[25] Cited by the Omaha *Daily Bee*, Aug. 16, 1876.

The nature of Wild Bill's difficulties in Clinton and Springfield has not been established, but perhaps the writer was thinking of the Davis Tutt fight, which is the only known trouble Wild Bill had in that place. A search of other records has failed to uncover any further reference to the allegation that Marshal Speers ordered Hickok out of town. On the contrary, Wild Bill made Kansas City his unofficial home for several years, and was reported to be there as late as 1876.

As earlier related, Wild Bill was approached by Sidney Barnett in Kansas City and engaged to appear in his Buffalo Chase at Niagara Falls in August, 1872. But by September he was back in Kansas City, where he was the center of attraction in an incident that could have had serious consequences.

On September 27, Wild Bill appeared at the Kansas City Exposition or Fair. There were an estimated 30,000 people on the ground at the time; during the day a number of Texans requested the band to play "Dixie," and when some of the onlookers protested, the Texans pulled their pistols. At that moment Hickok stepped forward "and stopped the music, and more than fifty pistols were presented at William's head, but he came away unscathed."[26]

It has been claimed that Hickok also prevented the James gang from robbing the cashier at the fairgrounds. As they were making the attempt, they "were met by Wild Bill, a pistol in each hand, in such a way as to cause them to make themselves scarce instanter."[27] This was not correct. The gang robbed the cashier on September 26 and got clean away.[28]

Hickok's movements from then on are not certain, but it is believed that he spent some months in Springfield, Missouri, remaining there until the spring of 1873. All available evidence thus absolves James Butler Hickok from the murder of Whistler and his companions, and this writer is convinced that the "Wild Bill" mentioned in the army report was Kress and not Hickok. Only Mari Sandoz has ever declared that "Wild Bill's Outfit" belonged to Hickok, and her evidence (that which she was prepared to divulge) is hearsay and not factual. No real motive has been offered to suggest why a man of Hickok's ability and reputation should involve

[26] Topeka *Daily Commonwealth*, Sept. 28, 1872.

[27] J. B. Edwards, *Early Days in Abilene*, 7. It is strange that Edwards should repeat this myth, because as early as April 20, 1926, Charles F. Gross had written and advised him that Hickok was not involved (Manuscripts Division, KSHS).

[28] Frank Triplett (ed. by Joseph W. Snell), *The Life, Times, and Treacherous Death of Jesse James*, 70.

himself in an incident that could easily have led to a frontier blood-bath. Certainly, knowing as he did how the military mind worked, a man of Hickok's experience would have immediately covered his tracks to protect himself from the soldiers—and the Indians.

⟶⊰ 12 ⊱⟵

The Women

MEN FOUND Wild Bill Hickok a fascinating character, and women even more so, which is why at this point, the year 1873, it is time that something was said of Hickok's lady friends—both the gentle and the wildcat variety.

Brown Paschal, an old-time Texas cowboy, recalled Hickok in Abilene:

> He came out of Ben Thompson's Bull's Head saloon. . . . When I came along the street he was standing there with his back to the wall and his thumbs hooked in his red sash. He stood there and rolled his head from side to side looking at everything and everybody from under his eyebrows—just like a mad old bull.[1]

Nobody else ever compared Hickok to a bull, but his good looks and handsome physique did suggest to women some sort of splendid animal. "Wild Bill," recalled Elizabeth Bacon Custer, "reminded me of a thoroughbred horse." Like so many others, Mrs. Custer was fascinated by the man. She went on:

> Physically, he was a delight to look upon. Tall, lithe, and free in every motion, he rode and walked as if every muscle was perfection, and the careless swing of his body as he moved seemed perfectly in keeping with the man, the country, the time in which he lived. I do not recall anything finer in the way of physical perfection than Wild Bill when he swung himself lightly from his saddle, and with graceful, swaying step, squarely set shoulders and well poised head, approached our tent for orders. He was rather fantastically clad, of course, but all that seemed perfectly in keeping with the time and place. He did not make an armoury of his waist, but carried two pistols. He wore top-boots, riding breeches, and dark blue flannel shirt, with scarlet set in front. A loose neck-handkerchief left his fine firm throat free. I do not at all remember his features, but the frank, manly expression of his fearless eyes and his

[1] Eugene Cunningham, *Triggernometry*, 249.

222

courteous manner gave one a feeling of confidence in his word and in his undaunted courage.[2]

In recent years it has been suggested that Mrs. Custer and Wild Bill conducted a love affair of several years' standing, but discussions with Custer experts, who have refuted the allegation, lead this writer to the conclusion that such allegations are untrue. There is some suggestion of a correspondence between them, but the evidence is not conclusive.

Naturally the impression which Wild Bill made on women did not extend to his male acquaintances. In fact his long hair and colorful dress seemed pretty effeminate to one man of a later generation, who even doubted that he was a man at all. Stuart Henry, the younger brother of the erstwhile Mayor of Abilene, noted:

In singular contrast to all we have said concerning his distinguished title to celebrity as a pistoleer, there seemed, odd to remark, his hermaphroditism. He suggested a southern type, though of New England strain. In looks and bearing he appeared feminine. He conducted himself as if courting this confusing, epicene pattern. Like his origin and manner of dueling, his looks surprised one. That softly rounded contour, that rather angelic countenance, were quite the opposite of the thin, rawboned Texas model. As his chest and hips measured large, he had, with his narrowly belted waist weighted by its brace of pistols, rather a female figure.

And, increasing his remarkable feminine pulchritude or resemblance to a Greek hermaphrodite, there should be noted, of course, his long hair around the shoulders of his white shirt. Long hair marked frontier men since the earliest day of the trappers. They had no conveniences for properly cutting locks. In fact, these constituted a protection from the weather and added warmth to the body in a life where overcoats provided a small feature.[3]

It should be pointed out that Stuart Henry was too young in 1871 to have noticed Hickok in such detail or appreciate the meaning of half the words he used. Doubtless his opinion was influenced by others who were baffled by the enigmatic Wild Bill Hickok.

The story of Mary Logan might also raise a question concerning Hickok's masculinity. Mary was a half-blood Sioux, so the legend goes, who met Wild Bill through her brother Indian Joe during the latter part of the fall of 1865. She fell madly in love with him

2 *Following the Guidon*, 160–61.
3 *Conquering Our Great American Plains*, 288.

and accompanied him on several hunting trips. J. W. Buel, in referring to this relationship, makes the following statement:

Notwithstanding this truly remarkable intimacy, in many particulars equally close as the most devoted man and wife, Bill always declared that the girl never lost her virtue, that her honesty was almost phenomenal, for she would readily have sacrificed her life rather than have forfeited the jewel of her chastity.[4]

Either Wild Bill did not appreciate the value of Mary's "jewelry" at this time, or Buel was pandering to Victorian prudery. The whole story sounds like a ridiculous fabrication. However, it is interesting to note that the name Logan is used, for the mother of Hickok's Kansas sweetheart, Mary Owen, was descended from a family named Logan. A coincidence perhaps, but only Buel could explain any possible connection.

The pulp magazines, seeking the sensational, have eagerly seized such episodes and taken them as complete fact. But the most cursory reading by any researcher will reveal that the great divergence of opinion regarding Wild Bill's looks and mannerisms depends on whether the writer of his time (or later) was a friend or an enemy. In this age a favorite adjective is "homosexual." There is absolutely nothing to show that Wild Bill was in any way inclined in this direction.

Mrs. Custer and others have described how, when he was at Hays City, Wild Bill was eagerly sought out by visitors, especially the ladies, and it has been alleged that trains made special or extended stops for this purpose. Among the mass of real and imaginary "recollections" there exists the following amusing anecdote by an unknown writer who claimed to have known Hickok in Hays:

HOW "WILD BILL" WAS CAPTURED
[From the *Chicago Tribune*]
I first saw Wild Bill in 1867, at Hays City, Kansas, a town which at that time, for general roughness, had no parallel on the plains. . . . a somewhat ludicrous incident occurred while he was holding the office of Marshal. . . . Hays City was a point from which the buffalo were easily accessible, many [excursion parties] . . . came there. At such times it was customary for the people of the town to gather at the depot upon the arrival of the train, to view the wealth and fashion of the East, as well as to enjoy the laughable incidents that invariably arose. Upon one occasion of this kind, among the sight-seers, was Wild Bill; his peculiar

[4] *Heroes of the Plains*, 86–87.

dress, fine form—ornamented with belt and revolvers—and long, waving hair, made him the center of attraction of a crowd of eager people who surrounded him. Presently a fashionably dressed young lady—an Ohio girl—with pretty face, and eyes that ought to capture anybody, ascertained that the handsome personage was no less a man than Wild Bill. Bent upon his destruction, she made her way to where he stood, and discharged her weapons about as follows: "Are you Wild Bill the Harper's Monthly tells about?" The astonished scout bashfully replied, "I believe I am." The mischievous eyes surveyed him complacently from head to foot, while their owner laughingly said, "Are you? Why my papa told me to come out here and marry some great man like you." The effect was wonderful, and for once in his life the man who had faced death almost time without number, and who could look into the muzzle of a "Colt's army" in the hands of an assailant without a quiver, was thoroughly frightened, and, too, by the harmless weapons of a pretty woman. Pistols were of no use in such an engagement, and to steal away and "blush unseen" was impossible. So, completely vanquished, he stood like the rural youth at his first "sparking," vainly trying to hide his feet and hands, until, tired of questioning a victim too overcome to answer, she bounded away to tell of her capture, and perhaps to find other "sons of the border" to conquer.[5]

One affair that was not platonic was that between Wild Bill and a woman called Indian Annie. Here the evidence becomes more reliable, although this woman has always posed something of a problem to historians. At one time it was believed that Wild Bill lived with her in Ellsworth during 1873, then deserted her and went east, leaving her with a small son. This is not true. His association with the woman took place in 1867. Whether or not she was the "wife" referred to by the press of the time is not certain, but it is known that in 1867 she lived in a small shack at the back of the Grand Central Hotel in Ellsworth, supporting herself mainly by doing odd jobs at the hotel and taking in washing. Hickok found something in her charms to attract him and spent some weeks with her on and off before drifting away, and there is nothing to prove that they ever met again. She was always referred to as "Mrs. Wild Bill Hickok," even though she did marry a man named Ben Wilson. They had one daughter, Birdie, and when Wilson died, Annie supported the two of them by doing odd jobs and fortune-telling. Annie died in the poorhouse in 1883, and the daughter was adopted by a man named Ben Spurgin.[6]

[5] Jefferson City *Daily Tribune*, Sept. 3, 1876. It has not been established from which issue of the Chicago *Tribune* this item was quoted.

[6] George Jelinek, *The Ellsworth Story* (pages not numbered).

There is a remarkable letter written by William E. Connelley on January 21, 1926, to Mrs. Ed Berry, Palacios, Texas, a copy of which is preserved in the Connelley Collection at the Denver Public Library. Explaining that Hickok had an Indian wife in Ellsworth, he went on:

. . . she had two children a boy and a girl. When she was unable to longer work and support her children she gave them homes with farmers near the Elk Horn. A man named Reuben Sparks furnished a home for the boy. My information is that he died at the age of fourteen. I have not been able to find the name of the person who furnished a home for the girl. I think you must be the girl, and I wish you would write me fully concerning your mother and her marriage to Wild Bill.

No reply to that letter has been found, but an Ira E. Lloyd informed Connelley that he knew "Indian Anna" at Ellsworth, and that she lived in a small house north of the old courthouse, where she took in sewing and washing. She had a small daughter whom the locals denied was Hickok's. This child later went to Oklahoma. Lloyd added that he knew her real father but he did not disclose his name.

At the age of eighty-six, the late Mrs. Bessie Beatty set down her childhood recollections of Annie:

In 1879, when a child eight years of age, I came with my parents, brothers, and sisters from the state of Iowa to the new little town of Ellsworth, Kansas. This was a newly settled country, windswept, treeless prairie, wild and desolate, compared to the wooded country with abundant fruit and beautiful flowers of the home I had lived in. Some years previous to this I was told the settlers had been in danger from the attacks of Indian Tribes.

While attending school, a young classmate asked me to go with her to the cabin where Mrs. Wild Bill Hickok lived, to watch her tell fortunes with cards. My young friend told me that she was an Indian woman called Indian Annie. I said, "No, I can't go with you, I'm afraid of Indians." She assured me that there were no other Indians there so I went to the little cabin where Indian Annie lived with her little daughter and stood in the doorway watching her tell fortunes.

Shortly after this Indian Annie and her little child went to live in the Country Home for destitute people where they lived until their death. They were laid to rest in the cemetery connected with the County Home.[7]

Although Mrs. Beatty was not aware of it, Birdie survived her mother. And so passes Indian Annie from the Hickok scene.

[7] Mrs. Bessie Beatty to the author, via George Jelinek, May 2, 1957.

Perhaps the most famous of the alleged Wild Bill consorts was Martha Jane Cannary—better known as Calamity Jane. Of all the women associated in any way with Wild Bill, she had the least to do with him, yet she is always spoken of in the same breath when Hickok's women friends are mentioned.

Portrayed as a dauntless buckskin-clad heroine of the Old West, Calamity Jane competes in legend with all the accepted heroes. She was said to be able to outshoot, outshout, and outswear most men—although contemporary evidence does little to substantiate this portrait.

Strangely, very little is really known about this remarkable woman. For instance, it has never been satisfactorily settled when and where she was born. The inscription on her tombstone in the Mount Moriah cemetery in Deadwood, South Dakota, reads simply: "Calamity Jane, Mrs. M. E. Burke. Died August 1, 1903. Aged 53 yrs."

This would place her year of birth as 1850; but in a little pamphlet published in 1896 entitled *Life and Adventures of Calamity Jane, by Herself*, she states that she was born on May 1, 1852, in Princeton, Missouri. The census for 1860 of Mercer County, Missouri, of which Princeton is the county seat, reveals that there were several families by the name of Conarray, including one with two children, a sixteen-year-old girl M. J. (Martha Jane?), and a child of seven.[8] Her own insistence that her real name was Martha Jane Cannary—without the second r—must be accepted as correct. The census writer undoubtedly used phonetic spelling. If, on the other hand, this *was* the future Calamity Jane, then her date of birth would be 1844.

Remaining in Princeton until 1865, the family then moved to Virginia City, Montana, taking five months to make the journey. From then on she disappears for a while, turning up in Wyoming in the early 1870's. Her appearance in the Fort Laramie area was recalled by John Hunton, who wrote:

About the time of the first appearance of Calamity Jane in this part of the country . . . in the fall of 1873 E. Coffey and Cuny started a large trading outfit five miles west of Fort Laramie on the north side of the Laramie River, where they carried on quite an extensive business selling goods, running a saloon and general road ranch.

In 1874 business got very slack with them and they decided to add new attractions, and for that purpose they constructed eight two-room

[8] Clarence S. Paine, "Calamity Jane—Man, Woman . . . Or Both?" The Westerners' *Brand Book* (Chicago), Bound Vol. II (1945–46), 77.

cottages to be occupied by women. They sent to Omaha, Kansas City and other places and in a short time had their houses occupied by ten or more young women all of whom were known as sporting characters.

Among this bunch was "Calamity Jane" who was of the type generally given her by magazine writers and newspaper correspondents. Her achievements have been very greatly magnified by every writer I have ever read, for she was among the commonest of her class. She seldom ever carried a rifle when riding horseback from place to place, and I do not think I ever saw her with both rifle and pistol. Her one redeeming trait was that she seldom spoke of what she had done or could with gun or pistol. I have no recollection of ever seeing her shoot at any object but I have seen her fire her pistol into space.

I am not sure when I first saw her, but I think it was in 1875, about the time Col. Dodge was getting ready to go to Jenny's Stockade. At that date my house was at Bordeaux, 27 miles from Fort Laramie on the Cheyenne road. My ranch was a general road ranch and place of entertainment. . . . Jane often stopped at my place, especially during the years of 1876, 1877 and 1878, while the Cheyenne and Black Hills stage coaches were in full swing, but I seldom ever saw her.

She went out with the Dodge expedition in 1875 and remained with the expedition until detected when she was ordered to remain with the wagon train until the train returned to Fort Laramie, which was in a short time. The wagon master, old Jim Duncan, demurred at the order, but saw to it that she went back to Fort Laramie.

She then resumed her old life at the Cuny and Coffey ranch and other places of similar character at Fort Laramie and Fort Fetterman until the organization of General Crook's army in May, 1876, when she and three other women of the same character were smuggled out with the command and remained with it until found out and ordered back.

After the battle of Rose Bud, in June, 1876, Crook's army lay idle on Goose Creek and Tongue Rivers until joined by General Merritt with the 5th Cavalry in July. Soon after being joined by General Merritt, General Crook ordered his extra wagons to be sent back to Fort Fetterman with the sick and wounded, and I know Calamity Jane was with it for I saw her on the way up to John Brown Ranch the same day the train arrived in Fetterman. She soon left Fetterman and I do not think returned that year, but she was in Fetterman in the spring of the year 1877 for a short time.[9]

No one has ever been definite about her appearance. One account says that she had blue eyes and black hair, and another that she had brown eyes and black hair. From her photographs she appears a large woman in build, not overly tall, with harsh, rawboned features. In fact she could almost have passed as a man. The theory

[9] Ed. by L. G. ("Pat") Flannery, *John Hunton's Diary*, II (1876–77), 109–11.

has been put forward that she was the victim of what medical science would call pseudohermaphroditism. This theory was evolved by Clarence S. Paine, who wrote:

I am fully cognizant of the errors in judgment which may derive from a too casual acceptance of the presence of this condition—a condition which in itself has not been finally defined by science and medicine. Moreover, in the absence of records of medical examinations it will remain impossible to prove the existence of any such disorder. On the other hand if we can, from such evidence as may be available—even circumstantial evidence—establish some semblance or proof, we shall have something which will serve to aid in evaluating the many deeds and misdeeds credited to Calamity.[10]

Obviously the woman's passion for male clothing and male company would indicate an unusual personality. Yet the female side of Jane never completely disappeared. It is claimed that during an epidemic of smallpox in Deadwood, it was Jane who bore the brunt of the nursing, for which the miners were eternally grateful.

Even the origin of the name "Calamity Jane" is in doubt. Jane's version given in the pamphlet is typical. Describing an Indian outbreak in Goose Creek, Wyoming, in 1873, she says that Captain Egan [James Egan of Fort Laramie?] was ordered out to quell the Indians. During the skirmish the captain was injured, and Jane brought him back to the fort. On recovery, Captain Egan called her "Calamity Jane, heroine of the Plains." Unfortunately the facts do not support the story. Egan heard it years later and denied it as did men in his command, and one writer has discovered that the only words that ever passed between them were when she was ordered to leave the soldiers alone because she was a bad influence on them.[11]

It was claimed in the 1920's that Martha Jane received her title from "Bill Nye in his Laramie Boomerang in the early days."[12] This does not settle the issue, for there were several "Calamity Janes." This, while adding confusion to the existing web of fable, does explain how she came to be credited with twelve husbands.

The alleged association between Wild Bill Hickok and Calamity Jane has been debated by historians for years. The hero-worshiping fraternity have steadfastly maintained that Wild Bill would have died rather than share a bed with Jane. The debunkers maintain

[10] Paine, "Calamity Jane—Man, Woman . . . Or Both?" *loc. cit.*, 79.
[11] Andrew Blewitt, "Calamity Jane," The English Westerners' *Brand Book*, Vol. V, No. 2 (Jan., 1963), 4.
[12] Lead *Call*, Aug. 9, 1927.

that Hickok was sexually promiscuous. Books written about Jane have done little to clarify the situation, for few of the writers have bothered to get beyond published material.

But the insistence that there *was* something between Wild Bill and Jane was finally brought to a head in 1941. On June 15 of that year, the Billings, Montana, *Gazette* published a story about a lady calling herself Jean Hickok McCormick, who claimed to be the daughter of Calamity Jane. To support this claim she produced a "confession" purportedly written by Jane. This was included in an old photograph album, which had been used as a diary. Its contents consisted of a series of letters written to the daughter in diary form. In the confession Jane said that she had been married twice, the first time to James Butler Hickok, a *cousin* of James Butler "Wild Bill" Hickok, who had also been employed in government service, and the second time to Clinton (she called him Charley) Burke, in 1891. According to the original *Gazette* story, Jane claimed that the cousin of Wild Bill was the child's father. This would seem to have settled the issue, but some odd things began to happen, once Mrs. McCormick's story received publicity.

The diary has undergone some changes. Calamity no longer states that the Hickok she married was a cousin, but *the* Wild Bill Hickok. To substantiate this claim, there is a wedding certificate— at least that is what it is called. It is in fact a page torn from a Bible. Her story goes on to state that in 1870 she warned Wild Bill of an impending attack by some desperadoes, tended his wounds, and ended up by falling violently in love with him. Hickok responded, and they decided to get married. On their way to Abilene they conveniently met the Reverends W. F. Warren and W. K. Sipes. The certificate reads as follows:

Sept. 1, 1870

ENROUTE TO ABILENE, KANSAS

I, W. F. Warren, Pastor not having available a proper marriage Certificate find it necessary to use as a substitute this Page from the Holy Bible and unite in Holy Matrimony—Jane Cannary, age 18. J. B. Hickok—31

Witnesses

Carl Cosgrove Abilene, Kansas

Rev. W. K. Sipes Sarasville, Ohio

Tom P. Connel Hays City Kansas.

This certificate has, apparently, appeared in several versions. Paine reports one dated 1873, and the Reverend Warren is alleged to be the same gentleman who later married Hickok and Mrs. Lake in 1876. A comparison of the handwriting on the marriage certificate issued to Hickok and Mrs. Lake with that shown on a photostat of the Bible certificate shows them to have been written by different hands, and none of the witnesses to the 1870 certificate have been traced. Robert Smith, Sarahsville, Ohio, informed the writer that a search of the church and other records revealed no trace of the Reverend Sipes. "But," he added, "the church records did not go back before 1890."[13]

The story of Jean Hickok McCormick is a strange one. She said she was born on September 25, 1873, at Benson's Landing, now Livingston, Wyoming. An English sea captain, James O'Neil of the good ship *Madagascar* owned by the Cunard Steamship Company, arrived and befriended Calamity, who had just given birth to the girl. When the mother and baby were fit to travel, they journeyed by ox team to Omaha, Nebraska, thence by train to Richmond, Virginia, where O'Neil and his wife adopted the baby and took her to England. When Calamity died, all of her papers and the diary were handed over to Captain O'Neil (some say by Reverend Sipes), and on his death in 1912 they came to the daughter. She kept them secret, even when she was married to a Robert Burkhardt. By accident, he found the diary and because of it divorced her. Then in France, during World War I, she fell in love with a young airman named Ed McCormick. They met in the hospital where she was serving as a nurse, and he was desperately ill from wounds received in action. They were married on Armistice Day, 1918; but forty minutes after the ceremony, he died, a matter of hours before the "cease fire" was sounded.

Back in the United States her movements are obscure. She never married again and would probably have disappeared entirely if she had not applied for an old-age pension from the United States government. To support her story she presented the diary and confession as evidence. The Columbia Broadcasting System's show "We the People" took an interest in her story, helped her to get her pension, and furthered her new-found fame. Mrs. McCormick appeared in several rodeos and shows, including the "Wild Bill Day" parade in Abilene. She died on February 21, 1951.

Joseph "White-Eye Jack" Anderson, who claimed to have known Jane when he was in the Black Hills, expressed his opinion:

I don't believe it. Of course there were several years in which I did not know about Bill's doings, nor those of Jane. . . . The last time I saw her

13 Robert Smith to the author, Oct. 25, 1958.

was in October, 1879, at Jack Bowman's ranch at Hat Creek. I was then leaving the Hills for Leadville. She was drinking at Jack's bar, and said: "Boys, I am married to George now, and am living a clean life." She was married to George Cosgrove, one of the men who came into the Hills with her ... from Fort Laramie.[14]

No further mention of Cosgrove has been found; neither is it known if such a marriage did take place.

There is no authenticated specimen of Calamity's handwriting known to exist which could be used as a comparison to that in the alleged diary. Therefore the statement that government experts examined the document and said it was genuine is nonsense. But it exists; we cannot deny that. Whoever compiled the diary originally was cunning, but not very clever.

For instance, I checked with the Cunard Steamship Company concerning the redoubtable Captain O'Neil, and was informed: ". . . no ship of the name of *Madagascar* was in our service at any time, nor has there been a Captain O'Neil among Cunard captains."[15]

The text of the diary is prepared for all sorts of questions, such as the insistence by Anderson and others that Hickok and Calamity ignored each other in public. Says Jane:

We met one day, and we both found we still loved each other better than ever. I forgot everything when I was near him. No one else ever knew—if anyone hinted such to me, I hauled off and knocked them down. He denied it also; we both lived a life of lies. He was meant for me, not Agnes Lake, or he would have stayed with her instead of coming back to me.[16]

[14] Correspondence with the late Raymond W. Thorp, who copied a number of excerpts from letters he had received from Anderson. It is interesting to note that the name Cosgrove (in a different context) is also mentioned by Anderson.

[15] Cunard Steamship Company to the author, Dec. 12, 1957. In a further attempt to unravel the mystery of the *Madagascar*, I enlisted the aid of Mr. T. M. Dinan of the Shipping Editors' Department of Lloyd's Intelligence Department, London, and together we checked the Lloyd's Registers for 1873–77 and 1893–96, both dates associated with Calamity's movements in connection with O'Neil. In 1893 she is alleged to have sailed in this vessel to Liverpool, England, as the guest of O'Neil. Two *Madagascars* were found, one French and the other English. The French vessel was on the Marseilles-Reunion run, and the English vessel was the one which left New York in June and sailed for Calcutta via Philadelphia, returning to New York on March 31, 1894. She then left for Java. She did not sail to Liverpool. The Captains' Register did not show Calamity Jane's James O'Neil. The only James O'Neil found died in Cape Town in 1918. The alleged photograph of O'Neil, which was published in a spurious "life" of Jane some years ago, brought the comment from Cunard: "The photograph . . . is one of Captain A. C. Greig, who served with the Cunard Line from 1906 until 1945." (Cunard Steamship Company to the author, Dec. 8, 1960.)

Calamity also states that she divorced Wild Bill in order that he might marry Madame Lake—but no papers have been produced to prove this.

There are many more discrepancies. As long ago as 1944, Clarence Paine suggested the diary was a fake.[17] Today that conclusion must stand.

This writer is uncertain how involved Mrs. McCormick may have been in the scheme to deceive, or if she honestly believed in the diary's authenticity. But facts are facts. Both the commercial and governmental bodies who so easily accepted the lady's claim and the documentation deserve some censure for not investigating and repudiating what was without doubt the most ingenious Western history fraud of the 1940's.

The final comment must surely come from the Hickok family itself. Ethel Hickok told the writer that in the 1940's the late Martha Dewey, a niece of Wild Bill, who had read the stories appearing in various newspapers, approached the Billings *Gazette* and advised them that the lady was an imposter. Furthermore, after a lot of cross-questioning, Mrs. McCormick finally admitted that she had not been born until 1880—four years after Wild Bill died!

Hickok's disappearance from the scene in 1876 did not seem to bother Jane much. She bummed her way around the frontier for the next twenty-seven years. It is claimed that she married Clinton Burke or Burk, in August, 1885. She first met him in El Paso, Texas, and a daughter was born on October 28, 1887. The child was later taken to a convent and disappeared. Burke also disappeared from her life in 1896 when he skipped out of Deadwood after embezzling his employer's money while employed as a hack driver.[18]

Despite repeated requests to be left alone, Jane's final years were not happy, and in 1903 her health failed. She was taken ill at Terry, South Dakota, and the proprietor of the Calloway Hotel took care of her. "I'm ailing—I guess I'm ready to cash in," she said. The man at first ignored her condition for he thought she was on another drunk, but later he became alarmed and sent for a doctor. News traveled fast, and with the doctor came friends from Deadwood. She grew weaker, resisted treatment, and finally became delirious, talking of a daughter who was married and living in North Dakota (the one placed in a convent?). Then on August 1

[16] Kathryn Wright, "The Real Calamity Jane," *True West*, Vol. V, No. 2 (Nov.–Dec., 1957), 23.

[17] Don Russell to the author, Dec. 3, 1957. Mr. Paine took the diary to one of the early meetings of the Westerners' organization in Chicago in 1944.

[18] Blewitt, "Calamity Jane," *loc. cit.*, 7.

she died. The cause of death was given as inflammation of the bowels, aggravated or induced perhaps by prolonged overindulgence in alcohol.[19]

Even in death Calamity Jane was not left in peace. Romantics among her friends (and, it is alleged, others with a macabre sense of humor) thought it a good idea if she could be buried next to Wild Bill in Mount Moriah cemetery, claiming that her last wish was "Bury me next to Bill," and this they did (although her grave is twenty feet from Hickok's). Not content with that, they changed the date of her death to a day later—August 2, the twenty-seventh anniversary of Wild Bill's murder.

Thus, the two were linked together in a relationship in death which had never existed in life.

But if Calamity Jane's marriage to Wild Bill was a fabrication, at least the same cannot be said of his marriage to Mrs. Agnes Lake Thatcher.

The story of this remarkable person would in many respects justify a book-length study. As a young woman she won international renown as a horsewoman, a tightrope walker, and for her performance as "Mazeppa."

However, her origin is in doubt. It was claimed by J. W. Buel, who interviewed her in September, 1880, that she was born in Cincinnati, Ohio, in 1832, and her maiden name was Thatcher. Agnes herself merely stated: "I was born the 24 of August 1832."[20] Wilstach, on the other hand, says that she was born in Alsatia in 1826, and her real name was Agnes Mersman. This latter information is corroborated by a press report published early this century which stated: "She was born in Doehme, Alsace, in 1826. Her parents' name was Mersman. She was about three when they came to this country and settled in Cincinnati."[21] A search of available records in Cincinnati has revealed that in 1840 there was a Henry Mersman, a "clerk from Germany" working at a store in town, but no mention was found of a daughter named Agnes. Several families named Mersman and Mersmann have been found, but so far no reference to an Agnes has been uncovered. She told Mrs. Hickok that "I have one Sister and One Brother in St. Louis[,] my Sister is heer [Cincinnati]."[22]

19 *Ibid.*, 8.
20 Agnes Lake Thatcher Hickok to Mrs. Polly Butler Hickok, Apr. 26, 1876, original in the possession of Ethel Hickok.
21 New Jersey *Mirror*, Aug. 31, 1907, copy supplied by William B. Secrest.
22 Original in the possession of Ethel Hickok.

(a) William A. Hickok, the father of Wild Bill, about 1850.

(b) Polly Butler Hickok, the mother of Wild Bill, from a portrait believed made in the early 1860's.

(c) Lorenzo Butler Hickok, brother of Wild Bill, from a portrait made in the mid-1860's.

This cover illustration from *DeWitt's Ten Cent Romances*, which fea-
tured the first dime-novel story about Wild Bill, was taken from the
February, 1867, issue of *Harper's New Monthly Magazine*, where it had
been used to depict the "McCanles Massacre."

In the second Wild Bill adventure to be published by DeWitt, the illustration is more typical of the period.

Samuel Strawhun, onetime Army teamster and courier, who caused a
riot in John Bitter's Beer Saloon in Hays City and was shot dead by Wild
Bill when attempting to restore law and order. From a rare family
tintype never before published.

Agnes Lake Thatcher, about 1871. She married Wild Bill five months before his death and mourned him until her own, thirty-one years later.

Reproducible copies of this old photograph are rare. The three center figures are Wild Bill Hickok, Buffalo Bill Cody, and Texas Jack Omohundro. The end figures have been variously identified, but it is believed that the man seated at Hickok's feet is Colorado Charley Utter.

Deadwood, Dakota Territory, about 1876, as photographed by Stanley J. Morrow.

Wild Bill's first grave, from a photograph made about 1876–77.

According to her son-in-law Gil Robinson and other sources, Agnes lived with her family in Cincinnati until her sixteenth or seventeenth year, when a circus came to town. Robinson says it was the Robinson and Eldred Circus, while other reports suggest that it was the Spalding and Rogers Circus.[23] With the circus was a young clown named William Lake Thatcher who, for theatrical reasons, dropped the "Thatcher" from his name and became plain Bill Lake. One day he saw Agnes swinging in the yard of her family home, and it was a mutual case of love at first sight.[24]

The couple ran away and, despite many setbacks, were finally married in the little town of Lafayette, Louisiana, some ten miles from New Orleans. Soon after the marriage Bill Lake left his wife in New Orleans while he joined the Rich Circus for a winter season in Mexico. This was a bare six years after the fall of the Alamo, and even then Mexico and the United States were boiling up for the war of 1846–48, and *Americanos* were not at all popular. The Mexican authorities closed the show and confiscated the animals and equipment. Lake barely avoided capture by hiding in a friendly priest's cellar. He arrived back in America with no money. He and Agnes then decided to return to Cincinnati to face the girl's parents, who were still none too pleased about their whirlwind romance and runaway marriage. Then came the problem of a career for both. For some time they tried various theatrical companies but had no success; then they heard that the Rich Circus was being reorganized. They stayed with the show for two years before moving on to join the Spalding (or Spaulding) and Rogers' Floating Palace, where they remained for eleven seasons. During this period the couple were blessed with a child. "My Daughter Emma was Born the 22d of February[,] Washingtons Birth Day; only not the same year," wrote Agnes, "she was Born in 1856."[25]

The family then returned to Lake's old show, the Robinson and Eldred Circus, and stayed with it until the close of the 1862 season. During the fall of that year Agnes got the chance to go to Europe, where she appeared in shows in a number of Continental cities in her role as "Mazeppa," acting the German version.

Back in America, the Lakes joined forces with John Robinson, and he and Bill Lake became partners, but it did not last long. Bill and Agnes broke with the Robinson circus and formed one of their own. Their young daughter showed the same talents as her mother

23 Gil Robinson, *Old Wagon Show Days*, 127. New Jersey *Mirror*, Aug. 31, 1907.
24 Robinson, *Old Wagon Show Days*, 127.
25 Original in the possession of Ethel Hickok.

and was soon an accomplished equestrienne, joining her parents in the ring.

Agnes Lake was a fearless woman, skilled as a dancer, lion-tamer, and "queen of the high wire." Largely through her efforts the show was a success. She had the honor of performing before the Emperor Wilhelm at the Old Victoria Theater in Berlin. So pleased was he with her performance that he gave her an autographed letter of thanks. She was a fairly well educated woman and was able to speak several languages.

The Lake show was a success wherever it went. Then tragedy struck. On August 21, 1869, at Granby, Newton County, Missouri, Bill Lake was shot "by a man named Killyou, and expired in a few moments. Killyou refused to pay admittance to the show, and was ejected by Lake, but returned in a short time, and seeing Lake near the entrance, drew a revolver, and shot him through the body near the heart. In the excitement, Killyou escaped, and $1,000 reward is offered for his arrest."[26]

Jack or Jacob Killian was captured and sentenced to only three years in the state penitentiary. He later met his death at the hands of a man named Bill Norton, a former sutler's clerk in the Civil War.[27]

In an odd, uncanny way, Agnes Lake's life was influenced by a succession of "Bills," all of whom brought tragedy.

The death of Bill Lake was a terrific shock to his wife, but she bore it with courage. When she felt fit to meet her employees, she called them together and told them that she intended to carry on with the show. She asked that if any of them wished to leave, they would give her two weeks' notice so she could fill their places. Nobody resigned.

Under her management the show prospered. Resolutely she refused to be put off by the fierce competition which she received from her male-owned rivals, and eventually she won their grudging respect.

So it was that she came to Abilene in 1871. During the short time the show was there, she made the acquaintance of the Marshal and went after him hook, line, and sinker.

There are many legends of how these two met, and the outcome of their meetings. Perhaps the most interesting, and certainly the most detailed, account was given by Wild Bill's friend Charles Gross:

[26] Topeka *Daily Tribune*, Aug. 28, 1869.
[27] Robinson, *Old Wagon Show Days*, 127–30.

Madam Lake . . . became infatuated with Bill . . . [and] I helped Bill by assuring her he was married and that I knew his wife in Ills. . . .

When Mrs[.] Lake the Widow of "Old Lake["] of Circus fame came to Abilene she set up her tent Just West of the D[rover's] Cottage on the vacant ground[.] Bill was on hand to Keep order. Bill was a Handsome man as you Know & She fell for him hard, fell all the way *Clear to the Basement*, tried her best to get him to marry her & run the Circus[.] Bill told me all about it. I said why dont you do it—He said "I Know she has a good show, but when she is done with the West, she will go East & I dont want any paper collar on[,] its me for the West. I would be lost back in the States.

Gross noted that something essentially feminine about her reminded Wild Bill of a horse collar, anyway. Gross concluded his remarks by stating that there was no legal reason for Hickok's refusal to marry Mrs. Lake, and that she was set on the idea because "she wrote to him after leaving Abilene I know[,] for the letters came to my care under seal to the Cottage."[28]

An examination of the letters from Agnes Lake to Mrs. Polly Hickok has revealed that Gross spoke the truth when he said that she continued to correspond with Wild Bill. There is no doubt now that there was a mutual feeling between them, for by 1873, Wild Bill's efforts to put Agnes off underwent a subtle change. Perhaps he felt that life was passing him by and that he should settle down. Unfortunately the letters he wrote to Agnes have not been found (if they still exist), and only from her comments can we guess his feelings.

She wrote to Mrs. Hickok on April 26, 1876:

My Daughter does not travle this Summer, as she will be confined sometime in August[;] she was Married last November to a Mr. Robinson[,] a Circus Proprieter and well of[f] hence my Marriage[.] I would never have Married as long as my Daughter remained single as it was my Duty to remain with her and take care of her; but now I am superceaded and she has a protector ahead of me: I loved James for three years before I married him [,but] I would not git Married before my Daughter did[.] I wanted to see her settled in the World first as I considered myself a minor consideration.[29]

After leaving Abilene, the show moved on to other parts of the West. In places it was not too well received, and in 1873, Agnes sold off her menagerie, apparatus and stud. One writer claimed

[28] Charles Gross to J. B. Edwards, Apr. 13, 1922, and June 15, 1925, Manuscripts Division, KSHS.
[29] Original in the possession of Ethel Hickok.

that her reason for selling out was the financial panic of 1873, which could well be true. Stories of her joining other circuses seem to be without foundation, and by the mid-1870's she devoted more and more time to her daughter's welfare. It is thought that she may have met Wild Bill in New York when he appeared with Cody, but her letters to the family do not mention this. Then, in February, 1876, she was in Cheyenne.

It is unlikely, in view of her comments to Mrs. Polly Hickok, that the meeting was a surprise; it was probably planned. Agnes was staying with some friends, S. L. Moyer and family. One day Hickok called at the house and the family discreetly withdrew to allow the couple some privacy. The result of the meeting was the following:

MARRIED.—By the Rev. W. F. Warren, March 5th, 1876, at the residence of S. L. Moyer, Cheyenne, Wyoming territory, Mrs. Agnes Lake Thatcher of Cincinnati, Ohio to James Butler Hickok, WILD BILL, of this city.[30]

The witnesses were S. L. Moyer and his wife.

The news spread quickly and evoked some interesting comment:

"Wild Bill," of Western fame, has conquered numerous Indians, outlaws, bears and buffaloes, but a charming widow has stolen the magic wand. The scepture has departed, and he is as meek and gentle as a lamb. In other words, he has shuffled off the coils of bachelorhood.[31]

Another commented:

Mrs. Lake came to Cheyenne ostensibly for recreation, but really to take advantage of the privileges which leap year gives the ladies. Hickok has always been considered as wild and woolly and hard to curry, but the proprietress of the best circus on the continent wanted a husband of renown, and she laid siege to the not over susceptible heart of the man who had killed his dozens of both whites and Indians. The contest was "short, sharp and decisive," and "Wild Bill" went down in the struggle clasping his opponent in both of his brawny arms, and now sweet little cupids hover over their pathway and sugar, cream and honey for a delicious paste through which their [they] honeymoon. Success and happiness attend them, and while on the road of life they may have every joy vouchsafed to mortals, and we feel confident that Mr. Hickok will see to it that they are never lacking for small Bills.[32]

In Cincinnati it was remarked: "The Wild Bill who recently mar-

[30] Cheyenne *Daily Leader*, Mar. 7, 1876.
[31] Cheyenne *Daily Sun*, Mar. 8, 1876.
[32] Omaha *Daily Bee*, Mar. 31, 1876.

ried Miss Agnes Lake is not the wild bill recently passed by the Ohio Legislation. We say it, and say it boldly."[33]

But one man had his doubts: the Reverend W. F. Warren, the Methodist minister who married them. He wrote in the remarks column of the church register: "I don't think the[y] meant it."[34] Agnes's letters, and the only two of Wild Bill's to survive, have proved him wrong.

The couple left for Cincinnati, where they spent two weeks with Agnes's relatives. There Wild Bill left her to return west; it had been agreed between them that he would make some money and then send for her so that they could plan a new life together out west. Agnes probably suggested that she get some kind of work meantime, for she knew she could get five thousand dollars a year and all expenses paid in a circus. But Wild Bill refused. "My husband says he did not Marrie me to work he only wants me to please him and not the Public; and that is what I am trying to doo," she wrote, "and iff duty and Love can doo it I will succeed."[35]

While waiting for James to send for her, Agnes busied herself looking after her daughter, despite considerable discomfort caused by a septic hand injured by an ice pick. "Loving James as I doo and being a Woman of tender feelings I dont see why we will not git along to gether," she wrote to Polly Hickok. "Dear Mother I want you to give me James exact Age as I want to put our Berths on our Marriage Certificate[,] he plays the Larkes with me so much that I wont put it down until I git it from you."[36]

Following Wild Bill's death, there was a long silence from Agnes, and it was November before she felt well and able enough to write to the family, and her moving letter is reproduced elsewhere.[37]

A year later Agnes was on the move again, and was reported to be in Cheyenne, where she had first appeared about June, 1877. It was reported that she returned east for a short while to visit rela-

[33] Cincinnati *Daily Enquirer*, Mar. 19, 1876.

[34] Marriage Record of the Methodist Church, Cheyenne, Wyoming Territory, 1876, Wyoming State Archives, Cheyenne, Wyoming.

[35] The date on this letter is indistinct, but it might be August 7, 1876. She refers to one she had just received from James, which "I will send with this so you can see where he is and what he is doing." It is possible that this was the letter he wrote on July 17 from Deadwood (see Chapter Fifteen). Apparently all the letters Hickok wrote to his wife were sent to the family to read, but were returned afterwards, because there is no trace of them among the family's collection.

[36] *Ibid.*, and Apr. 26, 1876. The reference to Wild Bill's age suggests that he lied to her about it—it has been claimed that he deliberately put it up to forty-five for the marriage certificate, which would seem a gallant gesture on his part.

[37] See Chapter Fifteen. Original in the possession of Ethel Hickok.

tives and then was back preparing for her trip to the Black Hills. On August 19 she set out for Deadwood, stopping for a while at Charley Dalton's ranch on Horse Creek. Charley and his wife joined her party, which was headed by a George Carson, a "frontiersman widely and favorably known." On September 7 they reached Deadwood, and on Saturday, September 8, she visited Wild Bill's grave. She examined it and remained there at length before returning to her friends, who stood some distance away to allow her privacy. On the advice of her friends she decided that the grave should remain undisturbed and that arrangements would be made to erect a fenced monument to Wild Bill's memory, in which kind action "Buffalo Bill, Texas Jack and Buckskin Charley will assist."[38]

Agnes let it be known that she was on her way to Havana, Cuba, via Cincinnati and New York, in company with her daughter. They intended to take two young horses they had trained in Cheyenne for the circus ring. Before leaving she sold her valuable gray racer Whalebone to F. C. Boulter for $862. It has long been rumored that Charley Utter sent a lock of Wild Bill's hair to his wife, but there is no record of a meeting between them.[39]

Back in Cheyenne, Agnes and George Carson took out a marriage license, but there is no evidence to suggest that they actually went through with the ceremony, for no mention of Carson has been found in connection with her after this date.[40]

In 1880, Agnes was reported once more in Cheyenne with her daughter, who was a "daring equestrian" with Barnum's Circus. "Mrs. Agnes Lake Hickok accompanies her daughter everywhere and is her constant companion. She has herself had 36 years of experience with the circuses, and what she don't know about them is not worth thinking about."[41]

The same newspaper, on July 19, 1881, printed this strange item:

A CHIP OFF THE OLD BLOCK.

The Sioux City *Journal*, of the 1st instant says: "A son of Wild Bill . . . is in the city on his way to join an uncle in the Black Hills. His mother was accidentally killed at Denver not long since, by a shot fired by a drunken man at somebody else. The young man himself is lame from a

[38] Agnes Wright Spring, *Cheyenne and Black Hills Stage and Express Routes*, 225; Spring, *Colorado Charley, Wild Bill's Pard*, 110–11.
[39] Spring, *Colorado Charley, Wild Bill's Pard*, 111.
[40] Laramie County Records, Book C, 21. A marriage license was issued to Mrs. Agnes Hickok and George Carson on Sept. 27, 1877 (Mary J. Carpenter, librarian, Carnegie Public Library, to the author via Mrs. Ethel L. Hutchins, Cincinnati Public Library, Nov. 18, 1959).
[41] Cheyenne *Daily Leader*, Aug. 3, 1880.

bullet lodged in his leg by a brother of his father's murderer, with whom he had an altercation. His step mother, Madam Lake, once lived at Cheyenne. She took charge of her husband's circus after his death, and while traveling with it was married to Wild Bill. It will be seen that a pay streak of tragedy runs through the whole family.

Efforts to track down this alleged "son" have failed. It could well be that the newspaper was repeating hearsay, for the content suggests that or a hoax.

In 1887, Mrs. Hickok's daughter Emma went to England with Buffalo Bill's Wild West. Her mother stayed in the United States and for a time ran a ranch near Salina, Kansas. Of Emma's appearance in London, it was noted: "Mrs. Robinson . . . rode before the Queen, who was so delighted with her performance that she sent her a bouquet of flowers."[42]

By the turn of the century Agnes Lake had faded into obscurity. Then in 1906 she was found living in New Jersey, where she gave an interview to the *Morning Telegraph*:

I am the first person who ever thought of a railroad circus in this country, and one of the first to put my ideas into execution. The railroad has done much to make the life of the circus performer easy. We used to have to ride over bad roads and sleep sitting up, sometimes arriving in town only a few minutes before it was time for us to enter the ring. It amuses me to hear people talk nowadays about being overworked. As for myself, I thrived on work. First, I gave the outside wire walking spectacle, then rode in the grand entree, was the chief feature of "Mazeppa," and also did another riding turn. Frequently I appeared in the concert as well. All this twice a day, with my only couch for the night's performance a carriage cushion.[43]

In August, 1907, while staying at the home of her son-in-law Gil Robinson, in New Jersey, Agnes became ill. She died on August 21, just three days from her birthday—her eighty-first, according to the paper. "She died of infirmities due to old age." It was announced that the funeral would "take place at the Robinson home Saturday, and the body will be placed in a vault until October, when it will be taken to Cincinnati and buried beside that of her first husband."[44]

So passed from the scene Agnes Lake Thatcher Hickok, the last link in the chain of Wild Bill Hickok's love life. From then on it was up to the fictioneers.

[42] Jersey City *Mirror*, Aug. 31, 1907.
[43] Jersey City *Morning Telegraph*, Aug. 23, 1907, clipping supplied by William B. Secrest.
[44] *Ibid.*, and Jersey City *Mirror*, Aug. 31, 1907.

--◦◦{ 13 }◦◦--

A Stage Career with Buffalo Bill

Long before he became a world-wide celebrity, William Frederick Cody, better known as "Buffalo Bill," had achieved a number of minor successes on the stage of New York, Baltimore, Chicago, and many other Eastern cities, presenting his dramas of Western life. Later he expanded his ideas into the field of the circus, and in 1883, "Buffalo Bill's Wild West"[1] was born. Among those who assisted Cody in his early career was Ned Buntline, the man responsible for persuading Buffalo Bill to take up acting as a profession.

Buntline was an interesting character. Born Edward Zane Carroll Judson, son of Levi Carroll Judson, at Harpers Field, New York, on March 20, 1821, he moved with his parents to Bethany, Wayne County, Pennsylvania, in 1826, where his father taught school, wrote books, and studied the law. Another move was made in 1834 to Girard Square, Chestnut Street, Philadelphia, and his father was admitted to the bar. Contrary to his father's wishes, Edward did not want to become a lawyer but preferred the sea. Following a violent quarrel in which Levi struck his son, Edward ran away from home in November, 1834, and became a common sailor.[2]

An accident in the East River, in which the Fulton Street ferryboat ran down a small boat, pushed Judson into the limelight. At great risk to himself he rescued the men from the boat, and for his bravery President Van Buren appointed the seventeen-year-old sailor acting midshipman on February 10, 1838.[3] This led to an exciting if controversial life at sea for some years; his only publicized reference to it was in his pseudonym of Buntline, which came from the rope at the bottom of a square sail—the "buntline." It is estimated that during his lifetime he wrote over two hundred novels. Always in some kind of trouble, Ned invariably contrived

---

[1] The word "Show" was never applied to Cody's "Wild West." The correct term, if asked, was always given as "Exhibition." (Don Russell, "Cody, Kings & Coronets," *The American West*, Vol. VII, No. 4 (July, 1970), 5n.)

[2] Albert Johannsen, *The House of Beadle and Adams and Its Dime and Nickel Novels*, II, 168.

[3] *Ibid.*

to make his ups and downs public property. Women, too, complicated his life, and he was credited with at least four marriages.

By the time Cody met him, Buntline was well established, but his appearance spoke of his perilous past. He was lame in one leg (a relic of an early scrape), and his tendency toward fatness combined with his lack of stature made him look grotesque.

In 1869, Buntline went west in search of material for his stories. It has been claimed that he was looking for Wild Bill, and as Hickok had already appeared in *DeWitt's Ten Cent Romances*, this may have been true. Hiram Robbins, the manager of the Buffalo Bill Combination that for a time included Hickok, recalled:

He would have been Buntline's hero, but for his disregard, I may say, dislike of notoriety. When Buntline came out in search of a real life hero, he saw Wild Bill in a saloon one night. Bill was dressed in regular scout fashion, with pistol belt and buckskin leggins. When he entered a saloon where Buntline had, according to his habit, stationed himself, he immediately awakened enthusiasm in the breast of the romancer. "There's my man," he exclaimed, and rushing forward he approached Bill and exclaimed: "I want you."

Now, in that country, it was not altogether polite for a man to rush up and say "I want you." There was something about it at that time which the rough and tumble man from the states did not fancy.

"What do you mean," exclaimed Bill, while his hand suggestively sought his pistol.

"I mean that I want you; that you are my man."

"Well, if you can take me, all right," Bill replied, drawing his pistol.

Buntline drew back, and realizing his rudeness said: "I am representing Street and Smith, of the New York *Weekly*, and am in search of a real, live Indian fighting hero. Seeing you, while my thoughts were on the subject, I recognized you as my ideal of such a character."

"That's all right," Bill replied. "That is a pretty good talk, but let me tell you, my friend, I'll just give you twenty-four hours to leave this community. I don't care what your business is, but I don't like your looks nohow."

Buntline, after inquiring around, learned that Bill was a man of his word, and left. Afterwards, meeting Buffalo Bill in Texas Jack's saloon, Buntline was presented to him. Buffalo Bill was a ward of Wild Bill, for when Cody was a boy, Wild Bill, conceiving a fancy for him, took him under his wild wing of protection. Buntline agreed that if Texas Jack would furnish the whiskey, a necessary incentive to Cody's free narration of Wild Bill's exploits, he would make both of them heroes. Jack, who had read Buntline's stories, readily agreed, and under a pretence of playing billiards, Buntline received from Cody many of Wild Bill's exploits, of which he made hurried notes, substituting Buffalo Bill for Wild

Bill. True to his promise, Buntline made heroes of both Buffalo Bill and Texas Jack.[4]

A hint of truth in the foregoing is found in an 1876 press report: "Wild Bill raised Cody to manhood's estate, after which the two separated over some personal difficulty, and have never been on good terms since. Wild Bill accuses Buffalo Bill of having given Ned Buntline incidents of his (Wild Bill's) life, and claiming them as his (Buffalo Bill's) own adventures."[5]

It is known that Buntline first met Cody when the latter was a scout for the Fifth Cavalry. Buntline expressed a genuine admiration for Buffalo Bill and his scouting friend Texas Jack, and repeatedly urged one or both to go east and appear on the stage. Cody did make a brief trip east and was introduced to an audience who reacted very favorably, but Cody was not convinced. Then, during the summer of 1872, Buffalo Bill was faced with the decision of his life. Either he could stay on the Plains, or go east and maybe make a fortune. Already at twenty-six he was a celebrity. Born on February 26, 1846, in Scott's Farm, near Le Claire, Iowa, he was the fourth of eight children born to Isaac and Mary Cody. His young life followed the pattern of the time: a trip on an emigrant train to Kansas, and later on one of the huge freight trains (where he claimed he met Wild Bill), and the rough frontier life which children of those days expected. He also claimed the distinction of being a rider on the Pony Express while still in his boyhood.

During the Civil War he further distinguished himself as a soldier on the Union side; but his greatest fame came after the war, when he won his name while supplying buffalo meat to the Union Pacific Railway Company, Eastern Division, construction crews during 1867–68. An excellent scout and guide, Cody was appointed chief of scouts to the Fifth Cavalry in 1868. His services as a guide for Eastern tourists were often requested.

Buntline's frequent requests to go east, however, put him in a quandary. Finally, he decided he would go if Texas Jack went with him. Jack was enthusiastic, and together the pair set out for Chicago, where they arrived on December 12, 1872.

Buffalo Bill made his debut on the American stage in *The Scouts of the Prairie*[6] at the Amphitheatre, Chicago, on December 16,

[4] "Wild Bill's Humors," interviewed in the *Arkansaw Traveler*, undated clipping supplied by Don Russell.

[5] Jefferson City *People's Tribune*, Aug. 23, 1876.

[6] Russell, *Buffalo Bill*, 193, points out that Buntline used his "Buffalo Bill's Last Victory: or, Dove Eye, the Lodge Queen," which had been serialized in the New York *Weekly*, as primary source material.

1872. But on the night of the *première*, Cody was too tongue-tied to utter a word. The minute he stepped onto the stage he was petri-fied. The audience greeted him with thunderous applause. As it died down, Buntline nudged Bill to speak. Cody gulped but re-mained silent. Buntline grew desperate. "Where have you been, Buffalo Bill?" he prompted. Cody look a little startled, then his eyes settled on a man in the audience named Milligan, with whom he had once gone hunting. "Why—why I've been out hunting with Milligan," he stammered. This brought the house down. Milligan was a popular figure, and Buffalo Bill's unwitting remark pleased the audience.[7] They took him and his company to their hearts, and from then on the performers could do no wrong. Except for the critics, no one in the audience cared that the scouts forgot their lines, or said and did the wrong things sometimes; all they were interested in was the fact that here was the *real* thing—and that was all they had come to see anyway.

But the critics were not so kind. Buntline's literary efforts were roasted, and the actions of the scouts were termed ridiculous by some. Others said that the American stage had reached an all-time low. But they could not deny one thing: good or bad, Buffalo Bill always played to a packed house.

All during the first tour of 1872–73 audiences were good, and press reports were for the most part favorable. In January, 1873, they reached Milwaukee and appeared at the Grand Opera House, where there appears to have been an addition to the program that has escaped general notice. It was reported: "Buffalo Bill found a host of admirers at the Opera House last evening. . . . Nobles was not wanting in his role of Wild Bill. The Dave Tutt of Mr. Carver should have consigned him to the Green Room for 40 hours; or until he obtains a fairer conception of the part."[8]

This is the first mention this writer has found of the use of "Wild Bill" in connection with the Cody-Buntline relationship, which suggests that Buntline had introduced characters from his first Cody "novel" "Buffalo Bill, King of the Bordermen," serialized in the New York *Weekly* in December, 1869.

By the time the troupe reached Harrisburg, Pennsylvania, they were already planning ahead for a new season. But Cody and Texas Jack were having trouble with Buntline. The three disagreed over

---

[7] There are many versions of this story, and perhaps it has some truth. An early biographer, Fred E. Pond (*The Life and Adventures of Ned Buntline*, 88), cites a similar story.

[8] Milwaukee *Sentinel*, Jan. 22, 1873.

the share of profits. The result was a break-up of partnership. The two scouts decided to carry on by themselves, and left Buntline to make his own plans.

The break-up between Cody and Buntline brought Buffalo Bill and Texas Jack closer together. Texas Jack had always sided with Cody in his arguments with Buntline, and had been the steadying influence on Buffalo Bill ever since they started. For no matter what history has made of Buffalo Bill, the fact is that he was an erratic character in all things. He drank too much, talked too much, and often lapsed into depressive moods. Several times he threatened to quit, and only Jack's quiet reasoning kept him on the stage. But when he had money, Cody's generosity knew no bounds.

Texas Jack was helped considerably in his gentle persuasion of Cody by Major John M. Burke, for the Major was one of Cody's truest friends. His early association with Cody in the stage productions had established a friendship between them that was lifelong. When Cody and Texas Jack split up in 1876, Burke joined Texas Jack and his wife; but he rejoined Cody when Buffalo Bill's Wild West was formed in 1883. A quiet, genial, and resourceful man, the Major made himself extremely popular with everybody. He became Buffalo Bill's shield against the cruel world of hard business and hard cash. In later years, when the Wild West had its bad times, it was Burke who bore the brunt of the attacks of Cody's creditors. Yet he never lost faith in Buffalo Bill—Cody was his life, and he idolized him to the end.

Texas Jack was the only one of the three scouts who never achieved the fame he deserved. He became the hero of innumerable dime novels and wrote a column for *The Spirit of the Times*, but his tragic death at the early age of thirty-three robbed him of his renown. And only one full-length biography has so far appeared on his life.[9]

Before pneumonia claimed him, Texas Jack had led an exciting life and had earned for himself a wholesome respect on the Plains. Born on July 26, 1846, at Pleasure Hill, near Palmyra, Fluvanna County, Virginia, he was the fourth child of John Burwell Omohundro (after whom he was named) and Catherine S. Baker Omohundro.

During the Civil War young John Omohundro served in the Confederate Army. Following the war he worked as a Texas cowboy. It was while on a cattle drive to Tennessee that he won his sobriquet. At a small town on the border of the state he and his fellow

[9] Herschel C. Logan, *Buckskin and Satin*.

drovers were welcomed by the townspeople. One of them asked him where he was from. "Texas," said Jack. "What's your name, son?" they asked. "Jack" was the reply, and they all cheered for "Texas Jack." And the name stuck.[10]

In 1869, Jack met both Wild Bill and California Joe at Fort Hays and later at Hays City. A firm friendship sprang up among all three; later at Fort McPherson, he met Buffalo Bill. Jack spent a lot of time at the fort or in the surrounding area, and as has been previously mentioned, he mixed a great deal with the Pawnees; along with Major Frank North, he was one of the few white men who earned their trust.

At Port Jervis, New York, on June 16, 1873, Buffalo Bill's troupe ended their first season. After the two scouts split with Buntline they returned to Fort McPherson, where for a short time they were guides on a hunting party. In company with several Easterners, among whom were E. B. Overton of New York and Scott "the hatter, of Chicago," they spent nearly a week hunting buffalo and elk, during which time they were joined by several "old scouts and companions." The army even supplied them with an ambulance and an escort, and the trip was a great success.

It was reported that "Buffalo Bill and Texas Jack are now on their way east to organize a company to make a tour of the Southern States early in the fall; after which they will return to New York and fill their final engagement in America, previous to their departure for Europe."

Before going to Europe, the story went on, Cody was to produce a new play "Buffalo Bill and Alexis on the Plains," in "which a number of horses will be introduced and several daring feats of equestrianism performed." An indirect reference was also made to the breakup of the partnership with Buntline: "The boys think they have made enough money for other people, and now propose to paddle their own canoe. They have learned the eastern country and the ways of the world sufficiently to hereafter be their own guides." Cody went to New York and Texas Jack to Boston for two weeks, and it was arranged to meet again in New York to resume business.

A most interesting remark came at the end of the article: "On the European theatrical trip, the scouts will be accompanied by James B. Hickok, the original 'Wild Bill.' They anticipate a more brilliant success in the Old World then they have yet met with in the New."[11]

[10] Ibid., 4.   [11] Omaha Daily Bee, July 27, 1873.

While it is understood that Cody had talked the proposition over with Hickok, it is not certain where they met. Fort McPherson seems to be the most logical place, for Hickok is reported to have made his headquarters there on several occasions. During the early months of 1873 the West was buzzing with reports published in several newspapers stating that Hickok was dead, the victim of murderous assassins. According to the accounts he was killed at Fort Dodge by two men whom he believed to be friends. While drinking with them in a saloon, the lights were suddenly extinguished and the firing commenced. One bullet pierced his brain, entering his skull in the center of his forehead, another hit him in the heel, and four more pierced his body in different places. The assassins then ran out and disappeared.

In Kansas it was stated that he had been murdered by friends or relatives of Phil Coe. Other reports said he was out west and had in fact written to his old deputy McDaniels (J. H. McDonald?). In Kansas City it was claimed that a letter had been received from "C" in Springfield, Missouri, stating that "I have seen the gentleman 'in flesh and blood' in this city to-day, and from his appearance should judge that he was not accustomed to 'laying in his gore' in saloons at Fort Dodge. His friends in Kansas City may be pleased to hear an authentic report concerning him."[12]

It was Wild Bill himself who put a stop to the rumor by writing two letters to the St. Louis *Missouri Democrat*. In presenting the first one, the paper referred briefly to the rumors, then published Wild Bill's comments:

SPRINGFIELD, Mo., March 13, '73.
TO THE EDITOR OF THE DEMOCRAT:
Wishing to correct an error in your paper of the 12th, I will state that no Texan has, nor *ever will* "corral William." I wish you to correct your statement, on account of my people.

Yours as ever.
J. B. HICKOK
OR "WILD BILL."
P.S. I have bought your paper in preference to all others, since 1857.

We take much pleasure in laying Mr. Hickok's statement before the readers of the Democrat, most of whom will be glad to learn from his own pen that he is still "on deck." But, in case you *should* go off suddenly, William, by writing us the particulars we will give you just as fine an

---

[12] For a selection of these reports, see The Laramie *Daily Sentinel*, Mar. 5, 1873; the Topeka Daily *Commonwealth*, Mar. 14, 1873; and the Dickinson County *Chronicle*, Mar. 20, 1873.

obituary notice as we can get up, though we trust that sad pleasure may be deferred for many years.

"Wild Bill," or any other man killed by mistake in our columns, will be promptly resuscitated upon application by mail. It is not necessary for the deceased to call in person. He will receive just as much—in fact, more—attention by simply writing.[13]

The second letter could not be found in a search of the weekly and daily editions of the paper, but it was copied by the Mendota, Illinois, *Bulletin* on April 11, 1873:

THE DEAD RETURNED TO LIFE
AUTOGRAPH LETTER FROM WILD BILL,
THE NOTED INDIAN SCOUT

[From the *Missouri Democrat*]

A few weeks ago we published an account of the shooting of Wild Bill by some Texans who decoyed him into a saloon under pretense of friendship and shot him from behind. We have seen no denial of the statement and never doubted its correctness until the receipt of the following letter minus the faintest smell of brimstone and bearing the well known imprint of Uncle Sam. We don't like to take anything back nor insist that a man is a ghost who handles shooting irons so familiarly and carelessly, but circumstances over which we have no control have modified our opinions and Wild Bill (William we meant to have said) is undoubtedly "korrect."

SPRINGFIELD, Mo., March 26th, 1873

I wish to call your attention to an article published in your paper of the 19th in regard to my having been killed by Texans. You say when I was murdered it was fulfilling a prophecy that all men of my kind should die with their boots on. Now I would like to know the man that prophesies how men shall die, or classes of men, so that the public may know who is right and who is wrong. I never have insulted man or woman in my life but if you knew what a wholesome regard I have for damn liars and rascals they would be liable to keep out of my way.

J. B. HICKOK, OR WILD BILL
from LaSalle County, Ill.

N. B. Ned Buntline of the *New York Weekly* has been trying to murder me with his pen for years; having failed he is now, so I am told, trying to have it done by some Texans, but he has signally failed so far.

J. B. H.[14]

13 Mar. 15, 1873.
14 Mrs. Georgia Gambrill, chief, Reference Department, St. Louis Public Library, to the author, Apr. 19 and May 14, 1962, tried to track down both letters, and eventually found the one published in the *Democrat* on Mar. 15, 1873. She suggested that the other letter might have appeared in the St. Louis *Republican*, which was a daily paper.

Following the publication of the letters, Wild Bill's movements, until he appeared in New York with Cody in the fall, are obscure. A report published in Wyoming in August stated:

Judge Thomas returned from Evanston yesterday, where he had been holding a term of court. . . . There was no trouble in convicting guilty men, it seems, in his court with an Evanston jury.

The following is some of the business disposed of . . . Wild Bill was convicted of riot and assault on the Sheriff and fined fifty dollars and costs.[15]

It is not known who this man was, although most authorities seem convinced that it was James Butler Hickok. Yet it was a common practice among certain individuals when involved in any difficulty to answer to a variety of names. One writer recalls that when a railroad terminus tough was arrested and asked for his name, "he usually answered that it was Slim Jim, or Wild Bill, or Lone Jack (with an oath)."[16]

When Wild Bill eventually set course for New York to join Cody, his arrival caused some excitement. Buffalo Bill recalled:

When I had arranged terms with Wild Bill to appear with my company, we were in New York playing an engagement, and I was stopped at the Metropolitan Hotel. Bill arrived in New York after dark, and being unacquainted with the city—this being his first visit there—he took a hack, instructing the driver to take him to the Metropolitan Hotel. Upon arriving at the house, Bill asked the driver his charges.

"Five dollars, sir," was the reply.

"And you wouldn't accept anything less, would you?" asked Bill.

"No sir, that's the charge and nothing less."

Bill then handed the driver five dollars, at the same time striking him a blow in the face that sent him plowing up the settlings in the gutter. A policeman very soon came after Bill, but bail being furnished by me, he was kept out of the Tombs; but the next day I paid a fine of $10 for him. This was his first experience in New York.[17]

When Hickok finally settled in at the hotel, he found Cody on his own. Texas Jack had made a dash to Rochester to get married. During the preceding season, he and Guiseppina (Josephine) Morlacchi, the female star of the show, had seen a great deal of each other, and finally on August 31, 1873, they became man and wife.

Born in Milan in 1846, Josephine was but six years of age when

15 Laramie *Daily Sentinel*, Aug. 4, 1873.
16 V. V. Masterson, *The Katy Railroad and the Last Frontier*, 157.
17 Buel, *Heroes of the Plains*, 160–61. Buel claims that Cody told him this story.

her parents placed her in a school at La Scala. During the next six years she was trained as a dancer, and made her debut at the Carlo Felice Theater in Genoa in 1856. Her skill as a dancer earned her an appearance at Her Majesty's Theater, London. Following some very successful appearances in Europe, Mlle Morlacchi went to the United States in 1867. By the time she played the dancing lead in *The Scouts of the Prairie* she was one of the toasts of New York society. Among her admirers was the notorious Jim Fisk. But from the start she had eyes only for Texas Jack.

When Texas Jack returned with his bride, he found Wild Bill in a highly nervous state about the business of acting. Cody had been giving him many pointers, and Hickok was beginning to unwind a little. Now that the whole troupe was assembled, the first engagement of the season was scheduled for Williamsport, Pennsylvania, on September 8.[18] For the first time Wild Bill would step onto a stage and face an audience.

There is some doubt concerning which of the Buffalo Bill Combination productions was chosen as the initial performance. There were at least two different plays in production during Hickok's appearance with the company. The most publicized version was *Scouts of the Plains* written by Fred G. Maeder, and it was perhaps Cody's most successful. The cast list, in true Victorian manner, gave the audience a preview of the "good" and the "bad":

BUFFALO BILL	W. F. Cody
TEXAS JACK	J. B. Omohundro
WILD BILL	J. B. Hickok
PALE DOVE (*Wife of Texas Jack*)	Mlle Morlacchi
JIM DAWS (*a renegade horsethief*)	Frank Mordaunt
AUNT ANNIE CARTER	Miss Jennie Fisher
ELLA	Miss Lizzie Safford
LOTTA	Miss Eliza Hudson
UNCLE HENRY CARTER (*a friend of the scouts*)	J. V. Arlington
NICK BLUNDER (*with song and dance*)	Walter Fletcher
TOM DOGGETT (*in cahoot with Daws*)	W. S. MacEvoy
EBENEZER LONGLANK (*Gov't Peace Commissioner*)	A. Johnson
TALL OAK (*a Kiowa, but on the square*)	W. A. Reid
BIG THUNDER (*a Comanche Chief*)	B. Meredith
BEAR CLAW (*a Comanche Brave*)	H. Mainhall
RAVEN FEATHER	J. W. Buck

[18] This date was given by the Rochester *Democrat and Chronicle* of Sept. 1, 1873, but a search of the local papers failed to reveal any trace of the performance (Mrs. Catherine T. Schulenberger, the James V. Brown Library, Williamsport, Pa., to the author, Nov. 7, 1960).

The second play was *Buffalo Bill, King of the Bordermen.* A recently discovered original copy of the program, which is undated, and appears to be a standard performance issue, reads as follows:

THE
PROGRAMME
ON THE TRAIL
The Scouts of the Plains!
BUFFALO BILL,
TEXAS JACK,
WILD BILL.

Dramatic Company, Tribe of Indians

Fred G. Maeder's Famous Western Drama
Buffalo Bill!
KING OF THE BORDER MEN!
In Three Acts

BUFFALO BILL	(by Hon. Wm. F. Cody)	Buffalo Bill Himself
TEXAS JACK	(by Mr. J. B. Omohundro)	Texas Jack Himself
WILD BILL	(by Mr. J. B. Hickok)	Wild Bill Himself
THE OLD VET, an 1812 Pounder,		
(Author of the Drama)		Fred G. Maeder
SANKEROOT SAM, Down on Snakes		Walter Fletcher
COL. JAKE McKANDLASS		Alfred Johnson
ALF COYLE, A Renegade		W. S. MacEvoy
MURTY MULLINS, The Sentinel		R. Wheeler
PERKINS, a Landlord		E. N. Watson
FLIPUP		W. G. Specke
STOCKWELL		E. Cunningham

INDIANS.

FIRE WATER TOM, a Drunken Red			J. V. Arlington
"Oof" "Oof" "Oof"		"Oof"	"Oof"
RAVEN FEATHER, a Sioux Brave			Jas. Johnson

BIG MAPLE, a warrior ⎫ By the
LITTLE ELK, the same ⎪ Tribe
WHITE ARROW, the same ⎬ from the
LITTLE PANTHER, the same ⎭ Plains

MA-NO-TEE, the Princess of the Ogllalla Sioux   Esther Rubens

LADIES

LILLIE FIELDING, the Rose of the Plains	Lizzie Safford
LOTTIE FIELDING, the Wild Bud	Eliza Hudson
MRS. FIELDING	Jennie Fisher
KITTY MULDOON, an Irish Girl	Rena Maeder

This copy of the program is owned by Ethel Hickok, who kindly allowed the writer to examine and copy it. It is printed on cheap paper of a greenish hue overprinted in black type. Someone has penciled a comment which is partly unreadable; the date October 15 is written, which suggests that that was the date a family member or friend saw the production. -

In this version of the play Mlle Morlacchi does not appear. On the back of the program a "Reconstructed Synopsis" presents a number of intriguing titles such as "Oath of Vengeance," "Judge Lynch and His Law," "Among the Vultures," "True Grit," and finally, "Buffalo Bill Keeps His Oath." The remainder of the space is devoted to "Facts about the Scouts," most of which is a quote about Wild Bill from Custer's *Life on the Plains,* published in the April, 1872, issue of *Galaxy.*

Having got Wild Bill on the stage, Cody was then presented with the problem of keeping him there. On one of his early appearances, the plot demanded that Hickok should sit down with the other two scouts and swap yarns. During the conversation a whisky bottle was passed between them, and as each took a drink from the bottle, he would spout a blood-curdling yarn. When Wild Bill's turn came, he took a mighty swig at the bottle and for a long moment sat still, a look of horror on his face. Then he swung his head sideways and spewed a mouthful of the liquid toward the wings. Amidst thunderous applause he roared: "Cold tea don't count—either I get real whisky or I ain't tellin' no story!"

Hurriedly Buffalo Bill sent someone out for real whisky, and the show continued. But Hickok had made a big impression, and the story goes that Cody kept him to his tea-drinking exhibition through every performance.

Yet Hickok did not like the notoriety he achieved, and cared little for his public. Some who saw him taking part in the parades to advertise the program believed him bored with the music, the cheers, and the excitement it engendered. All the time he was with Cody, Hickok was a source of amusement and vexation. When the company appeared at the Parshal Opera House in Titusville, Pennsylvania, on November 6, 1873, word reached the scouts that there might be trouble from the local toughs. Fearing that his guests might be parted from their money and their breath at the same time, the hotel manager asked them to use a side door to enter the hotel. The scouts agreed to this, and the arrangement worked quite well until Wild Bill grew tired of the moonlight flitting from one building to the other. Anxious to see how tough the bullies were, he deliberately sauntered into a billiard room where they were gathered. Buffalo Bill recalled that:

. . . one of the bruisers put his hands on his shoulder and said: "Hello, Buffalo Bill! We have been looking for you all day."

"My name is not Buffalo Bill; you are mistaken in the man," was the reply.

"You are a liar!" said the bruiser.

Bill instantly knocked him down, and then seizing a chair he laid out four or five of the crowd and drove the rest out of the room. All this was done in a minute or two, and by the time I got downstairs, Bill was coming out of the bar-room whistling a lively tune.

"Well!" he said, "I have been interviewing that party who wanted to clean us out."

"I thought you promised to come into the Opera House by the private entrance?"

"I did try to follow that trail, but I got lost among the canons, and then I ran in among the hostiles," said he, "but it's all right now. They won't bother us any more. I guess those fellows have found us." And sure enough they had, we heard no more of them after that.[19]

Little is really known of the private lives of the scouts between performances. Cody's family were then living in Rochester, New York, and he went home to visit them when there was sufficient time between engagements. Texas Jack's wife had an estate at Billerica, Massachusetts, to which they would disappear. Wild Bill seems to have spent his time in hotels, and no doubt made the most of his opportunities where women and gambling were concerned.

Buffalo Bill in later years recalled that Hickok had often warned him of the perils of gambling. He remembered that Hickok frequently gave the impression of being drunk or half-asleep when playing against a stacked deck; then he would finally choose his moment to pull a gun and show up the sharp. To Cody he declared, "When you play against a stacked deck, make sure you've got a hand to beat theirs." And he touched the butt of his revolver. He strongly advised Cody against gambling, warning him of the trouble it could cause—which, coming from Wild Bill, was a fine piece of irony.

On one occasion Wild Bill's sense of humor paid off. When the troupe reached Portland, Maine, where they were to appear at the

[19] *The Life of the Honorable William Frederick Cody, Known as Buffalo Bill,* 330–31. Don Russell has pointed out that Frank Bliss, who is usually credited with the authorship of this book, was in fact the publisher (*Lives and Legends of Buffalo Bill,* 271).

Music Hall on January 29 and 30, 1874, Hickok had difficulty in getting to sleep one night. As he tossed and turned he heard an unholy row coming from the next room. The clink of glasses and the occasional shout annoyed him. Jumping out of bed, he hastily pulled on a pair of trousers and went in to see what all the fuss was about.

He was met at the door by a thick cloud of tobacco smoke, and inside he found a number of city businessmen sitting around a table playing poker. One of them called out for him to sit in—it was a friendly game, he said. Wild Bill sat down and declared that as they didn't want him to sleep he would join in, but first they must show him the rudiments of the game.

Four hours later, after making a few carefully chosen blunders, Wild Bill arose from the table, having cleaned them all out. Open-mouthed, they sat and stared at him as he turned from the door and said: "Adios m'friends; better think twice after this before waking a man up and inviting him to play poker."[20]

This neat trick did not stop the men from enjoying the show, and the local press was compelled to admit: "We can only say today that Wild Bill, Buffalo Bill, Texas Jack and Morlacchi drew an immense audience to Music Hall last evening. The applause was frequent and hearty and Morlacchi's dancing aroused immense enthusiasm."[21]

Despite the huge amount of publicity he was getting, and his undoubted powers of attraction, Wild Bill was not a happy man. Hiram Robbins noted:

Wild Bill's actual merits made him a reputation, but with all of his daring exploits, which he modestly attempted to keep in the back-ground, he was not so well-known throughout the country as Cody. . . . I found it was necessary to assign Wild Bill, the actual hero, to a minor part, on account of his effeminate voice. Although he was a large and powerful man, he had a voice like a girl, altogether too weak for the part which he would naturally take.[22]

This remark by Robbins is strange. Evidently what he really meant was that Hickok's voice did not have the projection necessary to carry to an audience (at a time when acoustics were not considered and microphones were unheard of). Or perhaps Hickok himself lacked the enthusiasm necessary to put effort into his part —an opinion that seems to have been shared by others who claimed

[20] Logan, *Buckskin and Satin*, 90.
[21] Portland (Me.) *Advertiser*, Jan. 30, 1873.
[22] "Wild Bill's Humors," *loc. cit.*

255

that he had a powerful voice, but his heart was not in it. He ended up as a stammering, blushing, ridiculous figure—which for a man of his capabilities and temperament was intolerable.

News of his stage appearances reached his family in Homer and they endeavored to keep track of his movements, although it is not certain that any of the family ever saw the play. However, they did ask Agnes Lake what sort of an actor he was, and she wrote, "it would be hard to tel as he does not like it; but his Wife is a good Actres."[23]

There are dozens of legends of Wild Bill's escapades during his brief appearance on stage, but two in particular reflect his temperament.

On the American stage of the time it was common for actors to use loaded firearms when the need for real marksmanship arose. Shooting at glass balls was a popular feature. The weapons were always underloaded (about five grains of powder per bullet) and accidents were rare; wherever possible the shots were fired toward the wings and away from the audience. But Buffalo Bill wounded a small boy in a Baltimore theater with a carelessly aimed shot in 1878.[24] Legend has it that Hickok was bothered by the operator of a spotlight, and that in exasperation he shot the light out. It seems evident that this story stems from Robbins. He recalled that Hickok was quite content until the play appeared in Philadelphia, where they used a calcium light:

The light did not belong to the theatre but was owned by an outside man, from whom we rented it, paying him so much for every time it was turned on. It was thrown from above, and the manipulator occupied a place among the flies. One night Wild Bill conceived the idea that Buffalo Bill and Texas Jack were receiving too much light. Suddenly sensitive of his obscure part, he was determined that more blaze should be thrown on him, so one night just before the curtain went up, he climbed the ladder leading to the calcium light manipulator, and finding that gentleman at his post, said:

"Say, does Bill and Jack pay for this extra light business?"

23 Agnes Lake to Polly Hickok, Aug. 7, 1876, original in possession of Ethel Hickok.
24 Baltimore *American*, Sept. 10, 11, 12, and 14, 1878. Cody was riding off stage and fired his rifle in salute; by accident one of the balls hit a small boy in the chest as he leaned down over the gallery. At first it was feared the lad would die, but when Cody visited him and learned he would recover, he made arrangements for him to spend his convalescence at his ranch at North Platte. Doc Carver, without any attempt at verification, declared that the boy died and that paying for the funeral made Cody bankrupt (the late Raymond W. Thorp to the author, May 30, 1959).

The manipulator, thinking that he meant the management, replied, "Yes, they pay for it."

"Yes, that's what I thought. It makes them look pretty, don't it?"

"Well, it heightens the effect."

"That's what I thought. Now when I come out tonight, I want you to throw it on me."

"I can only turn it on when I am directed."

Bill always carried a revolver, and drawing it, he remarked, "Say, throw that stuff on me. If you don't I'll have to try you with this. I can kill you nine times out of ten from below, and if you don't throw the light on me when I appear, I'll try you one just for luck.

Bill occupied an obscure position in the scene where a cabin was being raided. Wild Bill, with a very meager part, occupied scene three. The signal for the calcium light was given, and it would have been grand, but the entire effect fell upon Bill, who, with his weak eyes, blinded by the intense light, stood for a moment and then yelled:

"Turn the blamed thing off."

The entire act was spoiled. Bill, in explanation, said that they had put something in the light to hurt his eyes.[25]

It seems evident that Wild Bill did not like his part of the bargain, and did all in his power to break his contract. There is a story, repeated even by Cody, that he deliberately upset the extras (the "Indians") by discharging his pistols close to their legs. Black powder, even in blanks, at close range can make some very bad burns, and Hickok was soon most unpopular. The extras complained to Cody who asked Wild Bill to stop it, and for a time he behaved. But Hickok was a rebel. The idea of the sham dying, acting, and false heroics turned him against the stage. The attacks on the extras may have been his way of expressing his disgust at the whole business.

He was just not cut out for the stage. Try as he might, Hickok could not settle down and be serious. He regarded the scouts' appearance on stage as ridiculous and repeatedly told his companions that they were making fools of themselves. Notoriety on the Plains was one thing, because with it went a great deal of respect; but this was something else. And, perhaps, Hickok was jealous of Cody's success and ease before an audience. Cody was a good mixer, but Hickok kept himself aloof in almost princely fashion.

The break finally came at Rochester, New York. Robbins tried to dissuade Wild Bill from leaving, emphasizing that they were all making good money, but Wild Bill declared that money was no object to him, "that he was merely sustaining Jack and Cody," and

25 "Wild Bill's Humors," *loc. cit.*

that it would be better for him to leave. "From my earliest acquaintance with the man," went on Robbins, "I had known that it was useless to argue with him, so I consented to his withdrawal."

Other reasons have been given for Wild Bill's departure. Ed Moore, an old soldier, told Connelley that Hickok left because a footlight exploded and nearly burned his eyes out. Since this story had a direct bearing on the reports that Hickok was going blind, I made a few inquiries.

The show went on at the Rochester Opera House on March 10, 1874. The house was so crowded that the reporter for the *Union* was unable to see the players and thus could not offer his readers any criticism of their efforts.

Two reasons for Wild Bill's leaving the show came to light. The records are somewhat scanty on this historic event, but John Fennyvessy, whose name still means theater in Rochester, shed some light on the mystery in his *The First 90 Years of the Rochester Opera House*.

One version was that on the second night of *The Scouts of the Plains*, Wild Bill was so mightily drunk that Cody and Texas Jack shipped him home and replaced him in the cast with Kit Carson, Jr.

The second version, which came down through the late Amy H. Croughton, historian and critic of the theater for the Rochester *Times-Union*, was something else. Miss Croughton's information came from William Thompson, a printer on the *Democrat* and *Chronicle* who, in his later years, clearly remembered Cody's and Hickok's appearance in Rochester.

Thompson's story was that on the second night of the show, Hickok received an urgent message from General Phil Sheridan, urging him to drop everything and join the troops at Fort Laramie. Cody and Texas Jack could not dissuade him, even in an argument at the railway station. In any event, he left, apparently uninjured and with his eyesight as good as it had been when he arrived.[26]

Wild Bill's departure was reported in the local press, who remarked on his alleged appointment with General Sheridan:

WILD BILL
HE LEAVES TROUPE FOR THE WESTERN FRONTIER—THE WAY HIS FRIENDS TREATED HIM

Having seen the stalwart form of Wild Bill (J. B. Hickok) passing down State street yesterday afternoon, and knowing that the troupe of scouts with which he has been appearing upon the stage for some time

[26] Rochester *Times-Union*, Feb. 28, 1958.

258

past had departed for Lockport where they performed last night, we ventured to approach the hero and enquire the reason why he tarried behind his fellows. Our hand was grasped with considerable warmth in his which appeared to be iron vice from which we were glad to be released. After devoting a few words not at all complimentary, to the blustering March winds that were whirling the snow through the streets, he began to relate why he was not with the troupe, and we should have had the whole matter explained then and there, had not an impudent youngster crying "*Union*" or "*Express*" come down the street with the loud cry of, "Oh! stag his nibs wid the long hair!" Now it is well known that Bill wears his hair in the flowing style prevalent on the frontier; and this, together with the tall form and manly deportment of the man, attracted the attention of the newsboy and caused him to give vent to several exclamations of no particular importance to the student of polite literature, but very well calculated to draw the attention of everyone within the sound of his voice to us. Bill was not at all affected by this strange proceeding. He remarked that he had witnessed it in hundreds of towns, so often, in fact, that it was an old thing to him. We suggested, however, that we should move along, to which he willingly consented. The few staring mouth-opened children of the pave who had gathered were soon left behind, and as we passed into Exchange Place, there was but one left, and he took to his heels because Wild Bill stopped and looked at him. We were then informed that Bill had received a call to the frontier. Recognized as one of the best scouts and Indian fighters that have appeared upon the great western frontier, his services are highly valued and eagerly sought for when there is danger of war with the Red man. Just now there is considerable commotion at Fort Laramie and some of the Indian agencies, especially the Red Cloud and Spotted Tail agencies. The Sioux has been seen in his war paint and General Sheridan thinks he may begin his attempt to seek the paleface in a few weeks. At this time and amid such scenes as these, the services of Wild Bill will be invaluable to the United States troops. It is this, together with a longing desire to return to the free, wild life he loves so well that has called our hero away. He will first proceed to New York where he has some business to transact, remain there a few days and then go direct to the frontier. Buffalo Bill, Texas Jack, and the other scouts did not like to have him leave, but when he said he must go, the noble-hearted fellows presented him with $500 apiece, and each gave him a splendid revolver, bidding him to make good use of it among the "Reds." He had nothing but kind words to speak of the boys, as he familiarly termed the other scouts. He wished them all manner of good fortune and was sure they would receive it. Wild Bill is a noble fellow, a true-hearted child of nature, one of those men which one occasionally comes in contact with and ever after retains a place in his memory. We shook hands with the hero, bade him good-bye, and wished him a pleasant journey to his far western home. He left at 12:15 this morning for New York.[27]

Hickok's business in New York is obscure, although there are stories of heavy gambling, and equally heavy losses. Robbins claimed that he joined a rival show under the direction of a man named Stevens, which he called the "Daniel Boone party." Hickok was offered fifty dollars a week to join them, merely to impersonate himself. After some hesitation he accepted, but it was a disaster. It was tactfully pointed out to Wild Bill that he was making a fool of himself, and after a moment's reflection, he agreed: "Blamed if it don't seem to me that way too. Guess Mr. Stevens will have to live without me."

Mr. Stevens also made a big mistake. Having extensively billed the scout in advance, he had to find a replacement, which turned out to be a tall fellow who "with the aid of a blond wig and a few extra touches" was transformed into "a complete scout." The deception was perpetrated in several places before Hickok found out about it and decided to take action. Claiming to be with him when Wild Bill set out on his warlike mission, Robbins wrote:

When we reached the town we went to a hotel and stayed in our rooms until time to go to the theater. Bill, with his long hair tucked up under his hat, seated himself immediately behind the orchestra. Stevens came out and introduced his Indian fighter. Just as the fellow bowed to the audience, Bill, with a bound sprang upon the stage, and with a blow of his ponderous fist, knocked the fellow down, and before the audience could realize what had happened Stevens and several other men who rushed out were sent spinning across the stage. The wildest commotion followed. Policemen attempted to arrest Bill and were knocked down. Finally a small officer crawled through a window, approached Bill and politely informed him that he was under arrest. Bill expressed his readiness to accompany the officer and was leaving the house with him, when several burly policemen, keen for the honor of arresting such a noted character, rushed up and attempted to sieze Bill. Stepping back, Bill drew his pistol, threw his lightning eye on the interlopers and remarked he was already under arrest, that it was wrong to arrest a man twice at the same time, and that an epidemic would soon spread unless there was an immediate change in the atmosphere. The atmosphere changed immediately. On our way to the police station, Bill slipped his pistol to me. The officer in charge would not accept a forfeit, and Bill was compelled to go into the lockup. I asked the officer if he would allow Bill to take whiskey with him into the prison, explaining his peculiarities, but he refused. I then asked if I could take him a lunch to which he agreed.

27 Rochester *Democrat and Chronicle*, Mar. 14, 1874.

The lunch consisted of a mere show of bread, meat and potatoes, the main feature being a cup of whiskey with a saucer over it. From then until day, Bill had to have a lunch every half hour. One of the officers declared that he had never before been introduced to such an active appetite. Next morning at court, no one appeared against Bill, and he was released after I had paid a light fine.[28]

This incident made a fitting finale to Wild Bill's brief appearance on the American stage. Never again would he invade the boards, which was perhaps just as well, because James Butler Hickok belonged completely to the West of the open plains, mountains, and streams. It was unthinkable that such a man could remain for long anywhere else.

[28] "Wild Bill's Humors," *loc. cit.*

--∙∢ 14 ⊱∙--

A Man about Cheyenne

FROM ITS EARLY DAYS IN 1867, when it was an end-of-track railroad boom town, Cheyenne had the reputation of being the wildest, roughest place on the continent. It was filled to overflowing with a crowd of roughs, killers, gamblers, and prostitutes such as had never assembled at any one place in America, except perhaps at Abilene. Like the citizens of that town, the reputable people in Cheyenne eventually set out to get law and order. In 1869, T. Jeff Carr was elected sheriff of Laramie County, in which Cheyenne was situated, but owing to some doubt concerning the legality of his appointment, Carr declined. The following year he was elected again by a large majority. From then until 1875, when he had to stand down because of a proviso in the law which prevented him from serving more than two successive terms, he was instrumental in bringing law to the territory. The 1876 elections came round and he was again elected sheriff. Carr spent his whole life in the service of the law, as sheriff, chief of police, or cattlemen's detective.[1]

By 1874, Cheyenne was beginning to settle down. Most of the visitors were "just passing through" and the police force was not often called upon to enforce the law, but the following year, when the prospective Black Hills miners gathered in Cheyenne in preparation for their search for gold, the place again abounded with tough characters. When Wild Bill arrived there during 1874 the town was pretty quiet.

Hickok's movements after he left New York have so far eluded the most diligent research. Certainly, no evidence has been turned up in Washington to suggest that he joined General Sheridan that year.

A host of wild stories have circulated about this period of his life. One claims that he got into a fight with two relatives of Phil Coe who were after his blood, and in a saloon gunfight (no specific town has been agreed upon, but Cheyenne seems favorite), he

[1] "T. Jeff Carr, the Detective," *Official Journal of the Police Authorities and Sheriffs of the United States*, Vol. IX, No. 108 (Mar., 1894).

shot and killed both. But there is no evidence to support this. Hickok himself had made it known that "no Texan has, nor *ever will* 'corral William,' " yet it was felt in some circles that he was ever on his guard against attack from friends of Coe.

Another story suggested that Hickok had lost his nerve and that, in order to repudiate this, he had telegraphed the editors of all the leading papers between Cheyenne and Abilene as follows: "I shall pass through your prairie dog villages on Tuesday. I wear my hair long as usual." This appears to be a variation of a tongue-in-cheek remark publicized in an inimitable Alfred Henry Lewis "Epic of an Unsung Ulysses," which at the time reached a wide public.[2]

Wild Bill's movements during the latter half of 1874 can be partially checked from the newspapers. In doing so, a certain amount of confusion is unearthed. The newspapers of Cheyenne and Denver, aided by exchanges with those of places in Kansas and Nebraska, spoke of plans for several hunting expeditions organized by certain wealthy Englishmen which would be guided by Hickok, Cody, and Omohundro. In order to clarify the situation, it is necessary to explain the movements of each of the scouts.

Buffalo Bill, according to one report, was to act as a guide to a certain Mr. Thomas Medley, a London millionaire, who was organizing a grizzly hunt. Accompanying him were several English lords. Cody was to leave his family in Rochester, New York, where his children were being educated, and come west and be joined at Corinne by Wild Bill, who was then said to be at Yosemite. Together they would join the party and go to Fort Saunders, Wyoming, to hunt mountain sheep and elk, and later to Fort McPherson to "chase the bounding buffalo." It was the Englishman's ambition to eclipse the success of the Grand Duke Alexis' buffalo hunt, and Medley was prepared to spend $20,000 for the purpose.[3]

Cody arrived in Omaha on July 17 and stayed at the Metropolitan Hotel. It was stated that "Bill is as handsome as ever; his long dark hair flows gracefully down his manly shoulders, while a pleasant smile continually plays upon his happy countenance; his immense diamond cluster pin sparkles on his immaculate shirt bosom, while a diamond ring on each little finger dazzles the eyes

2 Lewis, "How Mr. Hickok Came to Cheyenne," *loc. cit.*, 7.

3 Manhattan (Kan.) *Beacon*, July 22, 1874. A personal examination of available records in London failed to disclose a Lord Thomas Medley, and conflicting reports suggest that he was in fact a Chicago saloonkeeper. Don Russell remarked that Cody (who often got names wrong) said he was of London, but may actually have been a relative of Lord of the firm of Lord and Taylor, New York (Don Russell to the author, June 29, 1967).

of the observer; and an immense gold chain and trinkets, attached
to a costly watch, ornaments his vest." Cody remarked that his
theatrical partner, Texas Jack, was spending the summer and enjoying life with his wife at her "splendid farm at Bellerica, a short
distance from Boston."[4] From Omaha, Cody went to Denver and
by July 25 was in North Platte.

Wild Bill, meantime, was not in Yosemite. On July 18, Hickok
"passed through North Topeka . . . on his way to Cheyenne, where
he expected to join Buffalo Bill and Texas Jack, and proceed with
a party of English tourists to the Yellowstone country."[5] Later that
same day Hickok left the train at Kansas City, where he joined a
"party of about twelve English Lords and noblemen," who arrived
"by the Missouri Pacific train. The party are bound about 200 miles
west on a general hunting excursion. Wild Bill was picked [up] at
this place and taken along as scout."[6] On July 22 it was reported
that Wild Bill was in Cheyenne, and he then moved on to Denver.
On July 27 he left that city with a party of hunters. The press remarked:

Those English millionaire hunters, with "Buffalo Bill" and "Wild Bill"
for guides, who came out here to out-do the sporting achievements of
the Grand Duke Alexis, took the saddle last Monday, and by this time
have fairly commenced the extermination of all the wild game in the
Platte valley. Major Moore, with a company of cavalry, has gone out with
the party, merely to keep the Englishmen from destroying the redskins,
while exterminating the buffaloes.[7]

It is evident that the editor was generalizing, for Cody was not
on this particular hunt. From North Platte, he had gone on a hunt
on the Dismal River and was expected to be gone for some weeks.
But the hunt was cut short because Cody went to Fort McPherson,
where he was hired by Lieutenant P. H. Breslin of the Fourth Infantry as a guide at $150 a month for the Big Horn Expedition com-
manded by Brevet Lieutenant Colonel Anson Mills. Buffalo Bill
was with the party from August 7 to October 2, 1874.[8]

Early in August, Texas Jack left his wife and arrived in Denver

[4] Omaha *Daily Bee*, July 18, 1874. An undated clipping from an unknown newspaper in the possession of Ethel Hickok gives a similar description of Cody, only
the writer calls him "Wild Bill," and claims to have met him in Colorado. He was
reported to use "a pair of heavy Smith and Wesson revolvers, which shoot nearly as
accurately as rifles."
[5] Topeka *Daily Commonwealth*, July 21, 1874.
[6] Kansas City *Times*, July 19, 1874.
[7] Denver *Rocky Mountain News*, July 31, 1874.
[8] Russell, *Lives and Legends of Buffalo Bill*, 209.

on or about the eighth. There he was to meet the Earl of Dunraven, who had engaged him as a guide on a hunting expedition. On the tenth the party left for the Yellowstone. Texas Jack had first met the Earl at Fort McPherson in 1872, and they shared a mutual respect for each other.[9] Jack returned to Cheyenne from the Yellowstone about November 1.[10]

It is evident from the foregoing that Hickok, Cody, and Omohundro did not meet at all during their respective periods in Denver. Cody's and Omohundro's parties are now identified, but who Hickok acted for is not clear. By the middle of August he was reported to be in Missouri, where he was seen at the race tracks in Kansas City by Ed Moore. Moore reported that Hickok was wearing tinted glasses, and when it was pointed out to him that one of the lenses was missing, he threw them away in disgust. The spectacles were apparently worn as a result of the alleged accident in Rochester, which, as has been pointed out, could not be substantiated. But it should be noted that the report of Hickok passing through North Topeka on his way to Cheyenne also carried the comment: "Wild Bill is suffering with an affection of the eyes, caused by the colored fire used during his theatrical tour."[11] This suggests that he either mentioned the subject or was actually wearing glasses on the train.

This assertion that Wild Bill adopted glasses for a period has given rise to yet another legend concerning his appearance in Cheyenne not long after he left Cody. Again no date is given and the story lacks documentation, but it is evidently based upon an incident that occurred in 1874 or 1875. The most publicized version comes from Alfred Henry Lewis. To escape notice in the city Hickok wore dark glasses, piled his hair under his hat, and "concluded to creep about on his billiard cue" (adopted following a bout of rheumatism). He entered the Gold Room and engaged in a poker game, run by the notorious George Devol, a former Mississippi river-boat gambler and cardsharp. Accounts differ, but the general agreement is that Wild Bill found that he was being cheated. He expressed his disapproval by producing a pair of pistols and sweeping his hat and glasses off so that his long hair came down. The customers took one look at him and with the cry: "It's Wild Bill!" went through the doors and windows in "blocks of

[9] Logan, *Buckskin and Satin*, 120, 175.
[10] In tracing the movements of the scouts, I am indebted to Paul D. Riley for checking the Omaha press and for additional comment.
[11] Topeka *Daily Commonwealth*, July 21, 1874.

five." Hickok was left on his own, and the bartender nervously suggested a drink on the house, which he accepted. The next morning the manager of the establishment, accompanied by the town marshal, visited Wild Bill and suggested that they split two ways all the contents of the till which he had taken on the way out. Wild Bill graciously consented, and the three of them made their way back across the street from his hotel to the bar of the Gold Room.[12]

Aside from the humor of the above account, investigation into the affair has revealed that there were two Gold Rooms in Cheyenne. One was housed in Jim Allen's Variety Theater, and the other, the most famous, was run by Murray and Pierce. But no contemporary reference has been found involving Hickok in a fight in either. What may have sparked the story was an incident that only partially involved Wild Bill. According to J. W. "Doc" Howard, a former sergeant in the Fifth Cavalry, who had known Hickok for some time, Wild Bill had arrived in Cheyenne after leaving Buffalo Bill's show "because the lights affected his eyes, so he had to give it up." He was living in a room above Dave Miller's jewelry store. Howard was on the police force, and one of his first experiences might have been his last. As he was passing Jim Allen's Variety Theater, he heard:

... loud talking and [I] shifted my gun from the pocket holster into my right hand pocket and kept my hand on the gun. Just as I entered the main hall, I noticed Wild Bill leaning up against the door jamb. I passed by him to see what the quarreling was about. I saw Charley Rich grab the table to turn it over. The men around the table held it down, so he could not. He had been loser and wanted to put an end to the game. There was quite a lot of money on the table when I entered. I said, "What's the matter? Stop that!" With that, Charley whirled around, grabbed me by my slipknot necktie and tried to choke me. Then Wild Bill jumped in and grabbed me around the arms, so that I could not use my gun. Charley Boulder, a noted gambler, stuck his gun right into my stomach. I grabbed his gun and stuck it in my left coat pocket. I said, "Bill, let loose of me," and he said, "Doc, if Boulder had got you, I'd have got him." I took Boulder out and turned him over to Fallon, another cop who was peering in the window, afraid to come in.

Howard went in after Rich but was persuaded not to arrest him. Boulder went to another saloon and started drinking, so Howard arrested him. Sometime later Boulder killed two men and served ten years for killing one of them.[13]

12 Lewis, "How Mr. Hickok Came To Cheyenne," *loc. cit.*, 19.
13 J. W. "Doc" Howard, *"Doc" Howard's Memoirs*, 19–20. The name Boulder

The repeated references to Wild Bill and eye trouble bring up the fact that he evidently did suffer with his eyes. It has been alleged that he had trouble as far back as 1871; the theory has even been put forward that it was because of this that he did not see Mike Williams clearly and shot him on impulse, and that this explained his great mistrust of people until he knew for sure that they were friends. The controversy was generally publicized in a famous novel:

> When he [Hickok] had trouble seeing the spoor of the otter and mink up in the Yellowstone country, he slipped secretly to the army surgeon at Camp Carlin near Cheyenne. The doctor had looked very grave. It was advanced glaucoma, incurable, and in a few months he would be in total darkness.
>
> Sworn to secrecy—"There's a hundred as would brace me on any street, if it gets out how little I can see"—the doctor promised to do what he could, but it would be little.[14]

When I endeavored to establish the date of this interview, and to obtain a copy of the medical report, several unexpected difficulties arose. Neither the Adjutant General's Office in Washington nor the Armed Forces Medical Library had records pertaining to the alleged examination,[15] and other sources were equally unproductive. I then tackled the problem at source, and was informed:

> Here in America the progressive blindness of Wild Bill is no longer questioned by even the cursory investigator. Hickok made repeated trips to Topeka to a doctor about his eyes in his Kansas period, and the final evidence was in the medical records of Camp Carlin in the days when the material was in storage over at Virginia Avenue, Washington, D.C., in 1937–8. I've never checked on what has become of these documents since the material has been moved into the National Archives building.[16]

On my behalf the late Earle R. Forrest asked a friend in Washington for assistance, who took the matter to the highest level, but again the result was negative:

> Apparently your friend in England has written directly to the Archives in the past about Hickok. And perhaps others have too. In any event, the request for information about Wild Bill in the medical history of Camp Carlin has been considered a number of times.

bears a notable similarity to the Bowlby mentioned by Lewis and Buel as the owner of the Gold Room.

14 Mari Sandoz, *The Buffalo Hunters*, 259.

15 Dallas Irvine to the author, Aug. 15, 1956; Charles Roos to the author, Sept. 11, 1956.

16 Mari Sandoz to the author, Nov. 3, 1956.

The staff handling the reports has made intensive searches for the Camp Carlin material, without success. There is indication that such a record existed at one time in some warehouse in Washington prior to the transfer of a large group of records to the Archives. (By this I mean the administrative medical records of a Camp Carlin, which later became some other name.) Since the surgeon General's records have come to the Archives, that particular item has been searched for in vain. Presumably it disappeared before the Archives obtained possession.[17]

It is unfortunate that for reasons best known to herself, Miss Sandoz was not averse to causing confusion by producing references to historical characters that eventually turned out to be fictional, frequently involving others in months of fruitless research.[18] At this writing "no further information has been uncovered" by the National Archives relative to a medical report on James Butler Hickok.[19]

But lack of documentation does not eliminate the probability that something was wrong with Wild Bill's eyes. His brief affairs with the Cyprian sisterhood, both in the East and in the West, may have been in part responsible. Medical evidence suggests that gonorrhea, if transferred to the eyes, can produce a condition known as gonorrheal opthalmia. J. W. Buel stated that early in 1876, Hickok returned to Kansas City, where he "remained for some time inactive owing to an attack of opthalmia superinduced no doubt from the exposure he underwent while in the Black Hills. Dr. Thorne treated him for several months with such success that his eye-sight, which was for a time entirely destroyed, was partly restored, but he never again regained his perfect vision."[20]

Leander P. Richardson, who met Hickok at Deadwood in 1876, noted:

His skin was pallid from the use of powerful mineral drugs and his grayish eyes, which were just beginning to regain their power after almost being blinded by a terrible illness, were rather dull and expres-

[17] Frank J. Nivert to Earle R. Forrest, Dec. 11, 1956, original in the author's possession. The National Archives has confirmed that Camp Carlin (named after Col. E. B. Carlin, acting quartermaster) was constructed on Crow Creek near Fort D. A. Russell. This depot later became known as Camp Carlin; in 1871 the name was changed to Cheyenne Depot or the Quartermaster Depot at Cheyenne.

[18] Dr. John S. Gray to the author, Sept. 2, 1963. Dr. Gray had this experience with "Charley Reynolds." However, he did add: "On the credit side, I don't know anyone who has [so well] succeeded in capturing and communicating a feeling for Indian life."

[19] Elmer O. Parker, assistant chief, Old Military Branch, National Archives, to the author, Aug. 9, 1971.

[20] *Heroes of the Plains*, 181.

sionless in repose. One day afterward I saw them glitter with a sudden ferocity that was strangely luminous and I realized what this man must have looked like when his blood was up. But at our meeting, when he folded my hands in his big, strong fingers, his face was almost expressionless, and his eyes were more or less leaden.[21]

Old-timer Bill Sparks, who met Wild Bill in the early 1870's, recalled: "It was evident that he had been living indoors for some time for his face was slightly sunburned and the rims of his eyelids were red."[22]

At this date it can only be an educated guess from which disease Wild Bill may have suffered; therefore, I am grateful to an eminent professional ophthalmologist for kindly setting down his conclusions. He writes:

I doubt that it was gonorrheal ophthalmia—not that I doubt he had "G.C." [a medical term for gonorrhea]....

Regarding glaucoma and ophthalmia—your thoughts regarding gonorrhea were quite logical since that is the disease the term "ophthalmia" seems to be linked with most commonly today (but usually in regards to the form seen in the newborn) and, despite his family's protests, it's quite reasonable to assume that Wild Bill was a logical candidate for "G.C." Confusion regarding the two diagnoses stems from the fact that "ophthalmia" (a severe inflammation of the eye) is a broad term that includes many diseases—and especially did so in the 1800's when many conditions had not been better defined. Certain types of glaucoma (abnormally high pressure in the eye) might have been labelled ophthalmia, and various illnesses called ophthalmia at that time can lead to a secondary form of glaucoma.

When I asked Charles Snyder, librarian of the Lucien Howe Library of Opthalmology at the Mass. Eye & Ear Infirmary in Boston . . . what he felt doctors meant by "ophthalmia" in Post–Civil War U.S., his feeling was, "it could have been almost any painful or inflammatory condition of the eye." One suggestion of his that you might be interested in—trachoma. He states: "Granular conjunctivitis, ophthalmia, trachoma—call it what you will—was common on the Western Frontier. Jesse James suffered from it."

Anyway, it does not help to have only a diagnosis made at that time. We have to hope that the doctor that made the diagnosis at that time, was quite compulsive and kept very good records wherein he described all the symptoms and signs that led him to make the diagnosis (and this is probably asking too much for a frontier doctor in the 1800's).

[21] Leander P. Richardson, in a long letter to the editor of the New York *Sun*, refuting an article about Wild Bill. A complete copy of the letter was published in *True West*, Vol. XIII, No. 2 (Nov.–Dec., 1965).

[22] Ross Santee, *Lost Pony Tracks*, 248–49.

Another medical point that would be nice to have verified is whether or not Wild Bill did suffer from "rheumatism" or "arthritis" and, if so, from what sort, as some kinds of arthritis are associated with certain inflammations of the eye. (As a matter of fact, gonorrhea is one of things that can cause both—but, as I said before, the chronicity and course seems to be against that).

I do not feel that the spotlight exploding in or being directed at his eyes caused his problem. From what I have read, it would seem more likely to assume that he had an inflammation of the eyes that made them "photophobic" (quite sensitive to light) and that the bright lights aggravated his discomfort. The photophobia accounts for the wearing of the dark glasses.

This brings me to another point. Since the glasses could have been worn solely for protection from the sun and light and not for optical purposes, it is possible that Wild Bill did not need glasses to achieve his best vision. Furthermore, it is possible that he could have attacks that seemed to blind him—and still have good vision between them. I mention this because there are some people who do not believe Wild Bill had any eye problem at all—and seemed to base their arguments solely on visual acuity. . . . Well, first of all, as I mentioned, it is possible that he could have had some sort of eye problem and still have good vision. On the other hand, even if his vision was impaired, it would seem to me that by this point in his life his shooting was so instinctive that he could have performed remarkable feats of shooting even without a clear view of the target. While I must admit that in the realm of shooting I am no expert, certain of the episodes quoted in your chapter 17 would seem to support my feelings. For example, he could not use his central retina (and thus had to rely on the poor visual acuity to be had from his peripheral retina) when he stood *between* the fences of a road four rods wide and shooting *simultaneously*, hit each of the fence posts on *opposite* sides. . . .

I can't help but feel that there was definitely something about Wild Bill's eyes that bothered him—even if it was only some minor condition that he became overly concerned about. (And one can't blame him for that!) [There is an] episode where Wild Bill was dared to shoot it out with a "sawed-off buckaroo." But Hickok refused, saying his eyesight failed him. . . . While the account was supposed to show Wild Bill's cowardice, I cannot imagine Wild Bill being afraid of a "sawed-off buckaroo" unless he really feared that his eyes would let him down.

Hopefully some medical records will turn up that will allow us to say definitely whether or not there was something wrong with Wild Bill's eyes and that might even provide a clue as to what it was.

In addition to the foregoing, I discussed the subject with Mr. C.

R. Kay, a Consultant Optician to one of London's major hospitals, and himself a target shot. Mr. Kay believes that:

the trouble with Wild Bill's eyes may have been due to not one disease but a combination. If he had secondary Syphilis, this could have led to Iritis, giving him cloudy vision, photophobia, and pain in the eyes—it can also lead to glaucoma giving a diminution of the peripheral fields of vision. The idea of a central field loss does not seem possible as it would have been virtually impossible to shoot. Other possibilities are Trachoma or Conjunctivitis, which show some of the symptoms Wild Bill experienced.

Mr. Kay concluded, as did Dr. Stephens, that what Wild Bill really suffered with will remain a mystery, owing to the absence of medical records.[23]

By September, 1874, Wild Bill was back in Cheyenne as was his friend, Colorado Charley Utter. The discovery of gold in the Black Hills and the expected rush for transportation would create quite a demand. And Charley was not slow to check on the prospects.

Upton Lorentz, who later made his home in Comfort, Texas, recalled in 1936:

The writer first saw both Wild Bill and Utter in September, 1874, at a resort known as the "Gold Room," a combination theater, dance hall, gambling place and saloon, paralelling the Union Pacific Ry. line at Cheyenne, Wyoming. This resort was the noted meeting place for cattlemen and other early Western characters, and nightly Wild Bill stood at the end of a long bar, opposite the entrance from the south or railway side of the building, while the western end of the room was occupied by a raised platform for dancing. Between the bar and the platform were tables for games of various kinds, and also private gaming rooms at the side.

Never far from him, generally in front of the bar, could be seen Colorado Charley, a slight, well dressed man, with long fair curls to shoulder also, and perhaps but five feet six inches tall. It was said at that time that the position maintained at the bar by Hickok at the east end and Utter fronting him a short distance away, was a precaution against attack from enemies known to be looking for a chance to get the drop on Bill. . . . [Later] I mentioned to Utter of having observed him and Hickok at the "Gold Room" in Cheyenne some ten years before. He said he was only a friend to Hickok and never acted as a bodyguard.[24]

[23] Karl F. Stephens, M.D., to the author, Jan. 5 and 19, 1971; Mr. C. R. Kay to the author, April 19, 1974.
[24] "Colorado Charley, Friend of 'Wild Bill,'" *Frontier Times* (original series) Vol. XIII, No. 8 (May, 1936), 374–75.

Among the many who claimed to have known Wild Bill was Doc Carver, self-styled "Evil Spirit of the Plains" and "Champion Rifle Shot of the World." It is now believed that a great number of his Western claims are based upon a prolific reading of newspapers and books and a brief personal intimacy with a number of the plainsmen of the time.

Carver was born on May 7, 1840, at Winslow, Illinois. His full name was William Frank Carver. His father's name was William and, curiously, he also gave his other son the first name of William —William Pitt Carver. Contrary to what Carver told his biographer, his father did not hate him or make him run away from home as a child. The boy was educated in Winslow and then trained as a dentist by his father.

The term "Doc" sprang from his dental experience and not from his alleged "doctoring" of small animals as a child. Carver arrived at Fort McPherson, Nebraska, in July or August, 1872, and was already an established marksman. His shooting matches with Ena Raymonde, one of the finest shots among the women of the plains, indicated that she could teach him nothing about shooting, but he did teach her the rudiments of dentistry. Carver lived on the Medicine for a time, and his mother and brother came there to live in 1874. By the late 1870's Carver began to make a name for himself as a marksman, and for a time toured Europe, where he was well received. Following an unsuccessful partnership with Buffalo Bill, Carver had his own show, which somehow never achieved the fame and fortune of Buffalo Bill's—which may explain his bitter hatred and jealousy of Cody. Unfortunately, no corroboration has been found for his alleged association with Wild Bill.[25]

The Cheyenne *Daily News* twice mentioned Wild Bill in 1874. On October 7 it reported that "Wild Bill is among the number that will shortly go out to the Laramie Peak country exploring for gold," but on December 3 it noted that "Wild Bill is still in the city. He is a noble specimen of Western manhood."

Early in 1875 Wild Bill was still in Cheyenne. The city was in the midst of a local cleanup. The place was fast growing respectable. A story long in circulation tells how Wild Bill's name appeared on a notice listing him as a vagrant, and stating that he and all

[25] Paul D. Riley to the author, Mar. 28, 1971; Russell, *Lives and Legends of Buffalo Bill*, 297–300. For the result of Carver's fiction, see Thorp, *Spirit Gun of the West*. The late Mr. Thorp in good faith supplied a great mass of material, some of which appeared in the earlier edition of this book, but subsequent investigation has revealed its fictional qualities which, regrettably, were not realized by Mr. Thorp.

others with no visible means of support had twenty-four hours to leave, and if found within city limits after that time, would be forcibly ejected. He drew his bowie and slashed the notice to ribbons, stating that when he wanted to leave town he would.[26]

Doc Howard recalled that on one occasion Jeff Carr, "the hard boiled stiff that he was," saw Hickok on the street opposite Tim Dyer's saloon, and "he hollered across the street to Bill saying, 'Bill, I guess I'll have to run you out of town.' Bill was a cool, level-headed man. He just looked up, and said, 'Jeff Car, when I go, you'll go with me,' and he walked slowly down the street."[27]

A hint of something of an anti-Hickok feeling on the part of some people in the city can be found in a report published soon after Wild Bill's death. In a long article headed "Something about Wild Bill," the editor of the Cheyenne *Daily Leader* took it upon himself to deflate the Hickok legend by playing upon the fact that during his stay in Cheyenne, Wild Bill had done nothing except fill himself with whisky and fill the minds of greenhorns with wild stories of the fabulous riches in the hills:

"Wild Bill" . . . was one of those characters developed by the onward strides of the iron horse when the "Great American Desert" was spanned by the Pacific railways. Seven or eight years ago his name was prominent in the "Scare-Heads" of the border press and if we could believe half of what was written concerning his daring deeds, he must certainly have been one of the bravest and most scrupulous characters of those lawless times. Contact with the man however dispelled all these illusions, and of late years Wild Bill seems to have become a very tame and worthless loafer and bummer. Our city marshal ordered him out of town by virtue of the provision of the vagrant act, only a few months ago, but Bill cordially invited the officer to go to a much warmer clime than this and expressed the intention of staying here as long as he pleased. Bill delighted in joining a crowd of "tender-feet" at the bar and soaking himself with whiskey at their expense, while he stuffed them in return with Munchausenish tales of his thrilling adventures and hairbreath escape from red fiends and white desperadoes. In such moments he was the very personification of happiness.

He enjoyed the fullest opportunity for the gratification of this great weakness during the grand rush to the Black Hills, last spring. Although he had never been farther north than Fort Laramie, he could spin the

---

[26] Kansas City *Star*, Mar. 29, 1918 (book review of William Francis Hooker's *The Prairie Schooner*). This same Hooker, who called himself "Pizen Bill" in 1930 (although someone once remarked that "Windy" was more apt), claimed to have personally backed down Hickok in Cheyenne (Torrington [Wyo.] *Telegram*, Nov. 6, 1930).

[27] *"Doc" Howard's Memoirs*, 19.

most astounding yarns concerning the fabulous riches of the Hills, his favorite one being about how he, with a small party, had discovered a large cave near Custer City, which was full of diamonds and other precious stones, as well as tons upon tons of gold and silver.

Years ago, before wine and women had ruined his constitution and impaired his faculties, he was more worthy of the fame which he attained on the border.[28]

The wine and women of Hickok's last years were really the effect, not the cause, of his fall from grace. He was desperately trying to avoid the net of civilization which crept ever closer to him along the silver rails of the expanding railroad. Had Hickok been in Cheyenne during the late sixties and early seventies, there is little doubt that he would have been employed as a peace officer. But Cheyenne found Jeff Carr, and it was Hays and Abilene which claimed Wild Bill.

Since the editor of the *Leader* waited until Wild Bill was dead, and had never really known his full story, his outburst is not completely justified, and he might be classed as an early practitioner of that great American pastime—debunking popular heroes. But his comments concerning vagrancy are based upon fact.

On June 17, 1875, Wild Bill was charged with vagrancy, and a warrant for his arrest was issued the same day. A $200 bail bond was ordered and was returned and filed on June 18 and approved on June 22. By August 4 the charge had cost the county $5.25 in expenses. By November, when the case was to be tried, Wild Bill had disappeared, and a continuance was ordered. By June 12, 1876, Hickok had still not been apprehended, although he was known to be in town or near by preparing for his trip to the Black Hills. The case was again continued to the next term. When news of Wild Bill's murder was received, a clerk wrote across the docket entry, "Deft dead. Dismissed."[29]

One important conclusion to be drawn from this indictment is the fact that vagrancy in 1875 did not mean quite the same thing as it may today. Where gunfighters and gamblers were concerned, it could almost put them in a social class.

It was fashionable for gamblers and gunfighters of that time to "drift" from place to place. The description of "having no visible means of support" would be a difficult one to apply to them. Rely-

28 Aug. 16, 1876.
29 Laramie County Clerk of Court, Criminal Appearance Docket, Book II, 230, June 17, 1875–June 12, 1876, copy supplied by the Wyoming State Archives, Cheyenne, Wyoming.

ing as they did on their hands, eyes, and wits, provided the dexterity, keenness, and sharpness of all three were good, they were well able to support themselves.

Something of this view was shared by two old-timers who kindly set down their comments. Wrote the late L. G. "Pat" Flannery:

If Hickok was listed as a vagrant, the charge probably did not mean exactly what it does today. It may have been a general charge made against undesirable or dangerous characters which local authorities wanted to move on, but who had not committed any definite crime. It is not hard to understand why Cheyenne authorities might charge Hickok, the well known gun man and gambler, with vagrancy under that definition, hoping thereby to get him out of town to avoid possible trouble. But I doubt very much that Wild Bill was ever an ordinary tramp or down-and-outer.[30]

The late Russell Thorp added:

I am sure that Hickok was never known as a vagabond and vagrant. Had he ever been so classed, I surely would have known of it through my personal acquaintance with John Mill, a barber in Cheyenne, whose shop was regularly patronized by Hickok. Then there was Scott Davis, captain of the shotgun messengers on the Cheyenne Black Hills Stage and Express Lines, Jesse Brown, shotgun messenger, my father and others who were personally acquainted with him, and those men would have undoubtedly known of and mentioned Hickok as a bum or vagabond had he been one. His wife . . . lived in Cheyenne and both bore respectable reputations. Bill was always classed as a law and order man.[31]

It is probable that the charge against Wild Bill was not generally known even in his own time. Once the *Leader* had made its allegation against Wild Bill, the city marshal of Cheyenne, J. N. Slaughter, went to the *Leader's* rival, the *Daily Sun,* and denied that he had ever told Wild Bill to leave town.[32] To this the *Leader* replied on August 18, 1876:

WILD BILL AND THE MARSHAL

City Marshal Slaughter rushes into print with the statement that Wild Bill was never ordered to leave town, and by so doing confesses his ignorance of a matter which he should have been cognizant of. It may

---

[30] Letter to the author, Feb. 3, 1960.
[31] Letter to the author, Oct. 14, 1960.
[32] The files of the *Daily Sun* are incomplete for this period (about May–October, 1876) and despite considerable research all over the United States, copies have not yet been found. This is doubly unfortunate, because apart from the loss of the item in question, this paper is believed to have carried some detailed accounts of Wild Bill and his movements.

be true that Slaughter never ordered Bill to leave town, but we can prove that Bill was ordered out of town on several occasions by both city and county officers. We are not possessed of an "over-weening desire" to charge Marshal Slaughter with dereliction of duty, but if we ever make the charge we will substantiate it without any very great effort. By the way, was the Marshal afraid of Wild Bill?

Wild Bill had done little in Cheyenne to spark off bad feeling against himself, so the conclusions reached by Flannery and Thorp are probably correct. But the other allegations had deeper implications.

If we accept that whatever the cause, Wild Bill's eyes were bothering him, then he displayed an air of confidence that he obviously did not feel. It is alleged that several times, at risk of losing face, he laughed off would-be glory hunters by hinting that his eyes had "gone back on me." The assumption that this was cowardice was understandable, but perhaps others took it as a gesture of contempt for the individual concerned—that even without his eyes Hickok believed he could still beat them—and would not deem to waste his time and energy. Regardless of the reaction (and it is important to remember that no contemporary report suggests that Hickok backed down before anyone), Wild Bill Hickok never wasted time in explanation. He continued to maintain that princely aloofness that had marked him through life when he meant to make it obvious he wished to be left alone.

If we do accept that Hickok was suffering from a serious eye disorder, and hid his fears in tall stories and humor, often turned against himself, then in reality Wild Bill was a very brave man. In the face of total darkness, he maintained his ability to laugh at himself and tell stories in which he came off second best. The more lurid the stories the more interested his audience, and tales of diamond caves and huge monsters would have them agog. Invariably these tales would end with Wild Bill in an awkward predicament, and without fail someone would ask: "But Bill, if there was no escape, how did you get away?" "I didn't," he would reply amidst a roar of laughter, "I was killed!"

Hickok was seriously concerned about some of the bad stories about his exploits. He went out of his way to set the record straight. One person he spoke to about his reputation was Mrs. Annie Tallent, the first white woman to enter the Black Hills. She recalled the one meeting she had with him:

One day during the summer of 1875, while walking along one of the

276

principal streets of Cheyenne with a friend, there appeared sauntering leisurely along towards us from the opposite direction, a tall, straight and rather heavily built individual in ordinary citizen's clothes, sans revolvers and knives, sans buckskin leggings and spurs, and sans everything that would betoken the real character of the man, save that he wore a broad-brimmed sombrero hat, and a profusion of light brown hair hanging down over his broad shoulders. A nearer view betrayed the fact that he also wore a carefully cultivated mustache of a still lighter shade, which curled up saucily at each corner of his somewhat sinister mouth, while on his chin grew a small hirsute tuft of the same shade, and barring the two latter appendages he might have easily been taken for a Quaker minister. When within a few feet of us, he hesitated a moment, as if undecided, then stepping to one side suddenly stopped, at the same time doffing his sombrero and addressing me in good, respectable Anglo-Saxon vernacular substantially as follows:

"Madame, I hope you will pardon my seeming boldness, but knowing that you have recently returned from the Black Hills, I take the liberty of asking a few questions in regard to that country, as I expect to go there myself soon. My name is Hickok."

I bowed low in acknowledgment of the supposed honor but I must confess that his next announcement somewhat startled me.

"I am sometimes called Wild Bill," he continued, "and you have no doubt heard of me, although," he added, "I suppose you have heard nothing good of me."

"Yes," I replied candidly, "I have often heard of Wild Bill and his reputation, to say the least, is not at all creditable to him. But," I hastened to add, "perhaps he is not so black as he has been painted."

"Well, as to that," he replied, "I suppose I am called a red-handed murderer, which I deny. That I have killed men I admit, but never unless in absolute self-defense, or in the performance of an official duty. I never, in all my life, took any mean advantage of an enemy. Yet understand," he added, with a dangerous gleam in his eyes, "I never allowed a man to get the drop on me. But perhaps I may yet die with my boots on," he said, his face softening a little. Ah, was this a premonition of the tragic fate that awaited him?

After making a few queries relative to the Black Hills, which were politely answered, Wild Bill, with a gracious bow that would have done credit to a Chesterfield, passed on down the street out of sight, and I never saw nor heard more of him until one day in August, 1876, when the excited cry of "Wild Bill is shot!" was carried along the main street of Deadwood.[33]

Wild Bill's actual movements during the latter part of 1875 are obscure. He seems to have wandered in and out of Cheyenne

[33] *The Black Hills; Or the Last Hunting Ground of the Dakotahs*, 100.

where, despite the charge still outstanding against him, no one bothered him. Whether he wintered there is not certain. Probably he spent Christmas and New Year's there, joining in the general celebration, clinking glasses with the crowd to welcome in the United States' centennial year, 1876—his year of fate.

-—⚜ 15 ⚜—-

A Man Died in Deadwood

THE DISCOVERY OF GOLD in the Black Hills of Dakota in 1874 by General Custer's expedition almost caused a nationwide panic. William E. Curtis, special correspondent of the Chicago *Inter-Ocean* accompanying the expedition, spread the news in a dispatch to his paper which was published on August 27, 1874. From coast to coast the excitement mounted. General Sheridan, who had sponsored Custer's deliberate violation of the treaty with the Sioux, reiterated General Hancock's statement of two years before, that any invasion of the Hills by whites would be met with resistance by the military. But the would-be "Black Hillers" were not put off that easily, and soon they started to trickle through to the Hills.

The Sioux at first viewed this deliberate encroachment on their land with mixed feelings; later, when it was obvious that the whites meant to stay, they became angry and warlike. Under the treaty signed at the Fort Laramie peace council on October 10, 1868, the Sioux were to retain their lands, and no white man would set foot on them. The Black Hills were sacred to the Indians, and this violation of the treaty was to them a deliberate act of war. The whites were soon suffering attacks in reprisal.

By the middle of 1875, whites were beginning to converge on the Hills like a colony of ants. Soon it became impossible for the army to stop the rush, and it then had to offer protection. Custer City sprang up as a mining town, but soon died, and the men, estimated at 25,000 by some and only 15,000 by others, quit their digging and headed for a new camp—Deadwood Gulch.

The gulch was a dead-end canyon in which were located three camps—Elizabeth City, Crook City, and Deadwood. Of the three, Deadwood was the most prominent. It was situated at the head of the gulch, where the road ended, against the canyon wall. Laid out on April 28, 1876,[1] it consisted of one main street which weaved

---

[1] Cheyenne *Daily Leader*, Aug. 17, 1876. The same story indicates that town lots sold and unsold by that date were estimated to be worth $100,000, "and the city is yet an infant, being just three months old."

like a moving rattlesnake in and out among the tree stumps and pot-holes left by early arrivals. Strung along it were the familiar frame buildings of a frontier town, showing evidence of hasty construction from rough-hewn, still-green planks. The sidewalks were little better, but they did afford some slight protection from the ankle-deep dust of the street.

During the daytime the street was packed with jostling men, horses, mules, oxen, and every conceivable manner of conveyance. At night the sidewalks rang with the thud and scuff of thousands of boots, and the saloons did a roaring trade. A few hotels were visible, but it would be some months before decent establishments would spring up. For every store there were three saloons, and above the click of dice and poker chips rang the voices of the dealers and the players. Sometimes a gun thundered. The citizens of Deadwood were, like their town, completely lawless. Every man went armed, and scarcely a week passed without someone's dying of lead poisoning. The everyday excitement of gold-seeking found its culmination in the big event of the week—the arrival of the Deadwood stage, with Johnny Slaughter[2] driving. Down the street he came, yelling and cracking his whip, his coach rocking crazily on its leather thorough braces, his team exerting all their strength to get the last ounce of speed from their sweating bodies. Then, to a jangling of harness and screams of protest from the brake shoes burning on the iron rims, Slaughter would bring the team to a slithering halt, stirring up the dust and the thirsts of the cheering crowd of onlookers.

To this roaring, hell-raising outlaw town flocked all manner of creatures: gamblers, con men, pimps, pickpockets, and prostitutes, the latter becoming established very quickly.

Into this seething cauldron of humanity came the famous and infamous. There were California Joe, Colorado Charlie, Wild Bill, and later, Doc Holliday and Wyatt Earp. They all came like moths to a flame, drawn together in a bid for a fortune. Some came to dig, prosper, and depart; others came to die.

That spring of 1876 was a busy one for Wild Bill. Although he had finally taken the step into matrimony, he was faced with the grim fact that he was pretty much a failure as most men saw it. Admittedly the very name Wild Bill Hickok still commanded the respect of the great and the fear of the cowardly, and no doubt

---

[2] Johnny Slaughter was the son of Cheyenne's marshal. He was murdered in the spring of 1877, when five masked men held up and robbed his coach (*John Hunton's Diary*, II, 201–202).

would have done so for a long time to come. But Hickok must have realized that he was now fast approaching a stage in his life when he would want a more stable existence, to put down roots, and to settle. And if his eyes were acting up on him, it would only be a matter of time before some young fool would try to back him down to make a reputation. Hickok was the first to admit that bluff and a reputation could only go so far. Thus the gold rush to the Black Hills must have seemed the best way out. If he could once make a strike, he could return to his wife perhaps to retire or engage in less dangerous pursuits.

After spending a couple of weeks with Agnes in Cincinnati, during which time Hickok probably suffered with his eyes (he was reported to have recovered from a recent "illness" when he returned to Cheyenne, although in her letters to the Hickok family, Agnes never once mentioned James's suffering any form of eye trouble or other disorders), it was agreed that he should go west to try and make a strike and at the earliest opportunity, Agnes would join him. But some of the reports going around in the press suggested that "domestic life did not suit such a rover as 'Wild Bill.' Notwithstanding Mrs. Lake lavished all her available funds upon her handsome husband, he was not content. He went east to raise a Black Hills expedition."[3]

Agnes Lake Hickok, however, believed differently:

"[James] is very busy in St. Louis where he will remain until the middle of May and then he will go West again, and I expect to join him sometime in the Fall. He is going to take a party to the Black Hills and I expect to remain in this place [Cincinnati] until he sends for me[.] it is hard to part so soon after being Married but it is unavoidable and so I am Content.[4]

According to Howard L. Hickok, on his way to St. Louis, Wild Bill made a brief stop at his mother's home. He wrote that Wild Bill had accumulated $1,600. This

. . . would not go far in making a home consistent with the one his wife already had. He resolved to go into the Hills and win a stake more commensurate with a higher standard of living. He had old fashioned ideas of honor, and living on his wifes money was contrary to his ideas of honor and decency. After a happy two weeks he left Cincinnati and his new bride, and started for the Black Hills. He stopped at Homer on his journey west for a short visit with his mother and family. My mother

---

[3] Omaha *Daily Bee*, Aug. 16, 1876.

[4] Agnes Lake Hickok to Polly Butler Hickok, Apr. 26, 1876. Letter in the possession of Ethel Hickok.

told me of this visit. She and dad had been married but a short time and Dad and Lorenzo were still caring for the aged mother. Mother never spoke unkindly of Jim but one could tell she resented the fact that he did not leave some of the $1600 with the mother. . . . She said Jim wore fine clothes. No doubt with his mind on his new wife and a fortune to be won he did not exercise his usual consideration for his mother's welfare. With the confidence he had in his brothers, he did not consider it necessary to inquire into the state of the family finances. In all my years with Dad [Horace] I never heard a word of criticism of any one of his brothers and he demonstrated the pride he felt in his younger brother in all his conversation concerning him.[5]

By March 23, Wild Bill was stated to be in Cheyenne "at the 'Miner's Home' where he makes his headquarters. He is a trifle pale now because of a recent illness. . . . I had a conversation with him and he spoke of the prospects in the new El Dorado as soon as the weather opens."[6] The *Leader*, however, noted on April 14 that "Wild Bill still lingers with us and the same may be said of winter. He is in his element nowadays and makes a business of stuffing newcomers and tenderfeet of all descriptions with tales of his prowess, his wonderful discoveries of diamond caves, etc., which he describes as located 'up north.' "

Hickok did not linger long in Cheyenne. He moved to St. Louis as Agnes said, and began sending out information concerning his planned expedition. One of the few available issues of the Cheyenne *Daily Sun* carried the following in its issue of April 30, 1876:

BLACK HILLS AND BIG HORN EXPEDITION

Wild Bill (J. B. Hickock) sends us from St. Louis, circulars and posters announcing that he is raising a company for the Black Hills and Big Horn country, which will leave St. Louis, Jefferson City, Sedalia and Kansas City, on Wednesday, May 17th. He adds that for reasons which will be fully explained to all who make application to become members of the expedition, we deem it not prudent to start earlier than the above named time. He wants parties joining his command to be outfitted at [as] follows: One good rifle each, and 200 rounds of ammunition; one tent for two, four or seven men; camp supplies; one rubber blanket, two woollen blankets, and four to six months' provisions. Bill is not sure whether he will take the Cheyenne or Sidney route, but intends to purchase the supplies at one of the two places.

He says:

We hope to secure a large body of men for this expedition, not only

5 "The Hickok Legend," *loc. cit.*, 31–32. Horace Hickok and Martha Edwards were married in 1867, which suggests that Howard may have been confusing this visit with that made in 1869.

for better self-protection on the route, but also to enable us to get cheaper rates of transportation, and lower figures on our supplies, and make a formidable settlement in the famous gold region.

Even Wild Bill's chief critic, the *Leader*, found room to comment:

BLACK HILLS BREEZES

WILD BILL ORGANIZING AN EXPEDITION IN SAINT LOUIS

WILD BILL'S EXPEDITION

We have received circulars from St. Louis announcing that Wild Bill (J. B. Hickock) is organizing an expedition for the Hills, which will leave St. Louis, May 16, coming to Cheyenne by special train, coming here via Kansas City, Lincoln and Omaha. The expedition will go from here to Custer City, where it will stop about ten days and then probably proceed to the Big Horn Country. The fare from St. Louis to Cheyenne will be $25; and from St. Louis to Custer City $33.65.

Contracts have been made with our outfitting houses as to prices of outfits, and with forwarding houses as to freight rates, etc. The circulars give details as to the outfit required, and state that Wild Bill proposes to lead the expedition to points where plenty of gold can be found.[7]

The same newspaper eight days later noted that Hickok had written to a friend stating that he was working night and day to complete the organization of his Black Hills expedition. Apparently, there was some trouble "bucking" the Yankton route, for which agents were actively working in St. Louis.[8]

What happened next is not clear. Some have it that the Wild Bill expedition may have been confused with that of "Idaho Bill" and C. C. Carpenter scheduled to leave St. Louis on April 3,[9] but there is no doubt from the available newspaper evidence that Hickok was organizing such an expedition. Buel suggests one possible solution, although he seems careless of his dates. In relating Hickok's intentions and belief that the route from Cheyenne would be the most "expeditious and practicable; and his company was organized to proceed that way, where outfits could be had much cheaper than at Bismark," he stated that Wild Bill believed that not less than one hundred persons should go along, "and during this period of organizing he daily visited the writer, who was then city editor of the *Evening Dispatch*, and reported the progress of his scheme."

Buel then states that about one hundred men had joined at St.

[6] St. Louis *Republican*, Mar. 23, 1876.
[7] Cheyenne *Daily Leader*, May 3, 1876.
[8] Spring, *Colorado Charley, Wild Bill's Pard*, 89.
[9] *Ibid.*

Louis and "nearly as many more had enlisted under Carpenter at Kansas City, so that the two companies were consolidated and started to the Black Hills via Cheyenne on the 12th of April."[10]

Buel's comment might suggest that Hickok did not linger in Cheyenne until April 14, but in fact went to St. Louis before the end of March, organized his expedition, and returned with it on April 12, which prompted the comment in the *Leader*. But this does not agree with the printed references to his expedition, and Agnes throws a little more light on the subject. Unfortunately, the portion of the page which gives the reason for the postponement of Hickok's own expedition has been torn from the original—not deliberately, but probably through careless handling many years ago. However, here is her comment, which also throws some more light on their relationship over the years:

[James has] . . . put off the trip until the first of June. I will remit you his last letter from Omaha[.] I have not heard from him since and I feel so bad about it that I can not sleep at night, but the only consolation that I have is that he is where he can not communicate[.] iff I was sure it was that I would not feel so bad. But I am afriad that he is sick; and if so he will not write nor alow anyone else to do so. before we was Married I did not get a letter from him for five weeks; and the first [missing] that time he told my [the remainder is missing].[11]

On June 8 the *Leader* noted that "Wild Bill is among us again," but no further reference could be found to his expedition, the conclusion being that it was either abandoned or joined up with another one—Carpenter's, perhaps? Dubious sources have asserted that he did in fact lead such an expedition into the Hills and then returned to Cheyenne. But this is not corroborated.

Colorado Charley Utter arrived in Cheyenne in March, and it was noted: "He draws his rations at the Metropole."[12] During the next month he superintended the organization of his proposed Black Hills transportation line. Presumably he and Wild Bill met and discussed each other's plans, but Wild Bill left for St. Louis and Charley returned to Georgetown, Colorado, where he was reported to be completing arrangements for his wagon train. He was also organizing a pony express to be operated between Deadwood and Fort Laramie. In this venture he was to go into partnership with a man named Ingalls (possibly John James Ingalls) and an Eng-

10 *Heroes of the Plains*, 185–86.
11 Agnes Lake Hickok to Celinda Hickok, June 30, 1876. Letter in the possession of Ethel Hickok.
12 Cheyenne *Daily Sun*, Mar. 28, 1876.

lishman named Richard Seymour, better known from his own self-styled name "Bloody Dick" Seymour.[13]

Sometime in June, Charley and his brother Steve arrived in Cheyenne, and in company with Wild Bill prepared to set out for the Black Hills.

There is a great deal of confusion, fiction, and imagination to be found in printed versions of Wild Bill's last two months of life. Innumerable old-timers have come forward to claim intimate contact, but few of them can be considered reliable. At this late date it is hardly likely that a detailed picture of that trip can ever be accurately drawn. Despite some fictionalizing for a Western magazine in the 1940's, Joseph "White-Eye Jack" Anderson's claim to have been on that trip cannot be ignored. Thanks to his daughter, Mrs. Ellen Anderson Mitchell, I have been able to correct some of the fiction that crept in previously, and the revised extracts are used here.

At the time he was in Deadwood and later in Leadville, Anderson was known simply as "the Kid." Later he adopted the name John, which most of his family believed was his real Christian name, but in 1941 his daughter learned that his true name was Joseph Foster Anderson. He gained the name "White-Eye" when a burning buffalo chip landed on his left eye during a prairie fire, and although he kept his sight, his eyebrow turned snow white.

Anderson claims to have first met Hickok at Fort McPherson in the early 1870's, and found him a hard man to get acquainted with. Early in June, 1876, White-Eye and his brother Charley arrived in Cheyenne and made arrangements to get some form of conveyance to take them to Deadwood. They met up with Wild Bill, and thanks to him were able to join Utter's party. The Utter brothers had a four-horse outfit, while Wild Bill is alleged to have teamed up with a man named Pie, but the details are not clear.

Doc Howard made the claim that shortly before Hickok left Cheyenne, he asked him for a loan as "my remittance hasn't come from the East." Whether this was money from Agnes or some other source is not known. Howard agreed to the loan and staked him to $22.30:

He was very grateful and said he would pay it back as soon as he could. I remember saying, "Bill, if you ever get flush, pay it back; if not, forget about it." I thought a great deal of Bill. He was as good a friend as a man could have. He deserved much more credit than he ever got

[13] Spring, *Colorado Charley, Wild Bill's Pard*, 91–92.

for bravery and loyalty to all. After I staked him we said goodbye and he left with the gang in the morning.[14]

The party left Cheyenne about June 27 and set out for Fort Laramie. On the way they passed John Hunton's famous ranch at Bordeaux. In his diary for 1876, Hunton recorded Hickok's arrival at the locality; shortly before his death in 1928 he set down his recollections:

On June 30, 1876, "Bill" and a party of men who were on their way to the Black Hills mines, traveling with a four horse team and wagon, camped about two miles south of my ranch. The next morning they passed my place and "Bill" stopped long enough to say "How." He then said, "So long Jack" and went away. ("Jack" is the nickname by which Hunton was known in the early days). A few hours afterward Waddie S. Bacom, one of my men who had been out riding, came in and said, "Mr. Hunton, I met a man down the road who said he was 'Wild Bill' and wanted you to go to the place he camped last night and get his cane which he stuck in the ground at his head where he made his bed last night in the edge of a patch of bushes, and send it to him at Deadwood, by someone you can trust to deliver it to him. Be sure not to send it except by some mutual friend whom you both know, as he did not want to take any chance of losing it." I sent the man for the cane and he brought it to me.

In less than a month I heard of Bill's death. . . . I kept the cane until 1921 and then gave it to Miss Eunice G. Anderson, State Historian, to be deposited in the museum of the Wyoming Historical Society, where it is now deposited and can be seen.[15]

According to Anderson, the trip to Deadwood from Cheyenne took them two weeks. He recalled that early in July they arrived at Fort Laramie, where they were joined by about thirty wagons, all bound for the Black Hills. Along with this wagon train were a number of whores, ladies with the fascinating names of Big Dollie, Dirty Emma, Tit Bit, Smooth Bore, and Sizzling Kate.

At the fort, so White-Eye claims, the train gained another member—Calamity Jane. Despite some intensive research it has not been established that Jane was actually on this trip. It is known that she was tried in Cheyenne on a charge of grand larceny on June 9, but acquitted; that on June 10 she took a buggy ride, so she thought, to Fort Russell and ended up fifty miles away at the Chug, and finally reached Fort Laramie. From there she was reported at Forts Reno and Fetterman. Curiously, however, it was

[14] Howard, *"Doc" Howard's Memoirs*, 20.
[15] Vol. II, 115–16.

reported in the Deadwood paper that "Calamity Jane has arrived," on July 15, three days after the Hickok party are believed to have come in.[16]

White-Eye was adamant that during the trip Hickok hardly spoke to Jane at all, except to allow her access to his five-gallon keg of whisky, and all the women called him "Mr. Hickok" for he let it be known that he was only interested in his wife.

Anderson stated that on July 6 the party arrived at Jack Bowman's ranch at Hat Creek. There they met Buffalo Bill Cody, who was a member of an advance guard of the Fifth Cavalry. He greeted White-Eye as an old friend:

> "By God, it's the White-Eye Kid," and shook hands with me. He then asked me I would go along with the soldiers, as he was short of scouts, and said that he would see that I got $100 a month and board. I looked at Wild Bill, who had heard the offer, but I saw him shake his head in the negative, and refused.[17]

Students of Buffalo Bill will immediately question this statement, in particular its reference to Hat Creek. Buffalo Bill *was* at Hat Creek, but on July 17, when he killed the Indian Yellow Hair (sometimes called Yellow Hand). Jack Bowman's "Hat Creek" was in reality Sage Creek. In 1875 some soldiers were sent from Fort Laramie to establish an outpost on Hat Creek, western Nebraska. Instead, they got mixed up and established it thirty miles too far west on Sage Creek, eastern Wyoming. Even when the mistake was known, they continued to call it Hat Creek, and the name sticks to this day.[18]

Cody was at Sage Creek on July 7, and it is reasonable to assume that he did meet White-Eye and Wild Bill. Cody is also known to have been in Cheyenne for a brief stay during the early part of June or July and may have encountered Wild Bill there. But Cody himself did not mention the meeting in later years.[19]

Wild Bill became White-Eye's hero. Among his recollections are comments on Hickok's eyesight, marksmanship, and weapons, and in this latter respect it is difficult to fault him, because the pistols he claims Wild Bill had are of the type available at the time. He wrote:

> Wild Bill's far sight was practically gone when I knew him, and he

[16] Spring, *Colorado Charley, Wild Bill's Pard*, 95–97.
[17] These extracts are from the Joseph F. "White-Eye" Anderson manuscript now in the possession of his daughter.
[18] Spring, *Cheyenne and Black Hills Stage and Express Routes*, 122.
[19] Russell, *Lives and Legends of Buffalo Bill*, 221.

could hardly see at all in darkness. I used to bring him back to camp after he had played poker. Some of the boys said he was "moon blind." But every morning he had his target practise. His shooting was all done at 25 paces, and at that distance he could see perfectly, and never missed a shot at anything. He did not take aim at all. I have never seen him take aim when shooting at a target. He always carried his guns butts forward, as did all western men, especially gunmen. He often drew both guns at once and fired simultaneously. It was a simple twist of the wrist to bring out the guns when carried butts forward, and they came upward instead of having to come backward to clear the holster as "bad men" do in the movies.

Wild Bill had his old buffalo rifle. . . . it was a .56 caliber Springfield with three bands on the stock, called a needle gun.[20] At this time he had discarded the Colt Navy cap and ball pistols, and had two of the latest Colt .38 caliber cartridge sixshooters. the triggers were filed off and the hammers filed smooth, so that his thumbs would slip off easily. He had a whole case of cartridges and often used to practise, about every day. He liked these pistols much better than he had the old .44's used in earlier years, and kept them brand new.[21]

It is evident that Wild Bill and his companions reached Deadwood about July 12. There his arrival caused some comment, and old friends soon looked him up. Among them was California Joe, who spoke with him at length about Custer's death—neither man could believe that their old friend was gone.

California Joe had hardly changed since Wild Bill saw him last; his beard and hair were still matted, and he still had his great sense of humor. During the time Hickok remained in Deadwood he, California Joe, and Colorado Charley became a common sight on the streets and in the saloons of the rapidly growing city.

Wild Bill was only in Deadwood about twenty days, yet he would have needed a year to do all the things he is supposed to have done. For the first few days after his arrival Hickok busied himself locating a claim and sizing up the place. That his wife was never far from his thoughts is evidenced by the following letter, a copy of which is still preserved in Deadwood:

DEAD WOOD BLACK HILLS, DACOTA July, 17th 1876
MY OWN DARLING WIFE AGNES. I have but a few moments left before this

20 This was mistakenly called a needle gun, a common error on the Plains concerning the Springfield rifles embodying the long firing pin of the Allin-designed breechblocks. Hickok's rifle was apparently a custom Springfield sporter, 1870 pattern.

21 These revolvers were evidently the .38 rim- or center-fire *conversion* pistols from cap and ball .36 to the new Richards or Richards-Mason patents of 1871–72, or factory-made models under these patents.

letter Starts I never was as well in my life but you would laughf to see
me now Just got in from Prospecting will go a way again to morow will
write In the morning but god nowse when It will start my friend will
take this to Cheyenne if he lives I dont expect to hear from you but it is
all the same I no my agnes and only live to love hur never mind Pet we
will have a home yet then we will be so happy I am all most shure I
will do well hear the man is huring me Good by Dear wife love to Emma

J B HICKOK

WILD BILL[22]

Any doubts regarding Hickok's feelings for his wife are dispelled
by this note and by the one he wrote just before his death.

It is possible that the above letter was the one Agnes received
on August 7, at the same time she received one from Polly Hickok
and Celinda: "Your kind and welcome letter has this morning been
handed to me by the letter carrier, and while I was reading it he
handed me another from my Husband witch I will send with this
so you can see where he is and what he is doing."[23]

During his short stay in Deadwood, Wild Bill did little to attract
attention. Many newcomers were told that he was there, and re-
membering some of the tall tales about him, vaguely wondered
what his presence meant. To others his presence was cause for real
concern.

Deadwood was an outlaw town, and for the most part was run
by a strong lawless element. The great influx of gunmen, gamblers,
cardsharps, and others anxious to relieve the honest miners of their
gold dust led several of the more prominent and respectable citizens to take steps to bring law to the town. With noted killers like
Charlie Storms and Jim Levy in town, they feared an outlaw empire would spring up.

In the back rooms of several saloons furtive men discussed among
themselves Hickok's presence. If he became marshal, Deadwood
would be Hays and Abilene all over again. And they didn't want
that. As long as Deadwood was lawless, their illicit gambling dens
and other rackets could continue to rake in huge profits; once law
came, there would be a big cleanup.

How much attention Hickok actually paid to the rumors is unknown. His presence in the camp aroused great interest in the men,
and there were many eager to see him shoot. Old-timer Billy Rad-

[22] J. W. Buel reproduced an edited version of this letter, claiming that "it is at
present in my possession" (*Heroes of the Plains*, 188). However, the letter had been
published in several newspapers in 1877, presumably with Agnes's permission.

[23] Agnes Lake Hickok to Polly Butler Hickok, Aug. 7, 1876. Letter in the possession of Ethel Hickok.

dick recalled that someone placed several silver dollars on a stump about twenty-five paces away, and Hickok drew his revolvers and commenced firing before most people present were aware of his intentions. "I noticed that Bill was purty quick to walk over and pick up them plugged dollars, and I wondered about it at the time. But later when I learned that he had just got married to Agnes Lake, back in Cheyenne, I understood," he concluded with a sly grin, as if saying, "You know what I mean!"[24]

The brief period between July 12 and August 1 accounted for some of the legendary events which are still talked of and written about. If even half of these are true, Wild Bill was a very busy man. But stories involving him with embittered gunmen, one of which alleges that he backed down six men who had let it be known that he would not last to see another sunset, lack any form of documentation. There were other equally unreliable stories which wormed their way into his legend.

At every opportunity Wild Bill gambled, but he did not make a fortune at it. In his last days it is evident that he lost more than he won, which may account for a growing feeling of depression. Historians have not agreed on his favorite saloon haunts during this time. He is known to have frequented the Senate, Shingle's No. 3, and Mann's No. 10. Making the rounds of the saloons may have been a safety measure. If he kept on the move and had no established haunts, a potential enemy would have trouble planning a move against him. Perhaps he was just restless. Whatever the cause, Wild Bill Hickok was a changed man. He grew more depressed and spoke repeatedly of death, and once while riding into the gulch he turned to Charley Utter and said: "Charley, I feel this is going to be my last camp, and I won't leave it alive." Utter laughed as did his other friends, but Wild Bill did not.

Charley Utter, meantime, was busy with his pony express, which was welcomed both in the Black Hills and in Cheyenne. It was noted that the express between Deadwood and Fort Laramie "will make round trips hereafter. All mail matter arriving at Cheyenne for the Hills, for which they have orders, will be telegraphed from Laramie. The pony express must prove a great convenience and we hope it may be adequately patronized."[25]

Among the riders, apart from Charley and his brother Steve, were several notables, including "Bloody Dick" Seymour and Dick Street.[26]

[24] Leland D. Case to the author, Jan. 30, 1971.
[25] Cheyenne *Daily Leader*, July 22, 1876.

On July 22, in company with eight other men, Leander P. Richardson left Fort Laramie for the Black Hills. At Jack Bowman's ranch at Hat Creek he met Steve Utter, who gave him a letter of introduction to his brother Charley. Richardson reached Deadwood on July 31. His account of his brief sojourn in the place has met with critical comment, for he himself seemed curiously careless of his reporting—at least in later years. It is also evident that he had a sense of humor that was apparently not appreciated by some of his contemporaries. Once in a letter to the Cheyenne *Daily Leader* he declared that he had been killed by Indians, and was promptly branded "Puttyhead Richardson" by the editor.[27]

A perusal of Richardson's published comments in 1876 and 1877 indicates that he wrote for a varying readership, and therefore it is pertinent here to reproduce his two published accounts of Wild Bill and the impression he made upon him. In 1877 he wrote:

I had been in town only a few moments when I met Charley Utter, better known in the West as "Colorado Charley," to whom I had a letter of introduction, and who at once invited me to share his camp while I remained in the region. On our way over to his tent, we met J. B. Hickok, "Wild Bill," the hero of a hundred battles. Bill was Utter's "pardner," and I was introduced at once. Of course I had heard of him, the greatest scout in the West, but I was not prepared to find such a man as he proved to be. Most of the Western scouts do not amount to much. They do a great deal in the personal reminiscences way, but otherwise they are generally of the class described as "frauds." In "Wild Bill," I found a man who talked little and had done a great deal. He was about six feet two inches in height, and very powerfully built; his face was intelligent, his hair blonde, and falling in long ringlets upon his broad shoulders; his eyes, blue and pleasant, looked one straight in the face when he talked; and his lips, thin and compressed, were only partly hidden by a straw-colored mustache. His costume was a curiously blended union of the habiliments of the borderman and the drapery of the fashionable dandy. Beneath the skirts of his elaborately embroidered buckskin coat gleamed the handles of two silver-mounted revolvers, which were his constant companions. His voice was low and musical, but through its hesitation I could catch a ring of self-reliance and consciousness of strength. Yet he was the most courteous man I had met on the plains. . . . You have heard the expression "quick as lightning?" Well, that will describe "Wild Bill." He was noted all over the country for rapidity of motion, courage,

---

[26] Spring, *Colorado Charley, Wild Bill's Pard*, 97–98. "Bloody Dick" Seymour is something of a mystery man. Many believed him to be the son of an English lord or at least from a family of some prominence. His movements after 1876 are unknown.

[27] *Ibid.*, 108.

and certainty of aim. Wherever he went he controlled the people around him, and many a quarrel has been ended by his simple announcement, "This has gone far enough."[28]

Some seventeen years later, in a letter to the New York *Sun* refuting the claim of a man who said that Wild Bill was a cardsharp and that he had seen Hickok in Deadwood dressed "with his long yellow hair pouring down his shoulders, his sombrero cocked sideways on his head, and with two ivory-handled pistols in their holsters, swinging at either side," Richardson presented an entirely different picture. In place of the flamboyant figure he himself presented in 1877, he made Hickok look plain and attributed the gaudy raiment to Colorado Charley. Arriving in Deadwood, Richardson proceeded to Utter's camp:

Mr. Utter received me with wide open hospitality, and we started out to hunt up his partner. It was about the middle of a bright sunny afternoon, and we found Wild Bill sitting on a board which was lying on the ground in front of a saloon. His knees were drawn up in front of him as high as his chin, and he was whittling at a piece of wood with a large pocketknife.

"Get up, Bill," said Utter. "I want you to shake hands with a friend of mine."

Wild Bill slowly arose. He came up like an elevator, and he came so high that I thought he was never going to stop. He was unusually tall, and quite spare as to flesh, but very brawny and muscular. . . .

The last days of this man's life in Deadwood were interesting. I know all about them, because I was there. I was the guest of Wild Bill, and his partner was a natty, handsome, courageous little man named Charles Utter. He was called Colorado Charley, and was the dandy of that country. He wore beaded moccasins, fringed leggings and coat, handsome trousers, fine linen, revolvers mounted in gold, silver and pearl, and a belt with a big silver buckle. He was blonde with long hair and a moustache, and imperial, and "Calamity Jane," who bossed a dancehouse, had it as her sole ambition, aside from the consumption of all the red liquor in the gulch, to win him. Mr. Utter had one habit that was rather startling in that community. He took a bath every morning, and people used to come out and view the process with interest not wholly unmixed with wonder. . . .

Charley Utter . . . slept in a tent between fine California blankets, and he had a real mirror, and real combs, razors and wisp brooms.

Bill was less finicky about his quarters. He slept in a big canvas covered wagon, rolled up in an army blanket. Every morning, just before

[28] "A Trip to the Black Hills," *Scribner's Monthly*, Vol. XIII (Feb., 1877), 755.

breakfast, he used to crawl out, clad in his shirt, trousers and boots, tie his hair in a knot at the back of his head, shove his big revolver down inside the waistband of his trousers, and run like a sprinter down the gulch to the nearest saloon. In a few minutes he would come strolling back, with a cocktail or two stowed away where it would do the most good, and would complete his toilet. . . .

Utter's greatest hobby was neatness, a thing which most plainsmen knew nothing of. He positively would not permit Wild Bill, or California Joe, or "Bloody Dick," or any of the rest of them to enter his tent. That he declared, was a shooting point with him. One day Bill did not get home until after breakfast was over, and everybody gone. He brought with him a very superior article of Deadwood jag, and Utter's fine blankets, seen through the open flap of the tent, were more of a temptation than he could endure. Pretty soon the big fellow was snoring, calmly rolled up in Utter's bedclothing, and there we found him, Utter and me, when we came over to camp an hour or two later. "Colorado Charley" was at first amazed by the presumption of his partner. For a moment he stood and fervently cursed the unconscious sleeper, and then, catching him by the heels, dragged him bodily out of the tent upon the ground. After that he ran in, pulled out his blankets, and hung them up on the surrounding trees, all the time straining his vocabulary for fresh epithets to hurl at the offender. During the whole proceeding Bill stared at him with lazy lethargy, and then, with a parting grunt, climbed into his wagon and went peacefully to sleep again. . . .

Wild Bill was everything but a ruffian, under ordinary conditions. It was strange to note the control in which he was held by Utter. I was never quite able to decide to my own satisfaction whether Utter amused or awed him. But certainly I never heard anybody take "roastings" with as little concern as that with which Bill used to take the fierce tongue lashings of his dudesque little partner. I suppose, perhaps, they fully understood each other, and knew perfectly well that behind all the words there was an impenetrable wall of manly affection. . . .

It is true that he [Hickok] played cards a good deal. But he could not have cheated a blind baby. Almost every day his partner used to "stake" him to card money. If he ever won, nobody knew it. And, besides, the crowd that was congregated in Deadwood City in those early days was a fine sort of gathering for a poker sharp to deal with. It was probably by all adds the toughest outfit ever brought together in one community. . . .

One afternoon Bill, Utter and I were walking along the street when a row began in one of the shanties that did duty as a saloon. Everbody rushed in.

"Wait a minute," said Bill. "Pretty soon somebody in there will pull a pop, and you'll see 'em come out."

Pretty soon somebody did pull a pop, and the crowd came out. They came so fast that they brought the whole front of the building with

293

them. Bill said he thought it was a breach of hospitality for a man's guests to carry away the bulk of his house like that.[29]

Richardson also referred to the presence of California Joe around their campfire at night, and spoke at length of Wild Bill's story-telling. Most of the tales revolved around his experiences in New York, Boston, Philadelphia, and other places where his companions had never been. Any doubt which his companions had were re-ferred to Richardson, who verified his remarks, but wrote: "I love truth, but I do not yearn to obtrude my preferences so far away from home. They were great stories that Wild Bill told, and as his other hearers knew nothing about them, and I didn't contradict him, he had a very fair margin for the play of his imagination."[30]

Hickok's apparent indifference to personal danger was a point that intrigued Richardson. He watched him stand beside two men who shot it out without hitting themselves or anyone else, and hurl derisive criticisms at them for poor aim. Later, when they stood in a saloon and a row broke out, and Richardson made haste to beat the crowd out of the place when the proprietor threatened every-one with a sawed-off shotgun, Wild Bill stopped him. As the room cleared, Hickok said: "Young man, never run away from a gun. Bullets can travel faster than you can. Besides, if you're going to be hit, you had better get it in the front than in the back. It looks better."

Such prophetic words from Wild Bill prompted Richardson to ask him the question that scores of others must have wondered: "How can a man who is being shot at by two or three other men retain such complete control of his nerves as to shoot back with accuracy?" Hickok stared at him for some moments as if he had never given the matter much thought. "Well," he replied, "when a man really believes the bullet isn't moulded that is going to kill him, what in hell has he got to be afraid of?"[31]

Richardson also made a reference to the rumor connecting Hickok with the proposed cleanup of Deadwood. He said that Utter was quick to suggest that Wild Bill join him on a hunting trip after Indian ponies, which could be sold for a fair profit. Richardson noted his reaction:

Bill was silent.

[29] A verbatim copy of the letter was published as "Last Days of a Plainsman" in *True West*, Vol. XIII, No. 2 (Nov.–Dec., 1965), 22–23, 44–45. For the sake of chronology, I have rearranged some of the paragraphs.
[30] *Ibid.*
[31] *Ibid.*

"Joe will go along," resumed Utter, urgently, "and so will Richardson (I wasn't so sure about that), and a dozen others.

"Will you go?"

"Not a d——d foot."

"Why not?"

"Well, those fellows over across the creek have laid it out to kill me, and they're going to do it or they ain't. Anyway, I don't stir out of here, unless I'm carried out."

That was when I saw the quick flash of ferocity in Wild Bill's eyes. The conversation ended at this point. Everybody knew it was useless to argue with Wild Bill when his mind was set, and so everybody went on about his business as before.[32]

At this late date it is a matter of conjecture how much of the truth is to be found in Richardson's accounts. He was there, and he did have much to say in the contemporary press about Hickok, but his remarks leave much to be desired. It must be remembered that he only knew Hickok for two days, whereas his reports suggest it was a relationship of several weeks.

Hickok's preoccupation with death has some contemporary backing. A brief item published late in August states:

WILD BILL'S PRESENTIMENT

A week before Wild Bill's death he was heard to remark to a friend, "I feel that my days are numbered; my sun is sinking fast; I know I shall be killed here, something tells me I shall never leave these hills alive; somebody is going to kill me. But I don't know who it is or why he is going to do it. I have killed many men in my day, but I never killed a man yet but what it was kill or get killed with me. But I have two trusty friends, one is my six-shooter and the other is California Joe."[33]

Considering that Charley Utter was his "pardner," it is odd that Hickok should mention California Joe—unless Joe was the "friend" he spoke to. The publication of the story so soon after the assassination indicates that there was some truth in Hickok's alleged belief in his impending death.

On August 1, Wild Bill sat down and wrote to his wife, setting out his feelings for her and hinting at his premonition—indicating pretty clearly that he knew that he was going to die:

[DEAD WOOD BLACK HILLS DACOTA August 1st 1876]
AGNES DARLING, if such should be we never meet again, while firing my last shot, I will gently breathe the name of my wife—Agnes—and with

[32] *Ibid.*
[33] Cheyenne *Daily Leader*, Aug. 26, 1876.

wishes even for my enemies I will make the plunge and try to swim to the other shore.

[J B HICKOK
WILD BILL][34]

Later in the day Hickok went into the No. 10 saloon, where he was greeted by the bartender, Harry Sam Young. Young claimed in later years that he had first met Hickok in Hays back in 1869 and thanks to Wild Bill had secured employment with the government at Fort Hays.[35] When Wild Bill arrived in Deadwood, one of the first places he went in was Carl Mann's No. 10 saloon, and Young had been the first person he saw. Hickok quickly renewed their old acquaintance and gave his word to Mann that Young was a good boy and could be trusted.

On August 1, Hickok sat in on several games until the early evening. Each time he reserved the right to have his back against the wall—and no one ever refused him. In fact, it is part of the Hickok legend that he always insisted on this precaution, and at this date nothing has been produced to disprove or completely authenticate the story. However, it is in keeping with the actions Wild Bill adopted in public to defend himself against possible attack.

Later in the evening Captain William R. Massie, a former Missouri River pilot who had seen service on the Mississippi, walked in and joined the game. One of the players dropped out, and one of the bystanders took his place. It was Jack McCall. At the end of the evening McCall was broke, and Hickok took pity on him and gave him money enough for his supper. Then, bidding the company good night, Wild Bill made his way back to camp, and was soon inside his blankets.

It has been claimed that earlier in the evening Hickok had stood leaning on the doorjamb of saloon No. 10 watching the crowds bustling past, and had reflected again on his fear and premonition of death. Tom Dosier, one of his acquaintances, had tried to dissuade him from such thoughts, but Wild Bill shook his head and

[34] This text was first published in the Virginia Evening Chronicle, Aug. 4, 1877, as part of a poem written by Jack Crawford: "Wild Bill's Grave," and was preceded by the line: "Hear part of this letter—the last of this life" (quoted in Buel's Heroes of the Plains, 210–11). Wilstach claimed in 1926 that Gil Robinson owned two letters written by Hickok from Deadwood, so perhaps this was one of them, but its present whereabouts are in doubt.

[35] Harry (Sam) Young, Hard Knocks, 42–43. Claims that one Anson Tipple was the bartender are not substantiated. The Chicago Inter-Ocean, Aug. 17, 1876, states that "Samuel Young" was the bartender (see also Ramon F. Adams, Six-Guns and Saddle Leather, 713–14).

wandered away. Some have even hinted that Wild Bill possessed spiritualistic powers, because he often sensed danger and was able to beat his enemies. It is far more likely that years of experience on the plains, among men who held life cheaply, had taught him to be a good judge of men and characteristics—provided they were facing him at the time.

On August 2, Charley Utter was busy arranging final details of a race between his own express and one run by a man named Clippinger. One hundred copies of the *Daily Leader* were being dispatched by coach from Cheyenne to Fort Laramie, and then fifty copies each would be assigned to the rival companies to race the two hundred miles to Deadwood in three days.[36] So Charley was otherwise occupied when Wild Bill went down to saloon No. 10.

Noon came and went and Hickok dressed in his favorite outfit— a Prince Albert frock coat with all the trimmings—meandered into Nuttall and Mann's No. 10 shortly after noon. A nod to Harry Young, and he walked over to where Carl Mann, Charles Rich (the man who had caused all the trouble in the Gold Room in Cheyenne), and Captain Massie were already engaged in a game. There were then about eight people in the room.

At his approach, Mann hailed him and told him to sit down. Hickok hesitated and asked Rich, who had the wall seat, to change round. But he only laughed and told him not to worry—no one was going to attack him. Grudgingly Wild Bill sat down but a few minutes later again asked Rich to change seats. This time all the players good-naturedly ribbed him, and growling uneasily, Wild Bill sat down again. From where he sat, with Rich on his right, Mann on his left, and Massie right in front of him, Hickok had a clear view of the front door, but was conscious of the small door in his rear.

Having beaten Massie the previous evening, Wild Bill was now losing heavily to him. He looked over at Harry Young and asked for fifteen dollars' worth of pocket checks. Young left the bar and came over with them, placed them beside him, then returned to the bar.

Shortly before this, the front door swung open and a small, furtive man came in. Some say he was drunk, but others recalled that he gave no such impression as he came up to the bar. Jack McCall stared around. Facing toward him was Wild Bill, but he was busily examining his cards. Quickly he moved down the bar in case Wild Bill looked up—not that Hickok was likely to find much signifi-

36 Cheyenne *Daily Leader*, Aug. 2, 1876.

cance in his presence. Reaching the end of the bar, McCall stopped. He was only a few paces behind Hickok's stool.

Wild Bill's attention was on Massie. There was a friendly dispute between them, and Hickok was heard to remark: "The old duffer— he broke me on the hand."

Those were the last words he spoke. There was a loud bang, and a shout from McCall: "Damn you, take that!"[37] A smoking pistol was clutched in his right hand. The time was about 3:00 P.M.[38]

As McCall fired, Wild Bill's head jerked forward, and for some moments his body remained motionless. Then it toppled back from the stool to the floor. From his nerveless fingers spilled his cards: the Ace of Spades, the Ace of Clubs, two black eights, Clubs and Spades, and the Jack of Diamonds. Ever afterward they would be known as "Aces and Eights—The Dead Man's Hand."[39]

For some seconds no one fully realized what had happened. As the report of the shot died away, Captain Massie looked up, puzzled at the noise and the sudden numbness in his left wrist—unaware that Wild Bill was dead. Then he saw McCall, gun in hand, menacing the crowd, and as Hickok's body fell back, he realized what had happened.

Backing toward the rear door, McCall abused the crowd. "Come on ye sons of bitches," he snarled. But all except Carl Mann, on whom the pistol was leveled, ran out the front door. Snapping his pistol at George Shingle and Harry Young (both times it failed to fire), McCall ran out of the back door and mounted the first horse he saw. Unfortunately for him, the owner had slackened the saddle cinch because of the heat, and immediately the saddle turned over, sending McCall sprawling. Gasping for breath, he staggered to his feet and ran down the street, pursued by the excited cry: "Wild Bill is shot! Wild Bill is dead!" At a butcher's shop (said to have been Jacob Shroudy's) he hurried in and tried to hide, but someone used the muzzle end of a Sharps rifle to persuade him to come out, and he gave himself up without a struggle.

[37] Deadwood *Black Hills Pioneer*, Aug. 5, 1876. The word "damn" has not been found in any other accounts, including witnesses' testimony at McCall's trials.

[38] Wilstach gives the time as 4:10, but the *Pioneer* and others state it was "about three o'clock."

[39] The actual cards are disputed. Some have it that the fifth card was the Queen of Diamonds. A poker expert commented: "If Bill . . . had two pair *before* the draw, he was well on his way to a full house (3 of a kind plus a pair), which is the 4th highest hand one can get in poker. Mathematically, a full house appears once in 694 hands, so the odds (against getting one) are 693–1. If he had 2 pair *after* the draw . . . he held the third lowest possible hand, which shows once every 21 hands (Frank L. Forster to the author, May 15, 1971).

Back at the No. 10 some semblance of order was being restored. The doors were locked, and only friends of the deceased and people in authority were allowed in. A brief examination conducted by a hastily organized coroner's court, with C. H. Sheldon as foreman, established that the bullet had entered "the base of the brain, a little to the right of center, passing through in a straight line, making its exit through the right cheek between the upper and lower jaw bones, loosening several of the molar teeth in its passage, and carrying a portion of the cerebellum through the wound. From the nature of the wound death must necessarily have been instantaneous."[40] Having killed Hickok, the ball then lodged in Massie's left wrist.[41]

Word had now reached Colorado Charley, and he hurried into town, where he was joined by Doc Peirce,[42] a barber. The door to No. 10 was unlocked and they were allowed in. In describing the position of Wild Bill's body, Peirce wrote:

. . . he was lying on his side, with his knees drawn up just as he slid off his stool. We had no chairs in those days—and his fingers were still crimped from holding his poker hand. Charlie Rich, who sat beside him, said he never saw a muscle move. . . . When Bill was shot through the head he bled out quickly, and when he was laid out he looked like a wax figure. I have seen many dead men on the field of battle and in civil life, but Wild Bill was the prettiest corpse I have ever seen. His long moustache was attractive, even in death, and his long tapering fingers looked like marble.[43]

Ellis T. Peirce is remembered in Black Hills history with mixed feelings. But at this late date few people, if any, can improve on his recollections. His description of Wild Bill's death agrees with other accounts, and allowing for old-age lapses in memory, his version seems quite reliable. According to Wilstach, he served a two-year course in medicine in Pennsylvania prior to the Civil War. For this brief step into the medical profession he earned himself the title "Doc" on the frontier.

White-Eye Jack Anderson claimed that Wild Bill's coffin was

[40] Chicago *Inter-Ocean*, Aug. 17, 1876.

[41] It is evident that the ball was never removed. Massie claimed that it was still in his wrist as late as 1885, when it became a useful topic of conversation in barrooms (Cheyenne *Democratic Leader*, July 30, 1885, citing the Bismarck *Tribune*).

[42] Peirce was the correct spelling. In checking his letters to Frank J. Wilstach, The New York Public Library remarked: "Both the letter head and the signature show the use of Peirce as the spelling of Ellis Peirce's name" (Robert W. Hill, keeper of manuscripts, to the author, Jan. 6, 1966).

[43] Wilstach, *Wild Bill Hickok*, 284–85.

hastily constructed out of rough pine lumber, the outside covered in black cloth, and the inside with white, which "looked pretty good for a home-made coffin." The correspondent for the *Inter-Ocean* was far more sentimental:

. . . in a handsome coffin covered with black cloth and richly mounted with silver ornaments, lay Wild Bill, a picture of perfect repose. His long chestnut hair, evenly parted over his marble brow, hung in waving ringlets over the broad shoulders; his face was cleanly shaved excepting the drooping mustache, which shaded a mouth in death almost seemed to smile, but which in life was unusually grave; the arms were folded over the still breast, which inclosed a heart which had beat with regular pulsations amid the most startling scenes of blood and violence. The corpse was clad in complete dress-suit of black broadcloth, new underclothing, and white linen shirt; beside him in the coffin lay his trusty rifle, which the deceased prized above all other things, and which was to be buried with him in compliance with an often expressed desire.[44]

In 1925 it was alleged that the undertaker had stripped Hickok's body and found it covered "with knife and bullet wounds," but Peirce denied this:

The fact is I never undressed Bill. What was the use? He had no other clothes to put on. He was clean, except for clotted blood in his hair. I washed that out nice and clean; plugged up the hole where the bullet entered the back of his head; closed the perfect cross which the bullet made where it came out under his right cheek bone; fixed up and dressed his long fine mustache; cut a lock of hair from the back of his head which measured (if memory serves me right) about 14 inches in length; placed his right hand on his right hip where Bill always carried it, next to the stock of his Smith and Wesson gun;[45] placed his left arm across his breast; then put his fine Sharps' rifle in the box on the right hand side; I was thru."[46]

When asked what he did with the lock of hair, Peirce said he could not remember. But Richardson knew the answer. In his letter to the New York *Sun*, he wrote that "a lock of the dead man's hair was cut off after his body had been prepared for burial. Utter took half of the long brown strand and I have the other half to this day. It is glossy as spun glass and as soft as down. Near the roots there

---

[44] Chicago *Inter-Ocean*, Aug. 17, 1876.

[45] See note 53.

[46] Deadwood *Pioneer-Times*, Aug. 22, 1925. A year before Peirce had said: "We buried him in a rough coffin with his big Sharps rifle by his side. (His pistol, Utter, his partner, wished to keep). His left arm was laid cross-wise, beneath his back, just as he carried it in life. His right arm was extended downward by his side, with his hand resting on his rifle." (Sioux Falls *Daily Argus-Leader*, Aug. 9, 1924.)

is just a touch of roughness, where the life blood of a brave, great-hearted American man gushed out as the assassin's bullet burst through his brain." However, in a less melodramatic manner, Richardson wrote on November 1, 1876, to the Denver *Rocky Mountain News*: "Charley Utter . . . gave me a lock of the famous scout's hair. It is more than a foot long, and as fine and glossy as a woman's locks."

Richardson kept his lock of hair until 1907 when, through Gil Robinson, he presented it to Agnes Lake Hickok shortly before she died.[47] It is probably the same lock of hair now in the Wilstach Collection in The New York Public Library.

Wild Bill's funeral was set for the afternoon of August 3. According to O. W. Coursey, the pallbearers were Bill Hillman, John Oyster, Charlie Rich, Jerry Lewis, Charles Young, and Tom Dosier.[48]

All morning men had filed past the coffin for one last glimpse of the "Prince of Pistoleers." Colorado Charley, who intended to spare no expense for his friend, had gone into town the previous evening and had the following notice printed on neat paper inside a wide black border by the presses of the *Black Hills Pioneer*:

FUNERAL NOTICE

Died, in Deadwood, Black Hills, August 2, 1876, from the effects of a pistol shot, J. B. Hickock, (Wild Bill) formerly of Cheyenne, Wyoming.

Funeral Services will be held at Charles Utter's Camp, on Thursday afternoon, August 3, 1876, at 3 o'clock, P.M.

All are respectfully invited to attend.[49]

Following the service there was placed at the head of the grave a large board or stump on which was deeply cut: "A brave man; the victim of an assassin—J. B. (Wild Bill) Hickock, aged 48 years; murdered by Jack McCall, August 2, 1876."

Sometime later this was replaced by another headboard erected by Colorado Charley, which read: "Wild Bill—J. B. Hickock. Killed by the assassin Jack McCall in Deadwood Black Hills. August 2nd 1876. Pard we will meet again in the Happy Hunting ground to part no more. Good Bye—Colorado Charlie. C. H. Utter."

Wild Bill's grave at Ingleside, a romantic spot on the mountain-side, was surrounded within two years of his death by a growing

---

[47] Deadwood *Pioneer-Times*, Aug. 22, 1925.
[48] Sioux Falls *Daily Argus-Leader*, Aug. 9, 1924.
[49] The wording of this seems to vary. The Manhattan (Kansas) *Enterprise*, Aug. 23, 1876, substitutes the word "respectively" for "respectfully," and other papers spell Hickok in various ways.

Deadwood. The citizens decided to remove all the bodies to a new site at Mount Moriah, which would be a permanent cemetery.

Early in June, 1879, Colorado Charley made arrangements to go to Deadwood to have Wild Bill exhumed and removed to his new resting place. He let it be known that any attempt to disturb his friend without his being present would be a "shooting matter" so far as he was concerned. But first he had to face the law in Lead, where he was running a dance house. Indicted for "nuisance," Charley was sentenced to one hour's confinement in jail and a fine of fifty dollars and costs.[50]

During this time all sorts of wild rumors were buzzing around the country. Several unconfirmed rumors went round to the effect that Wild Bill's grave had already been opened and, worse, robbed. The Deadwood paper remarked on the rumors and was quickly followed by others. In Cheyenne it was reported:

WILD BILL'S GRAVE ROBBED

When Wild Bill, the noted frontiersman, the man who has "downed" during his lifetime, more fellow-creatures than he had fingers and toes, was buried in the old cemetery on the ridge in South Deadwood, his ivory handled revolvers and knife, according to the custom of the border, were laid away with his remains in the coffin. These implements of death were quite as famous as the owner himself, and the fact that they had been buried with the remains of their owner was kept a profound secret for a long time, but finally leaked out, and now it is said that some ghoul has gone through the grave and robbed it of these relics. When the sacrilegious act was committed we are unable to say, but that it was done is pretty well established in the minds of some people.

Robbing a grave is among the most dastardly acts in the catalogue of crimes and the man or men who despoiled the grave of Wild Bill deserves the fate of his cowardly assassin. The revolvers were made expressly for him and were finished in a manner unequalled by any ever before manufactured in this or any other country. It is said that a bullet from them never missed its mark. Remarkable stories are told of the dead shootist's skill with these guns. He could keep two fruit cans rolling, one in front and one behind him, with bullets fired from these fire-arms. This is only a sample story of the hundreds which are related of his incredible dexterity with these revolvers.[51]

And so began the last great speculation about Wild Bill's checkered career: what pistols *did* he have in Deadwood and what happened to them? Hickok's two large-caliber pistols were not buried in his coffin as the paper stated. His rifle was, and apparently also

[50] Spring, *Colorado Charley, Wild Bill's Pard*, 113–14.
[51] Cheyenne *Daily Leader*, July 1, 1879.

a small Sharps four-barrel derringer (at least this is the claim made for the weapon on show in Deadwood). Colorado Charley perhaps knew the whereabouts of those pistols, but there is no definite information available. A .44-caliber, finely engraved Colt revolver, "Model of 1850," with an ivory butt, is also in the region and is alleged to have been claimed by Hickok to be a gift from Kit Carson, and was only given up by Wild Bill shortly before his death because he needed the money to settle a board bill to a Captain Dobson. It has been described as so worn that there was a risk of multiple discharge if all the chambers were fired. Its present whereabouts is uncertain.[52]

To this date no one knows for sure what sort of heavy artillery weapons Wild Bill was actually carrying in Deadwood. White-Eye Jack Anderson's reference to a pair of .38 Colt revolvers converted from .36 percussion to cartridge are valid. Doc Peirce claimed that Hickok carried a pair of .45 cap and ball Colts, but Colt's did not make such weapons in that caliber, so it may be assumed that he was referring to a pair of .44 Army pistols, model of 1860. So far as is known, Wild Bill never had access to a Peacemaker—assuming that the weapon was then available on the frontier: production of this weapon had only reached about 22,000–25,000 by the time he died, and army and export orders had taken care of most of these. As for a .32 Smith and Wesson tip-up No. 2 Army revolver alleged to have been found on his body in saloon No. 10, there is no authentic proof of this weapon's ownership by Wild Bill. And of his two alleged .41 Williamson derringers there is no trace. It was even claimed, in 1879, that "those who should know, say that he never owned a pistol in the Hills."[53]

On August 3, 1879, three years to the day after Wild Bill's first burial, Colorado Charley and Lewis B. Schoenfield moved his body to its final resting place. The local press remarked:

As announced in these columns, Wild Bill's remains were exhumed

[52] Reference to the year 1850 suggests that the weapon was the Army revolver of 1860. Stamped on the cylinder of this model was "Patd. September 10, 1850," which referred to changes in design which were incorporated on all models manufactured during and after that year.

[53] O. W. Coursey claimed in the Deadwood *Pioneer Times*, Aug. 22, 1925, that the Hickok family in Troy Grove had one of the guns taken from Wild Bill's body, and quoted from a letter from Mrs. Louise Hickok mentioning the gun. The weapon in question is an 1851 model Colt Navy which was never used by Wild Bill but by his brother Lorenzo. It is part of family tradition that the Colt revolver in Troy Grove belonged to Wild Bill, but in letters written home in 1863, Lorenzo, then a wagon master in Missouri, refers to a pistol he had sent to his brother Horace. Serial number 143098, its year of manufacture was late 1862 or early 1863.

and reinterred in Mount Moriah Cemetery on Sunday last. For the information we have derived of the removal, we are indebted to Mr. Lewis Schoenfield, an old-time acquaintance of Bill's, and in whose memory Bill's many endearing qualities are still bright and green. Colorado Charley, a partner of Bill's at the time of his death, has purchased a lot in the new cemetery, and at his own expense procured a fitting monument of Italian marble, that is now daily expected, which will be raised over his new resting place as soon as it arrives. At 4 o'clock Sunday morning the body was uncovered and at 9 o'clock it was taken out of the grave. The body at interment weighed 180 pounds, but upon its removal it weighed not less than 300. There was no odor and no perceptible petrification had taken place, as it was hard as wood, and returned the same sound as when struck with a stick.

Everything in the coffin was found just as it was placed there, and the rumor that the grave had been rifled is all bosh. The only article buried with the body was a carbine, and that was in as good state of preservation as ever. There were no knives or revolvers buried with him as reported. . . . His hair was as glossy and silky as when in life, and a lock of it is now in the possession of Wm. Learned, musical director of the Gem Theatre. His moustache was hard, and seemed like his body to have been petrified and thus endeth the third and last chapter in the life of this truly remarkable man, whose true friends, and he seems to have many of them, still cherish his memory although three years have rolled past into eternity since they laid him in the tomb.[54]

Unfortunately, it now appears that Mr. Schoenfield's association with Wild Bill and his "memory" of his various deeds was not true. In a letter to his friends Dick and Brant Street (who had ridden for his Pony Express) which is now owned by Ethel Hickok, Charley (who signs himself "Charlie" on this occasion) declared that Schoenfield was a liar:

PLANTERS' HOTEL
DENVER, COLO., January 20 1880

DEAR DICK & BRANT

Yours of January 4/880 came to hand the day before I left Deadwood and Dick I was glad to hear from you. Well Dick I will explain all about that man Scholfield you spoke about. in the first place he is a dead beet and a bilk and I can prove it, he is a tender foot and wants to come into *noteriety*[.] he never seen Bill in his whole life nor was he in the Hills when Bill got killed. Well he made my acquantanship on the strength of Odd Fellowship[.] he claimed to be an Odd Fellow and was intraduced to me as such and when the City of Deadwood layed out the new burriel ground he took several contracts to move the boddies of parties

____

[54] Deadwood *Black Hills Times*, Aug. 5, 1879.

corpeses from the old ground to the new one and he came to me and wanted the contract to move Bill that was about six months before I took Bills boddy up[.] I told him when the proper time came that I would have him moved, and I did not want anyone to meddle with the grave and if they did that I would kill any one that I found tampering with the grave at all. Well on the 1st of August I went to the City Cleark and bought a burriel lot and on the 3rd I hired two men to dig him up[.] I bought a new outside box for the grave and paid the Expressman for hawling the boddy and Paid for digging the new grave[.] well the night before on the 2nd this man Schoolfield came to me and sayed he would go up and help the men dig Bill up. I told him all right he went to a Saloon and got some whiskey and took it up to help him along and I paid for the whiskey to. They went up early in the morning to dig, and I told them just as soon as they got to the coffin to come and get me for I would not allow any one to raise the boddy untill I was there[.] well they did so and I went up with some friends and we raised him and opened the coffin and found him just as I described to you before[,] so now you have the whole truth about the man Schoolfield *and* he is a liar. Well good By old friend

From CHARLIE H UTTER COLORADO CHARLIE

Dick answer this letter to Los Vages New Mexico.

A detailed description of the reburial of Wild Bill was given by John S. McLintock, who claimed to have witnessed Hickok's arrival in Deadwood in 1876, although some authorities believe that he did not actually reach the camp until 1877. His account of the reburial is interesting:

The body down to the hips was exposed. To our great astonishment it appeared to be in a perfect state of preservation. Being perfectly white, it seemed to have a coat of lime finish. The clothes, which were decomposed, had evidently been jolted to the sides while in transit to the new grave, leaving the upper portion of the body exposed. The manifold pleats in the fine linen shirt which he wore showed plainly on his form.

The writer took a stick the size of a cane and tapped many places on the body, face, and head, discovering no soft places anywhere. While the body appeared to be solid, petrified, the sound from the tapping was much the same as would result from the tapping of a wall, and not of solid stone. Some of the party were inclined to believe that the body was in process of petrification. Mr. Austin [William Austin, the cemetery caretaker] estimated the weight of the casket at five hundred pounds. While it was an extremely heavy load for four ablebodied men to carry up the hill, the writer would not place the weight above four hundred pounds, nor did I concur in the belief that it was a case of petrification, though there may have been such cases in existence. It was my belief that it was the result of a natural embalming or percolation of water containing embalming substances, depositing these in the tissues of the body.

After a close examination had been made by the four of us, the lid of the coffin was fastened down and the body of the great gunman, one of the greatest man-killers that the world had ever known, was for the second time lowered into a grave to be covered and lost to view. The wooden headboard was moved to the new grave, where it was practically destroyed by relic hunters whittling off pieces. In 1891, a statue was erected by J. B. Riordan, a sculptor from New York who chanced to be in Deadwood. This consisted of a rock pedestal with inscription, including the name of the sculptor, surmounted by a bust of Wild Bill. This was badly mutilated by relic hunters, and in 1902 another monument was placed over the grave. This is a life-sized Black Hills sandstone figure of Wild Bill. It was sculptured by Alvin Smith in a shop owned by H. W. Guyor, in Deadwood, and was erected in 1903. It also was badly defaced by relic hunters and the weather. It was tightly enclosed for protection with a heavy wire screen, but this was cut open by relic hunters, so it was removed about twenty years ago. . . .

It has been stated by the acting undertaker who was in charge of the original funeral, that Wild Bill's big Sharps rifle was buried by his side. This statement the writer knows to be incorrect, as he saw the gun in the coffin when it was opened on reinterment. It was not a Sharps rifle, but a carbine, or a short cavalry, fitted into an old-fashioned Kentucky rifle breech, with the name J. B. Hickok engraved on the wood. After his death his personal effects were disposed of, and John Bradley of Spearfish, South Dakota, purchased the Sharps rifle. He used the gun for many years afterwards in hunting for wild game. Subsequently it came into possession of Allen Toomey, of Spearfish, now deceased.[55]

Why many alleged photos of Wild Bill show him as a black haired bruinett is strange. He was a blond, as others, including General Custer who knew him well, have stated. His hair and moustache were of a tawny color.[56]

In 1892 a report went around that Hickok's remains were to be dug up; Charley Utter having "failed to pay for his lot in the cemetery where the remains of his friend lay, the cemetery company threatens to sell them to a New York museum agent."[57] Charley was furious, for he knew very well that he had paid for the lot, and

[55] There is some confusion here. The weapon Bradley had, which subsequently came to Allen Toomey, was in fact the Kentucky-type rifle. According to a short article headed "Wild Bill's Rifle," published in *Old West*, Vol. I, No. 4 (Summer, 1965), 53, the rifle is now owned by Toomey's niece, Mrs. Isabel Duffy, of New Orleans.

[56] *Pioneer Days in the Black Hills*, 283. Before the introduction of panchromatic and other techniques into photography, red, auburn, and ginger hair showed up black on the early wet- and dry-plate photographs.

[57] Central City (Colo.) *Weekly Register Call*, Oct. 28, 1892.

immediately went to Deadwood. His presence in town had a re-markable effect; the old books came to light and he was assured by the new cemetery association that Wild Bill would not be disturbed again. Apparently confusion arose when it was found that the old books did not record actual payments, but records did exist to show that Utter held the deed to the lot.[58] As late as the early 1950's a move was afoot to have Wild Bill removed from Deadwood and taken to Abilene, but the request was denied.

Back in 1876, it was some days before the outside world heard of Wild Bill's murder. The Cheyenne *Daily Leader* announced it on August 12, and out-of-state papers carried the story as much as ten days later. It is not known for sure how the news reached Troy Grove, but in 1896 his sister Lydia gave an interview which claimed to describe the events. The family say there are some inaccuracies, but it does indicate the great shock to the small community. Lydia apparently combined the reaction to the news as received by herself in Kansas and the family in Troy Grove:

I remember the day the paper came with the news of Bill's murder. . . . Mother had been a sufferer from inflammatory rheumatism for two years before that, and had not taken a step for eighteen months. My sister was standing at the gate when a neighbor came by and brought the Chicago paper giving an account of Bill's death. He handed it to my sister. She took it up and hurried into the house, hiding the paper in the kitchen behind a mirror on a shelf. Then, composing herself, she went in where mother was sitting.

"Mother," she said, "I am going over to the store a minute, and will be right back."

She put on her bonnet and ran to the little store about two hundred yards away to tell father[59] and one of my brothers. They all came back to the house together. When they entered the sittingroom there sat mother, the newspaper lying at her side, slowly rocking back and forth, while the blood from a hemorrhage of the lungs dyed the front of her light dress.

"I saw you get the paper, Linda," she said to my sister, "and when you did not bring it in I knew what was in it, so I went to get it."

She never fully recovered from it and she died two years later still mourning over Bill's terrible death.[60]

58 Spring, *Colorado Charley, Wild Bill's Pard*, 124.

59 This must have been a slip on the part of the reporter, because Polly Hickok did not remarry.

60 Chicago *Daily Record*, Dec. 26, 1896. The reporter assumed much from this interview. The family have never referred to Wild Bill as "Bill," but always as "James," "Jim," or "Uncle."

Agnes Hickok, too, shared their grief, and late in November the following letter reached Troy Grove:

CINCINNATI, Nov 12 [1876]

DEAR MOTHER AND SISTER

I suppose you think with the death of my beloved and lamented Husband you think that of [our?] friendship has ceased[,] but not so[.] I have had more trouble than I could live up to and tired nature gave way at last and I have not been able to write[,] but in future will do if God spares my life; my daughter has had a hard time of it, and the Baby is so cross that there is no rest with her night or day[,] and she has gone to Housekeeping and just got fixed nicely[;] and I am having the first leasure moment to Day Sunday that I have had for about 3 months[.]

Dear Friends I am longing to pay you all a visit this Spring before going West to remain next to the scenes that my beloved Husband loved so well[,] and try and end my days out West[.] I am going to the Black Hills and remain near his grave; I have been bothered to death with lawyers wanting a job on the case. I suppose you know that Jack McCall has been arrested and taken to Yankton to be tried for Murder, and friends of James told me not to get any lawyer as they was out there and would attend to all that needed attending to so you see my husband had Friends out there that Loved him as well as I do, God bless him. It is impossible for a human being to Love any better than what I did him. I can see him Day and night before me. The longer he is Dead the worse I feel. I am not quite so busy now that my daughter has got well[.] Now I have more time for Retrospection I greive all the time. My intention if nothing happens to take an overland route to the far West to ride Horse back all the way: I suppose you think it a funny notion so it is[,] but I am able to the task and not afraid to do it. How is our Dear Mother[,] has she recovered from the sudden news yet or not[?] I am anxious to see the mother of so noble a son as James was. Excuse bad writing as I have the Dropsy so bad that my hand is quite numb all the time[.] Out West it dont bother me at all[.] Give my love and a kiss to Mother and tell her that God willing I will see her in the spring[.] answer soon and believe me to be your Loving Sister

AGNES HICKOK

No further letters from Agnes to the Hickok family have been found, and it is probable that was the last one. Neither is there any evidence to suggest that she actually visited the family.

Reaction to Wild Bill's death among the newspapers of the day was mixed, but most of them carried comment favorable to Wild Bill, especially those published in places he was known to frequent. From Kansas City it was reported:

It appears that Bill died in just the way and manner he did not wish to die—that is, with his boots on. His life during the past five or six years has been one of constant watchfulness and expectation, as more than one reckless frontiersman had coolly contracted to take his life. But Bill was never off guard, and woe unto the wretched devil who failed to "get the drop" on the long haired William. More than one fool has had a bullet crushing through his brains from the ever ready pistol of this cool silent desperado. . . .

William Hickok was a quiet, courteous gentleman when sober, and seldom allowed himself to drink to excess. He dressed well, carried a small, fancy cane in his hand, and rather avoided than sought company. While he was a frontiersman in every sense of the word, he was not an Indian scout. He was well known in nearly every frontier town, and seldom went out on the trail. Gen. Custer speaks well of him. . . . He has many warm friends in this city, as well as all over the West, who will regret to hear of his tragic end, the end he has so long been expecting.[61]

Richardson declared that Wild Bill had tried the best he knew how to be respectable. "He shunned all disturbance, and took every means in his power to lead a quiet and inoffensive life. Among all his friends there is not one who does not give him credit for physical courage that was almost sublime."[62] Earlier he had written: "Bill Hickok was a desperado, and had a fair share of faults, but he also had good qualities, such as are seldom met in men of his stamp."[63]

Wild Bill's death prompted the editor of the *Leader* to add to his other criticisms: "Hickok, like all of his victims 'died with his boots on,' and the world has not suffered anything like any irreparable loss."[64] But such harsh criticism was rare, and among the editors who had known Hickok a genuine sense of loss was felt. Perhaps the most telling comment came from Hays City, scene of some of Wild Bill's more colorful exploits:

He never provoked a quarrel, and was a generous, gentlemanly fellow. . . . He was a dead shot, wonderfully quick in drawing and shooting, the latter faculty filling his enemies with a very wholesome respect, when in his presence. Living as he did in constant fear of his life, he always kept his revolvers with him, and had the fellow that shot him given him a fair fight, and not taken the cowardly advantage that he did, Wild Bill would not have been killed.[65]

The Hays City *Sentinel* reiterated the *Star's* conclusions and later, on February 2, 1877, remarked:

61 Omaha *Daily Bee*, Aug. 16, 1876, citing the Kansas City *Times*.
62 St. Paul *Pioneer Press and Tribune*, Sept. 8, 1876.
63 Cheyenne *Daily Leader*, Aug. 17, 1876.
64 Aug. 16, 1876.
65 Ellis County *Star*, Aug. 17, 1876.

Now, while Bill's friends and enemies are here to substantiate, and truthful historians to refute the lie, if given, is the time to tell the story of this man's wonderful exploits, that future generations may know of them and profit thereby.

Wild Bill was a character; undoubtedly a character. His life's career had been a checkered one; and the incidents therein are fraught with interest to the sensational public. Many stories are in circulation which are fabrications. For instance, we have read sketches of his life, in which it was asserted with the most refreshing stupidity, that while a resident of Hays, Bill had killed twelve men, and wounded and maimed whole batallions and regiments.

Bill was not a demon who delighted in taking life, and even if in truth he was a desperado, he was so by force of circumstances. During [his] . . . residence in Hays, Bill killed only three men; and a coroner's jury exonerated him from blame—partly through a reverence and fear of his prowess, and partly because he was blameless. . . .

The many tributes to his bravery, coolness, and generosity are not exagerrated. Bill was a quiet, peaceably disposed man,—never boisterous and quarrelsome—and never starting a row. But when Bill was once convinced of an adequate cause for taking hand in a row, there was always a funeral. This is where he differed from the generality of frontiersman. The ordinary ruffian, when involved in a row, would bluster around until, in the natural course of events, he would get shot; while Bill would perforate his opponent and then do his blustering at the funeral.

Few of the thousands of tourists who visit Deadwood each year and stand around the grave of Wild Bill really appreciate the part that he and his contemporaries played in the winning of the West. Overplayed by the false West of the dime novel, screen, and television, the real contribution of these men has long been lost. But each in his own way contributed something to the expansion of the United States.

It might be said that Wild Bill's death was a destiny fulfilled, that McCall's pistol (claimed to have had only one live round in it) was an instrument of fate, or that the last game of poker was the culmination of a chain of events predestined to end the career of the Old West's most colorful and controversial figure. It might also be said, with truth, that Wild Bill had outlived his time and had to die. His era was dying anyway; times were changing. Soon the day of the quick-triggered individual who held citizens in awe or terror, meting out his own justice (or injustice) to keep or break the peace, would be over, and the two-gun man a memory. For a nation was virtually being born around them, and there was growing a society that would frown on him and his kind, with no understanding of what made them or why. Yet in general, the ordinary citizens of the 1860's and 1870's had little to fear from such as Wild Bill, for his warlike attentions were never directed toward anyone unless provoked. The essential honesty, ability, and courage of James Butler Hickok during his most prominent years has already been emphasized. Yet facts are facts: with organized law, schools, hospitals, and all other amenities springing up wherever the railroad went, he and his kind were no longer needed.

Make no mistake: Wild Bill had not changed—society had. In an age of rough, tough humanity, Hickok, Tilghman, Masterson, and to some lesser extent the Earps, were the exceptions—which is why they are remembered. But it is hardly likely that they would appreciate their promotion to sainthood on modern television—probably they would be more interested in the profits being made in their names.

The real Wild Bill Hickok remains an enigma, a controversial character who will always to some extent baffle those who seek the man behind the legend. In an age when the ability to handle a gun meant the difference between life and death, he emerged the victor in all such encounters. Where others were coarse, harsh, and unwashed, he appeared clean, gentlemanly, well dressed, and well mannered. Yet his recklessness, zest for excitement, and amazing ability to find trouble—even without seeking it—made him truly a product of his time—a time that was short, both for him and for America. An ancient Wild Bill Hickok would have been unthinkable. Perhaps fate shared that view.

So passed James Butler Hickok, called Wild Bill, scout, pistoleer, peace officer, and showman. But peacemaker or killer, hero or villain, there *was* a man.

-◦◦{ 16 }◦◦-

A Fitting Death for an Assassin

JACK McCALL's only claim to fame was his cowardly murder of
Wild Bill Hickok. Who he really was did not interest people then
and does not now; but that one act earned him a sort of immortality—a place in history which he would most certainly never have
achieved from his own honest efforts.

Despite the mass of writing about the death of Wild Bill, no one
has yet come forward with the real reason behind McCall's bid for
fame. His own statement that he killed Hickok because Wild Bill
had killed his brother was quickly refuted, and it soon came out
that he was actually bribed to shoot Hickok. Although reference
was made to one of the men involved during McCall's trial, little
was done to apprehend them. It was McCall who paid the supreme
penalty, taking his secret with him to the grave. However, the appearance of more material in recent years throws a little more light
on the events which followed Wild Bill's murder.

Jack McCall was a man of many aliases. At the time of Hickok's
murder he was known as Bill Sutherland, but it was later established that his true name was John McCall. He was then in his
twenty-fifth year and believed to have been born in Jefferson County, near Jefferson Town, Kentucky, where his earlier years were
spent. Evidently the family lived in Louisville, for in 1877 his sister
Mary claimed that he had left his parents and three sisters there
and headed west.

There is some evidence to suggest that McCall was known to
early Nebraskans, for according to Galen Baldwin of Hitchcock
County, McCall was a member of a bunch of rustlers. Along with
such undesirables as "Big Jack," "Fat Jack," and "Long Jack,"
"Curly Jack" McCall tried to influence the electors when voting in
a new sheriff, by the use of six-shooter persuasion. But Baldwin
managed to lay him out with a piece of "two-by-four" as he came
through the door, gun in hand. At first they thought he was dead
but sometime later he was found to be breathing, and Baldwin's
wife nursed him back to health. Although all the people mentioned

by Baldwin who were involved in the election have been traced, there is no proof that "Curly Jack" was really McCall.[1]

It was also claimed by Doc Carver that he beat a man named "Buffalo Curley" in a buffalo-shooting contest. The beaten man was actually McCall, and he swore to kill Carver and "every other long-haired man on the plains." Unfortunately, like many other claims by Carver, this one cannot be substantiated.[2]

By his own admission, Jack McCall had been employed to carry the mail from Red Cloud to Deadwood, "a job which no one else would undertake," but this statement was made in a boastful manner to the press and has no basis in fact. It is probable that McCall's actual employment consisted of some form of laboring.

McCall appeared in the Black Hills in the wake of the gold-rushers of 1875–76. Newspapers later suggested that Jack reached Deadwood late in April or May, a month or more before Hickok arrived.

Following the shooting, McCall was arrested "after a lively chase by many of our citizens, and taken to a building at the lower end of the city and a guard placed over him."[3] Once the coroner's jury had established that "J. B. Hickock came to his death from a wound resulting from a shot fired from a pistol in the hands of Jack Mc-Call,"[4] preparations were made for a trial. But at one point in the day, the excitement over Wild Bill's death was forgotten when news came in that Indians had surrounded Crook City, and the arrival of a Mexican with the severed head of an Indian "cap[p]ed the climax[.] Wild Bill and every thing else was thrown in the Shade. The Greaser was Surrounded and carried through Town[.] when they reached the upper end of Town there was ful[l]y two Thousand men hooping and yelling[.] Such a Sight is Seldom Seen any where[.]"[5] It was later reported that the owner of the head, after begging money for exhibiting it, was shot down by an irate gambler, but this is not substantiated.

Later in the evening, when the miners had quieted down a little, the businessmen of the town set about organizing a trial for Mc-Call. After the evening performance at McDaniels' Theater, they took over the building and elected Judge W. L. Kuykendall as

---

[1] Cincinnati *Daily Enquirer*, Aug. 18, 1876. Culbertson (Neb.) *Progress*, May 14, 1925.

[2] Thorp, *Spirit Gun of the West*, 67–71.

[3] Deadwood *Black Hills Pioneer*, Aug. 5, 1876.

[4] Chicago *Inter-Ocean*, Aug. 17, 1876.

[5] Jerry Bryan, "An Illinois Gold Hunter in the Black Hills," (Diary, Mar. 13–Aug. 20, 1876), Pamphlet Ser. No. 2, Illinois State Historical Society (1960), 35.

president of the court. Kuykendall had resigned his position as secretary of the Wyoming Stock Growers' Association early in 1875 to join the gold rush to the Black Hills, and had eventually reached Deadwood. In later years he described how he organized the trial:

To observe the proper formalities, I was selected to act as chairman. After stating the object of the meeting to be the organization of a second miners' court to try the case next day, I stated that if any man present were not in harmony with the movement then was the time for him to leave. All remained. It was decided the jury should be selected by making out a list of twenty names of miners from each of the three mining districts, the name of each to be written on a separate slip of paper and well shaken in a hat, the twelve drawn therefrom to be the jury, lists to be made by a committee to be selected by the meeting when court convened next morning. On motion I was elected Judge, Isaac Brown, Sheriff, John Swift, clerk, Colonel May, Prosecuting Attorney, and Judge Miller, attorney for the prisoner. Both were able lawyers at that time, although without clients, for there was no law in force then or for months afterwards.

While willing to assume the responsibility, I refused to serve unless all those present agreed to be present with their revolvers when the court convened to see that a proper jury committee was selected and to remain through the trial and see the proceedings through to the end. I told them that if any of them would not do this, to retire immediately. Again all remained and by a rising unanimous vote pledged themselves. When the court convened the committee and jury were selected and sworn according to program.[6]

Prior to the selection of Judge Miller to represent McCall, the prisoner had chosen A. B. Chapline to represent him, but he had been too ill to act.

The trial was set for nine o'clock on the morning of the third. Together with those elected to fill official positions, three men were selected to inform the miners of the trial, one going up Deadwood Gulch, and the other two up and down Whitewood Creek. At the time set, McCall was led into court (McDaniels' Theater had again been given up for the purpose) and placed on the stage beside the judge.

Continued Kuykendall:

Officers and everybody except the prisoner were armed, and the theater was packed with men. The prisoner . . . entered a plea of not guilty, the trial proceeding under all forms of law. Evidence of the killing by

[6] *Frontier Days*, 187–89.

the prisoner developed an absolutely cold-blooded, cowardly assassination without any warning or extenuating circumstances whatever.[7]

According to the correspondent for the *Chicago Inter-Ocean*:

Never did a more forbidding countenance face a court than that of Jack McCall. His head, which is covered by a thick crop of chestnut hair, is very narrow as to the parts occupied by the intellectual portion of the brain, while the animal development is exceedingly large. A small, sandy mustache covers a sensual mouth. The nose is what is commonly called "snub," cross eyes, and a florid complexion, and the picture is finished. He was clad in a blue flannel shirt, brown overalls, heavy shoes, and as he sat in a stooping position with his arms folded across his breast, he evidently assumed a nonchalance and bravado which was foreign to his feelings and betrayed by the spasmodic heavings of his heart.[8]

From a list of names, each written on a slip of paper and dropped in a hat, a dozen were drawn by one of the committee. When this list was almost exhausted, the following twelve men were selected as having "formed or expressed no opinion for or against the defendant": J. J. Bump, Ed. Burke, L. D. Brookaw, J. F. Cooper, S. S. Hopkins, L. A. Judd, John Mann, J. H. Thompson, Alex. Travis, K. F. Towle, J. E. Thompson, and Charles Whitehead who was appointed foreman.[9]

The prosecution first called Charlie Rich, who testified that he had sat beside Wild Bill and seen McCall shoot him and say: "Take that!" Harry Young testified that he had supplied Wild Bill with fifteen dollars' worth of pocket checks and was returning to the bar when he heard the shot that killed Wild Bill, and turned to hear McCall shout, "Take that!" with his pistol in his hand. Carl Mann testified that he was part-owner with Jerry Lewis of the saloon, had been engaged in the poker game, and had seen McCall shoot Wild Bill; Captain Massie testified that he believed the ball which killed Hickok was still in his arm as it could not be found after careful examination of the floor and wall.

For the defense, Judge Miller produced McCall's employer, P. H. Smith, who testified that he had known McCall for four months and had found him "not a man of quarrelsome disposition, that he had always considered him a man of good character." He added that he had himself been introduced to Wild Bill in Cheyenne, and

[7] *Ibid.*
[8] Aug. 17, 1876.
[9] Deadwood *Black Hills Pioneer*, Aug. 5, 1876. Wilstach cites this list, but Connelley's published book shows a number of discrepancies.

had drunk with him. Wild Bill, he declared, had a bad reputation and had been the terror every place he had been.

The next witness for the defense, H. H. Pickens, said that he had known McCall for about four years and believed him to be a quiet, peaceable man. Wild Bill he described as a "shootist," known to be quick in using his pistol, who never missed his man and had a formidable list of killings to his credit.

Then Ira Ford stepped up and said that he had known McCall for one year—that McCall was liable to go on a spree just the same as anyone else. He added that Wild Bill had a reputation as a brave man who could and would "shoot quicker than any man in the Western country, and who always 'got away' with his antagonist."

More witnesses testified to McCall's good character, "the tenor of whose evidence was but a repetition of the foregoing. No attempt was made to show that Wild Bill had ever seen the prisoner."

In his own defense McCall cut quite a picture:

He came down from the stage into the auditorium of the theater, and with his right hand in the bosom of his shirt, his head thrown back, in a harsh, loud, and repulsive voice, with a bull-dog sort of bravado said: "Well, men, I have but few words to say. Wild Bill killed my brother, and I killed him. Wild Bill threatened to kill me if I crossed his path. I am not sorry for what I have done. I would do the same thing over again." The prisoner then returned to his place on the stage.[10]

In summing up his case for the prosecution, Colonel May attested that Wild Bill was a much-abused man; that he had never imposed on anyone; and that in every instance where he had slain men, he had done so either in the discharge of his duty as an officer of the law or in self-defense. But he agreed that "Bill's reputation as a gambler was bad."

After some further argument between counsel, the judge charged the jury and they retired to consider their verdict. It was agreed that the verdict would be given in saloon No. 10 where the killing occurred. McCall was placed under guard in a cabin at the rear of the saloon (with a convenient tree outside to cater for the expected verdict of "guilty"). A guard was placed in and around the saloon, with orders to shoot in case of any interference with the course of justice. Then word came that the jury had reached a verdict. All preparations were made, and McCall was brought in.

---

[10] Chicago *Inter-Ocean*, Aug. 17, 1876. It is not known who this observant and reliable correspondent was (he signed himself "Doc"), but it is fortunate for historians that he was on hand to provide the most detailed account available of McCall's Deadwood trial.

"When the prisoner was seated," wrote Kuykendall, "his feet beat a tattoo on the floor, and his teeth were chattering. He was a pitiable object of abject fear." The jury came in, and a hushed silence descended. The Judge asked the foreman for his verdict. The time was 9:00 P.M. Whitehead handed in the following verdict:

> DEADWOOD CITY, August 3, 1876.
> We the Jurors find the prisoner, Mr. John McCall not guilty.
> CHARLES WHITEHEAD, *Foreman*.[11]

The result of the trial was not well received:

The prisoner was at once liberated, and several of the model jurymen who had played their parts in this burlesque upon justice, and who had turned their bloodthirsty tiger loose on the community, indulged in a sickening cheer which grated harshly upon the ears of those who heard it. All lawabiding citizens feel that a terrible injustice has been done, and realize the fact that their only protection now is in forming "vigilantes." The first vote taken by the jury resulted in eleven for acquittal and one for conviction, and the single man [John Mann?] who desired justice was so intimidated by his fellow jurors that he was induced to sanction the iniquitous verdict. It was even proposed by one of the jurymen that the prisoner be fined fifteen or twenty dollars and set free.[12]

During the heated discussions which followed, some ugly rumors came out. Colonel May charged the jury with receiving bribes and further asserted that he knew the names of the men responsible. But it was to no avail. McCall was now a free man.

Colonel May left the courtroom vowing that he would seek justice elsewhere. Charley Utter, too, walked away in disgust. He was determined that McCall would get what he deserved. Some of the boys were for lynching McCall anyway, but Utter realized that that would not be the answer. Whatever plans he may have had for personal revenge are not known, for he was busily involved with his express and freighting business once the funeral was over.

As for McCall, he continued to hang around camp and was still a figure of interest. But one morning he received a shock. He looked up to see a large, angry-looking individual bearing down on him. It was California Joe:

Could California Joe have arrived in time, no doubt McCall would have been hanged; but he was down at Crook City, looking for Indians. . . . Joe came to Deadwood, and after hearing all the particulars of the killing of Wild Bill, walked down to McCall's cabin, and calling

[11] *Ibid.* The Deadwood paper used the word "jury" instead of "Jurors."
[12] Chicago *Inter-Ocean*, Aug. 17, 1876.

him out asked him if he didn't think the air about there was rather light for him. McCall's cheeks blanched, and he feebly answered he thought it was. "Well, I guess you had better take a walk then," said Joe, and seating himself on the side of the hill he watched the retreating figure out of sight.[13]

California Joe was not the kind of man to let the murder of a friend go unavenged—at any time he might provoke McCall and kill him in "self-defense." Jack took the hint and left Deadwood.

True to his promise, Colonel May relentlessly pursued McCall. From Deadwood, Jack went to Cheyenne and then to Laramie City. Once away from Hickok's known friends, he probably felt safer, or at least he grew more relaxed, and his new-found fame made him talkative, especially when he had been drinking. He started boasting of his deed, even alleging to one man at Horse Creek that he had killed Hickok because of a row over a card game.[14]

One evening, however, Colonel May and a stranger joined his audience. With May was Deputy United States Marshal Balcombe, and the officer arrested McCall. It was Tuesday, August 29, 1876, and the net had closed over McCall at last.

Although McCall had been tried in Deadwood by a judge and jury and found "not guilty," his trial was illegal. At the time of Hickok's murder Deadwood was an outlaw town, and its population had no right to be there, because the Black Hills had been set apart as an Indian reservation within the jurisdiction of the United States in 1868. Thus any acts of "justice" performed by the vigilance committee were not recognized by the United States courts.

It was at first decided to remove McCall to Cheyenne for a preliminary hearing before United States Commissioner Brunner, and then await a request from the Governor of Dakota Territory to have Jack put on trial at Yankton. When this news reached Cheyenne a great crowd awaited the arrival of his train on the thirty-first. As the train steamed in, the excited cry went up, "There he is!" and the crowd pressed forward. But Jack was not on board. The cause of the uproar was a drunken woman who was arrested by the Cheyenne police.[15]

At the last moment it had been decided to keep McCall in Laramie, and he was examined before Judge Blair. For his defense he had Attorney C. W. Bramel, with Attorney General Jenkins for the

[13] Cheyenne *Daily Leader*, Aug. 26, 1876.
[14] *Ibid.*, Aug. 30, 1876.
[15] *Ibid.*, Sept. 1, 1876.

prosecution.[16] McCall confessed to the judge that he was guilty of the murder, and the newspapers of Laramie, Cheyenne, and Denver were unanimous in their view that McCall should pay for his crime.

The *Leader* of September 1 stated that it was thought by the authorities that McCall might have killed another man after shooting Hickok:

The reason for this belief is that when McCall was tried in Deadwood he had but fortythree dollars on his person, while on the very next day he was sporting a costly gold watch and chain, and had also a large sum of money. An investigation of the circumstances is now being made, and startling developments may be expected.

The "startling developments" were never revealed and there does not appear to have been any follow-up story on McCall's sudden wealth. Despite the lack of proof, it is not unreasonable to assume that this money and the watch were part of his reward for killing Wild Bill. However, on August 30, McCall gave his version of the killing to a reporter of the *Daily Leader*, and it was copied by other newspapers across the country. On August 31 the paper reported:

MCCALL THE MURDERER.

McCall (and this we believe to be his real name,) is a medium sized man, and wears a light moustache. His brown eyes are slightly crossed, and restless, and he has an impediment in his speech. His manner is nervous and he shows every sympton of possessing an uneasy conscience. He is careful to always have the wall at his back when in conversation, as though afraid of being shot unawares. His story as related by himself is as follows:

"When I first met Wild Bill in Deadwood he asked me if I was not from Fort Hayes, Kansas, but I answered no, although I had seen Bill in Hayes, and easily recognized him in Deadwood as the man who killed my brother. At the time I shot him I was employed in carrying the mail from Red Cloud to Deadwood, a job which no one else would undertake.

["]On the day before the shooting I had a dispute with Bill about some gold dust which he had as good as robbed me of in a poker game. We quarreled some time about it and I finally slapped his face. He only laughed and said 'that is all right.' Between three and four o'clock the next afternoon I went into the Cricket saloon, where Bill and a party of men were playing cards, and after walking up and down a few times, stepped up to Bill, and telling him to 'look out,' shot him, the ball entering at his ear. When I warned him he smiled but made no effort to resist

[16] Denver *Rocky Mountain News*, Sept. 8, 1876.

or protect himself. I cocked my revolver and snapped it at the men he was playing with, but the d——d thing wouldn't go, although the cylinder turned. I rushed out of the saloon, mounted a horse standing near, and started off, but the saddle was loose and turned with me, so I was forced to surrender to a crowd of several hundred men.

["]I was arrested, lodged in jail and guarded by twenty-five armed men. Great excitement prevailed and I fully expected to be lynched, but another excitement caused by a Mexican bringing into town the head of an Indian diverted attention from me and preparations were made for a trial. I employed counsel, the trial was conducted in regular form, and I was acquitted. Soon afterwards I left Deadwood, came to Cheyenne, and went from there to Laramie, where I arrived Monday evening. I lost $700 here that night and think the thieves will be caught. I have three gold claims near Deadwood, and was intending to stay there this winter."

This is the story of the murderer, substantially as told by himself and we submit it to our readers as related. We are of the opinion that a Dakota judge and jury will give the man a full and fair trial, and that he will be meted out just punishment for his crime. Wild Bill had few friends, but he did not, in our opinion, deserve a dog's death, and if, as one witness will testify to-day, his murderer has stated that Bill never killed a brother of his, this can be proven, it will go hard for McCall, and the gallows will undoubtedly receive him.

So far as is known, this is the only statement in print by McCall explaining how and why he shot Hickok.

The wheels of justice were now turning in earnest. On September 9 a warrant for the arrest of Captain Massie was issued because he was considered an important witness for the prosecution. This was served on September 12 at Bismarck by United States Marshal Burdick. On September 14, before E. A. Williams, commissioner of oaths, Massie was placed on a five-hundred-dollar bail put up by D. W. Maratha. Following this, the Captain was ordered to appear at Yankton Court House on October 18. On September 19 he was released.[17]

William Rodney Massie was born on November 5, 1829, near Berger, Franklin County, Missouri, his home being on the riverbank. Massie grew up to be one of the most famous of the old-time Missouri and Mississippi river-boat pilots. His sojourn in the Black Hills at the time of Wild Bill's death was one of his few departures

[17] The United States *versus* John McCall, *alias* Jack McCall, trial documents, warrants, subpoenas, etc., including the Court Record Book (1876–77), of the Second Judicial Court, Territory of Dakota, at Yankton, on file at the General Services Administration, Federal Records Center, Kansas City, Missouri.

from the river. The late Raymond W. Thorp recalled that as a nine-year-old boy he met Massie at his home town of Miami, Missouri:

He came there on the *Electra* in 1905. When old Captain Al Ruxton told him I was determined to be a river man, he patted me on the shoulder and growled: "The steamboat days are gone, boy. You came along a little too late." He was lefthanded, and I didn't dream at the time that the arm he patted me with held the bullet that killed Wild Bill. I often thought of him later, when I was steamboating, and the Captain would say: "Here is where Bill Massie sunk the so-and-so, and here is where Bill Massie did this, and that."[18]

Massie died at St. Louis on January 29, 1910, and was buried at Bellefontaine Cemetery, where nearly all the old-time river-boat men were laid away.

McCall was indicted for murder at Yankton Court House on October 18. Following the reading of the indictment, he was asked if John McCall was his true name, and he said it was. He then added a plea of "not guilty."

Asked if he had counsel or means to employ one, McCall said that he had not. The Judge, Grenville G. Bennett, assistant justice of the Supreme Court, who was officiating in the absence of the Chief Justice, P. C. Shannon, suggested as his counsel Oliver Shannon (believed to be unrelated to the Chief Justice) and Colonel G. C. Moody. But as Moody was unable to take the case, he was replaced by General W. H. H. Beadle.[19]

A twenty-four-man petit jury was sworn in on October 19, and in a signed statement McCall stated that he had not had time to gather his witnesses, whom he named as John Weldon, Daniel Boyd, James Lamb, and George ———, "Whose sirname is now to him unknown." He also alleged that the day before he was killed, Hickok had engaged in an "affair with pistols with a certain man in Deadwood named Barker." The court agreed to McCall's request that the witnesses be produced, and warrants were issued for them. The case was then adjourned until November 27.[20]

On Friday, October 20, George M. Shingle was ordered to appear at Yankton Court House on the trial date on his own surety of $200.

McCall and his cellmate, McCarty, made a dramatic bid for freedom on November 9. They attacked their jailor, J. B. Robertson, and were only a few steps from freedom when Marshal Bur-

18 Letter to the author, Nov. 15, 1960.
19 The United States *versus* John McCall, Court Record Book, *loc. cit.*, Oct. 18, 1876.
20 *Ibid.*, Oct. 19.

dick and an assistant arrived. The lawmen quickly pulled their pistols and forced the pair to surrender.[21]

Realizing that he had prejudiced his case, McCall offered to turn state's evidence, alleging that John Varnes of Deadwood had paid him money to murder Hickok. A deputy United States marshal and a posse of five men headed for Deadwood, but Varnes had gone. It was claimed that Varnes was:

... charged with having procured the death of Wild Bill, by paying a sum of money to Jack McCall *alias* Sutherland, for the committing of the deed. It appears that some time ago Wild Bill and Varnes had a difficulty in Denver, and the animosity between the two augmented by a dispute over a game of poker at the 'Senate.'. . . a short time previous to the death of Wild Bill, at which time Bill interferred in a dispute between Varnes and another man. Bill covered him with his pistol and arrogated to himself the position of umpire, after which friends interferred and ended the difficulty.[22]

The disappearance of Varnes does not seem to have caused much concern. In fact his movements have remained obscure. Harry Young claimed that Varnes eventually "died in Denver, Colorado, an opium fiend," but no evidence has been found to support this.[23] A contributing factor in the lack of pursuit of Varnes can be found in the attitude of the state Governor, John L. Pinnington, who, as will be seen, was one of the people who signed McCall's petition to the President. A correspondent of the *Black Hills Pioneer* writing from Yankton on January 22, 1877, and signing himself "Doc" (possibly the same correspondent for the *Inter-Ocean*), made this telling comment:

By the way, the Deputy U.S. Marshal arrived the other day, and I was surprised to find that he brought no prisoners, but the reason, I have no doubt, was that he understood the position of Governor Pennington with regard to such matters. In a conversation yesterday the governor said that he was opposed to the re-arrest of persons tried and acquitted in the Hills, and thought that as we were trespassers, we should abide by the laws made unto ourselves, and persons tried under these laws should not have their lives the second time put in jeopardy for the same offence.[24]

During all the preliminary motions of September and October,

---

21 Yankton *Press and Dakotaian*, Nov. 10, 1876.
22 Cheyenne *Daily Leader*, Nov. 23, 1876, quoting the Deadwood *Black Hills Pioneer* of Nov. 11.
23 *Hard Knocks*, 212–13.
24 Deadwood *Black Hills Pioneer*, Feb. 10, 1877.

Colonel May had not been idle. It is believed that he contacted Agnes Lake Hickok who, according to the press, had engaged Colonel May to act for her, promising him funds. Perhaps he was one of the friends she mentioned to the Hickok family in her letter of November 12, but she did not send him any money. Late in November, Colonel George May became very ill, and without any funds of his own, was destitute. But the local Bar Association took care of him and paid for his room at the Merchants Hotel. The Colonel died on November 21, and was buried on November 23.[25]

The court convened on December 1, with P. C. Shannon presiding. The United States Marshal stated that he had been unable to find the witnesses McCall had asked for, and the prisoner was given a copy of the indictment and a list of the petit jury, plus the witnesses for the prosecution. The court advised him that he had two days in which to lodge any motions or pleas.

Following the Marshal's report that the witnesses had disappeared from his district, McCall's counsel requested that the trial be held over to the April, 1877, term so that the witnesses could be traced. The motion was denied when the court convened next morning, and the case was adjourned until the fourth, but not before "McCall used some language which was not very complimentary to the court when he was locked up yesterday after his failure to secure a postponement of his trial."[26]

Among the many people who assembled in the public gallery on the morning of December 4, when McCall's trial opened, was one who received many glances. Lorenzo Butler Hickok had traveled all the way from Troy Grove to represent the family at the trial, and was staying at the Merchants Hotel. When news of his brother's murder had reached Troy Grove, Lorenzo "took the old .36 Colt from his trunk and started for Dakota,"[27] but once he learned that McCall had been arrested he contented himself with witnessing his trial.

At 10:00 A.M. on December 4, Jack McCall's trial opened. He was led into court by Marshal Burdick and a couple of deputies. On his wrists were irons:

. . . which were, however, removed after he had taken his seat within the bar. He manifested no excitement or emotion, although there was a trace of anxiety exhibited in his general demeanor when first brought into court. . . . After he had been in court long enough to become ac-

25 Yankton *Press and Dakotaian*, Nov. 23, 1876.
26 *Ibid.*, Dec. 3, 1876.
27 Hickok, "The Hickok Legend," *loc. cit.*, 33.

customed to his new situation he put on a bold front and a careless air, conversing freely with his attorneys and carrying the manner of one who was arraigned for a trifling offense against the law. As the examination of the jury proceeded and the box began to fill with those who were to decide the question of life or death for him, McCall began to exhibit symptons of nervousness. He scanned closely with his sharp, eager eyes the faces of each juror as he took his seat and then anxiously awaited the appearance of the next candidate for examination as to his qualifications to act in the case.[28]

The twelve men eventually chosen to act as jurors were John Treadway (Foreman), Hiram A. Dunham, William Box, George Pike, Lewis Clark, West Negus, Charles H. Edwards, Isaac N. Esmay, Henry T. Mowry, Nelson Armstrong, James A. Withee, and Martin L. Winchell.[29]

Following the swearing in of the jury and the reading of the indictment, the court adjourned until 2:00 P.M. The judge ordered that the jury be taken to a room in the Merchants Hotel for lunch, where they were to remain throughout the trial guarded by deputies Henry C. Ash and F. D. Wysman.

When the court convened after lunch, William Pound, counsel for the prosecution, called George M. Shingle to the stand. Halfway through his evidence the defense requested that all prosecution witnesses be retired from the court until required to give evidence. The court agreed.

In evidence Shingle said:

I reside in Cheyenne and have lived there nine months. On the 2nd of August I was at Deadwood in the Black Hills. I knew a man named Wild Bill and had known him since 1866 by that name and by his right name, Hickock. He was best known by the name of Wild Bill. He is dead. He died in Deadwood on the 2d day of August, 1876. Deadwood is on Whitewood creek I think. It was at that time a place of 4000 population, I should think. On the 2d of August in a saloon at Deadwood kept by Carl Mann and Jerry Lewis, Wild Bill was there playing cards. There was a party of 3 or 4 others sitting at the same table. I was in the room at the time. I saw a man come in the saloon who is here now. It is the defendant here present. He walked towards the back door of the saloon. When within 3 or 4 feet of the door he turned and came up behind Wild Bill. He put a pistol within 2 or 3 feet of Wild Bill's head and fired. As he fired he said, "take that." The ball entered the back part of Wild Bill's head and came out of the right cheek entering the left wrist of Captain Massey. The shot killed Wild Bill almost instantly. He did not move and

[28] Yankton *Press and Dakotaian*, Dec. 5, 1876.
[29] The United States *versus* John McCall, Court Record Book, *loc. cit.*, 241.

said nothing. He sat in the chair a couple of minutes and then fell over backwards. I made an examination of Wild Bill and found him dead. The saloon stood nearly the same as this court house, with a door in each end and a bar and tables inside. The table where Wild Bill sat was nearly in the middle of the room. He was facing the bar. When the defendant came in I was weighing out gold dust. . . .

After firing the defendant walked backward toward the back door, with his revolver in his hand hold[ing] it up. As I went to look at Bill, McCall pointed the revolver at me and snapped it. I got out of the house. Carl Mann was the only one left in the house, and McCall. Saw the defendant half an hour later, when he was arrested. Was present at the trial, which was held in a theater building in Deadwood on the third day of August. McCall said to the court that he had killed Wild Bill and that he was glad of it, and if he had it to do over he would do the same thing—that Bill had killed a brother of his and he did it for revenge. The weapon used was a Sharps improved revolver 18 inches long with a piece of buckskin sewed around the stock.[30]

Cross Examined—"I said I was weighing out gold dust. The room where the bar was was twenty-four feet wide. The bar took up about 8 feet of the room and was twenty feet long. I was standing at the end of the bar. The room was about eighty feet long. Bill was sitting with his back to the back door and fronting the bar. McCall got around alongside of this partition and came up behind Bill. Captain Massie and Wild Bill were having a dispute about the game and I looked up, when I saw McCall in the act of shooting. Wild Bill was prospecting most of the time in the Hills. He did not keep a faro bank. I know of Bill killing three men, but in self defense and was tried and acquitted. He was a constant drinker. I saw the defendant in Deadwood, but was not acquainted with him. Wild Bill was sober when this shooting occurred. Could not say that McCall was drunk. I do not know that the man was staggering from drunkeness after the shooting. I saw him going up the street with his pistol in his hand, clearing his way, but I don't know he was drunk. The killing occurred about three or four o'clock p.m. Eight persons were in the room when the shooting occurred. The affair caused great excitement and a crowd gathered. McCall was acquitted on his trial in Deadwood. There were lawyers and a Judge present and a jury of twelve men. I was there through the whole trial. There was an attorney for the prosecution and for the defense. I don't know that there were any inducements held out to cause McCall to say that he had killed Wild Bill.[31]

Carl Mann was the next witness, and his statements agree with those of George Shingle:

---

[30] This alleged Sharps revolver has not been identified.
[31] Yankton *Press and Dakotaian*, Dec. 5, 1876.

I reside at Deadwood and was there August 2nd of this year. The place was then a town of two hundred houses. It is on White Wood creek. Gayville is about a mile and a half west of Deadwood gulch. Crook City is very nearly east of Deadwood—a little north of east. Bear Butte is a little north of east from Crook City. Deadwood may be about eight miles further west than Bear Butte. On the second of last August I had a house in Deadwood. There was a saloon there that some of them said that I was keeping. I do not know as I ought to answer questions about my keeping a saloon as it might get me into trouble. There was a building there which I had an interest in and I knew a man named Wild Bill. Saw both him and defendant that day at that building. Know of a shooting affair there that day. It was after dinner, about three o'clock probably. Three of us were playing cards with Wild Bill. I heard some body walking on the floor and as I looked up I saw defendant raise a pistol and fire it at Wild Bill's head. It kind of knocked Bill's head forward and then he fell gradually back. I saw where a bullet came out on his face before he fell. The pistol was from one foot to eighteen inches from Bill's head. It was a navy size revolver.[32] The same ball hit Capt. Massie in the arm. I slipped off to get something to defend myself with. All went out of my house. McCall pointed his pistol on me and head [had] it on me all the time. He went out before I did. Do not know of any inducements to defendant to confess. Heard men said that if McCall got up and said Wild Bill killed his brother the jury would clear him. Did not hear anybody say so to McCall. McCall said Wild Bill had killed his brother and he had killed Wild Bill. Did not hear him say anything about doing it again. Saw McCall only twice before this happened and in this house. Bill was there and McCall weighed out some gold dust to get some chips to play poker with Bill and the others. McCall won $23 or $24. Am not certain of the amount. He then went out and came back and played again. After playing a short time he took a purse from his pocket and bet five or six dollars and Bill bet twenty or twenty-five more. McCall shoved his purse further onto the board and says "I call you." Bill won and they came to the bar and asked me to weigh out $20 or 25. The purse was $16.50 short. Bill said "you owe me $16-25." McCall said "yes" and went out. He came back shortly after and Bill said "did I break you?" McCall said "yes." Bill gave him all the change he had, 75 cents, to buy his supper with and told him that if he quit winner in the game he was playing he would give him more. McCall would not take the money and went out in fifteen or twenty minutes.[33]

Further cross-examination of Mann revealed nothing new. If his comments on the game are the whole truth, then there seems little

[32] The nature of Hickok's wound and the close proximity to his head of the murder weapon suggests a Navy caliber pistol (.36). A .45 or .44 would have caused more damage.

[33] Yankton *Press and Dakotaian*, Dec. 5, 1876.

reason for McCall to hold a grudge against Hickok—unless he resented his help and later "bit the hand that fed him."

The court then adjourned until 9:00 A.M. on the fifth, when Captain William Rodney Massie was called:

I reside in St. Louis. Was present in Deadwood at the time of the death of Wild Bill. Was there at the time this man shot him. Did not see him die and do not know that he died immediately. We were seated at a round table playing cards. The house fronted south. I was sitting with my back partly towards the south and partly towards the wall. Bill was seated opposite me at the table. Mr. Mann sat on my right and Charlie [Rich?] at my left. Carl Mann's back was directly towards the front door and Bill's back was towards the back door. I saw the defendant first on that occasion. When the pistol report came I was looking down at the table and looked up and saw the defendant backing as if to get out of the back door. My left arm was resting on the table when the pistol was fired. I felt a shock and numbness in my left wrist. I heard the report of the pistol and looked up to see where it came from and saw the defendant with a pistol in his right hand. He was moving it about apparently to keep the crowd from coming upon him and was backing towards the back door. He was saying, also, "come on ye s——s of b——s." He intimidated the crowd with the pistol and it got out of the front door except Mr. Mann. I got out quick as I could and did not see Wild Bill fall. I looked up at the pistol and my eyes passed him. The ball was not found on examining my arm. It is there yet I suppose. I saw the defendant come into the same room a day or two before and around behind Bill and pull his pistol about two thirds out. There was a young man with him who put his arm around the defendant and walked him towards the back door.[34]

Captain Massie was also cross-examined without any new disclosures. It seems odd that several witnesses should claim that they had seen McCall half draw a pistol and then be led away, days before the shooting, and yet not warn Wild Bill of his danger.

William Pound then called Joseph Mitchell to the stand:

I reside at this time in Sioux City, but in the early part of August in this year was in Deadwood. At the time Wild Bill was killed I was putting the wainscoting in the same room. Saw the defendant there after the shooting but did not notice him before. The report of a revolver was the first that attracted my attention. I next noticed Wild Bill lying on the floor. McCall was standing by the back door. He pointed his revolver at me and told me to . . . come on. I then went out of the door at the rear of the building.[35]

[34] *Ibid.*, Dec. 6, 1876.
[35] *Ibid.*

General William P. Dewey and H. H. Reed gave evidence to prove the location of Deadwood, and E. F. Highee produced a map which showed that the western boundary of Dakota was thirty-five miles west of Bear Butte, and so placed Deadwood in Dakota. And the Yankton jailor, J. B. Robinson (or Robertson),[36] testified about the assault on him by McCall and McCarty.

The prosecution then closed its case. McCall's counsel gave notice that they had no witnesses for the defense. But a motion was made by Beadle and Shannon that McCall be discharged on the grounds that a true copy of the indictment had not been served by the prosecution. The prosecuting counsel countered by stating that such a document had been furnished, and after some argument the court adjourned, but ordered the defense to produce it next morning.

At 9:00 A.M. on December 6 the court convened and Oliver Shannon stood up and held out a paper, stating that it was the copy of the indictment handed to the prisoner on the day he was remanded.

All witnesses in the case had been for the prosecution, McCall being unable to produce any of his own. But his counsel must be given great credit for the way they conducted the defense. Both prosecution and defense now addressed the jury, and Justice Shannon, in his opinion and concluding remarks, said:

A true copy of the Indictment in the present case was delivered to the counsel of defendent (and in his presence, as positively sworn to by the U.S. Attorney) forty-seven days before the trial; secondly, a defective copy was delivered to the defendant himself, three days before the trial; thirdly, the plea of the 18th of October, could have been withdrawn, during the interval, for any advantageous purpose, but no attempt to do so was made—the defendant and his counsel thereby tacitly acquiescing (after abundant time for deliberation) in the propriety and wisdom of the original plea; and lastly, the defendant, without making any objection, went to the jury on that issue.

By having entered upon trial, and by having waited until the prosecution closed its case, the defendant was too late to make the objections referred to, concerning those copies; for, by such conduct and acquiescence, he has virtually admitted that he had a copy sufficient for all purposes intended by the act of congress.

As to the objection that the defendant should have been indicted and tried on the other side of this court, it is well settled that a trial for homicide, committed in an Indian reserve, must be had on the Federal side

[36] The newspapers referred to him as both Robinson and Robertson, but the Court Record Book states his name was Robertson.

of a Territorial court, and is governed by U.S. Statutes and the rules of the common law. . . .

It is therefore considered and adjudged that the motions for a new trial, and in arrest of judgment be, and they are hereby overruled.

By the Court,
P. C. Shannon, Judge.[37]

McCall, through his attorneys, objected and his protest was filed. At about 7:00 P.M. the jury retired. When they filed back into court at 10:15 P.M., the public gallery was full. Clerk of the Court A. J. Faulk asked for their verdict. The foreman John Treadway stood and amid silence handed over the written verdict of "Guilty as charged in the Indictment." McCall's counsel immediately objected to the verdict, and Jack was then led out by the United States Marshal.

Lorenzo Butler Hickok left the courtroom well satisfied with the verdict and confident that McCall would pay for his crime. Before leaving for Troy Grove, he told the press that "there was no truth in the assertion that Wild Bill shot the brother of McCall in Kansas."[38]

Several more sessions took place between the court and McCall, during which the minutes of October 18 were corrected in open court in connection with the alleged faulty indictment. In this document Hickok's name had not been used, only his pseudonym of "Wild Bill." But the document given McCall's counsel and the one used in the trial was correct. McCall's counsel continued to press for a new trial, but these motions were denied, and on December 23 the judge announced that he would pass sentence on McCall on January 3, 1877.[39]

When the court convened on January 3, 1877, the public gallery was densely packed. During the "delivery of the impressive language of the court," wrote the reporter for the *Press and Dakotaian*, "the prisoner seemed least moved of all present, though a slight quiver of the lips was perceptible when the judge dwelt pathetically upon the teachings and prayers of a mother." Asked if he had anything to say, McCall addressed the court at some length, but his plea was to no avail, and he was sentenced to death. Unfortunately, no transcript of what McCall said to the court has been found. Having objected to the sentence through his counsel, Jack was led out by United States Marshal Burdick.

---

[37] The United States *versus* John McCall, Opinion of the Court, *loc. cit.*
[38] Yankton *Press and Dakotaian*, Dec. 7, 1876.
[39] The United States *versus* John McCall, Court Record Book, *loc. cit.*, 256.

Even before the sentencing of McCall, his counsel had been busy trying to find loopholes in the judgment. Several men came forward late in December and signed statements alleging that the Bear Butte mentioned in court was in fact Bear Butte Gulch and not the mountain. A writ of error was submitted to the Supreme Court of Dakota Territory, but after an examination of the records of the Second Judicial Court, it was announced on January 20 that the verdict was upheld.[40]

On January 23, Beadle and Shannon advised Justice Shannon and William Pound that they were applying to the President for a pardon or commutation of McCall's sentence to life imprisonment. This petition, together with a covering letter signed by Oliver Shannon, was mailed on the twenty-fourth. In his letter Shannon stated that he did not propose to include a list of the jurors, as some of them lived forty to sixty miles away over the prairie country. Referring briefly to the introduction of maps in court and the affidavits attached, he asked for a speedy reply as the mails were frequently detained several days.

The first part of the petition was signed by John L. Pinnington, governor of Dakota Territory, and endorsed by William P. Dewey, one of the witnesses for the prosecution. It mentioned that McCall in his defense had claimed that he was drunk at the time the alleged murder took place and in fact had fallen down three times when crossing the street to the saloon. It was also alleged that while there was unquestionable proof of the killing, grave doubts existed when the history of the case showed a total absence of motive for the act—of vengeance, money, or anything else traceable to a natural cause. The Governor went on to allege that McCall's first knowledge of the killing "was whilst sitting on a log in the outskirts of the village, with five or six men around him, & when returning to consciousness was told that he 'had got into a bad scrape,' & when asked what it was, was told by them that he had killed 'Wild Bill.'"

The Governor's petition[41] was supported by one drawn up by Beadle and Shannon and was signed by a number of local businessmen, among whom was D. C. Nagle, speaker of the House of Representatives. It was claimed that McCall was born in New Orleans, that his occupation was hunter and miner, and that he had never

[40] Yankton *Press and Dakotaian*, Jan. 20, 1877.

[41] File No. F-307, Records Group No. 204 (Records of the Office of the Pardon Attorney, Washington, D.C.). For the full text of this and the other documents, see Joseph G. Rosa, "Alias Jack McCall: A Pardon or Death?" The Kansas City Westerners' *Trail Guide*, Vol. XII, No. 2 (June, 1967), 20–25.

been convicted of any crime. The petition consisted of a five-point declaration, pointing out that no logical reason had been found for the murder—"that he killed the deceased we have no doubt, but that he *murdered* him we do not believe." It was suggested that perhaps he was suffering from delirium tremens.

A reference was made to McCall's lack of friends and to the fact that the witnesses he wanted to testify in his behalf could not be found in time as they had gone gold-prospecting. "We have no word to utter about the deceased. We knew him only from reputation as 'Wild Bill' and propose that the grass that grows over his grave may be as green and beautiful as that of any other spot." In conclusion it was suggested that it was the state of society in Deadwood that contributed largely to McCall's downfall.[42]

With the dispatch of these petitions the wheels in Washington began to turn. On February 1 the Department of Justice sent the petitions together with a covering letter to William Pound, instructing him to communicate with Justice Shannon, obtain his opinion, and then render a report. In his lengthy reply of February 7 addressed to the Hon. Alphonso Taft, the attorney general, Pound completely demolished the defense's case and indicated clearly that McCall had had the benefit of every advantage:

I have never known a case where the interests of a prisoner were more carefully guarded by the Court than this one. Witnesses *were* sent for at the expense of the Government, where there were grave doubts as to their materiality, and the trial postponed nearly two months, and it was only after the Marshal made his return, and it was evident that no such witnesses as he desired could be obtained, that the trial proceeded.

Pound confirmed that when the case went before the Supreme Court the judgment of the District Court was unanimously affirmed by a full bench. McCall's alleged drunken state had been considered, but no mitigating circumstances were found by the jury. As for the attempt to excuse McCall's actions by pleading the situation that existed in Deadwood and the Hills, and to blacken Hickok's name, Pound went on:

[McCall's] counsel find it convenient to refer to the deceased as a "notorious character," and as one whose real name was only disclosed by the evidence. A reference to the indictment will show that both his real name and the *alias* of "Wild Bill" were used in it. But the name "Wild Bill" had been given to him and fastened upon him so that he was really better known by that than by any other, and without any discredit to

42 File No. F–307, Records Group No. 204, *loc. cit.*

331

himself. It is a part of the history of the war, that this man, by reason of his fearless and efficient service as a Union Scout among the guerillas of Missouri, Arkansas and Eastern Kansas, and by his contests with these same guerillas even after the war closed, when they so persistently pursued him, won this name of "Wild Bill," and he certainly had no reason, during his life to be ashamed of it. The same policy pursued him even to the Black Hills, his old enemies giving him a bad name whenever and wherever they dared to do it. Although the evidence was clearly inadmissible in a case like this, where the prisoner sought the deceased, and while in no danger, shot him from behind, I did not object to, and the court permitted testimony as to the character of the deceased for violence. One witness, for some years a passenger conductor on the Kansas Pacific Railway, who knew him there, ten years or more ago, and who had known him since at Cheyenne and in the Black Hills, said he was not a quarrelsome man and never quarreled unless forced into it. Other witnesses gave him the same character and no one gave him a different one.

How many *aliases* the prisoner has, it would be difficult to tell. Although declaring upon his arraignment that his true name was John McCall, he asserted immediately before sentence was passed upon him that it was not his true name. He seems to be a person of a depraved and wicked heart, without regard for human life, as was shown by a murderous attack upon the keeper of the jail here, in an attempt to escape, a short time before his trial. Coming, as it is now asserted from the south, he had conceived for some cause, or without cause, an especial hatred for "Wild Bill."[43]

Pound then described the events which led up to the shooting and its aftermath, concluding that he did not seek the life of "this unfortunate man, and if I should consult my own feelings and inclinations, I should prefer a substitution of imprisonment for life to the death penalty as a punishment for murder. The law of the United States recognizes the latter, however, and not the former, and upon my conscience I am utterly unable to see any extenuating circumstances in this case."[44]

During all these exchanges, United States Marshal Burdick had not been idle. Since part of his duties would be to arrange the actual execution and the building of a scaffold, he was anxious to learn the outcome of McCall's petition. On February 11 he wrote the following to the Hon. J. P. Kidder in Washington:

DEAR JUDGE:
I wish you would do me the favor to call at the office of the Atty Gen

[43] *Ibid.*
[44] *Ibid.*

at as early an hour as will suit your convenience after the receipt of this, and learn if you can whether McCall's sentence will be commuted by the President or not. Should you learn that it will be, please suggest to the Atty Gen the propriety of his *telegraphing* me to that effect, as I must commence preparations as soon as one week from tomorrow, and dont want to incur any expenses to the Government unless there is a necessity for it. It really seems to me that he ought to advise me by telegraph that the sentence will be commuted or that it will not be, as the case may be, that I may have time to make the necessary preparations, or that none need be made.

Very respectfully,
J. H. BURDICK
U.S. Marshal[45]

On February 14, Marshal Burdick received the death warrant, but he delayed his preparations awaiting official notification from Washington.

Jack McCall, meantime, seemed resigned to his fate. Shortly after his trial he had asked to see a priest and was visited by Father Elliot, a Catholic, who administered spiritual consolation in his cell. Later he was visited regularly by the Rev. Father Daxacher. He also read the Bible. "Doc," the reporter for the Chicago *Inter-Ocean* and the *Black Hills Pioneer*, wrote to the latter on January 22:

I visited McCall, (or rather Sutherland) the murderer of Wild Bill, in the United States prison, here. The man is the same taciturn, brutal being, and looked as forbidding as when I saw him on trial in Deadwood. There seems to be no contrition for his crimes, and he seems to regard his coming fate with stolid indifference.[46]

After due deliberation the following telegram was dispatched from Washington to the United States Marshal:

DEPARTMENT OF JUSTICE, WASHINGTON, Feb. 19 1877
To J. H. Burdick, U.S. Marshal, Yankton, Dakota Terr'y:
The Attorney General directs me to say to you that he has considered the application made on behalf of John McCall, convicted of Murder and declines to interfere with the sentence pronounced by the Court.
A. R. DUTTON, *Chief Clerk.*[47]

When the marshal broke the news to McCall he took it calmly, displaying the same indifference that had marked him since his

---

[45] *Ibid.*
[46] Deadwood *Black Hills Pioneer*, Feb. 10, 1877.
[47] File No. F–307, Records Group No. 204, *loc. cit.*

trial. Marshal Burdick then set about his unpleasant duty and made arrangements for the execution. At first intended to be private, it was finally decided to hold it in public on the school section north of the Catholic cemetery.

McCall spent a lot of his time, in the short weeks before his execution, answering letters from people interested in the Black Hills. He also received several visits from the Rev. Father Daxacher and continued his Bible reading. On February 6 one of his letters to a friend in Denver was published in the Cheyenne *Daily Leader*:

YANKTON D.T. Jan. 13th '77

DEAR FRIEND:
I received your letter and will drop you a few lines to let you know how I am getting along. I am in good health and spirits, hoping when this reaches you that you will be in the same. I have not heard or seen Jack Kelly since I seen you last. McCarty [McCall's cellmate] is here yet and will get his trial in April. I have got my trial and will be hung Thursday, the 1st day of March, 1877. I have not heard from any of the boys in the hills. We have had very cold weather here. But comfortable place here. I hope you will get out. You asked me if I thought it would pay to go to the hills in the spring. I think it would if you save your money and above all things let whisky alone. So farewell forever on this earth.

Yours,
JACK McCALL

Is it possible that in that reference to whisky Jack himself provided the only motive for the killing? His thoughts must have been very concerned with the events which led up to his sudden notoriety, for on February 21 he wrote to the *Press and Dakotaian* and offered an article for publication after his death, promising to hand it to the editor on the morning of his execution. But for reasons best known to himself, he destroyed his manuscript the night before he died. Useless though it was in altering his fate, it might have proved invaluable to historians. Perhaps his decision to take his motive for killing Wild Bill with him to the grave had something to do with the following letter from his sister, which was handed to him by the United States Marshal on the eve of his execution:

[MERCHANTS HOTEL]
LOUISVILLE, KENTUCKY,
February 25, 1877.

To the Marshal of Yankton:

DEAR SIR:

I saw in the morning papers a piece about the sentence of the murderer of Wild Bill, Jack McCall. There was a young man of the name John McCall left here about six years ago, who has not been heard from for the last three years. He has a father, mother, and three sisters living here in Louisville, who are very uneasy about him since they heard about the murder of Wild Bill. If you can send us any information about him, we would be very thankful to you.

This John McCall is about twenty-five years old, has light hair, inclined to curl, and one eye crossed. I cannot say about his height, as he was not grown when he left here. Please write as soon as convenient, as we are very anxious to hear from you.

Very respectfully,

MARY A. McCALL.[48]

No one will ever know the thoughts that went through McCall's mind when he read that letter, but upon "being shown the letter, McCall admitted it was from his sister in Louisville, Kentucky, where he also has a father and mother who had not heard of their wayward son for three years."[49] Jack answered the letter; it is not certain whether he wrote to his sister or to his parents, but it was noted that "To one of the latter he wrote a very feeling letter last night, in which he seemed fully reconciled to his fate."[50]

And now the day had come. The first legal hanging in the county was to take place. On the morning of Thursday, March 1, 1877, a number of newspapermen were admitted to the Yankton jail. It was 8:30 A.M. and McCall was in religious consultation with Father Daxacher and his assistant, J. A. Curry. McCall's fellow prisoners, McCarty and Allen, seemed more upset by the proceedings than McCall himself.

At 9:00 A.M. Marshal Burdick and two assistants, R. J. Stanley and Charles P. Edmunds (who later recalled that "McCall was a mild appearing fellow and not all the desperado type. . . . He was

---

[48] This letter appeared in Buel's *Heroes of the Plains* and has been copied by succeeding writers. A version given the author many years ago was headed "Merchants Hotel," and investigation carried out at Louisville revealed that the Directories for 1876–79 do show that a Miss Mary A. McCall was a housekeeper at the Merchants Hotel in 1876, and lived as a boarder at 300 Sixth Street near Broadway in 1877. She is not listed in 1878, but in 1879 she is shown as a grocer at 89 Tenth Street (Mrs. Dorothy Thomas Cullen, librarian, The Filson Club, Louisville, Kentucky, Dec. 29, 1958, and Jan. 26, 1959). The whereabouts of the original letter are unknown.

[49] Yankton *Press and Dakotaian*, Mar. 1, 1877.

[50] Cheyenne *Daily Leader*, Mar. 4, 1877, report dated Mar. 1.

a good prisoner."[51]), entered the cell and the Marshal read the death warrant to McCall who remained unmoved. His irons were then removed and he stepped quickly into his cell for a few moments, then returned to speak in whispered sentences with Father Daxacher. At 9:30 all was in readiness for the last journey. McCall said good-by to McCarty and Allen, both of whom displayed much emotion. Outside a drizzling rain did not prevent a large crowd's gathering in the hope of a brief glimpse of the condemned man.

Several carriages were lined up to transport the party to the scaffold. Marshal Burdick and Deputy Marshal Ash entered the first one, while McCall, Father Daxacher, Curry, and Phil K. Faulk (representing the local press) occupied the second. Edmunds recalled that he also rode with McCall, and on the way they passed the open grave, but McCall showed no signs of concern or fear.[52] Following behind was a long line of vehicles of every description, together with hundreds on horseback and on foot.

As the gallows loomed into view a great silence fell over the crowd. County Sheriff Baker and Town Marshal Leeper, who had charge of the policing of the crowd around the scaffold, had done a good job and there was no unnecessary pressure around its base.

Deputy Ash accompanied McCall up the steps to the platform. Jack then placed himself over the trap, still displaying a calmness and nerve that had marked him since his trial. His arms and limbs were bound and he knelt down to pray. He looked toward heaven as he prayed, then rose to his feet. Kissing a crucifix, he remained impassive as the black cap was placed on his head. As Marshal Burdick adjusted the noose, McCall asked for a moment in which to pray. Finally he said: "Draw it tighter, marshal."

At 10:15 the trap was sprung and Jack McCall was dead. Only at the last moment did he display any emotion, when the single, choking cry, "Oh God!" was heard as the drop fell.

Twelve minutes later Doctors D. F. Etter and J. M. Miller entered the boarded-up base of the scaffold to examine McCall. His head was drooped over his breast, and in his clenched fist, now turned blue, he still held the crucifix. Ten minutes later his body was cut down and placed in a neat walnut coffin. He was later buried in the southwest corner of the Catholic cemetery. There he remained until 1881 when the cemetery was removed. An examination revealed that he had been buried with the noose still around his neck.[53]

[51] Yankton *Press and Dakotaian*, June 6, 1936.
[52] *Ibid.*

In concluding its account of the execution, the local paper went on to state:

As a fitting close to the tragic drama we may say of "Wild Bill," notwithstanding his eventful and exciting career as a scout of the union army during the war, and on the frontier and the wild plains of the west, amongst wild and lawless whites, and still more savage redmen, he was still a quiet and unassuming man, peaceable and harmless, except when menaced by the cold glitter of the bowie knife or the deadly muzzle of the revolver. At such times his nerve and cool daring were unparalleled. As soldier, scout, marshal, sheriff and private citizen, his qualities enabled him always, by rapidity of execution and extraordinary fearlessness, to defeat and destroy his enemies when the odds were overwhelming. No open enemy could have taken his life, except by sacrificing his own, and it remained for Jack McCall to assassinate him in an unsuspecting hour, when his back was toward the enemy. Though his life was bloody and adventurous, yet he was the champion of the weak and oppressed; and if he was not a paragon of excellence, he was at least a man of brave impulses.

[53] This account of McCall's execution is based upon the report published in the evening edition of the Yankton *Press and Dakotaian*, Mar. 1 1877. See also the June 23, 1881, issue.

--◦❦ 17 ❧◦--

A Prince among Pistoleers

No HISTORY OF WILD BILL HICKOK would be complete without reference to the trait that, above all others, singles him out and places him in the limelight of fame—his remarkable skill with a pistol.

To get a pistol into action at great speed and with accuracy has been man's ambition ever since the earliest days of the weapon. The invention of Colt's revolver was the first decisive step in this direction. For the first time one man had the fire power of six. Armed with a Colt revolver, even the weakest and most cowardly man was the equal of all comers. The old-time swordsman and his romantic chivalry gave way to a new kind of character—the gunfighter.[1]

Although thousands of men carried pistols, few of them ever attained any real degree of accuracy, and even fewer were classed as "dead shots." Wild Bill Hickok, who was without doubt a great pistolman, much greater than most of the later figures of the gunfighting era, inspired many of the fables and tall tales woven into the gunfighter legend. Awe-struck journalists even dreamed up a title for him—"The Prince of Pistoleers."

It is not difficult to appreciate why Hickok, rather than any one of a half-dozen others, was singled out for such glory. He was the first of the so-called "fast guns"; he was both practical and spectacular in his original approach to gunfighting; and he was the first prominent figure to dominate this field. His worshipers, many of whom knew nothing of his pistol-fighting, saw him shoot, enlarged on what they saw, and firmly believed that he was capable of anything. In actual fact, his skill with weapons was rarely watched by competent judges, and consequently practical tests will only reveal how good he *could* have been.

Perhaps the first account on record of Hickok's shooting ability was published in *Harper's New Monthly Magazine* for February, 1867. Colonel Nichols expressed the desire to see Wild Bill shoot:

[1] For a detailed description of the evolution of the man behind the myth, see Rosa, *The Gunfighter: Man or Myth?*

338

"Would yer?" replied the scout, drawing his revolver; and approaching the window, he pointed to a letter O in a sign-board which was fixed to the stone wall of a building on the other side of the way. "That sign is more than fifty yards away. I will put these six balls into the inside of the circle, which isn't bigger than a man's heart." In an off-hand way, and without sighting the pistol with his eye, he discharged the six shots of his revolver. I afterward saw that all bullets had entered the circle.

When that story was published it received much skepticism from the press, but it was agreed that "[Wild Bill] is a dead shot with a pistol."[2] But Nichols' account set the stage for innumerable versions of the same incident, and to this date it is repeated. In 1931 in a fictional biography of Wyatt Earp, the author alleged that his hero had witnessed such shooting in Kansas City, only the distance that time was "possibly one hundred yards away," and the sign was on a saloon. Despite the fact that Market Square, where the incident is alleged to have taken place, is one hundred yards across,[3] no contemporary reference has been found. This writer believes that the Nichols story was still well known by the turn of the century, and probably formed the basis for a description of such shooting in Kansas City by Alfred Henry Lewis. Lewis alleged that Hickok paid a visit to Kansas City about 1874, and while wandering along "Battle Row" he noticed an Odd Fellows' sign painted black on white. The "O" of "Odd" showed "wood color inside the black," and Lewis went on:

It was years before when, to please a bevy of tender tourists and by permission of Mr. Speers, then chief of police, Mr. Hickok emptied his six-shooters into the centre of that "O." It was a finished piece of shooting; the tourists told of it about their clubs when safe in the East again. The "O" where the original white had been splintered into wood-color by those dozen bullets it had stopped, showed plain as print.[4]

Another version of this incident, which may be the origin of the Wyatt Earp yarn (it is believed that Earp never met Wild Bill), was written by Bat Masterson and published in 1910:

I remember one of Wild Bill's more numerous stunts used to be shooting the center out of the O's of the I.O.O.F. sign in Kansas City, across from police headquarters. Imagine a man amusing himself with that kind of target shooting in Kansas City today. I dropped in for a talk

2 Atchison *Daily Champion*, Feb. 5, 1867.
3 Stuart N. Lake, *Wyatt Earp, Frontier Marshal*, 43–44. The late James Anderson to the author, Aug. 12, 1956.
4 "How Mr. Hickok Came to Cheyenne," *loc. cit.*, 6.

with the chief of police of that town one day while Wild Bill was in a prime, and, chancing to notice the sign, asked what had happened to it.

The chief swore roundly and said it was the work of that blasted madcap, Wild Bill. It appears that Bill used to spend his winters in Kansas City and much against his will was required by the chief of police and the law to give up his shooting irons while he was in town. Bill hated the idea, for it naturally made him feel like a fish out of water. So he invariably used to relieve his feelings by emptying the guns at that hapless sign. He would repeat the operation in the spring when the guns were returned to him, saying it was to keep them from getting rusty.[5]

Regardless of the fictional qualities of the above accounts, the fact remains that such shooting, if questionable, is possible when performed by experts. Such an experiment was carried out on the writer's behalf by Jeff Cooper of Big Bear Lake, California, in cooperation with the Eaton Canyon Muzzle Loaders' Association of Pasadena, California. The results were published in the March, 1960, issue of *Guns and Ammo*.

Using a pair of .36 Colt Navy revolvers, model of 1851, a pair of .44 Colt 1860 Army revolvers, and a "New Model Army" Remington .44, with a load of 35 grains of Ffg black powder in the .44's and 25 grains in the .36's, the weapons were put to the test. Conical bullets were discarded in favor of round balls—partly for ease of molding and partly because competitions had shown them to be as accurate as conical balls (which ran the risk of being badly seated by the rammer).

The results of the tests at distances ranging from twenty-five to one hundred yards were quite impressive. Jeff Cooper concluded that "Ten successive shots in a two-foot circle at one hundred yards, off-hand, is possible with Hickok's weapons but very, very unlikely. With modern weapons it is difficult but not spectacular." Commenting on the claim by Nichols, Cooper said: "Barely possible for the weapon. Impossible under the conditions described."

Claims that Hickok could hit a dime edge-on, or drive a cork through the neck of a bottle with a bullet, together with the legendary feat of cutting a chicken's throat without breaking the bone, were also carefully considered by Cooper: "This would require one-caliber groups, center-to-center, with outside dimensions of 3/4" (.36 cal.) and 9/10" (.44 cal.). The chicken and the dime would be easier with the .44, while the whisky bottle would be easier with the .36. Barely possible for the shooter, using modern weapons. Impossible with Hickok's weapons."

[5] "A Few Scrapes," Denver *Republican*, July 17, 1910.

Experts do agree that a good cap and ball revolver could be effective at two hundred yards, but the accuracy at such a distance would depend upon many factors: skill on the part of the shooter, visibility, and windage. Some idea of the great respect with which the cap and ball revolvers were treated can be found in the exhaustive tests carried out by the British government at the time of the Crimean War in 1854. A Dragoon in .44 caliber was fired at a target 410 yards away twenty-eight times. The target was seven feet in diameter, and seventeen of the balls struck it. Two years before at Cape Town officers of the Twelfth Lancer Regiment had fired at and hit a target thirty inches square 177 yards away, shooting in competition with a rifle![6]

Most revolver shooting, however, is performed at short ranges, and in this respect the percussion revolvers used in the Old West were more than adequate for the task required of them. Even with the introduction of the Peacemaker in 1873, efforts were still made by the military to test the revolver to its limits, and it was found that the Peacemaker had a mean absolute deviation at 50 yards of 3.1 inches,[7] which would be enough for most "shootists."

The feats credited Hickok by the old-timers would fill volumes, even though most of them are nothing more than tall tales. But not all the stories are make believe. One that does have a ring of truth about it is told by Charles Gross about Wild Bill in Abilene. Having cause to visit Hickok's cottage one morning, Gross found him sitting up in bed with a pistol in his hands:

. . . to my surprise as soon as Bill was dressed, all but Coat & Hat—he went carefully to the door[,] looked all arround for several m[omen]ts & then Emptied one 6 shooter. He had the one in Each hand, returned to the room[,] cleaned & reloaded it, then went to the door & Empt[i]ed the Other one & reload[ed] it the same way. Bill used powder & Ball—We had pistols then with Metal Ca[r]trides but Bill would not use them[.] he used powder & Ball, moulded his own bullets & primed Each tube using a pin to push the powder in so he was sure of powder contact and before putting on the Cap he looked at the interior of Each Cap[.] now this [was] all strange to me & new too, for I had roomed & slept with Bill all [the] time he was at the [Drover's] Cottage (2 months or more) & he never did it there, so I said, did you get your Guns damp yesterday Bill? he said "*no*, but I aint ready to go yet & I am not taking any chances, when I draw & pull I *must be sure*. . . ." I went fishing with Bill once at Hoffmans Dam & when we got in the Buggie Bill threw on

[6] *United Services Gazette*, Dec. 4, 1852. *British Army Despatch and Nautical Standard*, Dec. 15, 1854.
[7] Rosa, *The Gunfighter: Man or Myth?* 185.

2 extra pistols and on our way home we stopped at a clear spot by some Cotto[n] woods & he and [I] put up a piece of paper on a tree as near the size of a mans body as we could guess & about the h[e]ight of Navel —(a 6 foot man)[.] the paper was about 6 in long with a spot in the Center half way. We stepped off 20 feet & he asked me to "wait a few moments," he Kind of slouched and did not appe[a]r to be looking at anything[.] he said "Keep talking & then suddenly without any hesitation in your talk, say *Draw* (Kinder qu[i]ck)[.]"

He shot six times so quick it startled me, for his 6 was in his Holster when I said "Draw[.]" I was looking directly at him and only saw a Motion & he was firing. No use to ask how he drew[,] I dont Know[.] I only saw his arm was not straight & stiff[.] there was a preciptible Curve to his arm, but very slight—Every shot was in the paper and two in the spot, but all of them within one inch of an up & down line like this[:]

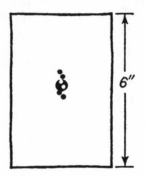

We put up another paper and Bill tried his left hand with the result that all were in the paper but none in the spot but all of them [on] the up and down line, Each almost over the other or in the same hole. I said Not quite so good Bill—He said "I never shot a man with my left hand Except the time when some drunken Soldiers had me down on the floor & were trampling me & then I used both hands. I do not recall that I ever heard Bill say "Killed[.]" He always said "shot[.]" . . . Bill said "Charlie I hope you never have to shoot any man, but if you do[,] shoot him in the Guts near the Navel. *you* may not make a fatal shot, but *he* will get a shock that will paralize his brain and arm so much that the fight is all over[."][8]

Gross's reference to Wild Bill's habit of frequently reloading his pistols shows that Hickok took reasonable precautions. A temperature change at night, cooling the pistols, might easily draw moisture into the chambers—a common fault in the day of salt-laden

[8] Charles F. Gross to J. B. Edwards, June 15, 1925, Manuscripts Division, KSHS. The reference to a fight with soldiers could be an authentic quote from Wild Bill concerning the killing of Private John Kile.

black powder, which often caused misfires. Hickok no doubt spoke with the voice of experience. However, it is not clear whether Hickok actually fired his pistols or drew the charges—anyone who has tried to unload a cap and ball revolver in this manner will appreciate the problems. Assuming that Hickok fired each pistol to clear the chambers, the question naturally arises: "Why wasn't the chief of police fined for discharging a firearm within city limits?"

Among the many who claimed to have witnessed Hickok in action with a pistol was Leander Richardson. The day after he met Wild Bill:

> I asked to see him use a pistol, and he assented. At his request I tossed a tomato-can about 15 feet into the air, both his pistols being in his belt when it left my hand. He drew one of them, and fired two bullets through the tin can before it struck the ground. Then he followed it along, firing as he went, until both weapons were empty.[9]

Another alleged witness to Wild Bill's prowess with a pistol was Robert A. Kane. Writing in 1906, he claimed that he met Hickok in Milwaukee, Wisconsin, when he was with Buffalo Bill's theatrical company. But Wild Bill was not with Cody when he played Milwaukee.[10] Possibly Kane was mistaken in the town; nevertheless, his description of Hickok's skill is interesting and worth repeating:

> Along in the '70s W. F. Cody (Buffalo Bill), Wm. A. Hickok (Wild Bill) and Texas Jack, as members of Buffalo Bill's "Prairie Waif" Company,[11] played a three-nights' engagement in Milwaukee, Wisconsin. Several of the local marksmen, including myself, called on the celebrities at their hotel, where in a little social session shooting and shooting methods were discussed. Mr. Hickok treated us with great courtesy, showed us his weapons, and offered to do a little shooting for us if it could be arranged for outside the city limits. Accordingly the early hours of the afternoon found us on our way to the outskirts of the city. Mr. Hickok's weapons were a pair of beautifully silver plated S.A. [single-action] .44 Colt revolvers. Both had pearl handles and were tastefully engraved. He also had a pair of Remington revolvers of the same calibre. The more

---

[9] "A Trip to the Black Hills," loc. cit., 755.

[10] Cody played in Milwaukee in January, 1873, and May, 1874, both times when Hickok was not with the show (Mrs. Lynn Murphy, Milwaukee Public Library, to the author, June 20, 1960).

[11] Russell, Lives and Legends of Buffalo Bill, 285, indicates that this "thoroughly successful drama" opened in Chicago on September 5, 1881, so could not have been the play Kane saw.

showy pair of Colts were used in his stage performance. On reaching a place suitable for our purpose, Mr. Hickok proceeded to entertain us with some of the best pistol work which it has ever been my good fortune to witness.

Standing on a railroad track, in a deep cut, his pistols cracking with the regularity and cadence of the ticking of an old house clock, he struck and dislodged the bleaching pebbles sticking in the face of the bank, at a distance of about 15 yards.

Standing about 30 feet from the shooter, one of our party tossed a quart can in the air to a height of about 30 feet. This was perforated three times before it reached the ground, twice with the right and once with the left hand.

Standing midway between the fences of a country road, which is four rods wide, Mr. Hickok's instinct of location was so accurate that he placed a bullet in each of the fence posts on opposite sides. Both shots were fired simultaneously.

Located midway between the two telegraph poles he placed a bullet in one of them then wheeled and with the same weapon planted another in the second. Telegraph poles in this country run about thirty to the mile, or 176 feet distant from each other.

Two common bricks were placed on the top board of a fence, about two feet apart and about 15 yards from the shooter. These were broken with two shots fired from the pistol in either hand, the reports so nearly together that they seemed but one.

His last feat was to me the most remarkable of all: A quart can was thrown by Mr. Hickok himself, which dropped about 10 or 12 yards distant. Quickly whipping out his weapons, he fired alternatively with right and left. Advancing a step with each shot, his bullets striking the earth just under the can he kept it in continuous motion until his pistols were empty.[12]

As late an 1912, writing in *Outdoor Recreation* for November, Kane declared: "I am prepared to believe any story of his skill or prowess that does not conflict with the laws of gravitation and physics."

The .44 Colts and Remingtons to which Kane refers offer in themselves cause for speculation. The Colts were either cap and ball Armies, or Springfield Armory conversions, Richards-Mason conversion to the rim- or center-fire cartridge, or (very remotely) a pair of 1873 New Model Army revolvers (Peacemakers) in the special .44 Henry rim-fire. Since there is little likelihood that Hickok used a Peacemaker, the former types of weapons must apply.

[12] (Letter to the editor), "The D.A. *vs.* S.A. Controversy," *Outdoor Life*, Vol. XVII, No. 6 (June, 1906).

The Remingtons, however, would be more acceptable in cartridge form, for by 1872 the company was selling its "Improved Army Revolver," a .46-caliber five-shot weapon that preceded their famous six-shot Army revolver of 1875. Prior to 1872, and during the late 1860's, a number of Remington percussion revolvers were converted to .46 caliber. In 1855, Rollin White was granted a patent for revolvers with bored-through cylinders, and he had in turn granted exclusive rights to Smith and Wesson to produce revolvers on his principal, which remained effective until April 3, 1869, when the patent expired. Remington had been one of the first companies to convert their revolvers on this principle by payment of a royalty, but after that date all the manufacturers began to produce cartridge weapons of their own.[13]

On the subject of Kane's evidence, Jeff Cooper and his team were much happier. The shots at poles would be "distinctly possible with Hickok's weapons, easier with modern weapons." And the shots at bricks would be "relatively easy for both gun and shooter." The quart can stunt would have been "easy for the weapon. Difficult to faintly possible for the shooter, depending upon the angle and velocity with which the can was thrown."

This writer has seen "plinkers" at work on tin cans and has himself tried with varying degress of success shots at cans thrown down on the ground and shot at to make them "jump about." The results were very encouraging. However, I would agree with Mr. Cooper that a great deal depends upon the ability of the man behind the trigger.

Tests carried out in the 1920's with the old cap and ball weapons in .36 and .44 revealed that in the hands of a good shot, and with the proper loading and attention, especially with round balls, a marksman could put six shots inside a circle five inches in diameter at fifty yards. But again, emphasis was placed on the fact that weapons had to be carefully loaded, the bore kept clean, and plenty of grease placed around the balls after being rammed into the chambers.[14] The sights on the old-time weapons left a lot to be desired, but for the task required of them, the weapons performed very well.[15]

However, among the mass of adulation for Hickok's shooting prowess, there exist comments from others that express doubts.

[13] John E. Parsons, *The Peacemaker and Its Rivals*, 10; John E. Parsons, *Smith and Wesson Revolvers*, 3–4, 41–54.

[14] Roy C. McHenry, "In Re: Wild Bill Hickok," *American Rifleman*, Vol. LXIII, No. 25 (June 1, 1926), 865.

[15] Rosa, *The Gunfighter: Man or Myth?* 184–88.

One such debunking of Wild Bill's skill came from Charles B. Roth, a member of the Denver Posse of the Westerners:

The usual pistol targets in Hickok's day consisted of the backs of envelopes. These envelopes were 4" x 4". The stamp was affixed on the back, in the exact center, and was around an inch square. The stamp was the "Bullseye." They customarily shot at ten yards, 30 feet. With the distance and target of this kind, a modern pistoleer would shoot the stamp completely away, but [none of] the Hickok targets I had . . . showed more than one shot in the stamp, with the others scattered clear around the sixteen square inches of white space.[16]

Mr. Roth later volunteered the information that the targets had been owned by a newspaperman, Chauncey Thomas, and that he did not know where they were today, when they were actually made, or any other authentic information about them. This is unfortunate, because a great deal of what Thomas wrote is suspect, and these targets must therefore be considered in the same light.

Certainly, contemporaries of Wild Bill were mixed in their opinions of his marksmanship, but there seemed to be a general opinion that when Hickok shot at a man he was in a class by himself. Luther North, brother of Frank North of the Pawnee Battalion of Indian scouts fame, rated his brother one of the finest pistol shots on the plains. He recalled that Wild Bill, his brother Frank, and a man named John Talbot used to meet about twice a week at Talbot's Roadhouse (between Cheyenne and Fort Russell) in the early 1870's, and compete in target-shooting. According to Luther, Frank invariably won, closely followed by Talbot. "I never saw Wild Bill shoot with his left hand either, although he was always called a two-gun man," wrote Luther. He later wrote that Wild Bill "was very deliberate and took careful aim closing his left eye. If he could shoot from the hip he never did it there. . . . Wild Bill was a man of Iron Nerve and could shoot straight enough to hit a man in the right place when the man had a gun in his hand and just between you and me not many of the so called Bad Men could do that."[17] To Charles B. Roth, Luther said that Hickok once remarked to his brother: "Frank, you can beat the hell out of me shootin' at pieces of paper, but I can beat you when it comes to hittin' men." And that was true: Hickok's greatness consisted in being able to shoot while being shot at.[18] To Nichols he made the

16 Letter to the author, July 18, 1956.
17 *Man of the Plains*, 150–51, 310; Luther North to Richard Tanner, Dec. 31, 1930, MS1345 Tanner, Manuscripts Division, NSHS.
18 Charles B. Roth to the author, July 18, 1956.

comment that is as true today as it was in 1865: "Whenever you get into a row be sure and not shoot too quick. Take time. I've known many a feller slip up for shootin' in a hurry."

It has been claimed by some writers that most of Wild Bill's pistol prowess was performed with a pair of .41-caliber Williamson[19] derringers, the same pair he is reputed to have carried in concealed pockets in his waistcoat or vest. As has been pointed out, at the time of his death no trace of these weapons could be found, and the whereabouts of these pistols today is questionable. However, the late Raymond W. Thorp wrote on this subject in the August, 1926, issue of *Outdoor Life*. He said in part:

Wild Bill's derringer was a .41-caliber Williamson, heavily engraved and plated in gold, which he was wont to carry reposing in a vest pocket under his long black coat. This gun saved his life many times, under circumstances in which a long-barreled six-shooter would have been impossible of operation, such as close card games, etc. In 1875, in Denver, Colo., Wild Bill gave this gun to Buffalo Bill, telling Cody at the time that it had accounted in all for the lives of twenty-seven men. Colonel Cody later gave this weapon to his friend, a noted gun collector, named Clark, who gave it to his son, M. C. Clark, himself a collector of famous guns. I understand that M. C. Clark is a gun collector no more, but has quit the hobby. . . . But I am not thru with Hickok's derringer. This was sold by Mr. Clark to another noted collector, a friend of mine, Waldo L. Rich.

Mr. Thorp later told this writer that when Mr. Rich died he asked his family for the Williamson, but he never received it—instead he was sent a Colt Theur No. 3 which had no connection with Hickok at all. The present owner of the Williamson is not known. In his letter to *Outdoor Life*, Thorp confirmed that the Hickok family were concerned over the disappearance of Wild Bill's revolvers when he died:

I have a letter written by his sister [probably Lydia] in 1915, saying that "He often told us that in case he was killed, he would send home his six-shooters, etc., as he had had arrangements made to have a box shipped to us with these guns and other paraphernalia, but he did not do this, and we, none of us, have anything that was ever owned by James. Charlie Utter told L. B. (Wild Bill's older brother) that he had gotten James' six-shooters from the railroad officials [?], and to write to him and he would send them, and altho L. B. wrote, they were not sent.

[19] Patented in 1866, the Williamson was produced in .36 and .41 calibers. It was unique in that it was designed to fire fixed rim-fire ammunition or powder and ball.

347

The foregoing raises many interesting points, in particular the reference to "railroad officials." No clue is given as to what was actually meant by this. Some might conclude that Utter meant the legendary presentation pistols from the Kansas Pacific, or perhaps it merely meant that the pistols had been shipped to Utter by railroad express. In his correspondence with this writer, Mr. Thorp was unable to add any further details.

Wild Bill seldom wore holsters in later life. For the most part he carried his pistols in his belt, or in a silk sash or his waistband, and wore them butts-forward for a "twist" or "Cavalry" draw. Both pistols would be drawn in an inverted or twist motion. The right hand is turned under the right-hand butt, the index finger slips into the trigger guard, and the thumb folds over the hammer spur. The pistol is drawn and spun forward, so that the weapon is cocked by its own weight. Coming straight out in this way, the weapon is automatically lined up on its target. This draw would be useless when wearing pistols under a coat, so it seems logical to accept the theory that Hickok wore shoulder holsters with a Prince Albert, or, as has also been suggested, carried his pistols as described, but used a cross-draw.

Hickok was a two-gun man, and unlike many of his contemporaries, he could use both. While it seems evident that his left-handed shots were not as good as his right in all respects, the fact remains that he was ambidextrous.

Basically two guns meant one in reserve. If a man was really good, he rarely needed the second gun—but the second gun had its practical value also. In the days of the percussion revolvers, which were slow-loading, and sometimes subject to spent caps jamming the action, such a setback could be the difference between life and death. Sometimes the pistol had to be stripped down in order to remove the obstruction, and in a time of crisis, such a situation could prove fatal. Even a broken mainspring was less serious than the effects of a spent cap, for the user could improvise if necessary by striking the hammer with a rock and setting off the cap. To combat this, Colt milled a groove in the recoil shield so that as the cylinder turned the caps dropped away. But this provision was by no means foolproof. Remington and other solid-frame revolvers rarely suffered from this danger, but in the latter's case, the small cylinder pin rapidly became fouled and frequently stuck, rendering the weapon inoperative. With the introduction of metallic ammunition, the two-gun man slowly disappeared, but few gunfighters were caught without a reserve or "hide-out" gun, just in case.

Despite the legends built around the old-time gunfighters, few of them ever notched their pistols. This was certainly true of the men who made reputations. A notched gun was the weapon of the braggart, attracting nothing but trouble for its owner. Besides, notching destroyed the balance and comfortable grip, which were both vital factors in the game of life and death.

While the gunfighter was basically a product of the cattle-driving days, drovers or cowboys for the most part were poor shots with a pistol, but generally adept with a rifle. Cowboys were known to pull their pistols and shoot with alarming rapidity at whatever took their fancy, but they seldom could hit a barn door from the inside. This is not surprising. Working an average of sixteen hours a day (Sundays included), cowboys had little time for fast and fancy pistol practice. With a wage of forty dollars a month (most of which was spent on hell-raising or repayment of debts to the boss), they could ill afford to buy silver-plated pistols or shoot off thousands of rounds of ammunition; and their work-hardened, rope-scarred hands, calloused by years of rough labor, were not at all suitable for an art that demanded supple yet strong hands. So gunfighting was left strictly to the professionals. Crazed steers, rattlesnakes, or bears on the prod might induce cowboys to blast off a few rounds, as might a spree in town—but pistol practice on each other was a rare thing. One look at such as Hickok meandering around in his shirt sleeves with a brace of six-shooters was enough to convince them that they were outclassed.

Thus it was that part of the Hickok legend was built on his ability to handle a pistol. Wild Bill, whose two guns spelled death from either hand—whose reputation spoke volumes for him, and constantly forced him to resort to his weapons or his fists to keep it— let all men know once and for all that if he was forced to pull his gun, he did so with one object: to kill.

A Chronology of Wild Bill

1837 Born at Homer, La Salle County, Illinois, on Saturday, May 27, the fourth son of William Alonzo and Polly Butler Hickok.

1847–49 In between schooling, works on neighboring farms and lives with his brothers in small cabin.

1851 Oliver leaves for California and James takes his place on a local farm. Aids his father in assisting escaping slaves.

1852 William Alonzo Hickok died on Wednesday, May 5. Remaining sons and two daughters take over running the home and farm.

1854 Finds employment with company building Illinois and Michigan Canal. Falls out with employer over latter's cruelty to livestock and pushes him into the water. Returns home but anxious to go to Kansas.

1856 James and Lorenzo set out for Kansas to establish family claim. Lorenzo returns and James becomes involved with Free State movement.

1857–58 Joins General James Lane's Free State Army. Meets Will Cody on wagon train. Elected village constable of Monticello Township, Johnson County, Kansas, on Monday, March 22, 1858. Friendship for Mary Owen, but relationship ended by family interference. Journeys with Lorenzo to Leavenworth and becomes teamster for Russell, Majors, and Waddell.

1859 Believed to have come home for harvest and then returned west, where he met Kit Carson and stayed at the Cody home in Leavenworth during the autumn and winter.

1860 Pony Express started on Tuesday, April 3. Cody becomes a rider, but Hickok remains a coach and freight driver. Attack on a relay station by Indians in September. Hickok leads a band of riders to recover stock. Cody joins in. Joseph A. "Jack" Slade joins victorious riders in celebration and kills a stage driver in a brawl.

1861 Friday, July 12, kills David C. McCanles at Rock Creek. Cleared of murder. Joins Union Army in Civil War as a teamster. Wins name of "Wild Bill."

1862 Wagon master, sharpshooter, and spy.

1863 Spy behind rebel lines. Spends some time at Rolla and in constant touch with his brother Lorenzo, a government wagon master.

350

1864 Employed as a detective in Springfield in March. In April appointed a scout, with headquarters at Springfield at $5.00 a day. Acts on orders of Captain R. B. Owen and General Sanborn. Engaged in spying during battle of Westport.

1865 Scouting for General Sanborn; mustered out in June. Kills Davis Tutt in Springfield on Friday, July 21. Tried for manslaughter, but defended by John S. Phelps and aided by Owen. Meets Colonel George Ward Nichols, who decides to write up his exploits for publication. Runs for marshal of Springfield but loses.

1866 Witnesses the shooting of James Coleman in Springfield. Ordered to Fort Riley by Owen; believed appointed deputy United States marshal. Captures deserters and mule thieves. Guide for General Sherman, and escorts tourists on plains. Meets General Custer and California Joe.

1867 Chases more deserters and signs on as a scout for the United States Army. Joins Hancock's expedition to Indian country. Scouts for Custer. *Harper's New Monthly Magazine* publishes Nichols' story of his exploits, and "Wild Bill" is a celebrity. Meets Henry M. Stanley and the *Harper's* artist Theodore R. Davis. Davis unimpressed with Hickok, but Wild Bill proves his ability when capturing some deserters. Well-known figure in Leavenworth and Kansas City. Lives for a short time with Indian Annie in Ellsworth; familiar figure in Hays and friend of United States Marshal Whiting. Tuesday, November 5, is unsuccessful candidate for sheriff of Ellsworth County against Captain E. W. Kingsbury (Hickok also stood for marshal of Ellsworth in July, but lost to Chauncey B. Whitney who was elected town constable).

1868 March 13, his friend, Jack Harvey, dies. March 28, Wild Bill, in his capacity as a deputy United States marshal, takes some prisoners from Fort Hays to Topeka, accompanied by Buffalo Bill Cody. Meets Bill Tilghman. Attraction at Hays City for tourists. Scouts for Tenth Cavalry. Misses Washita battle and is snowed up on the Canadian River with General Penrose. Rescued by Buffalo Bill.

1869 February, wounded by Indians and leaves scouts. Visits mother's home at Troy Grove. Returns west and acts as a deputy United States marshal in May, by removing mule thieves from Fort Wallace to Topeka. Attraction in Hays City. August, elected sheriff of Ellis County. Tuesday, August 24, shoots Bill Mulrey (or Mulvey), who dies on August 25. Monday, September 27, kills Samuel Strawhun in a saloon brawl. Sunday, October 3, attempts to obtain the prisoner Bob Connors from the post commander of Fort Hays and is refused. Sunday, October 10, Wild Bill prevents a lynching in Hays. Tuesday, November 2, loses the election to succeed himself as sheriff by 89 votes to 114. Visits Topeka.

351

1870 January, his friend Charles Whiting dies in Topeka. February, gets involved in a brawl and is fined for disturbing the peace. Leaves town but returns late in April. May 2, appears in Junction City and serves a subpoena on two witnesses in a forthcoming court case. Signs the return as "J. B. Hickok, Deputy U.S. Marshal." Goes to Texas with Colonel Ginger's Circus and quits at Sherman. Makes a trip to Hays and is mixed up in a saloon brawl with a number of Seventh Cavalry troopers during the night of Sunday–Monday, July 17–18. Kills one and wounds another in self-defense. Leaves town ahead of irate citizens, disappears for a time, and eventually reappears in Topeka, where it is believed he first met Mrs. Cody. Displays marksmanship for local residents. Gambles frequently.

1871 Appears in Junction City, displays marksmanship for English emigrants. Believed next appeared at Fort Harker. Offered job as marshal of Abilene, accepts, and is appointed on Saturday, April 15, 1871, at $150 per month. Meets Charles Gross, an old friend by whom he was recommended for the job, John Wesley Hardin, Ben Thompson, and the ill-fated Phil Coe. Mrs. Agnes Lake Thatcher arrives in August with her circus, and falls for Wild Bill, but he puts her off. October 5, kills Coe in a street fight; Mike Williams is also killed when he runs into the line of fire. Foils an attempt on his life during November while on a train ride to Topeka. This act is applauded by the newspapers, as is his conduct as marshal of Abilene. Wednesday, December 13, is dismissed because the city no longer needs him.

1872 Leaves Abilene and goes to Georgetown, Colorado, to stay with Colorado Charley Utter, and later moves to Kansas City. Here he meets Colonel Sidney Barnett, who persuades him to appear in a grand Buffalo chase at Niagara Falls. The show takes place on Wednesday, August 28, and again on August 30. September 27 at the Kansas City Exposition, Wild Bill annoys Texans by refusing to allow the band to play "Dixie." Late in the autumn the Indian Whistler is murdered. A Wild Bill is blamed, but this was not Hickok.

1873 It is reported in March that Wild Bill has been killed, but he writes to the newspapers denying his death. Persuaded by Cody to join his Combination, and arrives in New York late in August or early September. Unhappy in show business.

1874 March, leaves troupe at Rochester, New York, intending to go west. Before leaving, Hickok is interviewed by local press and meets Mrs. Lake once more. Keeps up continuous correspondence with her. Reported in New York City in rival show to Cody, which he leaves but returns to wreck when he finds out that an actor is to play "Wild Bill." Visits Cheyenne and Denver, where he is reported to be acting as a guide for English tourists. Goes to Kansas City and Wyoming.

1875 Back in Cheyenne, where in June he is charged with vagrancy. In the summer he meets Mrs. Annie Tallent and asks about the Black Hills. It is claimed that he was ordered to leave the city but refused. His eyesight gives him some trouble, and he visits Dr. Joshua Thorne in Kansas City for treatment.

1876 His continuous correspondence with Agnes Lake leads to romance. Both appear in Cheyenne in March and are married there on the fifth. They honeymoon in Cincinnati. Wild Bill leaves wife to go to St. Louis to organize band of miners for the Black Hills. Abandons project and reappears in Cheyenne, where together with Charley Utter and his brother Steve, he organizes a trip to Deadwood. They are joined by Joseph "White-Eye Jack" Anderson and his brother Charlie. The party stops briefly at John Hunton's ranch on Friday, June 30. It is claimed that Calamity Jane joins their train at Fort Laramie. During a halt at Sage Creek about Friday, July 7, the party is believed to have been met by Buffalo Bill, who is once more scouting for the Fifth Cavalry. It is claimed that Cody was in Cheyenne at the same time as Hickok, but there is no record of a meeting. In Deadwood, Wild Bill meets Leander P. Richardson, who persuades him to demonstrate his pistol prowess. Wednesday, August 2, Hickok is assassinated by John McCall in saloon No. 10, and is buried on the afternoon of August 3. McCall is tried for murder by an illegal miners' court and acquitted. McCall leaves town and is later arrested in Laramie and tried legally for murder in Yankton, on December 4–6. Convicted of murder.

1877 Wednesday, January 3, McCall is sentenced to be hanged. Sentence is carried out on Thursday, March 1.

1879 Wild Bill is reburied on Mount Moriah on Sunday, August 3, in his final resting place.

Bibliography

I. Books and Pamphlets

Adams, Ramon F. *Six-Guns and Saddle Leather*. Norman, Okla., 1969.

Armes, Col. George A. *Ups and Downs of an Army Officer*. Washington, D.C., 1900.

Arthur, John Preston. *History of Watauga County, North Carolina, with Sketches of Prominent Families*. Richmond, Va., 1915.

Athearn, Robert G. *William Tecumseh Sherman and the Settlement of the West*. Norman, Okla., 1956.

Baldwin, Elmer. *History of La Salle County, Illinois*. Chicago, 1877.

Beecher Island Annual, Vol. V (Forty-Ninth Anniversary Edition, 1917).

Bloyd, Levi. *Jefferson County History: Rock Creek Station*. Fairbury, Nebr., n.d.

Buel, J. W. *Heroes of the Plains*. New York and St. Louis, 1882.

Burke's General Armory. London, 1884.

Burkey, Rev. Blaine, *Wild Bill Hickok the Law in Hays City*. Hays, Kan., 1973.

Cody, William F. *Life of the Honorable William Frederick Cody, Known as Buffalo Bill, the Famous Hunter, Scout and Guide: An Autobiography*. Hartford, Conn., 1879.

Connelley, William Elsey. *Quantrill and the Border Wars*. Cedar Rapids, Iowa, 1909.

———. *Wild Bill and His Era*. New York, 1933.

Coursey, Oscar William. *Wild Bill*. Mitchell, S.D., 1924.

Cunningham, Eugene. *Triggernometry*. Caldwell, Idaho, 1941.

Custer, Elizabeth Bacon. *Following the Guidon*. New York, 1890.

Custer, George Armstrong. *My Life on the Plains*. New York, 1874.

Dawson, Charles. *Pioneer Tales of the Oregon Trail*. Topeka, Kan., 1912.

Dykstra, Robert R. *The Cattle Towns*. New York, 1968.

Ebbutt, Percy G. *Emigrant Life in Kansas*. London, 1886.

Edwards, J. B. *Early Days in Abilene*. Abilene, Kan., 1940.

Eisele, Wilbert E. (Ross Lyndon). *The Real Wild Bill Hickok*. Denver, Colo., 1931.

Gard, Wayne. *The Chisholm Trail*. Norman, Okla., 1954.

Hardin, John Wesley. *The Life of John Wesley Hardin*. Seguin, Tex., 1896.

Heisler, E. F., and D. M. Smith. *Atlas Map of Johnson County, Kansas.* Wyandotte, 1874.

Heitman, Francis B. *Historical Register and Dictionary of the United States Army.* 2 vols. Washington, 1903.

Henry, Stuart. *Conquering Our Great American Plains.* New York, 1930.

Hickok, Charles Nelson. *The Hickok Genealogy, Descendants of William Hickocks of Farmington, Connecticut.* Rutland, Vt., 1938.

History of Greene County, Missouri. N.p., 1883.

Howard, J. W. ("Doc"). *"Doc" Howard's Memoirs.* Denver, Colo., ca. 1931.

Hungerford, Edward. *Wells Fargo: Advancing the American Frontier.* New York, 1949.

Hunt, Lt. Col. R. H. *General Orders No. 11.* N.p., February, 1908.

Hunter, John Marvin (editor). *The Trail Drivers of Texas.* 2 vols. San Antonio, Tex., 1920–23.

Hunton, John. *John Hunton's Diary.* Edited by L. G. "Pat" Flannery. 3 vols. Lingle, Wyo., 1956–60.

Jelinek, George. *Ellsworth, Kansas, 1867–1947.* Salina, Kan., 1947.

——. *The Ellsworth Story—90 Years of Ellsworth and Ellsworth County History.* Ellsworth, Kan., 1957.

Jennewein, J. Leonard. *Calamity Jane of the Western Trails.* Huron, S.D., 1953.

Johannsen, Albert. *The House of Beadle and Adams and Its Dime and Nickel Novels: The Story of a Vanished Literature.* 2 vols. Norman, Okla., 1950.

Kuykendall, W. L. *Frontier Days.* N.p., 1917.

Lake, Stuart N. *Wyatt Earp, Frontier Marshal.* Boston, 1931.

Lockard, F. M. *The History of the Early Settlement of Norton County, Kansas.* Norton, Kan., [1894?].

Logan, Herschel C. *Buckskin and Satin.* Harrisburg, Pa., 1954.

McLintock, John S. *Pioneer Days in the Black Hills.* Deadwood, S.D., 1939.

McCoy, Joseph G. *Historic Sketches of the Cattle Trade of the West and Southwest.* Kansas City, Mo., 1874.

Masterson, V. V. *The Katy Railroad and the Last Frontier.* Norman, Okla., 1952.

Meline, James F. *Two Thousand Miles on Horseback: Santa Fe and Back: A Summer Tour Through Kansas, Nebraska, Colorado and New Mexico, in the Year 1866.* New York, 1868.

Miller, Nyle H., and Joseph W. Snell. *Why The West Was Wild.* Topeka, Kan., 1963.

Milner, Joseph E., and Earle R. Forrest. *California Joe.* Caldwell, Idaho, 1935.

Monaghan, Jay. *Civil War on the Western Border (1854–65).* Boston, 1955.

Morden, J. C. *Historic Niagara*. Niagara Falls, Ont., 1932.

North, Luther. *Man of the Plains: Recollections of Luther North*. Edited by Donald F. Danker. Lincoln, Nebr., 1961.

Otero, Miguel Antonio. *My Life on the Frontier*. 2 vols. New York, 1935.

Parsons, John E. *The Peacemaker and Its Rivals—An Account of the Single Action Colt*. New York, 1950.

———. *Smith and Wesson Revolvers*. New York, 1957.

Payne, Bayard H. *Pioneers, Indians, and Buffalo*. Curtis, Nebr., 1935.

Pictorial and Genealogical Record of Greene County [Missouri]. N.p., n.d.

Pond, Fred E. *Life and Adventures of "Ned Buntline," with Ned Buntline's Anecdote of "Frank Forester" and Chapter of Angling Sketches*. New York, 1919.

Price, John M., Samuel A. Riggs, and James McCahon, Commissioners Appointed by the Governor, Under an Act Approved February 18, 1867. *The General Statutes of the State of Kansas*. Lawrence, Kan., 1868.

Robinson, Gil. *Old Wagon Show Days*. Cincinnati, Ohio, 1925.

Roenigk, Adolph (editor). *Pioneer History of Kansas*. Lincoln, Kan., 1933.

Root, Frank A., and William Elsey Connelley. *The Overland Stage to California*. Topeka, Kan., 1901.

Rosa, Joseph G. *The Gunfighter: Man or Myth?* Norman, Okla., 1969.

———. *They Called Him Wild Bill: The Life and Adventures of James Butler Hickok*. 1st ed. Norman, Okla., 1964.

Russell, Don. *The Lives and Legends of Buffalo Bill*. Norman, Okla., 1960.

Sandoz, Mari. *The Buffalo Hunters*. New York, 1954.

Santee, Ross. *Lost Pony Tracks*. New York, 1953.

Savage, Richard (editor). *Stratford-upon-Avon Parish Registers: Baptisms (1558–1652); Marriages (1558–1812); Burials (1558–1652/3)* London, 1897–1905.

Spring, Agnes Wright. *Cheyenne and Black Hills Stage and Express Routes*. Glendale, Calif., 1949.

———. *Colorado Charley, Wild Bill's Pard*. Boulder, Colo., 1968.

Stanley, Sir Henry Morton. *My Early Travels and Adventures in America and Asia*. London, 1895.

Steckmesser, Kent Ladd. *The Western Hero in History and Legend*. Norman, Okla., 1965.

Sternberg, Charles H. *Life of a Fossil Hunter*. New York, 1909.

Tallent, Annie D. *The Black Hills; Or the Last Hunting Ground of the Dakotahs*. St. Louis, Mo., 1899.

Thorp, Raymond W. *Spirit Gun of the West—The Story of Doc W. F. Carver*. Glendale, Calif., 1957.

Tilghman, Zoe A. *Marshal of the Last Frontier*. Glendale, Calif., 1949.

———. *Spotlight—Bat Masterson and Wyatt Earp as U.S. Deputy Marshals.* San Antonio, Tex., 1960.

Townshend, R. B. *A Tenderfoot in Colorado.* Norman, Okla., 1968.

Triplett, Frank. *The Life, Times, and Treacherous Death of Jesse James.* Edited by Joseph W. Snell. Chicago, 1970.

Verckler, Stewart P. *Cowtown Abilene, The Story of Abilene, Kansas (1867–1875).* New York, 1961.

Wallace, Irving. *The Fabulous Showman.* London, 1960.

Webb, W. E. *Buffalo Land.* Cincinnati, 1872.

Wetmore, Helen Cody. *The Last of the Great Scouts: The Life Story of Col. William F. Cody "Buffalo Bill."* London, 1901.

Wheeler, Homer W. *The Frontier Trail.* Los Angeles, 1923.

Whitney, Maj. Gen. Courtney. *MacArthur—His Rendezvous with History.* New York, 1956.

Williamson, J. W. *The Battle of Massacre Canyon.* Trenton, Nebr., 1930.

Wilstach, Frank Jenners. *Wild Bill Hickok—The Prince of Pistoleers.* New York, 1926.

Young, Harry (Sam). *Hard Knocks.* Portland, Ore., 1915.

Zornow, William Frank. *Kansas: A History of the Jayhawk State.* Norman, Okla., 1957.

II. Magazines and Articles

Barnes, Lela (editor). "An Editor Looks at Early-Day Kansas—The Letters of Charles Monroe Chase," Kansas State Historical Society *Quarterly*, Vol. XXVI, No. 2 (Summer, 1960).

Beardsley, J. L. "The West's Top Triggerman," *Guns*, Vol. II, Nos. 4–16 (April, 1956).

Blancett, Truman. "The Old Frontier," Denver *Post* (March 22, 1931).

Blewitt, Andrew. "Calamity Jane," The English Westerners' *Brand Book*, Vol. V, No. 2 (January, 1963).

Bryan, Jerry. "An Illinois Gold Hunter in the Black Hills" (Diary, March 13–August 20, 1876), Pamphlet Series No. 2, Illinois State Historical Society, Springfield, Illinois, 1960.

"The Case of James Butler Hickok, *alias* 'Wild Bill,' " Westerners' *Brand Book* (Chicago), Vol. III, Nos. 2–3 (April–May, 1946).

Cody, Louisa Frederici. "Memories of Buffalo Bill," *Ladies' Home Journal*, Vol. XXXVI, No. 7 (July, 1919).

Connelley, William Elsey. "Wild Bill—James Butler Hickok: David C. McCanles at Rock Creek," Kansas State Historical Society *Collections*, Vol. XVII (1926–28).

Cooper, Jeff. "How Good Was Hickok?" *Guns and Ammo*, Vol. II, No. 3 (March, 1960).

Cooper, Wilbur (Jack Rohan, editor). "Hickok-Hoakum Case Goes to Jury," *The American Rifleman*, Vol. LXXIII, No. 26 (June 15, 1926).

Cushman, George L. "Abilene, First of the Kansas Cow Towns," Kansas

State Historical Society *Quarterly*, Vol. IX, No. 3 (August, 1940).

Dykstra, Robert R. "The Last Days of 'Texan' Abilene: A Study in Community Conflict on the Farmer's Frontier," *Agricultural History*, Vol. XXXIV, No. 3 (1960).

Forrest, Col. Cris. (editor). "Wild Bill's First Trail. As He Told It," *De-Witt's Ten Cent Romances*, No. 10 (December, 1867).

Hance, George W. "The Truth About Wild Bill," Topeka (Kansas) *Mail and Breeze*, December 20, 1901.

Hansen, George W. "True Story of Wild Bill–McCanles Affray in Jefferson County, Nebraska, July 12, 1861" (with supporting articles by Addison E. Sheldon and William Monroe McCanles), *Nebraska History Magazine*, Vol. X, No. 2 (April–June, 1927).

"Historical News and Comments," *Missouri Historical Review*, Vol. X (October, 1915–July, 1916).

Hunter, J. Marvin, Sr. "Reminiscences of Colonel Lewis Ginger," *Frontier Times* (Original Series), Vol. XXX, No. 2 (April–June, 1953).

Kane, Robert A. (letter to the editor). "The D.A. *vs.* S.A. Controversy," *Outdoor Life*, Vol. XVII, No. 6 (June 1906).

King, Paul. "Wild Bill–Peace Officer in Hays," *The Aerend*, Vol. V, No. 2 (Spring, 1934).

Laurent, Louis Charles. "Reminiscences by the Son of a French Pioneer," Kansas State Historical Society *Collections*, Vol. XIII (1913–14).

Lewis, Alfred Henry. "How Mr. Hickok Came to Cheyenne: An Epic of an Unsung Ulysses," *The Saturday Evening Post*, Vol. CLXXVI, No. 37 (March 12, 1904).

Little, E. C. "A Son of the Border," Topeka *Mail and Breeze* (September 13, 1901).

Lorentz, Upton. "Colorado Charley, Friend of 'Wild Bill,'" *Frontier Times*, Vol. XIII, No. 8 (May, 1936).

M'Afee, E. C. "Wild Bill's Reputation as 'Bad Man' Overrated," Springfield (Missouri) *Leader* (February 1, 1920).

McHenry, Roy C. "In Re: Wild Bill Hickok," *American Rifleman*, Vol. LXIII, No. 25 (June 1, 1926).

Mann, E. B. "Wild Bill Hickok," *The American Rifleman*, Vol. XCV, No. 4 (April, 1947).

Masterson, W. B. ("Bat"). "A Few Scrapes," Denver *Republican* (July 17, 1910).

Montgomery, Mrs. Frank C. "Fort Wallace and Its Relation to the Frontier," Kansas State Historical Society *Collections*, Vol. XVII (1926–28).

Nebraska History Magazine, Vol. VI, No. 3 (July–September, 1935). [The whole issue is devoted to the Battle of Massacre Canyon.]

Nichols, Colonel George Ward. "Wild Bill," *Harper's New Monthly Magazine*, Vol. XXXIV, No. CCI (February, 1867).

Nordin, Dr. Charles R. "Doc W. F. Carver, 'Evil Spirit of the Plains,' The

Wizard Rifle Shot of the World and His Career on the Nebraska Plains," *Nebraska History Magazine*, Vol. X, No. 4 (October–December, 1927).

Odd, Gilbert. "Adah Helped K. O. Heenan," *Fighters and Their Women*, London *Evening News* (August 31, 1963).

Paine, Clarence S. "Calamity Jane—Man, Woman . . . Or Both?" The Westerners' *Brand Book* (Chicago), Bound Vol. II (1945–46).

———. "She Laid Her Pistol Down; or, The Last Will and Testament of Calamity Jane," The Westerners' *Brand Book* (Chicago), Bound Vol. I (1944).

Preston, Paul. "Wild Bill, the Indian-Slayer: A Tale of Forest and Prairie Life," *DeWitt's Ten Cent Romances*, No. 3 (July, 1867).

Putnam, John H. "A Trip to the End of the Union Pacific in 1868," Kansas State Historical Society *Quarterly*, Vol. XIII, No. 3 (August, 1944).

Richardson, Leander P. "A Trip to the Black Hills," *Scribner's Monthly*, Vol. XIII (February, 1877).

Riley, Paul D. "Red Willow County Letters of Royal Buck, 1872–1873," *Nebraska History*, Vol. XLVII, No. 4 (December, 1966).

Robbins, Hiram. "Wild Bill's Humors," *The Arkansaw Traveler*, n.d.

Root, George A. "Reminscences of William Darnell," Kansas State Historical Society *Collections*, Vol. XVII (1926–28).

Rosa, Joseph G. "Alias Jack McCall: A Pardon or Death?" The Kansas City Westerners' *Trail Guide*, Vol. XII, No. 2 (June, 1967).

———. "Are These the Hickok Guns?" *Guns Quarterly*, Vol. I, No. 1 (Spring, 1960).

———. "Incident at Rock Creek," The English Westerners' *Brand Book*, Vol. II, No. 4 (February, 1956).

Russell, Don. "Cody, Kings & Coronets," *The American West*, Vol. VII, No. 4 (July, 1970).

Ryan, Captain John. "Ten Years with General Custer Among the American Indians," *The Newton* (Massachusetts) *Circuit* (August 20 and September 3, 1909).

Settle, Raymond W. and Mary Lund. "Waddell and Russell: Frontier Capitalists," Kansas State Historical Society *Quarterly*, Vol. XXVI, No. 4 (Winter, 1960).

"T. Jeff Carr, The Detective," *Official Journal of the Police Authorities and Sheriffs of the United States*, Vol. IX, No. 108 (March, 1894).

Uhlarik, Carl. "The Myth of Wild Bill Hickok, "*The Prairie Schooner*, Vol. XXV, No. 2 (Summer, 1951).

Watson, Elmo Scott (editor), and Theodore R. Davis. "Henry M. Stanley's Indian Campaign in 1867," The Westerners' *Brand Book*, Bound Volume II (1945–46).

Wright, Kathryn. "The Real Calamity Jane," *True West*, Vol. V, No. 2 (November–December, 1957).

III. Newspapers

Where only one or two references were made to a newspaper, the actual dates are given; in all other instances the months or years checked are shown.

Abilene (Kansas) *Chronicle*, 1870 and 1871.
Atchison (Kansas) *Daily Champion*, February 5, 1867.
Atchison (Kansas) *Weekly Free Press*, March 2, 1867.
Austin (Texas) *Democratic Statesman*, October 12, 1871.
Austin (Texas) *State Gazette*, December 25, 1852.
Austin (Texas) *Weekly State Journal*, October 26, 1871.
Baltimore (Maryland) *American*, September, 1878.
Beatrice (Nebraska) *Express*, February 13, 1873.
Blue Hill (Nebraska) *Leader*, June 20, 1952.
Brenham (Texas) *Banner*, October 19, 1871.
Brownville (Nebraska) *Advertiser*, July 25, 1861.
Burlingame (Kansas) *Chronicle*, March 28, 1868.
Central City (Colorado) *Weekly Register Call*, October 28, 1892.
Cheyenne (Wyoming) *Daily Leader*, 1874–77 and 1880–85.
Cheyenne (Wyoming) *Daily News*, October 7, December 3, 1874.
Cheyenne (Wyoming) *Daily Sun*, 1874–76.
Cheyenne (Wyoming) *Democratic Leader*, July 30, 1885.
Chicago (Illinois) *Daily Record*, December 26, 1896.
Chicago (Illinois) *Inter-Ocean*, August 17, 1876.
Cincinnati (Ohio) *Commercial Gazette*, September 16, 1885.
Cincinnati (Ohio) *Daily Enquirer*, 1876–77 and September 16, 1885.
Cincinnati (Ohio) *Times-Star*, September 15, 1885.
Clyde (Kansas) *Republican Valley Empire*, August 2, 1870.
Culbertson (Nebraska) *Progress*, May 14, 1925.
Deadwood (Dakota Territory) *Black Hills Pioneer*, 1876–77.
Deadwood (Dakota Territory) *Black Hills Times*, 1879.
Deadwood (South Dakota) *Pioneer-Times*, 1925.
Denver (Colorado) *Field and Farm*, June 1, 1895.
Denver (Colorado) *Post*, March 22 and August 8, 1931.
Denver (Colorado) *Rocky Mountain News*, 1873–77.
Dickinson County (Kansas) *Chronicle*, March 20, 1873.
Ellis County (Kansas) *Star*, June–August, 1876.
Ellsworth (Kansas) *Reporter*, March 28, 1872.
Evanston (Wyoming) *Daily Sentinel*, 1873–76.
Fairbury (Nebraska) *News*, August 13, 1965.
Fort Scott (Kansas) *Democrat*, September 29, 1859.
Hays (Kansas) *Daily News*, November 11, 1929.
Hays City (Kansas) *Railway Advance*, 1867–68.
Hays City (Kansas) *Republican*, April 10, 1897.
Hays City (Kansas) *Sentinel*, August, 1876 and February 2, 1877.
Jefferson City (Missouri) *Daily Tribune*, September 3, 1876.

Jefferson City (Missouri) *People's Tribune*, August 23, 1876.
Jersey City (New Jersey) *Mirror*, August 31, 1907.
Jersey City (New Jersey) *Morning Telegraph*, August 23, 1907.
Junction City (Kansas) *Daily* and *Weekly Union*, 1866–71.
Kansas City (Missouri) *Daily Journal of Commerce*, August 25, 1869, and June 25, 1889.
Kansas City (Missouri) *Star*, June 15, 1913, and December 14, 1947.
Laramie (Wyoming) *Daily Sentinel*, 1873.
Lawrence (Kansas) *Daily Tribune*, 1868–69.
Lead (South Dakota) *Call*, August 9, 1927.
Leavenworth (Kansas) *Daily Bulletin*, February 13, 1867.
Leavenworth (Kansas) *Daily Commercial*, 1862–63.
Leavenworth (Kansas) *Daily Conservative*, 1862–63.
Leavenworth (Kansas) *Daily Times*, 1862–63.
Leavenworth (Kansas) *Times and Conservative*, 1867–72.
Lincoln (Nebraska) *Daily State Journal*, July 2, 1872.
London (England) *British Army Despatch and Nautical Standard*, December 15, 1854.
London (England) *Evening News*, August 31, 1963.
London (England) *Times*, January, 1872.
London (England) *United Services Gazette*, December 4, 1852.
Manhattan (Kansas) *Beacon*, July 22, 1874.
Manhattan (Kansas) *Enterprise*, August 23, 1876.
Manhattan (Kansas) *Independent*, 1867.
Marysville (Kansas) *Enterprise*, May 18, 1867.
Mendota (Illinois) *Bulletin*, March 18, 1869, and April 11, 1873.
Milwaukee (Wisconsin) *Sentinel*, January 22, 1873.
Neodesha (Kansas) *Citizen*, July 28, 1871.
Niagara Falls (New York) *Gazette*, 1870 and 1872.
Omaha (Nebraska) *Daily Bee*, 1874–76.
Oxford (Kansas) *Times*, 1871.
Portland (Maine) *Advertiser*, January 30, 1873.
Rochester (New York) *Democrat and Chronicle*, March 14, 1874.
Rochester (New York) *Times-Union*, February 28, 1958.
St. Louis (Missouri) *Weekly Missouri Democrat*, 1867 and 1873.
St. Louis (Missouri) *Republican*, March 23, 1876.
St. Paul (Minnesota) *Pioneer Press and Tribune*, September 8, 1876.
Saline County *Journal*, 1871–72.
Salt Lake City (Utah) *Desert News*, December 24, 1868.
Sioux Falls (South Dakota) *Daily Argus-Leader*, August 9, 1924.
Springfield (Missouri) *Missouri Weekly Patriot*, 1865–67 and 1872.
Sycamore (Illinois) *True Republican and Sentinel*, 1863.
Topeka (Kansas) *Daily Commonwealth*, 1970–71.
Topeka (Kansas) *Mail and Breeze*, September–December, 1901.
Topeka (Kansas) *State Record*, 1869–70.

Topeka (Kansas) *Weekly Leader*, April 2 and August 13, 1868.
Westport (Missouri) *Border Star*, October 29, 1859.
Wichita (Kansas) *Eagle*, September 14, 1876.
Wichita (Kansas) *Weekly Beacon*, October 28, 1874.
Wichita (Kansas) *Weekly Eagle*, August 9, 1872.
Yankton (Dakota Territory) *Press and Dakotaian*, 1876–77, 1880, and 1881.

IV. Manuscripts and Other Materials

Abilene (Kansas) Minute and Council Records Books, 1870–72, Microfilm copy, Manuscripts Division, Kansas State Historical Society.
Anderson, Joseph F. ("White-Eye"). Manuscript in the possession of Mrs. Ellen Anderson Mitchell, Fresno, California.
Bascom, C. J. "Some Early Sketches on the U[nion] P[acific] between Junction City and Sheridan, now Lisbon," undated typed manuscript, Manuscripts Division, Kansas State Historical Society.
Buel, J. W. Letter to Horace D. or Lorenzo B. Hickok, March 9, 1881. Original owned by Ethel Hickok.
Census, 1860. "Jones Territory—36" Territory of Nebraska. Microfilm copy, Archives Division, Nebraska State Historical Society.
Connelley, William Elsey. Collection of letters, clippings, manuscripts, bound copies of his Hickok manuscript, and other typed copies of letters and books, The Western History Department, Denver Public Library.
Court House and Officers of Ellis County, Kansas, 1867–1942. Typed manuscript, Manuscripts Division, Kansas State Historical Society.
Edwards, Cyrus, to J. B. Edwards, April 8, 1926. Papers of J. B. Edwards, Manuscripts Division, Kansas State Historical Society.
Department of State Permanent Marshal's Commissions, Vol. 3. Applications and Recommendations for Public Office, 1861–69. Records of the Department of State, Washington, D.C.
Governor's Correspondence (1869), Manuscripts Division, Kansas State Historical Society.
Gross, Charles F., to J. B. Edwards (1922–26 correspondence), Manuscripts Division, Kansas State Historical Society.
Hardin, John Wesley, to his wife Jane, June 24, 1888, copy on file at the San Marcos, Texas, Library.
Harmon, Edith. "The Hickok Family," unpublished genealogical record.
Hickok, Howard L. "The Hickok Legend," unpublished manuscript in possession of his son, Major James Butler Hickok, U.S.M.C.
Hickok, James Butler, letters written to his family from Kansas (1856–58), in possession of his niece Ethel Hickok, Troy Grove, Illinois.
Laramie County Clerk of Court Criminal Appearance Docket Book II, copy supplied by the Wyoming State Archives.

Little, Theophilus. "Early Days in Abilene," typed manuscript, *ca.* 1910, Dickinson County Historical Society, Abilene, Kansas.

National Archives, Washington, D.C.:

Fort Hays Letter File (1867–69) Microfilm copy, Manuscripts Division, Kansas State Historical Society.

Fort Wallace Letter File (1867–69) Microfilm copy, Manuscripts Division, Kansas State Historical Society.

Muster Roll, Companies I and M, Seventh United States Cavalry, July–August, 1870, Old Military Records Division (Office of the Adjutant General).

Records of the Office of the Pardon Attorney, No. F-307, Records Group No. 24, National Archives, Washington, D.C. The United States *vs.* John McCall *alias* Jack McCall. Trial documents, including warrants, the Court Record Book, and other documents, of the Second Judicial Court, Territory of Dakota, at Yankton, 1876–77, on file at the General Services Administration, Federal Records Center, Kansas City, Missouri.

Records of the Quartermaster General, 1861–69.

Records of the Social and Economic Records Division, Group 75, M21, Roll 108, and M234, Roll 661.

Records of the U.S. Army Continental Commands, 1821–1920 (Department of the Missouri, District of South West Missouri, Records Group No. 393).

Red Cloud Documents, W885.

Pawnee Agency Documents, Vol. II, Microfilm copy, Archives Division, Nebraska State Historical Society.

Philip, W. D. Notes made from an interview with Matt Clarkson, copy on file, Manuscripts Division, Kansas State Historical Society.

Raymonde, Ena. "Diary of Ena Palmer Raymonde," The Ena Palmer Raymonde Ballentine McLeary papers, Archives Division, Nebraska State Historical Society.

State Penitentiary Record Book (showing details of sentence and when released or executed), Manuscripts Division, Kansas State Historical Society.

Utter, Charles H. ("Colorado Charley") to Dick and Brant Street, January 20, 1880. Original owned by Ethel Hickok.

Index

365